THE ROMAN THEATRE
AND ITS AUDIENCE

Street musicians playing a tambourine, cymbals, and an aulos on a small stage.
Second-century BC mosaic from the 'Villa of Cicero' at Pompeii, and now at the
Naples Museum, believed to be a copy of an earlier Hellenistic painting.

THE ROMAN THEATRE
AND ITS AUDIENCE

Richard C. Beacham

London

First published 1991
Paperback edition first published 1995
by Routledge
11 New Fetter Lane, London EC4P 4EE

© 1991, 1995 Richard C. Beacham

Typeset in 10/12 pt Monotype Garamond by
Megaron, Cardiff

Printed and bound in Great Britain by
T.J. Press, Cornwall

British Library Cataloguing in Publication Data

A catalogue record for this book is available from the British Library

ISBN 0-415-00067-X
0-415-12163-9 (pbk)

For my parents

CONTENTS

ILLUSTRATIONS

PREFACE

My first serious encounter with the Roman theatre occurred not in the usual way through study of its legacy of playtexts, but from viewing the wall paintings preserved at Pompeii and Herculaneum which some scholars believe depict ancient stage sets. I was fascinated with the possibility (but soon aware too of the problems) of using such evidence to place the viewer imaginatively as a spectator within the Roman theatre, in a way which the contemplation of other sources in isolation was never likely to do. The wall paintings, in providing an entirely different type of evidence, judiciously interpreted, could greatly enhance the understanding derived from ancient commentaries, ruins, and playtexts.

Starting from this premiss, it was only natural that my interest focused from the beginning upon the physical aspects of the Roman theatre. This encompassed not just its architecture, but extended beyond that to the elements of performance; the enactments taking *place* in time and space. I first determined through study of the paintings together with analysis of the written evidence what I thought was a plausible format for the temporary stage upon which Roman drama was first performed. Timely assistance from the Nuffield Foundation then enabled me to test whether my ideas 'stood up', by constructing a full-scale replica stage, together with hypothetical scenic apparatus, and producing Roman plays upon it. This in turn allowed me to explore at first hand both the physical expression of Roman dramaturgy – the plays in action – and how this functioned and was modified in the presence of a contemporary audience. Together with the experience of translating plays for such occasions, these experiments raised a great many further questions, as well as some tentative answers about the nature of the ancient audience.

The purpose of this book is to record some of the results of these investigations in the context of a more general account of the Roman theatre including, indispensably, its audience. I do so in the hope that it will add something different and useful to complement the far more comprehensive studies already available on Roman drama and the remains of its permanent theatre buildings. In attempting to provide the general reader with an accessible survey of the Roman theatre, while giving the specialist an account of my particular studies, I hope the results will be found by each to be more useful than frustrating. I am well and uncomfortably aware of what through limits of space, format, and indeed, knowledge, I have had to leave out or deal with less fully than I would wish. In particular, I have not been able to give any extended critical interpretations of the surviving playtexts, having chosen instead to detail the larger theatrical context of such plays, while offering a fuller account of how one of them might be staged. Fortunately such critical textual analyses are the subject of a number of works currently available including some highly perceptive and innovative studies that have appeared in recent years.

People who involve themselves in theatre history soon realize that to study a theatre is to study the entire age in which it existed, since this casts light upon theatrical activity and in turn is mirrored by it. When the theatre in question spans a period of a thousand years, the problem of context and background is formidable. I have attempted to sketch in such aspects of Rome's history as are essential to make intelligible what I have to say on theatrical topics; the result is necessarily a compromise. I urge general readers understandably dissatisfied with the sparse details I provide, to supplement them through further reading of Roman history, which will enrich their understanding of its theatre.

I would like to thank the institutions and individuals that have helped me in my work and in preparing this book. A grant from the United States' National Endowment for the Humanities first enabled me to study Roman wall paintings in detail. Generous support from the British Nuffield Foundation provided for the construction of a replica Roman stage, and grants from the University of Warwick, and from Warwickshire Arts Council have supported a series of productions upon it. The British Academy awarded me a stipend to assist in preparing this book, and the University of Warwick granted me study leave to complete it. I am grateful to Erich Segal for inspiring in me an abiding interest in Roman drama as his student and teaching assistant at Yale, and more recently for his kind support and invaluable advice on matters of translation and staging. I am indebted to the student actors with whom I have produced Roman drama for many of the insights and staging details that I record and analyse. I am grateful to Mr Neil Monro-Davies for his research assistance, and extensive help in preparing the manuscript for publication.

Richard C. Beacham
June 1990

THE ROMAN THEATRE
AND ITS AUDIENCE

1

AN AUDIENCE IN SEARCH
OF A THEATRE

Theatre is a self-conscious activity. The audience and performers come together to participate in a form of interaction which is governed by certain tacit understandings about the nature and limits of what will take place. The rules conditioning this activity – conventions – determine such things as its purpose, the place and duration of the activity, the spaces designated respectively for performers and spectators, and the limits of what may be said or done on either side. More subtle distinctions govern the aesthetic quality of the presentation; broadly speaking its 'style'. All theatre involves an element of 'make-believe', but this varies enormously from one type to another. How close are the language, appearance and behaviour of the performers to 'everyday life'? What use is made of costumes, props, and scenery? Is a set text followed, or do the actors improvise; are they permitted under the accepted conventions to step out of their roles? What distinctions are meant to be drawn between 'real' actions and exemplary ones?

Because of its self-conscious nature – it does not just happen – theatre tends to leave a certain amount of evidence behind. Such things as dramatic texts, buildings, lists and accounts chronicling its activity, occasionally bits of scenery costumes or props, and sometimes pictorial representations accumulate in its wake. The theatre historian readily examines and analyses such flotsam and jetsam, in order to identify these passing acts of theatre, as they existed in a particular period and place, and to understand what they were like.

At the same time, however, it is important to bear in mind that a failure to discover such material cannot itself be seen as conclusive evidence that no theatrical activity had taken place. At particular periods of its evolution, theatre will generate different types of evidence, and in its earlier phases, may leave behind nothing at all, or at least nothing so substantial as to survive the corrosive forces of mutability and time. In such circumstances one must proceed cautiously in attempting to determine what the theatrical practices of a particular society *may* have been like both by contemplating the evidence of its

1

own later practice to suggest what happened earlier, and by considering analogies with other societies for which more information exists.

Our knowledge of early Rome is very incomplete. Except for fragmentary accounts from a few scattered sources, most of our information comes from Livy, who is writing in the age of Augustus, centuries after the events he describes, has strong biases, and often must be treated with the greatest caution. He records that the Romans had their first experience of theatre in the middle of the fourth century BC, when they witnessed performances by an invited troupe of Etruscans. Although the event he describes may well be true, his implication that it was the first encounter of the Romans with any form of scenic art, must, I think, be viewed with scepticism. Livy has a particular fondness for determining first causes in the interest of demonstrating how as he puts it, from 'small beginnings' great (and frequently unwholesome) things have evolved.[1]

It is hardly credible that, whatever instructive example the Etruscans may have set, the Romans were not already familiar with some form of theatrical activity and, indeed, probably had been for a long time. As Aristotle was the first to point out, the impulse towards imitative activity is fundamental – shared indeed, with animals – and will be evident in even the most primitive societies long before its expressions are formalized and defined as 'theatrical art'.[2] In addition to its certain occurrence in the course of everyday human exchange, it provides too, a ready and universal means of communication, which the Romans, located as they were in the midst of other peoples speaking a variety of languages and dialects, might be expected to have developed to rather a high degree.

In a society which greatly venerated its past, and in which literacy was lacking, an oral tradition of storytelling would have been greatly important; a sacred and indispensable practice which we are surely safe to assume would have displayed some form of embryonic dramatization as the narrator used appropriate gestures and vocal 'colouring' to enhance his performance. Similar elements would have been evident in the formal public speaking which was at the centre of Roman political life. The art of oratory was nurtured and recognized to be of supreme significance throughout Roman history, not only for obtaining public office, but for exercising effective power both within the institutions of the Roman state, and in times of political crisis, outside of them as well. Later commentators – including a number of the most renowned orators – frequently compared its skills and reception to those of theatrical art.

The rituals too which were central to Roman worship – the repetition of carefully defined exemplary gestures and verbal formulae – must themselves have formed a repertoire of proto-theatrical acts. Ritual, like theatre, is a self-conscious activity, whose participants meticulously record the necessary details and must follow them scrupulously if the rite is to be effective. The ritual is simultaneously a real event, taking place at the moment of its enactment, and also a timeless replication of itself. Ritual often contains too within its symbolic framework of words and gestures, representative and mimetic elements bordering on the theatrical.

Dance too would have figured prominently in Roman life. It would almost certainly have exhibited strongly mimetic features modified and conditioned by music and rhythmic movement, but still, despite such stylization, suggestive of actions or events whose representation would be understood by both audience and performers. It was out of such dance that Greek drama is thought to have been generated (whatever the details of that process may have been) and it is not far-fetched to speculate that, at least with regard to the presence of quasi-dramatic elements, early Roman dance displayed some broadly similar qualities.

These assumptions about the pre-theatrical practices which may have been evident in Roman society, are only that: they are informed by very little unequivocal evidence. They do, however seem reasonable; more so, certainly than the alternative of supposing that theatrical art was suddenly revealed to a fourth-century Roman audience as a foreign entity for which nothing in their own experience or practice had prepared them. In fact, when we turn to such facts as we possess concerning the theatrical activities of Rome's neighbours, these tentative suggestions begin to appear over-cautious.

There is one further example of an early Roman practice bordering on the theatrical to consider: one which later Roman commentators apparently saw as a precursor of dramatic art. The so-called Fescennine verses, popular amongst the early Romans, are mentioned by several writers, including Horace in the Epistle to Augustus, in which he briefly surveys Rome's literary tradition.

> Our old-time farmers – steadfast folk of frugal wealth – after the harvest was stored, sought refreshment at holiday time for both the body and the soul, which bore such toil in anticipation of its end. Together with children, faithful wife, and the friends who shared the work they appeased the earth with a pig, Silvanus with milk, and each man's guardian spirit, who is mindful of the brevity of life, with flowers and wine. Our licentious Fescennine verse came into use by this custom, when earthy abuse poured forth from one side, then the other. Such freedom, innocent and jolly, was welcomed each recurrent year, till the jokes became cruel, and soon overtly savage, and stalked through innocent homes, fearless and unchecked. The slanderous tooth drew blood and even those who were spared felt concern for the welfare of all. Finally a law was passed, with a penalty forbidding abusive slander in poems.

3

When the stick was brandished, men soon changed their tune, and turned back to more decorous forms of speech. . . . Our old Saturnian verse ran dry and decency suppressed so crude a poison. Yet many traces lingered on and remain today from our uncouth past.[3]

The sense that Horace conveys of a simple folk, practising honest, rustic arts before sinking into corruption is of course a most frequently recurring theme amongst Roman writers. Yet the suggestion of the existence of a form of satirical, bawdy and improvised holiday pastime is lent credibility both from concurring references by other Roman writers, and by what may be thought to be analogous pre-dramatic practice in early Greece, of which we have some scant knowledge.

In his account of the Etruscan actors who first performed in Rome in the mid-fourth century, Livy apparently contrasts the professional performance which ensued, based on their example, with 'the earlier practice of exchanging repartee in irregular unpolished improvised lines similar to the Fescennine verses'.[4] Horace's account is echoed too by Tibullus, who relates how a farmer, resting from his work, would sing improvised verses to the music of the pipe, and, painting his face red, would perform a clumsy dance in honour of the gods.[5] Rather a similar scene is evoked by Vergil in a passage comparing Roman and Athenian practice, and referring to wine festivals honouring Bacchus, in which the participants wore crude masks and laughed wildly while improvising their bawdy verses.[6] Elsewhere the Fescennines are given a particularly sexual connotation. There are references to their use at weddings, and a possible derivation of the word itself suggests that it may relate to a form of black magic by which the phallus is evoked to ward off evil and ensure fertility.

This invites comparison with the so called *phallica* of Greece; a species of ribald rural entertainments of great antiquity. Aristotle describes them as improvised licentious entertainments originating with the leaders of phallic ceremonies and songs.[7] He also describes how comedy developed out of such derisive singing that mocked and satirized unpopular members of the community: a custom which strongly echoes the scant details we have for the Fescennines. Out of such revels a form of primitive farce may have evolved, of the sort which evidently became widely popular in the Greek world, extending at an early date to Sicily where it is thought to have been given literary form possibly as early as the late sixth century BC.[8] We know from the survival of numerous grotesque terracotta figures, usually sporting an oversized phallus, that these entertainments were widespread, and extended into the areas of southern Italy colonized by the Greeks.

There are grounds therefore for suspecting that there already existed in early Rome, prior to the development of more advanced forms of theatre, some sort of proto-farce, its origins lost in pre-history. It would have drawn upon the mimetic elements immanent in everyday life, enhanced perhaps by the special festive mood induced by holiday and celebration. At such times, encouraged by drink and the relaxation of normal constraints, the community would indulge and entertain itself in play: rude improvisations, suggestive joking and ribald mockery of prominent citizens. Probably lacking any coherent plot, such revels would have been characterized by rough verse or abusive banter, some crude music, and a bit of suggestive dance: the sort of thing not at all uncommon at stag-parties today.

This seems at any rate, a reasonable hypothesis. It is strengthened by the evidence of what may have been a somewhat more advanced form of farce practised by a people living to the south – the Oscans – with whom the Romans were in close contact from at least the fourth century. Associated with the town of Atella in Campania, and frequently referred to therefore as *Atellanae*, these Oscan farces were originally unscripted rural entertainments, based on stock characters and situations, and relying heavily on slapstick and buffoonery. Their performers wore exaggerated masks. These entertainments were later taken up by the Romans and, as we shall see, left an indelible mark upon their written comedy which, indeed, they may have surpassed in popularity. There are frequent references to their continuing performance at Rome, well into the imperial period, and this very continuity makes it difficult to draw distinctions between their later form (they became scripted early in the first century BC) and what they may have been like when the Romans first encountered them.

In briefly describing the evolution of dramatic practice at Rome, Livy seems to indicate that the *Atellanae* were introduced to Roman audiences at an early date:

> After the new rule governing plays had been substituted for merriment and uncontrolled jesting and the 'game' had gradually turned into a profession, the young citizens abandoned to the actors the performance of plays and returned to the old custom of exchanging jokes set in verse; their performances were later called 'after-pieces' and were worked into plays, especially Atellane plays. These Atellane entertainments were derived from the Oscans and were kept by the young citizens in their own control, unpolluted by the actors.[9]

Livy's use of the term 'after-piece' (*exodium*) is somewhat ambiguous, since from other sources it seems clear that the *Atellanae* were themselves used as farcical tags following the performance of the main *piece*.[10] Perhaps his purpose is simply to establish a connection between a form of indigenous Roman farce, based on 'old custom', and

5

the not dissimilar *Atellanae* which displaced it and which continued to be popular in his own day. Although the Oscan language in which the farces were originally performed was an Italic dialect, it was evidently incomprehensible to ordinary Romans, and the farces would have been translated or modified to make their language intelligible to a popular audience. However, this difficulty would have been mitigated by the nature of their material: short, crude and boorish, highly physical, and largely improvised without written dialogue.

The characters of the *Atellanae* were traditional, probably clown-like 'grotesques', characterized and motivated by some basic appetite (gluttony, lust) or dominant quality (stupidity, anger). The few character names that have come down to us, together with an indication of their type, suggest a form of stereotyped buffoonery similar perhaps to that of *commedia dell'arte*: Pappus, an old man, Bucco, a braggart, Dossenus, a trickster, and Maccus, a clown. The most intriguing of the names to be recorded is that of Manducus, who appears to have been a ravenous ogre, with great snapping jaws.[11] There seems to have been an emphasis on coarse or obscene jests, horseplay, and slapstick, effective in holding a primitive rustic audience.

It is impossible to say at what point the Romans first encountered these Oscan farces, or indeed whether (as Livy may imply) they evolved a related form of entertainment themselves, independent of any example from their neighbours. In any case, by the mid-third century, the Oscan territory had been firmly within the Roman orbit for some time and when, in this period, the first literary comedy appears at Rome, some of its characteristics may plausibly be thought to have been influenced by the *Atellanae*.

Prior to Rome's southern expansion, the Oscan lands formed a sort of buffer between Roman territory and the area of southern Italy which had been extensively colonized by the Greeks (as early as the ninth century BC), and in which a thriving Hellenistic culture was well established: *Magna Graecia*. Although the whole of the region did not finally fall under Rome's sway until after the war against the Greek city of Tarentum, and its ally, Pyrrhus, king of Epirus (282–270), ample opportunities would have existed earlier for contact and exchange. Indeed, by the end of the fourth century Roman power already encompassed the Greek cities of Campania.

Long before then, however, Greek culture had begun to exercise significant influence upon Rome. It was reflected in the forms of prayers and certain rituals, and in the formulation of the earliest codified law as recorded in the Twelve Tables, dating traditionally from 450 BC. Its influence is evident too in extensive Latin borrowings from the Greek language which came to be thought of as native, and in the setting up of the earliest Roman festivals. Greek art was reflected in

Roman practice, and the stories of Greek myth were reworked into Roman versions.[12]

Theatre was a thriving institution throughout the Hellenistic world, and nowhere more so than in the Greek cities of southern Italy, which appear to have enjoyed regular visits from touring companies, and also mounted local productions of Greek dramatic fare. Syracuse had a permanent theatre dating from the fifth century, and in the course of the fourth, theatres were widely constructed both in Sicily and in *Magna Graecia*. Archaeological and literary evidence exists for structures at numerous locations, and from depictions on vases it is clear that Greek tragedy was widely performed (particularly the plays of Euripides) as well as, perhaps, revivals of Aristophanic comedy.[13]

It is most unlikely that Rome of the mid-fourth century was in any position either geographically or culturally to benefit directly from such a sophisticated theatrical culture. Roman visitors may possibly have

1 Representation of a farcical scene depicting Heracles, engaged in an act of abduction, from a *phlyax* vase now at Lentini. It features a raised stage (with steps to the ground level) and a decorated backdrop to the rear.

been bemused observers from time to time of performances in Greek theatres, but they would have brought back only travellers' tales of practices, entertaining perhaps to recount to their families and friends, but aesthetically too advanced to be understood or to influence the growth of whatever crude drama was germinating at Rome. However, there was another, rather more accessible form of dramatic fare, widely practised in the Greek-speaking areas of southern Italy and Sicily; one which was possibly sufficiently similar to the type of rude farces which may have existed at Rome to have exercised some influence upon their staging. There had apparently developed an independent western Greek tradition of farcical dramas, the *phlyakes*, which are thought to be illustrated on some 200 fourth-century vases found in the area, the so-called '*phlyax* vases'.

The vases show a simple platform stage, which sometimes has an overhanging roof, stairs connecting it with the ground level, and some sort of background, either of wood or cloth. This backdrop frequently has a doorway opening from it onto the stage, occasionally windows, and is sometimes enhanced with simple, possibly painted decoration. The platforms stand on posts, which occasionally have draperies hung between them. In addition to doorways, the vases sometimes depict other stage properties, including small porches and altars, as well as various objects relating to the particular scenes and characters depicted, such as weapons, baskets, chests, tables, chairs, etc.

The scenes depicted on these vases and the manner in which they are represented give us our first glimpse of actual stage practice in ancient Italy, greatly expanding the understanding gleaned from sparse and uncertain literary accounts. As a series of veritable 'snapshots', these vases frequently record what is almost certainly meant to be the actual performance of scenes from domestic farces and burlesques on mythological themes, probably of a partly improvised sort. Less often, they represent the artist's conception and distillation of the central conflict or meaning of a plot, without faithfully recording an actual moment from its staging. The masked characters are generally grotesque, wearing padded costumes and tights; the males invariably outfitted with a prominent phallus. Various garments are worn over the tights, including cloaks, tunics, armour, as well as props appropriate to the particular characters portrayed, such as a lion skin and club for Heracles, or a lyre for Apollo.

The subject matter of the *phlyakes* is broadly divided into two types: that parodying myths, or, on a more sophisticated level, its presentation in tragedy; and depictions of comic scenes from everyday life. The former are devoted to such subjects as the labours and adventures of Heracles (a particularly popular character), the wanderings of Odysseus,

2 Actors enacting a *phlyakes* farce based on the story of the centaur Chiron and Achilles. The stage has a roof extending over it. The vase is now in the British Museum.

and events from the great cycles of the Trojan War, or the House of Atreus. Some of these have been shown to satirize the way in which particular stories had been presented on the tragic stage. The domestic scenes show moments of conflict or intrigue employing a cast which would form the standard *dramatis personae* of later Roman comedy: clever slaves, masters ripe for tricking, drunken or love-struck sons, desirable girls and shrewish wives. Occasionally there are representations of dancing satyrs and maenads, sometimes in the company of Dionysus, who often figures in other scenes depicted on the vases.[14]

Although the *phlyakes* are not believed to have been given lasting literary form until the beginning of the third century (according to tradition by Rhinthon, an inhabitant of the Greek city of Tarentum, prior to its domination by Rome), the compelling evidence of the fourth-century vases demonstrates the existence of a lively tradition of unscripted comic theatre widely practised by Rome's southern neighbours. No evidence exists that it directly influenced activities at Rome, but, in the light of some marked similarities between its subject matter and staging and the earliest surviving Roman drama a century later, some connection at least seems plausible.

In the case of Rome's northern neighbours, the Etruscans, speculation rests on firmer ground. The Romans were decisively influenced by the Etruscans, who, indeed had ruled them until the overthrow of the last of the City's three Etruscan kings, traditionally held to have taken place in 508 BC. It was under Etruscan political and cultural dominance in the sixth century that Rome's early character was formed, with Etruscan practice providing the model for political institutions, laws, the organization of religious rites, temple architecture, and the earliest forms of Roman art. Rome's fundamental social organization too, was originally based on Etruscan practice: a patrician aristocracy with total power; beneath it, a sub-stratum of clients and slaves.

The Roman aristocracy rose up against the Etruscans and expelled them, and they lost naval supremacy to the Syracusan Greeks in 474, as well as, subsequently, control of Latium. They were decisively defeated by Rome in 285 BC. But Etruscan influence remained strong, and long after the dissolution of the archaic social structure, the legacy of earlier Etruscan dominance was evident throughout Roman culture. It seems logical to turn to the Etruscans for further circumstantial evidence about the nature of early Roman theatre.

Both literary and archaeological material suggests the existence of some form of Etruscan theatrical tradition. Wall paintings show a variety of masked performers, musicians, acrobats, and dancers as well as spectators sitting on benches. A reference to an Etruscan composer of *'tragoediae Tuscae'* dates only from the first century BC, but there is no compelling reason to think such playwriting was a late development.[15]

The most likely expression for the earliest Etruscan drama to have taken would have been the form of satyr drama. Some paintings certainly show performers impersonating satyrs, which because of their close association with drama in the Greek world, from which the Etruscans would have acquired them, suggests a theatrical context.[16] Dionysian themes became particularly prevalent in Etruscan art in the late fifth and early fourth centuries, but earlier, in the late sixth, satyrs already figured prominently on vases and as architectural decoration both in Roman and Etruscan examples. This was the period in which satyr drama is believed to have developed at Athens, prior to the appearance there of the earliest tragedies, traditionally held to have been introduced at the Dionysian festival in 534 BC by Thespis. The cultural contacts which the Etruscans evidently had with Greece may have encouraged some related development in Italy.

This provides some further context for returning to Livy's account of the introduction, in September 363 BC, of scenic games which were held in honour of Jupiter in the hope of propitiating the gods during a pestilence:

As the violence of the malady was appeased neither by human remedies nor by appeals to the gods, scenic shows were introduced, a novelty for this warlike people, which up till then had known no spectacle except the circus. These shows were on a small scale, like all beginnings. Dancers were summoned from Etruria and danced gracefully in Etruscan style to the strains of the piper, without any song or any gestures in imitation of songs. The young citizens took to imitating them, at the same time exchanging among themselves jests in improvised verse, with gestures to match their words. The innovation was a success and grew in favour by dint of frequent repetition. The native artists received the name *histriones*, *ister* being the Etruscan for player.

What was it, exactly, that the Etruscan performers presented at Rome? The indication we get, in Livy's subsequent description of what the native players performed (presumably influenced by Etruscan example) is unfortunately ambiguous, and greatly disputed. He writes, 'They now performed "*satura*", rich in [poetic, musical?] measures, written with music for the piper, and with appropriate movement.'[17] '*Satura*' is generally translated as 'medleys', and was used later by the

3 Wall painting probably from the fifth century BC, depicting Etruscan performers. The 'Tomb of the Leopards', Tarquinia.

11

Romans to designate satire. Even in antiquity, no one seemed certain what its derivation was. One fourth-century grammarian, who wrestled with the problem, gave several alternatives, one of which noted, 'In former times the name satire was given to a song composed of different kinds of poetry . . . the word satura comes from the name of the satyrs, because this poem contains jests and indecencies like the licentious words and actions of satyrs.' Another ancient commentator, Evanthius, was more confident, pointing out that after the Fescennines were regulated, 'another type of piece arose, the *satura*. It is so called from the satyrs, gods, as all know, always merry and unrestrained; and it is a mistake to look for another derivation. This satura, while it attacked the vices of the citizens with biting jests which were rustic in tone, did not mention individual names.'[18]

The word '*satura*' eventually came to mean (in addition to 'satire') something composed of different things: a mixture; but although Livy's words may imply that the performances had a certain variety of form or content, this does not exclude the possibility that the Etruscan model for them (and thus the origin of the word) may indeed have been some form of satyr drama. As further evidence suggesting that the Etruscans may have introduced satyrs at the games, there is the third century BC testimony of Rome's first historian, Fabius Pictor. He left a description of the form of the original *Ludi Romani*, which, as the ancient commentator Dionysius of Halicarnassus, who recorded Fabius' account noted, was derived 'not just from what he had heard but from what he knew at first hand'. In his account, Fabius described the procession from the Capitol to the Circus Maximus. Included in it were choruses of *satyristai* (men dressed as satyrs), performing a dance similar to the Greek satyr dance, the *sikinnis*. They imitated and mocked the other participants, in a manner which recalls the theatrical jestings referred to elsewhere, and which may have been the survival of an Etruscan custom originally introduced by them into the games on the occasion described by Livy. In commenting on Fabius' early account, Dionysius adds that he too has seen *satyristai* in funeral processions, dancing the *sikinnis*, and from another account by the historian Appian we know that such performances had taken place at the triumph of Scipio Africanus in 201, and were definitely of Etruscan origin.[19] The notion, therefore, that the Etruscans introduced the Romans to satyr drama in 363 is worth taking seriously.

Viewed as a whole, the evidence for the nature of early theatrical activity at Rome is short on facts, but allows at least a general impression to emerge. What we perceive is a rough, largely improvised form of comedy, plausibly developing out of bawdy festive occasions, probably influenced by more structured farces performed by Rome's neighbours the Oscans, and possibly too by the *phlyakes* which were so popular in

Magna Graecia. These early Roman entertainments were characterized by satirical abuse, expressed in uninhibited jesting and crude verse. The presenters may have imitated the particular objects of their humour, or more generalized rustic 'types' without achieving any very complete impersonation, much less a 'character'. The performances were essentially plotless, comic 'turns', which probably took shape in response to a good deal of audience comment and encouragement. It seems likely that they took place in the midst of other holiday diversions; singing, dancing, acrobatics, conjuring: essentially 'fair-ground' entertainments. Apart from its apparent lack of plot, the quality which most distinguished Roman theatrical expression from what we know of, for example, contemporaneous Greek dramatic modes, was its emphasis on the musical element, evidently an expression of popular taste, and one which would certainly strongly characterize later Roman drama.

The Etruscan example may have given such entertainments a more specifically religious content (the context would in any case have been a religious holiday) by merging bawdiness and worship in the particularly apt form of satyr drama. This, as Livy suggests, could have provided the impetus towards more structured and professional activity without, however, entirely displacing the old, evidently well-loved abusive jesting, which continued as a somewhat subversive pastime. 'After the new rule governing plays had been substituted for merriment and uncontrolled jesting and the "game" had gradually turned into a profession, the young citizens abandoned to the actors the performance of plays and returned to the old custom of exchanging jokes set in verse.'[20]

This picture, unfocused and lacking in detail, but broadly discernible in outline, suggests the state of theatrical affairs at Rome in the middle of the fourth century BC. Unfortunately, further definite information is entirely lacking until 240 BC, the date at which, traditionally, scripted drama was held to have been introduced at Rome by Livius Andronicus. His namesake, the historian Livy, passes over the intervening century with barely a phrase; 'After a few years Livius [Andronicus] took the bold step of abandoning the *satura* and produced a play with a plot.'[21] If there is little more that we can add to our knowledge of Roman theatre during this period, we can at least develop further an understanding of the Roman audience and the changes it had undergone by 240, the date which also marks the conclusion of the first Punic war.

Earliest Roman society had been modelled on the Etruscan division between an all-powerful aristocracy on the one side and, on the other, a large lower order composed of everyone else: slaves, peasants and craftsmen, as well as artisans, dancers, and musicians. Within this system, the family was an extremely important and discrete economic, social, and religious entity, whose head exercised virtually unlimited authority over his wife, children, slaves, and property. The Romans gradually evolved a further distinct category, the plebs, in addition to the Etruscan division of masters on one hand, and clients, servants, and slaves on the other. Partly in reaction to this, the early patrician aristocracy was greatly concerned to maintain strict lines of demarcation between the social groups and to avoid further erosion of their separate identities. Thus the patrician order was a closed group, based upon birth. Newcomers in Rome could only join the plebs, and no marriage was allowed between the two orders.

In the beginning this aristocratic social system was directly based on the ownership of land and agricultural production. The patricians were reluctant to depart from such ancient custom, which, as they passionately believed, provided not only the material basis for their superior position, but its moral and spiritual foundation as well. Consequently they tended to distance themselves from ordinary life, and particularly its developing urban expression; holding themselves aloof for example, from commerce and the crafts. According to one tradition, Romulus himself had forbidden the Romans to abandon farming and military service in favour of the crafts and trade. According to later Roman historians, such things, having low social esteem and moral worth, had been practised primarily by foreigners, particularly Etruscans, in early Rome.[22]

In time, by way of extending and consolidating their status as an independent order, and to avoid remaining essentially a peasant substratum, the plebs began to involve themselves in urban commerce, and crafts. As part of this process, the codification of law in the twelve tables of 450 BC was highly significant, since it set social distinctions between groups and individuals not solely on the basis of birth but on property as well, thus greatly benefiting wealthy plebs. At about the same time, 445 BC, the ban on marriage between plebs and patricians was abolished. Over the next two centuries, until the first Punic war (264–241), the position of the plebs continued to improve and individual members were able to acquire wealth, power, and social prestige. The fact that it was also a period of continuing military conflict and territorial expansion for Rome greatly increased their 'bargaining power'; their ability to demand reform in exchange for providing essential support to the state. In the course of the fourth century and until the Punic wars, there was a stream of social and political measures which greatly benefited the position of the plebs, giving them at times decisive control of public affairs, and allowing their members to obtain the highest political offices.

The earlier system of patricians and plebs was displaced by a more complex one, composed of an elite whose membership was based on wealth, property, and consequent political office and, beneath it, a variety of lower strata. 'There were rich farmers who held land in the captured areas, minor craftsmen and traders, smallholders and agricultural workers, who were more dependent upon the rich landowners and might be their clients, freedmen, who were generally engaged in occupations in the city, and slaves, who were no longer automatically members of the patriarchal family group as they once had been.'[23] This new, more diverse, and balanced social arrangement resulted by the early third century in an end to overt conflict and the beginning of a period of relative domestic peace.

In addition to providing a glimpse both of the later Roman audience and the cast of characters which performed before it, what significance might such changes have for the development of theatre at Rome? The victory of the plebs allowed the evolution of an elite interested not solely in land and practical agrarian pursuits, but also in finance, trade, crafts and, ultimately, the arts. At the same time, however, amongst conservative elements of society, and particularly the old aristocracy, such things were viewed with suspicion, as morally threatening and not legitimately 'Roman'. 'Perhaps due to the social divisions marked by the so-called struggle of the orders, the upper class in Rome developed an attitude that regarded the fine arts as frivolous, foreign, and unsuited to the practice of a serious public figure. The fine arts, practiced by foreigners and inferiors, could serve for adornment, occasional entertainment, or public ritual.'[24] Such an attitude inevitably conditioned the practice and reception of theatre at Rome.

In the course of the wars through which, by the mid-third century, Rome had consolidated its position and power in Italy, further changes of far-reaching consequence occurred. Instead of a single city-state, itself largely dependent upon an agrarian economy, the Romans now had a large and complex system in which there were a variety of peoples, and many urban centres, including the old Greek cities in the south. This expansion brought with it a further development of commerce and the arts, and the strengthening of the groups involved in such things. It also meant that the native Romans were exposed to far more advanced and sophisticated forms and social expressions of art than anything existing at Rome.

In the course of the third century the numbers of traders and craftsmen in Roman society, as well as foreigners, greatly increased, together with their social importance. As a result of conquest and disruption they were augmented by ever-larger proletarian masses in the city itself, and by a greatly increased slave population.[25] In the period following the Punic wars new conflicts were to arise, not as earlier from antagonism between the plebs and patricians, but between the economically dominant and secure social groups and those of the dispossessed which formed at Rome and increasingly determined its character.

It is important to emphasize that the victory of the plebs, and the enactment of thoroughgoing social reform had not led to democracy, and Rome could in no way be compared to Athens of the fifth century BC. It continued for the rest of its long history to be ruled by an aristocratic social system, but one that changed its character and its balance from time to time. Indeed members of the aristocracy came to dominate even the popular assembly which earlier had been a stronghold of the plebs, by exercising influence over their clients whose support they required for political advancement. But it remained important for ambitious office-seekers to secure broad support from the general population, and while holding more minor posts, to take measures to ensure future electoral prospects. There were more than fifty annually elected offices.[26] It was a capital offence to seek office by openly offering gifts, but other means were at hand for impressing and gaining the favour of the public at large. One highly effective and widely used method was through the liberal provision of lavish entertainments, including of course, the scenic games.[27]

By the early second century, there were probably 2–300,000 adult male voters in the citizen body. Because however, many of these were widely dispersed throughout central Italy, the residents of Rome itself (those who actually could be mustered to vote) had a disproportionate influence on public affairs, and were the object in turn of intensive electoral manipulation. Public gatherings where argument and oratory could be used to impress and win support were crucially important, as was any gesture or deed which might win favourable publicity for a candidate. Thus, regardless of their level of personal taste or refinement, and indeed despite whatever moral reservations or antipathy they might have felt towards the theatre, ambitious members of the aristocracy had strong pragmatic reasons for supporting it. These same practical concerns however, and the way they were expressed, both limited and to a degree determined the type of theatre likely to be officially encouraged or to find popular favour. For politicians the theatre was a means to an end; not a place for direct political debate, or the explication and exploration of ideas of immediate public concern. Unlike the great Athenian plays of fifth-century Athens, at Rome (where direct democratic expression was far more circumscribed) drama was to provide entertainment, not enlightenment; it could please and impress, but ought not to unsettle the audience by raising troublesome issues or questioning fundamental principles as understood by those exercising social and political hegemony.

The audience in turn became conditioned both by the holiday atmosphere and the purpose to which the games were put, to expect pleasurable diversion and essentially escapist fare. In time this would inevitably tend to place a premium on spectacle in staging and a degree of sensationalism in dramatic content, with more thoughtful works and nuanced presentation finding little encouragement. Undoubtedly (as I shall suggest later) there were exceptions to this pattern, but generally speaking it appears to have determined virtually from the beginning and throughout its long history, the balance of Roman theatrical practice. By its very nature, theatre as an institution is extraordinarly slow to change, and both the conservative bias of Roman society and the particular constraints under which its theatre operated would have greatly encouraged such inertia.

According to the very few details we have (none of them altogether reliable) Livius Andronicus came as a slave to Rome, one of numerous 'half-Greeks' (the term used by Suetonius) who migrated to the city in the course of the third-century wars of expansion.[28] Like others, he found advancement, catering to a developing interest in Hellenistic culture amongst the Roman aristocracy, by teaching and giving lectures on Greek literature, and eventually obtained his freedom. It was said that his home had been the ancient Greek city of Tarentum in *Magna Graecia*, and if true, it was an apt origin for the founder of Roman drama, since by all accounts the city was (some Romans would have said *literally*), 'theatre-mad'. In 282 a ship with a Roman envoy arrived in the harbour at Tarentum when most of the population was revelling in the theatre. The Tarentines were so drunk that they attacked the ship without even knowing its origin or purpose. On another occasion, when a Roman delegation addressed them in the theatre, the people were so bemused (or conditioned by the comedies they habitually saw there) that they treated the Romans like clowns, laughing at their togas and funny accents. In the war which, not surprisingly, ensued, Tarentum sought help from the Greek king Pyrrhus of Epirus. His first measure was to order all the places of public entertainment closed in order to gain the Tarentines' attention and get them to take the war seriously; an austerity measure so dire that many inhabitants preferred to leave the city, some doubtless emigrating to Rome.[29]

In the course of this war (which ended in 270), and subsequently during the first Punic war (264–241), the Romans were involved in virtually continuous contact with Greek society in southern Italy and Sicily, and brought back with them their first ambivalent taste for Hellenistic culture, together with a good many Greeks ready to cater to it. The changes which resulted in Roman society from this contact were profound and permanent and one of the first expressions of this took place in the theatre. As Horace pointed out two centuries later:

When Greece was captured, she herself made a slave of her savage subduer and introduced her fine arts to the rustics of Rome. . . . Only late did he turn his talent to Greek writings.[30]

One of the immediate consequences of the conclusion of the first war was that the audience at Rome pressed for more numerous and more varied and spectacular entertainments, and this is the context in which Andronicus' earliest production in 240 of a translated Greek play at the *Ludi Romani* should be seen. Indeed, at about the same time (240 or 238) a second occasion for the presentation of plays was established (the *Ludi Florales*); apparently as a deliberate political act intended to please the plebs.[31] Judging by the surviving titles of his plays, Andronicus met this demand with Latin versions of Greek works fashioned to entertain an unsophisticated audience. The eight titles of his tragedies include some of the most thrilling and accessible mythic material ever dramatized by the Greeks. *Achilles, Ajax*, and the *Trojan Horse*, for example, dealt with well-known events from the Trojan War, likely to appeal to the bellicose Romans, while the stories of *Aegisthus* and *Tereus* readily lent themselves to blood-curdling 'pot-boilers'.

The nature of Andronicus' comedies (judging from only three titles, and at most, some thirty-two words), is less evident. *Gladiolus* means roughly, 'the blade', or, perhaps 'the little soldier'; the title *Ludius* may be a term for a scenic dancer; and, most intriguingly, there is *Virgo* or *Verpus*: 'the maid', or 'the circumcised man'. Although considered to be less successful at comedy, Andronicus' style (judging from the fragments) had much in common with surviving examples of later comic works which enthralled the Romans. We detect for example, a taste for alliteration, catchy rhymes and sound patterns, and the use of word-play and proverbs. There is a hint of whimsy, and even a classic evocation of the comic spirit: *'adfatim edi bibi lusi'* 'I have eaten well, drunken, and made merry!'[32]

It seems logical to assume that the elements which characterized these earliest works of Latin literature were composed of both something old and something new. As far as Andronicus' tragedies were concerned, the subject matter, the plots based on Greek dramatic form, the tragic rhetoric and possibly some of the poetic meters may have been a novelty for the Roman audience. However, in the case of comedy, despite Livy's assertion that he 'abandoned' the *satura*, it would have been perilous for Andronicus to frustrate the Roman taste for music, song, dance, and the jesting verbal style, particularly the alliteration and word-play to which Latin so readily lends itself. No doubt the relative decorum of Greek New Comedy models (assuming that Andronicus made use of them) was greatly compromised too by traditional bawdy and farcical elements which were an indispensable crowd-pleaser. In fact, from the titles, it is impossible to determine either the extent to which New

Comedy conventions influenced Andronicus' innovations in comedy, or whether his works adapted their texts.

One possibility is that he turned not to Greece itself for his inspiration, but to the comic traditions of *Magna Graecia*, and his native Tarentum. Although the illustrations of the *phlyakes* found on vases are limited to the fourth century BC, evidence that a related form continued at Tarentum in the third century is provided by similar, *gnathia* vases.[33] Moreover, the first literary *phlyakes* are known to have been composed at Tarentum by Rhinthon from about 300 BC. These mythological burlesques were appropriately termed '*hilarotragoedia*', and may have been somewhat more elevated than the farces depicted on the earlier *phlyax* vases: the few titles we have suggest they took as the subjects of their parody such Greek originals as *Orestes*, *Iphigenia in Aulis*, and *Iphigenia in Tauris*, and dealt with the story of *Amphitryon* and the ever-popular deeds of *Heracles*, as well.[34]

In addition to his dramatic compositions, Andronicus introduced the Romans to a masterpiece of Greek literature, Homer's *Odyssey*, translating it into Latin. This continued to be used at Rome for centuries, although it seems to have been valued more for its antiquity than its excellence. Horace named Andronicus as one of the early Roman poets he found 'old-fashioned, often crude in diction and frequently flat', adding, 'now note, I'm not condemning the poems of Livius [Andronicus] or saying they ought to be destroyed, those lines I remember [my teacher] rod-wielding Orbilius bashing into me when I was little. I'm just surprised to hear them called flawless, little short of perfect, incomparable.' In a similar vein, Cicero compared Andronicus' *Odyssey* to some makeshift experiment by Daedalus, and said that his plays were not worth a second reading.[35]

Nevertheless, one of the few reliable facts we have about Andronicus' career documents the success and esteem he enjoyed in his day, and tells us something as well about the position of theatre in Roman society at the end of the third century. In 207 BC, during the second Punic war (218–201 BC), a consultation of the Sibylline books advised that a hymn be composed and performed throughout the city by a chorus of boys and girls. This was during the consulship of Livius Salinator who, another source tells us, had been Andronicus' master; possibly because of this connection, as well as his fame as a poet, Andronicus was given the prestigious commission. When subsequently an important victory was won at Metaurus, a grateful public by way of honouring Andronicus 'because he both wrote and acted in plays', bestowed on his acting and playwriting colleagues the right to use the temple of Minerva on the Aventine hill as a meeting place and shrine.[36]

The composition of the hymn and the manner of its presentation hints at the adoption by the Romans of a Greek practice, as does too, the

19

official recognition and awarding of civic honours to members of the theatrical profession. It is likely that a *Collegium* of dramatic poets and actors had already existed at Rome for some time, and that the real significance of the notice is evidence of such an organization having won state support. Probably composed in part of 'half-Greeks' and provincial emigrants such as Andronicus (who, as noted earlier, may have lived at the margins of Roman life, both socially and economically) it would have provided its members with an important sense of identity and an effective professional body at a time when major innovations were taking place both in their own status and in the form and social role of theatrical entertainment, including the occasion for its performance. A suggestive model for such a guild existed in the Artists of Dionysus, to which Greek members of the theatrical profession belonged, and which toured widely, taking part in festivals and performing in theatres in the Hellenistic world, possibly including southern Italy. We know very little about the Roman association, but it apparently had a long history, and brief references from the first century BC, indicate that it was a close-knit, rather proudly self-conscious group, whose members read their works to one another. Like other professional bodies, it may have enabled its members formally to develop their skills and advance professionally, since Cicero notes that actors could be promoted to clerks and even eventually rise into the equestrian order.[37]

Apart from its obvious benefit to its members, there were good political reasons for providing formal support to the profession. The Roman authorities had recognized the importance of maintaining civic morale during the dark days of the second Punic war, when Hannibal was regularly ravaging the countryside, Rome's armies were annihilated, and the city found itself besieged. To augment the *Ludi Romani* and *Ludi Florales*, additional games were instituted in the form of the *Ludi Plebeii*, which may have included scenic entertainment from their founding in 220 (and certainly did by 200); the *Ludi Apollinares*, established in 212 and probably scenic from the start; and the *Ludi Megalenses* inaugurated in 204, which soon became pre-eminently scenic. Although intended in part to satisfy the popular demand for more numerous and spectacular entertainment, the games (and by extension the plays presented at them) were also of great religious importance.

The *Ludi Florales* had been set up in response to a command in the Sibylline books to secure the protection of the goddess Flora (at a time when it was also politically expedient to shore up plebeian support); the *Ludi Apollinares* were established in obedience to an augury revealing how to defeat Hannibal after the Roman disaster at the battle of Cannae; and the *Ludi Megalenses* were initiated in honour of the recently introduced cult of the Phrygian goddess, the *Magna Mater*, who alone (the Sibylline oracle advised), could drive the Carthaginians from Italy.

Thus, both in their origin and subsequent celebration, the games were an expression and function of Roman religious life, and even when this is not directly reflected in the subject matter of the plays, it still undoubtedly conditioned the expectations and response of the audience. The Romans of this period were dominated by the demands of religion in a way which we today can hardly comprehend; indeed, even in antiquity their preoccupation with gods and rituals caused comment. The Greek historian Polybius, writing in the second century BC, pointed out that

> the greatest advantage of the Roman social structure . . . lies in my view in their attitude towards the gods. What is in other peoples a reproach is precisely what forms the foundation of the Roman state – an almost superstitious fear of the gods. At Rome religion plays this part in both public and private life: its significance is hardly conceivable.[38]

Religion provided the ideological basis for society and, as determined by an elite, exercised direct and decisive control over its expressions and development. The Roman people generally were both the objects of this control and willing participants in its functions, but the organization of religion at Rome was directed by the aristocracy, who furnished the state priests, and took on the task of determining divine will and laying down the measures necessary to fulfil it. They fervently believed that the welfare of the state was utterly dependent upon the rigorous observance of sacred obligations, and unlike the situation briefly attained in fifth-century Athens, these neither encompassed nor were mitigated by an ethos of free expression or philosophical enquiry, least of all in a volatile medium of public activity such as the theatre.

The games enjoyed a particular status and could make special claims upon the audience by virtue of their religious basis, but at the same time, their content and performance was severely circumscribed, and subject to tight control. A revealing example of this is seen in the practice of 'instauration', whereby if the play were in some way interrupted, or there was the smallest omission or mishap, it had to be repeated from the beginning just like any other formal religious ceremony.[39] Dramatic art by virtue of its role as a function of religion acquired an aura of sacred magic which heightened its significance for the audience. The religious element became a part of the spectators' experience of the performance. This sense of occasion was enhanced too by the plays' actual content, which was frequently based on the same myths that informed religious belief.

All citizens had the right to attend the games, which were free; women also attended, as too did slaves, who were not, however allowed a seat. While quintessentially religious, to attend them was also to be on holiday, with the expectation of being entertained. This was an important part of their social function, consciously determined by the leaders of the Roman state, and reflected in the nature of the event. This concern tended to enhance the impressive and spectacular aspects of the performances, at the expense of other qualities. Unlike the great theatrical festivals of the Greeks, at Rome the scenic games were only notionally competitive, with the emphasis not on a contest for artistic excellence (much less on free ethical debate), but on impressing and pleasing a crowd out for a good time.

Provision of the games and their management was the responsibility of the elected officials. The *Ludi Romani, Florales*, and *Megalenses* were given by the two *curule aediles*, the *Ludi Plebeii* by the two plebeian aediles, and the *Ludi Apollinares* by the praetor *urbanus*. In addition the two consuls were expected to provide some show during their year in office, and other officials acted as patrons from time to time. Since the games were an important and useful public activity which it was the obligation of the public magistrates to present and pay for, it is not surprising that the state extended its official recognition to the theatrical personnel responsible in turn for their execution and success. The games included a variety of activities in addition to drama – circus races, animal fights, boxing, and the like – and members of the *Collegium* may have helped to organize and run these as well as theatrical events per se.[40] It is unlikely that at the end of the third century the number of days officially set aside for scenic games amounted to more than about a dozen. In addition to the annual recurrent games, there were *ludi extraordinarii* (which might well be scenic) held to mark particular events such as the celebration of a military success, or an end to some natural disaster; funeral games in honour of deceased notables; and even occasional *ludi privati* individually sponsored by a donor anxious to impress the public. Even so, despite the evident tendency during and after the second Punic war for an increase in theatrical opportunities at Rome, it is difficult to believe that playwrights or performers were able to secure a living entirely from work at the games.

Recognition of their guild would have been a useful and welcome gesture to members of a vulnerable profession not otherwise greatly esteemed at Rome, but other means would have been necessary to eke out a living. One likely possibility would have been work as a private tutor or teacher (such as Andronicus found), which someone with a knowledge of Greek literature might reasonably hope to obtain from the growing numbers of Romans interested in Hellenistic culture. A fair proportion of the guild might be expected to have the necessary background. Other opportunities would have been found in piecemeal work: singing, dancing, giving private performances or lessons, and composing works on commission. Polybius noted that it had become the custom as Romans grew in sophistication to provide cabaret entertainment of various kinds at grand dinner parties – a natural opportunity for guild members, particularly if they were known from appearances at the public games.[41] Finally, although there is little direct evidence to prove it, it seems altogether likely that plays were toured in the Italian provinces, where in some cases (the cities of *Magna Graecia*), they could be confident of a hearing before an audience of experienced theatre-goers in, moreover, the convenience of a permanent purpose-built theatre. The evidence of impressive monumental building in the course of the second century BC, especially in towns and cities boasting an important religious shrine (where scenic games would have been appropriate) indicates abundant local resources to attract such tours. Membership in the *Collegium* at Rome would have been very useful (or perhaps even a prerequisite) for benefiting from these opportunities.[42]

We possess a few facts about the works and career of one of Andronicus' fellow playwrights, Gnaeus Naevius, which complement and extend somewhat our perception of the state of theatrical affairs at Rome at the end of the third century. Naevius was born about 260, and according to the Roman author Aulus Gellius (writing in the second century AD), came from Campania, possibly from the old Oscan city of Capua.[43] If so, when he subsequently arrived in Rome at the end of the first Punic war (in which he fought), and began to produce plays in 235, it is convenient to think of him as representing the second long-established Italian theatrical tradition, that of native Oscan farce, the *Atellanae*, just as Andronicus had borne with him the dramatic heritage of *Magna Graecia*, especially the *phlyakes*.

He specialized in comedy, most of which he evidently translated from Greek originals; indeed a number of the thirty surviving titles are in Greek, and others suggest Greek characters or locations. Having fought in the war, much of which took place in Sicily and *Magna Graecia*, and possibly having grown up in Capua at the edge of Hellenistic civilization, he probably could have informed his works with an intimate knowledge of Greek life and customs. Nevertheless the few fragments hint that he was not slavishly bound by his originals nor reluctant to insert a bit of Italian local colour; in fact, Terence speaks admiringly of Naevius' neglect being more worthy of emulation, than the 'murky accuracy' of his critics.[44] He was particularly fond of titles ending in the suffix, *-aria*, which may indicate a desire to signal his audience that the comedy in question is a stage piece with a plot (despite whatever irrelevant but crowd-pleasing buffoonery he may have used as leavening), as opposed to the plotless predecessors which may in the last decades of the third century have still been more familiar to them.[45] Thus we find such plays as *Carbonaria* (the charcoal-burner); *Corollaria* (the flower-dealer); *Tunicularia* (the man with the short-tunic) and, intriguingly, *Testicularia*, which, together with *Triphallus* indicates that phallic humour still held its own at Rome. Other titles translate as 'The Madmen', 'The Night-Hawks', 'The Soothsayer', and 'The Trick'.

On the basis of the few surviving fragments it seems clear that such plays, in addition to the jests, word-play, and whimsy which the Romans evidently demanded of their comedy, also made use of characters and situations common both to Greek New Comedy and to the later comedy of Plautus and his descendants. Thus we can identify in Naevius' ensemble such favourites as a swaggering soldier, a flatterer, a difficult old man, and a young man in close pursuit of a courtesan. The plots evolve around exposed infants, drinking parties, slaves in fear of a whipping, sons wishing to be rid of their parents, and the inevitable complications arising from twins. One fragment from the *Tarentilla*, (the girl from Tarentum) sketches a beguiling scene between a courtesan and, presumably, a group of love-struck soldiers; 'Like a ball among a ring of players, she puts herself at the disposal of all; to one she nods, to one she winks, one she fondles, one she hugs, to one she gives her hand to clasp, another's foot she presses with her own, she sings a duet with one while signalling a message to yet another.'[46]

Like Andronicus, Naevius also wrote tragedies; indeed two of the seven surviving titles, *Danae* and *Equos Troianus*, indicate that he tackled (perhaps by way of deliberately inviting comparison) subjects also dealt with by the Tarentine playwright. Other works include an *Andromache*, an *Iphigenia*, and a *Hector*. The few surviving lines indicate rather a self-consciously ponderous diction. Nevertheless, he was clearly popular both in his own lifetime and later; Horace notes almost two centuries after his death that 'Naevius is in our hands and stays in our minds almost like yesterday.'[47] In addition to his tragedies and comedies, which, based on Greek settings and probably on Greek originals, may be termed *fabula palliata* ('plays in Greek dress'), Naevius is also credited with inventing a form of drama based on the famous deeds of Roman legend and history, the *fabula praetextata* (which took its name from the purple-bordered toga worn by Roman officials). In doing so he was catering to the desire of his Roman audience to see its own heroes bodied forth on stage, in the same way that the Greeks had celebrated theirs. In a period of ever-increasing Hellenization, when Romans were beginning both to admire and to hope to emulate the achievements of Greek culture, such a development is hardly surprising. At the same time, however, it ran counter (as did so many attempts to incorporate Greek ideas and practice) to the stern Roman sense that such things were not altogether fitting, and possibly even subversive of public morality.

The Twelve Tablets proscribed death for the slander of living persons, and also severely punished political allusions, which according to Cicero was extended to include direct reference in the theatre to any living Roman.[48] One of Naevius' 'history plays', *Romulus*, set safely in the heroic past, was unlikely to have caused controversy; but another, the *Clastidium*, may well have offended powerful interests at Rome. The play almost certainly dealt with the battle of Clastidium of 222 BC, in which M. Claudius Marcellus defeated the Gallic leader Viridomarus in single combat.[49] The Claudii Marcelli were a powerful family, and it has been conjectured that they acted as Naevius' patron; encouraging him to glorify their virtue and deeds, possibly while taking a swipe at their political rivals.[50] Nothing was more important to the Roman aristocracy than ensuring that, as Polybius noted, 'the memory of public bene-factors remains alive in the people and is passed on to children and to children's children'.[51]

What seems certain is that Naevius found himself in deep trouble with one such family, the Metelli, over a line which might well have come from the *Clastidium*. 'Fato Metelli Romae fiunt consules', he wrote; 'by fate [i.e., not by ability] the Metelli become consuls at Rome'. The family responded, both in word, 'dabunt malum Metelli Naevio poetae'; 'the Metelli will give a whipping to Naevius the poet', and in deed: Naevius is reported to have been imprisoned and subsequently exiled. This may not have been entirely a result of his insult to the Metelli (one of whom was Consul in 206 at about the time the events took place); the playwright apparently offended other aristocratic families as well.[52]

One conclusion to be drawn from this is that although by the end of the third century the audience at Rome appears to have found a theatre, some powerful members of that audience found it not altogether to their liking. Along with their religious and recreational qualities, the games were political occasions as well. The aediles who were usually responsible for organizing them were politically ambitious men at the beginning of their careers, who had to endeavour to please the large public audience of potential voters as well as powerful political patrons. Not infrequently, to ensure brilliant games they added to the state contribution from other sources.[53] In turn, they must have placed considerable pressure upon the playwrights. These found themselves in the difficult position of having to entertain a popular audience whose prior experience of theatre was conditioned by satire and ribald abuse, and who would have been quick to pick up (or even misconstrue) political references, while simultaneously avoiding offence to religious or political interests. When one considers as well the need to balance native and Greek traditions in composing new works or translating old ones, and the infrequent opportunities for practicing their craft, then the challenge facing playwrights at Rome seems truly daunting. The example of Naevius set an unhappy precedent.

One of his fellow playwrights, who eschewed tragedy and avoided too the quicksands of the *praetextata*, inserted a sympathetic, though guarded, reference to Naevius in the midst of one of his own comedies; 'I have heard that a barbarian [i.e., non-Greek] poet has his face fastened to a column, with two gaolers [chains] lying on him all day'.[54] This playwright at least, seems to have understood how to surmount the difficulties attendant on writing for the Roman audience; he rarely attempted either to edify or to educate, but always to entertain it: his excellence lay in giving the spectators who crowded into the makeshift theatres to attend his plays exactly what they wanted. In Titus Maccius Plautus, the Romans found a playwright and, as far as posterity is concerned, the Roman theatre found its authentic voice.

2

THE FAMOUS COMIC
PLAYWRIGHTS OF ROME

Imagine one of those astronomers who scans the heavens, year after year, diligently listening for the radio signals which will prove the existence of intelligent life somewhere out there, almost inconceivably remote in time and space. At length, one day, out of the inter-stellar static, a few faint, but intelligible sounds are heard. With quickening excitement, he adjusts his receiver and continues to search. Suddenly, to his utter astonishment, all his dials light up, and at full volume a signal comes blasting in, full of outrageous jokes, animated conversation, witty monologues, and ribald accounts of zany goings-on: the sound portion of some extra-terrestrial version of 'Monty Python's Flying Circus'! This suggests something of the thrill one might feel in discovering the lively works of Plautus after the important but somewhat dispiriting task of sifting through the fragments of his playwriting predecessors. All at once, with the earliest Latin writer of whose work we have complete examples, there is something which we both recognize and respond to at once: Comedy; in so many ways almost as we often encounter it today. The discovery astonishes and delights us; it even makes us laugh. Plautus, the most successful comic writer of antiquity, also, manifestly, made the Romans laugh;[1] to understand why and how, we need to consider in further detail developments prior to and during the period when Plautus appeared on the scene – and stole it!

Important and pervasive change in Roman society resulted from the wars and conquests of the third century BC, and, largely as a consequence of these, greatly increased contact with Hellenistic culture. Although from the earliest days Rome had engaged in extensive commercial activity with the Greek cities to the south, such communities were now being systematically integrated into Roman society. Earlier, in the long period of domestic upheaval, during which a *modus vivendi* was painstakingly achieved between the upper and lower strata of Roman society, cultural influence and assimilation had been limited. But now, under the new conditions of social and political stability and of greatly expanded economic activity which characterized the end of the

27

third century, much more extensive contact took place. The Romans observed examples of Greek values and practices both in the neighbouring communities which had come under their control and in the City itself; sizeable numbers of Greeks lived in their midst as merchants, itinerant scholars, artists, and household slaves.² The virtual juxtaposing of a culturally more advanced society with one relatively more primitive but confident and ambitious, produced a powerful reaction.

The results of this intimate contact were very extensive, penetrating ultimately almost every area of Roman life; one of its earliest expressions was the arousal of deep interest in Greek literature and, consequently, an impetus towards the development of works in Latin. Initially (as noted in chapter 1) this took the form of translation, as Roman society responded to a felt need 'to acquire for itself . . . [Greek] society's heritage of linguistic, scientific, and literary experience in order to extend its own knowledge and attain a higher level of cultural life'.³

This process through which Roman life was deeply affected by Greek values and practices was characterized by a strongly ambivalent reaction on the part of the Romans themselves. Espousal of Greek influence was rarely whole-hearted, and often qualified with complex expressions of jealousy, resentment, and an attitude which vacillated between feeling a moral superiority to the 'decadent' Greeks on the one hand, and an admiration and desire for the many achievements of their more advanced culture on the other. Plautus' contemporary, Cato the elder, epitomized the former attitude, fearing that Roman morality and customs would be severely compromised by injudicious imitation of the Greeks, advising that one should 'observe, but not examine' the literary works of that 'perverse and corrupting race'.⁴ In the Hellenistic world the Romans encountered not only artistic but religious and philosophical ideas as well, whose tenets often were at odds with their oldest and most cherished beliefs. Nevertheless, despite the warnings and strictures of Cato and his adherents a sizeable and influential portion of the Roman aristocracy (augmented by large numbers of *nouveaux riches*) readily sought both to possess examples of Greek art and to emulate Greek literature and espouse Greek philosophy, seeing in such things 'an opportunity for the legitimation of claims to world rule and of their own pre-eminence in society through an ideological system adequate for the new age'.⁵

The evidence for such 'approach/avoidance' is particularly pronounced in Roman theatrical practice. The development of dramatic art in the period following the introduction of scripted works modelled on Greek originals in 240 BC, has been accurately characterized as 'the Hellenizing of the Roman Stage'.⁶ The Roman audience had placed before them, with increasing frequency at their festivals, a dramatic fare based on the plays of Greek authors. At the same time, this audience (attending during a holiday, and intending to be entertained) was likely to resist works which seemed too 'foreign' to it, or which failed to deliver the type of situations, characters, and humour, that it had long enjoyed. Plautus, along with other ambitious Roman playwrights, had to perform a balancing act, presenting plays, part of whose appeal must have been that they satisfied the new fashion for things Greek, while at the same time taking care not to make excessive demands on the sophistication of their audience, or neglect altogether its established taste for traditional fare.

The scant evidence we have about Plautus' life suggests that he came from Sarsina in Umbria, an area that had been under Roman rule for about a decade before his birth in 254. After coming to Rome he is supposed to have worked in the theatre, possibly as an actor, but later became a tradesman, fell into debt and, after labouring for a period in a mill, began to write plays whose success allowed him to return to the theatre as a popular playwright. He is thought to have died in 184.[7] Such a background, and the absence of any mention of a patron, may provide a hint at understanding Plautus' approach to his craft. He had to 'please to live', and his criteria for success were likely to be based less on notions about the excellence of his models, or skill in rendering superior Greek works faithfully into Latin, than on winning the approval of the audience; the exploitation of a talent to amuse derived from practical experience on the stage.[8]

Of the twenty-one works by Plautus surviving wholly or in part, all are believed to be based on Greek New Comedy texts, by such writers as Menander, Diphilus, and Philemon. These had been composed as much as a century earlier, and may well have formed part of the repertoire presented by itinerant Hellenistic companies, known to have performed in southern Italy. Perhaps it was as a result of direct or indirect contact with such troupes that Plautus obtained his original texts.[9] But instead of translating them directly into Latin, Plautus as he freely admitted, 'transformed' them into his 'barbarian' versions.[10] These adaptations were conditioned by his own abilities and preferences, which in turn reflected (probably to a significant degree) the taste and pressure of his public. In examining the results, we can gain some understanding both of the playwright's skill and the character of his audience.

In effect, Plautus' treatment of his originals amounted to a cultural transposition by which the product of one society was made accessible to another which was limited in its ability to absorb or respond to such material. Straightforward translation (even allowing for the necessary compromise common to all translation of having to find expressions equivalent in meaning in the second language) was inadequate: the originals had to be rendered by Plautus into a form of entertainment expected and accepted by his audience and appropriate to the occasion and format in which they took place. The Greek New Comedy plays which Plautus took as his point of departure were essentially mild-mannered, sober, and urbane intrigues. Often the plot centred on the love affair of a well-to-do young man, who after some not too unseemly adventures discovers that the object of his affections is (despite first impressions) a fit choice for marriage. 'By intrigue or by the fortunate discovery that she was a long-lost cousin, or at least the long-lost daughter of a family friend, boy almost invariably got girl, though seldom before learning an edifying lesson or two.'[11]

The plot is generally plausible and the characters, although exaggerated for comic effect, sympathetic. The language is refined and sensible, and the jokes decorous, indeed in some surviving examples, all but undetectable. On the evidence of such plays and fragments, buffoonery on stage or belly-laughs in the audience were rare.

Plautus took these works, and quite apart from whatever changes he wrought upon their plots (a subject of endless scholarly debate),[12] made

> the characters more laughable and grotesque; he gradually increased the amount of song and dance, making the plays almost musical comedies with gay and festal conclusions: he added Roman references and did not hesitate to break the dramatic illusion; he increased the quantity and vulgarity of his jests; by eliminating a certain amount of exposition and repetition of information, he sought to introduce more suspense and surprise into his plays.[13]

The characters found in his New Comedy models are in Plautus' hands more vigorously drawn and more cynically motivated. In place of the more subtle characterization found in the Hellenistic playwrights, Plautus tends to prefer caricatures, funnier but less sympathetic than their predecessors. Their language is cruder, more ribald, and playful, but also much richer in complex and sometimes fantastical imagery. Their intrigues tend to be less plausible but more energetically pursued. Plautus is fonder of such devices as soliloquies and overheard conversations. His plots abound in trickery and, serving as its mischievous agents (and foils), he greatly increased the role of slaves.

These slaves are threatened (and often presented in pairs as rivals threatening each other) with extreme violence: pain, beatings, threats of torture are not only a source of fun, they become one of the chief motivations of the plot and action. Such violence is neither prevalent in Plautus' Hellenistic models, nor when present given such prominence through emphasis and repetition. In transforming them, he seems deliberately to have increased both elements of violent verbal abuse and threats of dire physical punishment.[14] Of course, violence was a part of everyday existence for the Roman audience. Slaves were indeed tortured, even executed for trivial offences, without recourse to law: as mere chattels, their well-being was entirely at the will and whim of their masters.[15] But Plautus is not otherwise greatly concerned with verisimilitude, and he rarely dwells on matters of direct social or political concern (however important they may be in providing a general context for evaluating his plays); his exuberant comic fantasy easily slips away from such moorings.

It seems certain that all these changes constitute a response to Roman spectators who (though by no means innocent of theatrical experience) were less refined than those for whom the plays had originally been composed; an audience conditioned both by custom and occasion to more lively humour and less thoughtful amusement. In particular, the increased violence may suggest that Plautus

> is catering for a fondness for abuse which had been formed by the Fescennine verses and the Atellane farces, and, secondly, he is, rather regrettably we may feel, pandering to the rather cruel streak in his audience which accounted for the later popularity of the bloody sports of the amphitheatre.[16]

As noted in the previous chapter, early Roman theatre was generated in large part out of unscripted popular entertainment, including both the indigenous Fescennine songs and farcical forms of theatre practised by peoples to the south. Although the earliest examples of the Greek *phlyakes* were probably no longer a living influence, the *Atellanae* continued undiminished and indeed survived into the Empire after assuming literary form. In addition, although it is impossible to determine their nature in any detail, the musical ribaldry of the *saturae* was also a vital presence.[17] We discerned the influence of such popular forms in the few remnants of Andronicus and Naevius, and the evidence for them in Plautus' works is very persuasive.

It is very likely that the example of popular entertainments (and the pressure exerted by an audience whose taste had been both indulged and influenced by them) are responsible for many of the most characteristic qualities of Plautine drama; particularly those that most markedly distinguish it from his ostensible New Comedy models. They help to account for his marked fondness for low comedy and stock types, for the replacement of the serious ethical and romantic concerns found in his models with fantasy themes and obscene schemes. In addition to the inclination towards coarse and sometimes indecent humour, slave protagonists, and verbal violence and threats, Plautine elements include the use of disguises and crude deception, slapstick, a preference for fooling over the development of emotional interest, and a fondness for a festive conclusion. Even Plautus' middle name, Maccius, appears to be a Romanization of the clown, Maccus, known to have been one of the stock characters of the *Atellanae*: perhaps Plautus acquired the nickname in the course of his own work in the theatre, referred to by the scraps of biographical information we possess.[18]

Another likely legacy of popular drama taken up and developed by Plautus may be discerned in his use of music and mastery of a great variety of metrical forms. Plautus strives to create mood and enhance the emotional impact of characters' language through close attention to sound; alliteration, rhyme, assonance, word-play are all abundant, and these are presented in a great variety of both spoken and lyric meters. Passages which in his Hellenistic models were dialogue, are transformed into song, which in performance probably would have been accompanied by heightened gesticulation and dance. Such songs were an important element in the development and organization of his plays.

> Plautus, in turning a comedy of straight dialogue into a musical comedy, discarded the structural principle of act division, whereby the action progresses through discrete units, each with the introduction of new material and each with its own rise and fall in dramatic tension. Plautus replaced this with a musical structure, of which the only indication left to us is the variety and order of metres: he used *senarii* [iambic lines of six feet] for plain dialogue (A), iambic, trochaic and anapaestic *septenarii* [seven feet] and *octonarii* [eight feet] for sections which were chanted or spoken to musical accompaniment (B), and lyric metres of all types for the songs (C). The action then develops in sections which are dominated by songs, typically in the sequence ACB.[19]

This metrical richness and dexterity, unmatched by any other Latin author, tended to increase in the course of his career, possibly reflecting 'a more penetrating knowledge of the mass of his audience and a better grasp of his medium [as] he moved in the direction of greater freedom from his sources'.[20] Plautus' models had very limited metrical variety, and music was confined to the choral intermezzi separating the acts. He abandoned such breaks (possibly to avoid losing the attention of his audience),[21] but reintroduced music into the body of his plays with, as time went on, ever greater portions of his text accompanied by the piper or *tibicen*.

Although such changes and innovations must surely have helped ensure the success of his plays in performance, they did little to endear him to generations of critical classicists who too often considered him at best a hack translator and adaptor of what (in their absence) were believed to be the sublime comedies of the Greek New Comedy playwrights. Many scholars appeared to be far more concerned with what Plautus might have read than with what he wrote.[22] Typical of such critical evaluation was that of Gilbert Norwood in 1932.

The construction of some among his plays is so incredibly bad that even stupidity alone, even ignorance alone, even indifference alone, seem insufficient to explain it. We can but suppose that he neither knew nor cared what drama is, and was concerned with nothing save to amuse an audience that knew and cared not indeed less, but no more. He took for this purpose amusing Greek plays and happened to produce excellent matter only when he happened to put in little of his own.[23]

Norwood's dismissive critique, widely shared, suffered a major setback when the sands of Egypt began yielding up original examples of New Comedy, which were revealed to be, alas, something less than the anticipated masterpieces that scholarship had predicated and prejudice had accused Plautus of having corrupted. In essence, Plautus had been attacked for not being a good realist playwright; only recently has a fresh approach begun to recognize him not for what he never aspired to be, but for what he was: a superbly gifted comic craftsman who mastered and employed every theatrical skill for the benefit and appreciation of an audience which had already acquired an impressive degree of experience and some sophistication in responding to dramaturgical technique.[24]

This rehabilitation derives from a proper appreciation of the elements of performance, and the manner in which these can invigorate and redeem what may seem silly or lifeless on the page.[25] Critics often castigated Plautus for his use of 'unrealistic' devices, such as eavesdropping and audience address, and the manner in which these disrupted the text so that, according to them, the excellence of Greek originals was 'smothered by barbarous clownery, intolerable verbosity, and almost complete indifference to dramatic structure'.[26] By contrast, Niall Slater has this to say on the same subject.

The eavesdropper on the page is a virtual cipher; on stage he is a powerful presence, coloring and shaping our perception of the scene and characters he overhears even when not commenting aside. Improvisation may proceed by fits and starts; as narrative text, such false starts and interrupted action may seem awkward indeed, yet such an approach comes alive in performance.[27]

The influence which dramatic tradition and audience taste exercised upon Plautus' plays extended beyond modifying their content and structure to determine as well the aesthetic of actual performance. Roman theatricals, evidently from earliest times, had involved a substantial element of audience participation, whether in the form of robust repartee between spectators and performers, or playful references to members of the community (subsequently curbed by official stricture), or the more subtle expression of a psychological sharing in the spirit of fun appropriate to a holiday situation. The nearest recent equivalent might be the atmosphere and type of performance often found in music hall or British working men's clubs.[28] However formal the rites attending them may have been, performances themselves are likely to have encouraged a sense of fun and freedom from ordinary inhibitions and social restraints; indeed as noted earlier, some such impulse may have led to the increased frequency of theatrical games to provide recreation and maintain morale during the second Punic war.

The sense of a holiday spirit is frequently evoked in the plays of Plautus (often explicitly in their prologues) and has been very usefully analysed as a major factor in understanding the nature and appeal of his comedy. An important element in such a spirit was the 'saturnalian' sense

> when the customary restraints of law and morality are thrown aside, when the whole population give themselves up to extravagant mirth and jollity, and when the darker passions find a vent which would never be allowed them in the more staid and sober course of ordinary life.[29]

Traditional unscripted drama, much of it improvised and allowed to respond to the dynamic of the particular occasion as well as the mood and reaction of the audience, must have been well suited to such circumstances, and it is not far-fetched to suppose that the audience would have been conditioned to associate their manner of presentation with the very concept of theatre.

The introduction by Plautus and his fellow playwrights of new dramatic fare (and a consequent style of performance) derived from a different theatrical tradition may well have reflected the desire of at least a portion of their audience for such innovations. Yet, at the same time, it would have been perilous to have catered exclusively to the taste of a Hellenist minority if in doing so a playwright sacrificed essential popular support. Some compromise was called for, not just as I have outlined in subject matter and dramatic style, but in actual performance as well. In effect, new works of scripted comedy were presented according to the conventions appropriate to traditional improvised farce.[30] The taste of the audience was gradually changed, and their response and understanding 'educated' in performance itself by presenting new wine in old skins; new dramatic content insinuated into familiar dramaturgic forms.

It has been noted by critics that one of the recurrent 'conceits' of Plautus' plays is that the characters make up the comedy as they go along: they contrive the very plot in which they take a part. Probably this directly reflects the legacy of a more tentative dramatic fare: improvised, non-literary entertainments long favoured by his audience, which the actors are thought to have assembled on the basis of stock characters and situations, some well-worn but ever-popular bits of comic business, and the barest outline of a scenario. We trace the influence of such performances in Plautus' deliberate choice to 'make believe' that his own plays are unscripted; taking shape in the presence of an audience which in turn assists in their formation. In Plautine drama no attempt is made to maintain 'dramatic illusion' in the usual sense of the conventions of realism; characters frequently acknowledge the audience, their own function as actors, and the play itself.[31]

In such moments we can discern not merely an attempt to continue to use tried and tested methods but, beyond this, the expression in dramaturgical terms of a tension between the conventions of an 'upper class comedy imposing its criteria from without and a native comedy vigorously resisting from within the intrusion of foreign standards'.[32] This tension results in a remarkably self-conscious form of theatre. There is no question of suspension of disbelief; the spectators and performers are simultaneously inside and outside the world of the play. Such double vision, constantly reinforced in the course of performance, could, while indulging traditional tastes, gradually acquaint an audience with the conventions of an alien drama, whose qualities could be noted and commented upon both to edify and amuse the spectators. In the *Rudens* for example, Daemones rather pompously expresses the sort of noble sentiments characteristic of New Comedy, which are then identified and debunked in an aside to the audience by Gripus, who harbours a robust scepticism more characteristic of popular entertainments.

> 'Before now I've seen comic actors mouthing sage sayings like this and winning applause for preaching these wise morals to the audience. But when everyone left and headed back home, not a single one acted as the actors had urged.' (1249–53)

This sense of theatrical self-awareness permeates Plautus' plays. For example, in the *Miles Gloriosus*, the slave Palaestrio is observed working himself into the role of 'clever slave'. The old man, Periplectomenus, urges the audience to pay attention as a convention takes shape before their very eyes:

> 'Well, look at him! Standing pensive, pondering profundities with wrinkled brow. Now he knocks upon his head – he wants his brains to answer him. Look – he turns. Now he supports himself with left hand on his left thigh. Now he's adding something with the fingers of his right hand. Now he slaps his right thigh – what a slap! . . . Look – he shakes his head. No, no, what he's invented doesn't please him. He'll cook up a plan that's well done – not half baked – I'm sure of that . . . Bravo! *Molto Bello*,[33] standing slavewise and theatrically.' (200–5; 207–8; 213)

In the *Truculentus*, the soldier reminds the audience knowingly of the behaviour expected from his comic 'type'; 'Do not expect, spectators, an account from me of my battles' (482). In the *Pseudolus*, Simo similarly eschews his conventional role; 'I've decided now to ambush Pseudolus in a different style than it's done in other comedies, where it involves lying in wait with clubs or whips: I'll go right in and bring the twenty minas that I promised him' (1239–42). A little earlier in the same play, the pimp Ballio brushes off the insults he received, noting that it comes with the part.

> *Simo*: 'What did he say? What was his story? Come on, what did he tell you?'
> *Ballio*: 'Oh, mere theatrical nothings; the usual line of abuse a pimp gets in comedies, stuff schoolboys know. He said I was nasty and wicked and a liar.'
> *Simo*: 'Gee, he didn't exaggerate!'
> *Ballio*: 'Indeed. Consequently I took no offence.' (1080–4)

Such examples could be multiplied many times over, as Plautus uses the very idea of scripted comedy as a source of fun, subverts the conventions of New Comedy illusion, and encourages the audience to join in the creation of his play. The bi-focal awareness induced by the juxtaposing of scripted and improvisational modes encourages the spectators simultaneously to perceive and to 'see through' the dramatic form of the 'new' comedy being presented to them. It also engenders a sense of pervasive irony (enhancing normal comic subversion), which allows Plautus' characters by commenting upon the play-in-progress and their roles within it to establish a mood in which even the 'serious' passages may, a moment later, be undercut with a joke.[34]

Characters who rise to the delivery of moralistic *sententiae*, do not maintain their dignified attitude for long. The prologue of the *Captivi* promises an unconventional 'improving' play of high moral tone; 'not a hackneyed work . . . no filthy lines . . . no mendacious pimp, or wicked courtesan, or braggart soldier', but then, in his next breath goes for a laugh in pointing out that all the violence will take place off stage, and if anyone wants to 'have a go' he will happily arrange something memorable for him (54–66). Pseudolus pauses to utter some 'Roman thoughts' about mutability and the vain folly of human affairs; 'it all ends the same; while we're worrying and scurrying, death sneaks up upon us', then returns to the fray. 'That's quite enough of philosophy; I'm talking too much and too long. By the immortal gods, that lie I spun just now was good as gold!' (685–9).

Such an ironic attitude complements Plautus' habit of striving for immediate comic effect in performance, often at the expense of any 'literary' notions of character consistency or dramaturgical logic. The dramatic development is set aside while characters tell jokes, engage in irrelevant banter, and interject anachronistic topics to entertain their audience. In the *Curculio*, for example, the property manager of the company makes a cameo appearance to comment on the play, straddling the real and illusionistic worlds by noting that one of the *dramatic* characters is such a rogue, he doubts whether 'I'll get back those costumes I hired out' (464).[35] He then passes the time (sounding remarkably like a contemporary Roman taxi-driver) by giving the audience the 'low-down' on the 'interesting' parts of town.

References to Roman customs and institutions suddenly poke through the plot of a story ostensibly set in Greece, or characters recite the verbal formulae of Roman religious ritual.[36] The plot may stop, but the 'play' and the show must go on, as the audience is treated to the pleasures of parody, recognition, and identification. A 'Greek' character will suddenly turn Roman with a topical allusion or even leave the play altogether to deliver a few critical comments about the Greeks.[37] Serious scenes are spiced with indecorous indecencies, as an actor steps out of character to perform a comic routine, or engage in obscene banter and abuse with another. Words are coined, played with, tossed about, and phrases turned; sometimes to release a flash of bizarre imagery, but often purely for the funny sounds they make.

> Roles are taken up and dropped, transferred and subverted. Eavesdropping scenes turn into play-within-the-play, and all the while some improvising player struggles, not always successfully, to hold this unruly, boisterous, but vital enterprise to some narrative thread. This is far more than a burlesque of sentimental Greek comedy, as is often charged; it is a theatrical reconceptualization.[38]

The chief agent of this dramaturgical self-consciousness is usually the 'clever slave' who fashions the play around him to become simultaneously its author and hero.[39] He fills this role by virtue of his wit and intelligence, triumphing over adversity and the social facts of life in a way that no actual Roman slave could ever do. Indeed, according to Donatus, it was forbidden for Roman slaves to be depicted in plays as cleverer than their masters;[40] Plautus' slaves could do so since all the plots and characters are, notionally, set safely and unthreateningly in Greece: in the time-honoured tradition of ethnic and minority humour, a Plautine play is one extended 'Greek joke'. Masters are tricked, freedom is won, and so long as the play lasts, in the words of a slave in the *Casina*, 'we victims are victors; it's our lucky day!' (line 510). The audience (which unlike that in Greece, was not limited to the middle and upper classes, but comprised all elements, including slaves), enjoys the pretence of the *actors'* theatrical improvisation while, in the process, admiring and experiencing a mildly subversive 'saturnalian' pleasure in the *characters'* ex tempore ability to salvage something redemptive from their dramatic situation, and get away with it.

The clever slave does indeed enjoy impunity. In the surviving plays nothing dire ever actually happens to him despite circumstances of ever-present danger. As Segal points out, Plautus' protagonists make a point of positively disdaining and mocking the fates which, but for their success in fashioning unlikely, anti-realist plots, would tumble down upon them.[41]

The same indulgence and eventual amnesty is extended in the plays to another social group normally subject to severe restraint in Roman society: freeborn sons. Under the law, the *pater familias* held the literal power of life and death over his children. 'He could sell them into slavery, his consent to their marriage was needed, and he could bring about their divorce if he wished. The children could own no property . . . anything they acquired belonged to the father.'[42] Yet in the plays, sons frequently contrive and enjoy a victory over their fathers, especially when one is paired against the other as rivals for the affection of a young girl.[43] In such situations the behaviour of the father is presented as degrading and ludicrous, and his eventual humiliation at the hands of his son – unthinkable in real life – must have been a particularly potent source of pleasure, providing brief comic relief from one of the most deeply seated of all psychological repressions; one greatly intensified in Roman society by the full weight of sacred custom, the *mos maiorum*.

The enjoyment of such guilty psychological pleasures is eased for the audience by being partly exonerated through the plays' appeal to poetic justice. In the fragile fantasy world conjured up on stage the bad guys, the authority figures (who have compromised their legitimacy in some way), the rapacious lechers, unscrupulous soldiers, and other abusers of desirable social norms are punished, while the – by contrast merely mischievous – authors of their correction enjoy a general amnesty announced at the play's conclusion. Today is a holiday: it's 'fun and games'; but tomorrow, as the performers frequently remind the audience, is another day. Their little brief authority, the delight and higher justice it sometimes brings, ends with the conclusion of these lively, but unlikely revels.[44]

The festive frame of mind, as well as the aesthetic conditions in which it can be indulged – the rules of the game – are the object of careful preparation by Plautus, principally in his prologues. We are fortunate indeed to possess these. They provide an invaluable opportunity to gain an impression of the Roman audience 'caught in the act'; to sense and savour the nature of the theatrical occasion, and to observe both by what means Plautus inducts his spectators into his aesthetic realm and, by inference, what he conceives it to be. In doing so, we should remind ourselves that the perception and meaning of any theatrical experience for an audience is made up of all the elements present when it takes place: the representation of the (written or improvised) scenario through the actions and language of the performers; their costumes; the scenic elements; the type and location of the building or place set aside for performance; its amenities, organization, and personnel. The audience 'makes sense' of all these individual factors within the larger social and cultural context in which it experiences them.[45] Plautus' prologues (occasionally supplemented by material in the body of a play) allow us to glimpse some of these components.

The first thing we sense is the presence of a large, potentially unruly crowd whose attention and goodwill the playwright, acting through the speaker of the prologue, is concerned to obtain. Only once it has settled down can it be prepared for the entertainment at hand. Most of the prologues begin with a call for quiet, sometimes proposing a pact with the spectators in exchange. The *Miles Gloriosus* is typical; 'Now folks, if you'll be kind and hear me out, then I'll be kind and tell you what our play's about' (79–80).[46] In the *Amphitruo* a more formal contract is drawn up by Mercury, promising the audience prosperity and happiness in exchange for quiet attention. In some plays, this call leads to the delivery of friendly advice or instructions to the audience and theatre personnel. In the *Miles* anyone who doesn't wish to listen is asked to leave and make room for those who do. In the *Captivi*, an individual spectator is singled out and urged to come forward where, if no space to sit is available, he can stroll about: the prologue is not going to exhaust himself with shouting. In the *Asinaria*, the speaker hopes that attention will benefit the audience, the company, the managers, sponsors, and himself, and commands the herald to do the job for which he is paid.

The most elaborate instructions (and the best picture of the audience) are found in the prologue to the *Poenulus*. After pointing out that he wants the spectators to sit comfortably and eat their fill of the play (noting however, that they would have been wiser to have had a proper meal before coming), he bids the herald do his duty by announcing the play, then continues,

'Let no ripe whore sit on the stage, no lictor[47] or his rods make a sound, no usher amble about in front, or show anyone to his seat while an actor is onstage. Those who slept idly at home for too long, should now stand patiently, or sleep moderately. No slaves should crowd in – let them either leave room for freemen or put up the cash for their freedom – otherwise, go home to avoid double-trouble: a beating here and a whipping at home when their masters return and find things neglected. Let nurses look after their tiny tots at home – don't bring them to the show, lest the nurses go dry, and the kids die from hunger, or bleat for food like goats. Women should watch silently, laugh silently, curb their tuneful prattle, and take their babble home, so as not to plague their husbands both here and there.' (17–35)

After noting in a more formal vein that the directors of the games have ordered the competition be conducted fairly,[48] he returns to his earlier tone to interject, 'Oh, and one thing more, which I almost forgot: while the play is on, attendants attack the bakery! Now's your chance, while the tarts are hot, charge!' (41–3).

Plautus takes care to ensure his play a good reception both by stimulating the spectators with this friendly banter (very much as a contemporary night club 'warm-up man' might work on the audience before the main event) and by encouraging them with reminders of the mood appropriate to a holiday. The *Asinaria* promises 'a clever comedy full of fun and jokes and laughter' (13–14); the *Casina* urges, 'Away with sorrowing, thoughts about your borrowing . . . the games are underway, and even bankers get a holiday!' (23; 25). In some plays the audience are assured that not only will they enjoy themselves, they will also have a 'good' time watching an improving play. In the *Captivi* the prologue promises a moral work, which will profit the audience to hear; in *Casina* they are told that the heroine will prove chaste and suffer no indecency in the play.[49]

As references to the herald suggest, part of the function of the prologue is simply to announce the play. This sometimes (but not always) includes a statement giving information about the title and author of the Greek original. It is not known how plays given at the festivals were publicized, though word of mouth is likely to have played a part. How effective this was is open to doubt; the prologue to Terence's *Hecyra* (on the third attempt to perform it) may imply that some confusion about the nature of the play had contributed to the spectators' premature departure to a rival entertainment. At the performance of his *Heautontimorumenos* however, Terence's prologue remarks, 'I would now say who wrote it and who was author of the Greek play, if I didn't think that most of you already know' (7–9).

A further, more subtle aspect of this process of induction, observed in some of the prologues, involves setting the aesthetic scene by gradually eliding the world of the play into the environment of the theatre. In performance the dramatic realm evoked by the imagination is never completely separate from the ambience in which the performance is taking place; rather each permeates the other, and this fanciful cohabitation set up in the mind of the spectator frequently begins in the course of the prologue. In the *Truculentus*, it is introduced in the opening lines.

'Plautus proposes a paltry part of your great and gracious precincts in which to erect an Athens without architects! What about it? Will

40

you give it to him or not? They nod. I see that *public* property is mine at once. How about if I ask for a bit of your *private* property? They don't nod. By Hercules, how the good old ways are maintained, with your swift response in saying "no"! . . . I shall transform this very stage into Athens while we present this comedy.' (1–8; 10–11)

Similar playfulness with scenic convention occurs at the beginning of the *Menaechmi*. The prologue points out that although comic writers customarily pretend that the story takes place in Athens, he can affirm that though the plot be 'Greeky', it is not in fact 'Attic' but actually 'Sicilyish' (7–12). He relates the narrative background, then notes (punning in passing on the bodily and metrical meanings for 'foot'); 'I must return by foot to Epidamnus' to continue the story 'while remaining right here'. He pauses to joke that while in Epidamnus, he will gladly conduct business for any in the audience who wish to commission him, but warns 'if he doesn't provide the fee, he'll get nothing for it; and if he does, he'll get *less* than nothing!' (54–5)[50] This whimsical mood (and its evocation of the theatrical mingling of illusion and reality) continues as the speaker concludes with a further explicit reminder first of dramaturgic convention, and then of the stock *dramatis personae* who are presented and 'exist' within it.

'This city is Epidamnus while the play takes place; when another is enacted, it will become another town. It's just the same as households change: now a pimp lives here, now a young man, now an old one, now a poor one, a beggar, a king, a parasite, a prophet.'

In introducing a play, prologues sometimes poke fun at the generic qualities characterizing it. In the *Mercator*, this takes on particular irony, since it is spoken not by a 'neutral' figure but by Charinus, the play's central character, who – simultaneously occupying both real and fictive 'space' – proposes to inform the audience both about the plot, and his passion. His ambiguity (worthy of Pirandello) intensifies, as he asserts that 'I shall not imitate those other lovers I've seen in comedies, who confide their woes to the night, the day, the sun or the moon . . . it is to you rather that I shall tell them' (3–5; 8). After indicating the author and title of the Greek original, he begins to relate 'his' story, pausing to criticize his own inadequacy in the role, digressing to comment on the verbosity of lovers, then upon his own. 'So you should not be angry at my super-loquacity now: it was bequeathed me by Venus, that same day she gave me my love. To which I must now return, and continue my tale' (37–9).[51]

Similar generic self-consciousness is found elsewhere. In the *Captivi*, the prologue appears on stage together with the play's two principal characters who stand in chains, and are referred to as he explains the plot. On concluding, he reassures the audience that, despite its high moral tone, the play will indeed be a comedy; 'it would almost be wicked of us, decked out in this comic gear, suddenly to try to present a tragedy' (61–2). A more extensive example of the same notion (and also of the coexistence of the roles of performer, character, and presenter) is provided by Mercury in the prologue to the *Amphitruo*:

> 'you shall hear the plot of our tragedy. What's that? Making a face because I said it will be a tragedy? I am a god; I shall change it! If you wish, I'll transform it from tragedy to comedy without altering a line . . . I shall mix things up: let it be a tragi-comedy! But it wouldn't suit for me to make it a proper comedy, since there are kings and gods about. What to do? Well, since it's got a slave role, I'll make it just like I said: a tragi-comedy.' (51–6; 59–63)

In the same passage, Plautus gives the character in his script (who, we recall, is represented as if he were improvising a speech by the god Mercury at the performance of a play) an even more paradoxical function. The character refers to his own 'real' existence as a humble actor, who, like his fictive master 'Jupiter', lives in fear of a whipping.[52]

> 'For in fact, that Jupiter who sent me here fears punishment no less than any of you: his mother was mortal, so was his father, so it's hardly surprising he's worried about himself; me too, who am the son of Jove: if Dad's in trouble I fear I shall be too.' (26–31)

A little later Mercury speaks of Jupiter's concern for actors, notes that he will perform in this comedy, and then uses the idea of personification of a god playing an actor to comment once more upon theatrical convention. 'What? Does that surprise you? As if Jove turning actor were a novelty! Why only last year he came to assist the actors on this very stage when they summoned Jupiter' (89–92). In the prologue to the *Poenulus*, Plautus again presents the pretence of a performer possessing a persona apart from the character he portrays. 'Well, I'm going to get costumed up. Follow things patiently . . . so farewell and stay with us. I'm going; I want to become somebody else now' (123; 126). The same idea occurs implicitly in many of the epilogues when the actors ask for applause. In the *Cistellaria* it is made explicit as the epilogue refers to the departing characters:

> 'Don't expect, spectators, that they'll return here to you. None will show himself; all will finish their business inside. When that's done, they'll remove their costumes. Then any who made mistakes will be whipped, and those who didn't will get a drink.' (782–85)

What emerges from the prologues, together with much complementary evidence from within the body of the plays, is the sense of a consummate control of the theatrical medium, through which both audience and performers are involved in a carefully coordinated and integrated aesthetic act. This event, which is structured out of a subtly balanced arrangement of real and imagined elements, depends for its success equally upon the manipulative skills of Plautus and his actors, and on the receptive mood and conspiring imagination of his festive audience. And as the Prologue of the *Captivi* demonstrates when he notes; 'all this will be fact for us, fiction for you' (line 52), the performance requires a self-conscious willingness both to 'make-believe' – assuming the role assigned – while, simultaneously, preserving an ironic detachment and the sense of fun which that provides. Plautus was admired for centuries for his skill as a playwright,[53] but his success was crucially dependent on his Roman spectators through whom he was able to create 'an almost unparalleled unity of purpose between playwright, actor, and audience'. That audience was

> widely travelled . . . self-confident, sophisticated, thoroughly accustomed, thanks to their experiences in forum, court, and comitium, to every facet of artistic verbal ritual . . . one of the great theatrical audiences of all time . . . their expectations would have been a major force in shaping Roman comic tradition.[54]

It seems likely that the career of Plautus' successor, Caecilius Statius, was itself shaped both by the pressure of his example and by the audience with which he had enjoyed so close a rapport. Only a few facts about Caecilius' life and work have been preserved – not always from reliable sources – together with a mere 300 lines and some 42 play titles. This is particularly unfortunate since he was held in high regard by later Roman commentators, including Cicero, who (despite some reservations about the purity of his Latin) ranked him first among Roman comic writers. Even Horace, who regarded Plautus with scorn, esteemed him for his 'dignity', and noted that his plays were still packing the theatres.[55]

Thought to have been born around 219, like Plautus, he came from northern Italy; indeed Jerome claimed he was a Gaul, and Aulus Gellius (writing in the mid-second century AD) believed that he began his career at Rome as a slave.[56] He died about 168 BC, which means that as a younger man he is likely to have known Plautus (or certainly, to have observed his work at first hand), while at the end of his life, Caecilius is reported to have befriended the young Terence and helped him to get his first play, the *Andria*, produced.[57] It is from Terence that we learn that his own manager, Lucius Ambivius Turpio, had earlier been instrumental in saving Caecilius' career, 'restoring to the stage a poet who otherwise would have been driven by his adversaries from his calling and work in theatrical art'. Through Turpio's effort and encouragement, Caecilius' plays were eventually able to win popular approval, but only after a period in which they 'had been rejected, or barely survived'.[58] Why had the audience withheld its support?

As the case of Terence, discussed below, reveals, theatrical controversy centred on the question of the manner in which playwrights used the original Greek texts in fashioning their own plays for presentation; in particular, the extent to which traditional Roman elements were retained (and popular taste indulged) at the expense of fidelity to the style and format of Hellenistic New Comedy models. Thus the problem which Caecilius faced early in his career (*c.* 195–185/180) must have been broadly either that his works were deemed too 'Hellenistic', or not 'Hellenistic' enough. But which? In the Terentian prologue in which Ambivius Turpio claims credit for saving Caecilius from his 'adversaries', he goes on to suggest that now, years later, he seeks to do the same on behalf of Terence, and urges the audience 'not to allow dramatic art through you to be determined by a few'. He seems to be suggesting that the broad mass of spectators are in danger of being manipulated by an unrepresentative clique, but making allowance for Turpio's special pleading (and the fact that, as he notes, the audience had twice earlier abandoned the play for which he now seeks a hearing) it might equally well have been the case that these few were in fact merely acting as influential exponents of prevailing popular opinion. Unless Turpio is disingenuous, one must assume that those opposing Terence now are the same sort who earlier threatened to destroy Caecilius' career.

There is, as we shall see, little doubt that Terence faced popular resistance from those who disapproved of his renunciation of the Plautine approach for a different formula through which he shifted the balance towards greater Hellenization – without however, acting as mere translator. In occupying this ambivalent ground, he left himself open to attack from the other side: from those Hellenophile purists who felt he corrupted good Greek plays. On balance, I think that Caecilius early in his career may have made the same error which later plagued Terence: he innovated too drastically against established tradition by producing plays which through deference to a growing but still minority taste, were too 'Greek' for the general public.

The 'few' who might well have seen it as their responsibility to protect established practice – while in doing so supporting popular taste – would logically have been other professional poets and theatre personnel with a stake in preserving the status quo: the same who would later oppose Terence. Such people had been formally honoured with official recognition as a *Collegium* only a few years before Caecilius appeared on the scene. In a period of rapid proliferation of theatrical activity (and the steady advance of Greek influence) this singular institution[59] would have been well positioned and motivated to guard their craft jealously, and could certainly have snuffed out any unwelcome innovations from a provincial newcomer, particularly one who may have been a slave, and almost certainly (unlike Terence) lacked powerful patrons to promote his work.[60]

If this analysis is correct, it suggests that although Caecilius' later, successful works may have exhibited some nominal Hellenizing, on balance they were more traditional than novel: more like Plautus than Terence, let alone that most refined and orthodox of New Comedy playwrights; Menander. This assertion is reinforced by the meagre textual evidence that survives. It is true that in taking his plots, as was customary, from Greek originals (and probably adhering to them more closely than Plautus)[61], Caecilius exhibits an increased preference for Menander. We may (on inadequate evidence) possibly discern a trend. Sixteen of his forty-two titles may be found in the list of Menander's works, while earlier for Plautus the number is only three out of twenty-one and in the case of Terence rises to four out of six. But Caecilius' style was radically different from that of Menander. This was the considered opinion of Aulus Gellius, who was able to compare the work of the two poets closely.[62] Although an admirer of Latin comedies 'whose wit and charm you might think could not be surpassed', Gellius points out that the impression fades when such works are scrutinized along with their Greek originals. Comparing passages from the *Plocium* of Caecilius with the Menandrian version, he is moved to exclaim, 'good gods, how dull and lifeless, how very different Caecilius appears from Menander!'

> 'Quite apart from the charm of treatment and the diction . . . which is not at all the same in the two works, I note the general fact that Caecilius has not tried to repeat, even when he might have done so, some of Menander's brilliant, apt and clever lines; but rather, passed over them as of no value and instead thrown in some farcical stuff. And what Menander took from real life; simple, true and delightful, Caecilius for some reason has omitted.'

Leaving aside the question of Gellius' strong subjective preferences, in comparing for ourselves the two passages which he records, we do note marked differences. An old husband complains that his wife (rich, ugly, and troublesome) has forced him to sell an attractive slave girl whom she considers a rival. Menander's character presents the situation in a straightforward descriptive account; in Caecilius' version the same basic information is conveyed through a series of colourful metaphors and playful images. The husband compares his life to a besieged fortress, wishes his wife dead, and describes himself in the mean time as a living corpse. He uses the familiar verbal devices of alliteration and assonance, and the repetition of similar words. 'Ita plorando, orando, instando, atque obiurgando me obtudit'; 'she bombarded me with crying, sighing, prying and vilifying'.[63] The passage builds to a final comic climax in which the old man impersonates his wife mocking him as she gossips to their neighbours.

Gellius compares a second shorter passage in which 'Caecilius chose to be ridiculous rather than appropriate and fitting to the character represented', and in a third, more serious scene from the same play, he contrasts the 'sincerity and realism' of Menander with Caecilius' use of 'the language of tragic bombast'. In reviewing these passages, we note again striking affinities with Plautus. In the second scene the playwright has used the Menandrian context as the occasion for entirely independent and fanciful treatment, substituting 'the mimetic language of the extraordinary, the paradoxical, the burlesque'.[64] In the third example, Caecilius condenses nine lines in the original into only four, giving them impressive emphasis and gravity.[65]

Gellius characterizes Caecilius' style as 'lacking in grace and dignity', and notes the introduction of what he terms *mimica*: 'farcical stuff'. Such a critique transcends textual analysis to imply a style of performance. From other uses we can determine that (apart from its specific use to identify a theatrical genre, mime, which I discuss in chapter 5), *mimica* suggests a highly expressive acting style using physical gesticulation and pronounced vocal inflexion to create an exaggerated, caricatured impersonation; the antithesis of the lifelike portraits for which Menander was famous.[66] This is precisely the type of characterization that Plautus' performers seem likely to have used in enacting the roles and speaking the lines which he gave them. In doing so they continued a popular tradition older than Plautus, and older too than scripted drama at Rome. Gellius concludes his comparison by chastising Caecilius for 'not following a guide with whom he could keep pace'; in fact, however, I believe he did: he followed the taste of his audience.

Shortly before his death, Caecilius was said to have met Terence (who, if the story is true would have been about eighteen years old), and impressed by the *Andria* which the aspiring playwright read to him, supported the youth's application to the aediles to have the play produced.[67] It appeared in 166. According to the same account, Terence had been born in Carthage about 185 BC, and came to Rome as a slave, where he was given a good education by Terentius Lucanus who set him free. He was then taken up by a circle of aristocrats interested in literature and Greek culture. These are said to have included members of highly prominent Roman families, including Scipio Aemilianus and Gaius Laelius,[68] both of whom were about the same age as Terence, and went on to distinguished political careers. Terence produced his six plays between 166 and 160, in which year he sailed to Greece evidently to obtain further examples of Greek plays. He died on the journey before returning to Rome.

Terence was born at the time of Plautus' death and presented his last play a mere twenty-five years later. And yet, in almost every way, the surviving works of Rome's two greatest comic playwrights display a radically different approach to their craft and, by implication, to their Roman audience as well. 'In style, structure, characterization, and moral outlook Plautus . . . and Terence are about as different as two poets working in the same genre can be.'[69] In attempting to identify and understand such differences we need to consider the role of both personal and public factors, that is, to assess the manner in which the innovations in Terence's work may reflect his own aesthetic preferences and principles on the one hand and, on the other, the pressure and changing taste of his audience.

A portion of that audience was increasingly influenced by Greek culture as Rome's contact with the Eastern Mediterranean expanded and deepened after the conclusion of the second Punic war in 201 BC. Although Greece itself had been nominally granted its freedom by Rome in 196, the Macedonian Wars ensured that Rome's military and commercial involvement there remained substantial. Meanwhile, in Rome itself, the influence of Greek culture grew apace, tending all the while to erode traditional norms and attitudes in Roman society as religious and philosophical ideas took root which often contradicted ancient custom. It was within that portion of society most directly charged with preserving traditional practice – the aristocracy – that contact was most extensive, through education, commerce, and foreign travel. Not surprisingly, the ranks of the aristocracy were deeply divided on the subject, with opposing and passionately held positions taken up by the conservative circle of Cato the elder on the one hand,[70] and the adherents of the Scipio family on the other. The conflict was joined directly or indirectly in a great many areas of Roman life; we find evidence of it in Terence's work and the controversy it generated.

Although literary works had been imported piecemeal for decades, the first great collection of Greek literature, the library of the kings of Macedon, was brought to Rome in 167 (the year before the presentation of Terence's first play) by the victorious general Lucius Aemilius Paullus. His natural son, Publius Cornelius Scipio Aemilianus, was adopted into the family of Publius Scipio, the son of Scipio Africanus (the victor over Carthage), and these important works are thought to have been left to the younger Scipio and his descendants; shared perhaps with the powerful family of the Fabii, descendants of Paullus' other son, Quintus Fabius Maximus Aemilianus.[71] Scipio Aemilianus received an extensive education from Paullus, who collected for this purpose outstanding Greek teachers, grammarians, philosophers, and artists.

When he matured, Scipio Aemilianus was renowned for his knowledge and espousal of Greek culture and regarded as one of the most enlightened and refined men of his day. He gathered about him a circle of Greek artists and philosophers, whose work he actively encouraged. Even Cato, fervently anti-Greek, praised him in noting that 'he alone has wisdom, the rest are empty shadows'.[72]

A prominent portion of the aristocracy was acquiring literary and artistic sophistication, and their interest and influence extended to dramatic art, both because of its potential for advancing a political career and as an expression of the Greek culture they espoused. As early as 194 at the urging of the elder Scipio, special seats had been allotted to senators at the scenic games,[73] which while indicating support by members of that class for the theatre, may also suggest their desire to establish a distinction between themselves and the larger popular audience. For the first time, we detect evidence of a stratified audience and may perhaps infer a tension in the role of theatrical producers between the need to entertain the majority,[74] while acknowledging the taste and expectations of an influential minority.

Terence moved amongst the aristocratic circle centred on the Scipios, and, indeed, two of his plays, the *Hecyra* and the *Adelphoe*, were performed in 160 at the funeral games of Paullus which the younger Scipio organized. One of the consuls then was Lucius Anicius Gallus, who had fought alongside Paullus in the Macedonian campaign. Seven years earlier, just before commencing his career, Terence may well have been present at Anicius' triumph, at which (displaying his own interest in Greek culture) the general presented Greek tragic actors and choral dancers performing before an elaborate *skene* erected for the celebration.[75] For this same occasion we have striking evidence (if somewhat lacking in detail) of the type of difficulties which such foreign innovations could meet with in the boisterous and sometimes xenophobic Roman audience; problems not unrelated to the sort which subsequently plagued the presentations of Terence's own works. The proceedings evidently came close to general mayhem when the Romans were confronted by unfamiliar Greek fare which they either misunderstood, or perhaps regarded with contemptuous mockery. Possibly the performance was too refined for the festive mood of a triumph; in any case, the audience was dissatisfied, and turned the performance by the hapless Greeks into a confused burlesque and near riot.

Although a self-conscious and educated elite may have espoused and encouraged through their patronage the development of serious domestic drama more closely modelled on Greek example, this risked antagonizing popular taste, the strength and nature of which may be seen in the institution of the *Floralia* celebrations which began to occur annually after 173. At this spring festival a different sort of theatrical fare was presented – the mime – whose popularity would eventually surpass and displace orthodox drama.[76] This was unscripted (and probably virtually plotless) entertainment, which later became notorious for its obscenity and licence. Unlike literary drama, it was presented without masks and included female performers in what were evidently un-inhibited and exuberant celebrations. Perhaps, as Beare points out, 'short, amusing, topical, utterly unrestrained by any considerations of technique or decency, yet capable of adopting on occasion the most sententious style, the mime came nearer than any other form of drama to the real tastes of the Roman populace'.[77] If so, we can begin to understand why the utterly different type of entertainment offered by Terence (however buttressed by his aristocratic patrons) struggled to win popular support.

From the same prologue (that of the *Hecyra*) in which as noted earlier, Terence's manager Lucius Ambivius Turpio recalled his troubles in presenting the works of Caecilius, we learn that in the work at hand the spectators' attention ('populus studio stupidus') was so difficult to hold that on two previous occasions they literally stopped the show.

> 'When I began to present it the first time, the pomp of the pugilists, the massing of their mob, the commotion, the clamour of the women constrained me to depart prematurely . . . I produced it again. The first act went well, but then came the cry that a gladiatorial show was on offer: the audience crowded in with such tumult and struggling for position that I was not able to maintain mine own.' (33–5; 37–41)

Evidently the majority of the audience sometimes had scant regard for the comedies with which Terence proposed to please them, particularly when more festive fare was on offer. Unlike Plautus, who used his prologues for friendly and engaging banter with his spectators, from the first (*Andria*) to the last (*Hecyra*), the Terentian prologues were employed to lecture on dramatic technique, argue with his critics, defend his craft, and plead for a fair hearing. Why then were his plays so vulnerable, and the support of his audience so tenuous?

The prologues suggest that Terence was criticized for a number of alleged faults. In the *Heautontimorumenos* (163 BC) he cites the complaint that his work 'relies on the genius of his friends rather than his own ability' (24), and he returns to the same criticism three years later in the *Adelphoe*; that he 'is continually assisted in his writing by men of high rank' (15–16). Terence does not directly refute the claim, suggesting first that the audience must judge for themselves the merit of his work, and later that his supposed supporters are, after all, the same men who have been called upon to assist the general population in both war and peace. It is possible, of course, that members of an educated coterie (perhaps even Scipio himself) may have tried their hand at dramatic composition (as indeed did later prominent Roman statesmen), and felt it unwise to publicize the fact.[78] A more likely interpretation, however, is that Terence's rivals (possibly older, more established members of the *Collegium*) were envious of his patronage, and perhaps also wished indirectly to criticize the 'foreign' innovations that such cosmopolitan supporters encouraged, without tactlessly attacking the taste of their superiors. Thus the charge may in part reflect the more general controversy engendered by the impact and assimilation of Greek culture.

Another, related criticism cited in the prologues was that Terence had produced inaccurate versions of his Greek originals. In the *Andria* he identifies the source of this and similar charges as a 'malevolent old playwright' (7) who from references elsewhere is known to have been one Luscius Lanuvinus.[79] Indeed, Terence notes that because of the need to answer such abuse he is constrained to use his prologues not to explicate the plot but to defend himself from jealous slander. Luscius had accused him of composing the *Andria* by combining two plays of Menander into one. In fact, all that Terence appears to have done was to add to his version of the Menandrian original characters who may possibly have been found in a second play by the Greek playwright.[80] In defending himself he cites precedent in the practice of Plautus, Naevius, and Ennius. This may be a somewhat disingenuous appeal, since the types of change made by these writers (much extraneous material added to scenes, introduction of topical allusions, extensive rewriting) are not the sort of which, apparently, Terence stood accused.

The same charge is cited in the prologue to the *Heautontimorumenos*, to the effect that Terence has 'spoiled many Greek plays while making a few in Latin' (17–18). Again, Terence cites the precedent of 'good' writers, and pledges moreover to produce 'new plays free of defects' (29–30), while promising to identify by contrast the faults of his rival unless Lanuvinus 'puts an end to his abuse' (34). Indeed, his defence may be interpreted as a covert counter-attack on traditional dramatic fare, with the implication that his own innovatory approach is superior to that of his predecessors. He promises a play 'of quiet action' (36), written in 'refined language' (46), and liberated from the usual stock characters of 'the running slave, the angry old man, the gluttonous parasite, the brazen trickster and the greedy pimp' (37–39). In deliberately citing and banishing such old favourites from his play, and alluding to his contrasting treatment, Terence was in effect challenging his audience to raise its standards.

In his next play, the *Eunuchus* (161 BC), Terence makes good his threat to retaliate, accusing Lanuvinus, despite 'translating well', of 'composing badly' and thereby of 'turning good Greek plays into bad Latin plays' (7–8). He therefore implies that accurate translation is insufficient (claiming that Lanuvinus has recently 'ruined'[81] a play by Menander, the *Phasma*) and that his own compositions may actually be superior to their Greek originals. This recalls the distinction Terence made earlier in the prologue to the *Andria*, (20–1) between the creative 'negligence' of such writers as Plautus, and the 'murky accuracy' of others.

Terence admits that he has introduced into his version of Menander's *Eunuchus* two characters – a parasite and a braggart soldier – from another of the Greek playwright's works, the *Kolax*.[82] Lanuvinus had accused him of stealing these characters from a play by Naevius and Plautus, and Terence uses the charge to remind his audience again that such characters and others (notwithstanding his attempt in the *Heautontimorumenos* to dispense with them) are constantly recycled in comedy. 'In fact nothing is said that has not been said before' (41). His implicit intention (or claim) is to express things more eloquently and in more carefully crafted works than those of his predecessors and rivals, including Lanuvinus whose faults Terence once again threatens to detail in subsequent prologues should his slanders continue. They did, and in the prologue to *Phormio* (performed six months later, in September 161) Terence indicates that the conflict had intensified, with Lanuvinus seeking to end his career by 'driving him from his calling' (19). His rival continues to claim that Terence's plays 'are thin and trivial' (5). Again, Terence evokes the concept of aesthetic quality, suggesting that Lanuvinus' popular success was due less to the merits of his play than to the skill of those who presented it. In further urging free competition between the 'followers of dramatic art' for 'the prize' (17) he may again imply that the excellence of his work lies not in fidelity to Greek models but in the intrinsic and independent artistry of its Roman author. However cautiously, Terence is in the process of staking out his claim (the first by a Roman writer) to be judged as an autonomous creative artist.

How perilous such innovation might be is demonstrated only a few lines later when Terence first recalls that on another occasion the performance of his play had to be abandoned because of 'uproar', and then, having appealed for 'attentive silence', concludes by judiciously flattering the audience for 'your goodness and sense of fair-play' (34).[83]

In the *Adelphoe* of the following year, Terence cites (as we noted) the charge that he benefited from the support of well-placed patrons. He also records that his 'rivals' have unfairly criticized and attacked his latest play, and urges the audience to judge whether it be condemned or praised. He freely admits that he has lifted an entire scene from a comedy by Diphilus and 'used it, translated word for word, in the *Adelphoe*' (10–11), which was itself based on a work by Menander. Once more Terence invites the spectators to evaluate the merit of his action, and concludes by again exhorting them to support the 'poet's efforts at composition' by hearing the play with an open mind.

The same plea is particularly emphatic in the prologue of Terence's last play to be performed (after, as noted, two abortive attempts); the *Hecyra*. Indeed, its venerable speaker, Lucius Ambivius Turpio, characterizes himself as a 'suppliant' in the opening sentence, and his entire speech is shaped as an appeal to the equability of the audience, with references to its 'fair-mindedness' (28), 'intelligence' (31), 'power to bestow grace on scenic entertainments' (45), and finally (evoking two particularly potent terms of praise in the Roman moral lexicon), its 'authority' (47) and 'faith' (53). The spectators are urged for good measure not to allow Terence (and by implication themselves) to be 'unfairly mocked and ensnared by foes' (54). Such an approach in this and the other prologues seems calculated to define and place a special responsibility upon the audience: not simply to be silent and attentive, but indeed to rise to the challenge of Terence's art. Envious rivals denigrate the young poet's worthy and innovative work, and at the same time implicitly insult the intelligence of the audience and impugn their capacity to appreciate his artistry. The persistence of this theme together with the hard evidence of failed presentations indicates that Terence's comedies did indeed make special demands on his audience. Analysis of the plays themselves confirms and adds substance to this suggestion.

Terence's use of the prologue to put forward critical concepts about the nature of dramatic composition is an important and influential contribution to European drama, as well as a marked departure from previous Roman practice as exemplified by Plautus. His concern was not to induct the audience into a theatrical 'world', nor to provide the sort of information which would ease their passage through the plot. Moreover, and again unlike Plautus, he seems to expect the attention of the spectators to be held by the ideas and situations set out in the story and its sometimes convoluted development, without recourse to the buffoonery, topical injections, and extended irrelevant banter which the earlier playwright evidently deemed necessary to ensure popular approval. His plots are, to be sure, standard New Comedy fare: it is in details of their handling, characterization, language, and ethos that Terence departs from earlier Roman practice. As one commentator has succinctly described it, all of Terence's plays except the *Hecyra* share the following elements of plot:

> Two young men, often brothers, are engaged in love affairs. One of them loves a courtesan, the other wishes to marry a young woman, who is either poor but freeborn, or ostensibly a courtesan. The father opposes his son's marriage or even wants him instead to marry the daughter of a friend or relation. The young woman turns out to be freeborn or the daughter in question, and all ends well.[84]

Terence places his emphasis on realism and plausibility, qualities for which Menander was himself greatly esteemed. Although we have no specific texts through which to compare his treatment with an extended passage from a Greek original, from such examples as we do possess of the works of Menander it seems clear that Terence is much more faithful to the tone and details of his models than were either Plautus or Caecilius. Such changes as he made served to broaden their appeal to common human experience, displaying in place of 'stock comic types and scenes, a universalism that derives from fidelity to human truth rather than hackneyed formulas'.[85] This was a considerable achievement for an artist working within a conventional and confining dramatic tradition, which was not only foreign in origin but had previously been experienced by his audience only in the significantly 'compromised' versions of his predecessors.

In fact, the range and variety of human activity represented within the format of New Comedy was so restricted and repetitive that unless one chose to enliven the presentation, as Plautus did with the use of material extraneous to the plot and its characters, the scope for original expression or being 'true to life' was severely limited. ' "Everyday experience" for some comic characters is only that which is sanctioned by repeated appearance on the comic stage'.[86] One way to mitigate this without disrupting the dramaturgical integrity of a work was to increase its philosophical content; to evoke and explore moral themes and questions directly relevant to the concerns of the audience. Menander's spectators were likely to have been familiar with the ideas of the peripatetic philosophers with whom he is sometimes linked. These, as recorded in the treatises of Aristotle and his followers, were themselves a systematic investigation of ethical ideas that had long informed popular notions of morality, so it is hardly surprising that, deliberately or not, we find echoes of them in dramatic works intended for public performance.[87] However, successfully to transfer such material as it was embodied in a Greek dramatic text into the very different context of the Roman theatre would have been a daunting task.

Nevertheless, there is clear evidence of such an attempt by Terence. His most often quoted line, 'I am a human being, and nothing human is foreign to me' (*Heautontimorumenos*, 77), is as typical of his tone and outlook as Plautus' 'Man is a wolf to other men' (*Asinaria*, 495) is of his.[88] The stock characters that Plautus recycles with such delight are in Terence more realistically (or, at least, far less cynically and farcically) drawn and, certainly for a modern reader, what they lose thereby in comic potential they gain in empathy. Even Plautus' grasping and rapacious courtesans become in Terence's hands kindly and generous.[89] When a Plautine son is inconvenienced by his father, he is apt (with never a guilty thought) to wish him dead; in Terence, he merely wishes him too tired to get out of bed![90] In his fourth century AD commentary, Donatus found this disinclination to present characters 'true to type' remarkable, and the modern reader is also struck by Terentian verisimilitude. 'For we have on stage kindly mothers in law, a modest daughter in law, a husband at once tender to his wife and devoted to his mother, and a virtuous prostitute.'[91]

One consequence of this different approach to characterization is to enhance the ethical potential and relevance of the plays. Characters less defined by type are less confined in 'allowable' behaviour and attitude. They can be drawn in more subtle hues than the stark contrasts used to depict Plautus' single-minded figures, and may be motivated in more complex and ambiguous ways. Such an approach, moreover, would have been in tune with the times, since, as noted, Rome was now undergoing considerable social and cultural upheaval as traditional values and modes of thought were subjected to the doubt and scepticism engendered by extensive contact with the Greeks. A Terentian character frequently finds himself in situations in which, like individuals and groups within the volatile and changing population of Rome itself, he 'bends rules and softens lines that define social structure' and must be prepared 'to improvise with laws and customs'.[92]

This loosening of both dramatic stereotype and conventional comic morality was accompanied by greater sobriety in language and more decorous use of theatrical form. In Terence there is none of the exuberant metrical variety so abundant in Plautus; few puns, indecencies, irrelevant jokes or sudden outbursts of song. There is no emphasis on punishment and torture, no extravagant flights of verbal fantasy, alliteration, assonance or invented words. Instead Terence sought to write pure and elegant Latin, which was simple, flexible, and concise, but also capable of irony and wit: the language spoken perhaps by the cosmopolitan circle with which he associated. Staging conventions are more realistically employed. The plot is rarely interrupted for comic asides, nor for audience address, topical allusions or slapstick. Nevertheless, Terence's plays are not mere pale emanations of their Greek models, but still recognizably Roman. Together with the works of Plautus, 'they share the freer Roman outlook on sex, the Roman zest for life, the optimism inspired by Rome's victory'.[93]

They are, however, undeniably less robust and festive than the fare to which the holiday audience was accustomed. Plautus' works were carefully crafted to cater to the mood and occasion; his characters, as we saw, were simultaneously contemporary Roman fairground performers and denizens of a recognizable (if topsy-turvy) Roman milieu nominally decked out with Greek trappings. Terence's dramatic realm is less bound by time or place; more universal to be sure, but also less immediate and compelling. It is not surprising that his audience was at times distracted, either by the attractions of rival holiday entertainments or by the taunts of the likes of Lanuvinus who, sensing how tenuous Terence's hold upon it was, used the opportunity to chastise him for taking liberties with his Greek texts. Of course, it is hardly likely that the portion of the audience who abandoned Terence for a circus show were greatly upset by his failure faithfully to translate Menander; such critical concerns were 'Greek' to them. But by occupying a middle ground – neither the traditional stance exemplified by Plautus, nor the philhellenic position of Lanuvinus who evidently favoured direct translation – Terence was vulnerable to attack from both sides. And, like the society from which it was drawn, his audience was itself increasingly varied and fractious.

What is remarkable about Terence's short career is not that he encountered difficulties but that, notwithstanding these, he evidently enjoyed significant success and frequent opportunities to present his plays.[94] That they were not howled from the stage suggests that the taste and sophistication of the Roman spectators (who, in the days of Plautus had acquired considerable experience and critical acumen in his 'rough and ready' theatre) had continued to develop and mature. If Terence's experience proves that, broadly speaking, it would be inaccurate to think of its standards as 'refined', or on a par with Greek concepts of excellence, it also provides some measure of their resilience and breadth as, for the first time, a Roman playwright both invited and provoked direct comparison with the revered artists of the Hellenistic theatre.

3

EARLY ROMAN STAGES

In attempting to understand and interpret the staging of dramatic fare during the first two centuries of theatrical activity at Rome, the first fact to bear in mind is that the archaeological remains of Roman theatres, found abundantly throughout the Mediterranean world, are by no means a reliable guide. From the introduction of drama at Rome, until more than a century after the death of Plautus, all Roman theatres were temporary structures, built for particular occasions and then dismantled, leaving not a rack behind. Such wooden stages were erected in the city frequently during this period, and according to Vitruvius, writing after the construction in 55 BC of the permanent theatre of Pompey, they were still were being built in his day in great numbers both at Rome and elsewhere, even in towns of only moderate size. Wooden stages continued to be constructed in the imperial period; the last reference to one is in the time of Claudius, but they may well have been used to the end of antiquity.[1]

It was these early stages that shaped Roman drama, and were shaped by it, including the surviving plays of Plautus and Terence, and which may therefore provide crucial evidence for understanding such works not as texts on the page, but as actions intended to take place in a particular architectural format that they in turn and time modify. Before suggesting what such temporary stages may have been like, it is necessary briefly to consider the type of theatre architecture (and dramatic art) already existing elsewhere in Italy, which the Romans would have encountered and been influenced by in developing their theatre.

There were, of course, a large number of permanent theatres in *Magna Graecia* and Sicily, and somewhat later in Campania and Samnium, which could have influenced practice at Rome. However, when it ultimately appeared, the permanent form of the free-standing, architecturally unified Roman theatre, with its characteristic elaborately ornamented stage facade (the *scaenae frons*) was markedly different from the Hellenistic structures preceding it.[2] It seems likely therefore that any formal evolution must have occurred chiefly within the temporary theatres. Later remodelling of Hellenistic stages into the Roman type was always drastic; we look in vain for any transitional phase in the archaeological record.[3] The temporary stages left no tangible trace, and so on the basis of the structural remains alone, the permanent Roman stage would seem, implausibly, to have appeared without any evident architectural antecedent.

It is likely, then, that the temporary stages provide a hypothetical 'missing link' between the earlier Hellenistic and later Roman, stone theatres. This fact alone makes them potentially an extremely valuable source of information about Roman theatrical practice generally. Because over a long period of intense theatrical activity the Romans did not construct any permanent theatre (which in the early period could only have been based on Greek example), they were able gradually to evolve and determine a theatre structure which directly reflected their own experience and understanding of theatre, instead of simply espousing Hellenistic norms. The frequent construction of temporary stages gave the Romans a continuous opportunity to mould these structures to reflect their own theatre as it developed, in its particular social and aesthetic context. By examining what they chose to use, to adapt, or to forgo entirely from the theatrical practice of their neighbours we may discern the conditions and attitudes which governed those choices. The architecture may provide a record which can be interpreted analogously to the comparison of Roman with Greek drama, to reveal differences between the two cultures and their conception of theatre.

We know a good deal about the final result, the permanent form of the Roman theatre (which will be discussed in chapter 6) but what can be learned about the temporary stages that preceded it? We may begin by examining the indirect archaeological evidence provided by these permanent theatres of *Magna Graecia* and Sicily; the examples which the Romans themselves would have had at hand. Nearly all such theatres appear to have been of the *paraskenia* type: a raised stage (or perhaps in the earliest period, an acting area upon the ground itself) which had a facade (the *skene*, or scene building) behind it, and two projecting wings (the *paraskenia*) containing doors, on either side. Such a theatre form may date from the earliest Athenian structures, or at the latest, appeared during the fourth century BC. It seems to have continued to be built and used in southern Italy after it had been replaced for the most part in other parts of the Hellenistic world by the *thyromata* stage, which had a straight facade with openings into which decorative panels could be placed, but no projecting wings.

In Sicily the earliest theatres for which there is archaeological evidence date from the second half of the fourth century, and have been found at some half-dozen sites. About the same number exist elsewhere in Sicily, and are thought to date from the second half of the third century, after which construction of new theatres seems to have ceased, some being converted much later to the Roman *scaenae frons* model.[4] In addition to these remnants, we know from literary evidence that a theatre already existed at Syracuse in the fifth century, although the surviving structure is later. All of these theatres were constructed in urban locales and in the midst of other public buildings, all are located in a natural enclave (they are not free-standing structures), and all are situated so that there is a panoramic view behind the scene building. They were of various sizes, accommodating between 1,250 and 14,000 spectators. The facade of the scene building facing the audience through which performers entered onto the acting area could be quite high, ranging from 17 to 26 metres. In front of this there apparently was usually a wooden stage, 1–2 metres high, the front wall of which was decorated with columns or pilasters, with painted wooden panels (*pinakes*) placed between them.

The situation in *Magna Graecia* was similar. Seven theatres have been found, and in addition a further example (at Tarentum) is known from literary references.[5] The oldest of these date from the second half of the fourth century, and no new theatres appear to have been built after the early third century. They ranged in capacity from 1,200 to 6,500 spectators, all were located in urban areas near the public *agora*, and close to temples. Both here and in Sicily, on the basis of written evidence, it seems likely that the buildings were used for public assemblies as well as for theatrical entertainment. In all cases where physical remains have been studied, the structures in *Magna Graecia* appear to have been of the *paraskenia* type. Again as in Sicily, all these theatres except one made use of a natural enclave or hillside. The exception (at Metapontion) is notable, since, like the later permanent Roman theatres, it was built up artificially on a flat site, and, moreover, the upper levels of the auditorium were reached by flights of steps from entrances in the circumferential facade of the structure. This too became a feature of later Roman practice, and is otherwise unknown in Greek-inspired theatres.

The remains of theatres found in the neighbouring territories of Campania and Samnium are of particular interest because of their proximity to Rome. Although no theatres have been found here as old as those in Sicily or *Magna Graecia*, there is evidence of an increasing interest in Greek-inspired theatre-building in the course of the second century (when these areas were firmly within the Roman orbit), with structures found (or known from literary sources) at seven sites.[6] This was the same period in which we know that an abortive attempt was made (in 154 BC under the consuls V. Messala and C. Longinus, who had been given a contract by the censors) to construct a permanent theatre in Rome near the Palatine hill. It was also at this time that theatres were constructed by Rome's neighbours within Latium itself, at Gabii and Lanuvium.[7]

Most of the theatres built in Campania and Samnium were on the Greek model with *paraskenia*, probably a significantly raised stage, and an auditorium formed from the natural topography; but there were significant exceptions. The remnants at two sites (Cales and Teanum Sidicinum) suggest an artificially built-up structure, and a written inscription from Capua, dated 108 BC and referring to a group of magistrates having sponsored the construction of a 'theatrum terra exaggerandum',[8] indicates that it too was a free-standing building. Another factor, also evident in later Roman practice, was that several of these theatres were built in combination with a temple located somewhat higher and orientated towards the axis of the theatre. All the theatres of Campania and Samnium are found in urban sites, except that at Pietrabbondante, which is located in a religious sanctuary. Only the capacity of the theatre at Pompeii has been calculated: it accommodated an audience numbering 5,000.

In addition to such Hellenistic stone theatres, the Romans had before them the example of the much simpler temporary stages used to present the *phlyakes*, which were described in chapter 1. From the vases we know that these featured an overhanging roof above the stage itself (which the Greek-inspired theatres lacked), a simple raised platform for performance, and a backdrop of wood or cloth which was sometimes decorated, and through which doors gave access onto the stage. Often stairs are shown connecting the stage to the ground. Unlike the more formal arrangement of space which characterized the Hellenistic theatres, all of which had a large orchestral area interposed between the separate structures of the stage building with its raised stage and the auditorium, the *phlyakes* frequently show an exchange of actions taking place between the actual stage and open ground in front of it. This difference undoubtedly reflected the type of drama performed in either theatre, the one literary, the other unscripted.

In the performance of Greek New Comedy, a raised stage separated the actors in the play itself from the orchestra to which the chorus (now performing interludes entirely separated from the dramatic action) was confined. This chorus (unlike that used earlier in fifth-century Greek tragedy and old comedy), 'far from being a bridge between audience and stage as it once was, tying the theatrical space together . . . now functions as a framing device, cutting off the world of illusion from that of the spectators'.[9] The actors were set off from the chorus, and both actors and chorus from the audience. No such use of architecture formally to support illusion is suggested by the *phlyakes*; on the contrary, everything we know about them suggests their self-conscious theatricality, with a strong improvised element, almost certainly a good deal of direct exchange between actors and audience, and encouragement of the notion that the spectators were actually taking part in the creation of the play and performance.

The Romans, through their awareness of these two distinct types of theatre, each having generated its own architecture, had the opportunity to adopt from each those elements appropriate to their own conception of theatre, and then in the course of time to modify them as theatre practice evolved in Roman society. What can be determined about the choices they made, and the reasons for making them?[10] Solely on the basis of the extant comedies we can begin to construct a model of the early Roman stage by identifying the minimal elements necessary to stage these plays. They were performed on a wooden stage, which Plautus refers to either as the *proscaenium*, or the *scaena*. These are not, however, exact terms, since *scaena* could also be used to designate the scene building, or indeed, its scenic facade, and the latter meaning is also a possible translation of *proscaenium*.[11] In Plautus' *Poenulus* (17–20), the prologue states, 'let no ripe whore sit on the stage [*proscaenium*], no lictor or his rods make a sound, no usher amble about in front, or show anyone to his seat while an actor is onstage. [*scaena*]'.[12]

The stage was backed by the scene building. The front of this building, facing onto the stage, had three openings which could be fitted with serviceable, possibly folding, doors. References to such doors and their functioning abound; they were an indispensable element of the comic action.[13] In addition, entrance onto the stage was afforded from either side, and used by characters when they refer to coming or going to off-stage areas (the harbour, the forum), other than through the doors. There is textual evidence for a roof above at least one of the stage doors, which could be reached from inside the scene building but which projected out on the stage side above the doorway. In Plautus' *Amphitruo* (1008 ff.) Mercury climbs up onto the roof to empty pots of water on Amphitryon standing outside at the door below; 'I'll climb out on that roof there . . . I'll go inside . . . then I'll go up on the roof.'[14]

In other plays by Plautus the doorways may have been somewhat enhanced architecturally. For example, in *Asinaria* (817) we read, 'Didn't I tell you to clean the spiders' webs off the columns? Didn't I tell you to rub those door knobs till they shone?' Probably the doorways occasionally had a small raised porch, the *vestibulum*, attached to them. In *Mostellaria* (817–19) there appears to be an explicit reference to one. 'Do you see this porch in front of the house . . . ? And take a look at these posts! How solidly they're made, and how thick!' This is the only unequivocal suggestion in a surviving comedy[15] of an actual porch, which may, nevertheless, have been imaginary. But there are many instances in the plays when the presence of such an area, set off in front of the doors (probably with a few steps descending to the stage), would have been plausible. It would have been useful both as a convention for presenting a number of notionally 'interior' scenes to the audience, and invaluable for staging the numerous eavesdropping passages.

The area in front of the three doors was thought of, conventionally, as an open street which the characters normally refer to as *platea*; less frequently as *via*.[16] The doorways function as entrances to houses thought of as located along the street. In addition, the plots of the plays frequently make use of a passageway conceived as being behind the houses. A back alley, *angiportum*, is regularly referred to, and it appears to have been thought of as an open area affording access to the rear of the houses (or to the gardens, often referred to as behind them). It was used as a theatrical convention to account for necessary movement of the characters when that movement could not take place openly (for reasons of plot) on the street into which, also conventionally, the houses were thought to open: the stage. Because the actors did indeed need to make just such concealed movements in the course of the performance, it is logical to believe that the conventional concept would in fact have been realized in terms of actual stage structure: a narrow passageway (not visible to the audience, or to onstage characters) running just behind the stage facade. There are frequent references to the *angiportum*, e.g.:

> 'He's already inside. He didn't come this way. He went around by the back passage and through the garden in order not to be seen by the servants.' (*Asinaria*, 741–3)

> 'I went off that way through the back passage to our garden, and opened the garden gate from the back passage and led out all our forces.' (*Mostellaria*, 10043–4)

> 'Go that way through the back passage to the forum; have the girl come back to me the same way through the garden . . .
> . . . Return to me through the back passage, and enter through the garden there.' (*Persa*, 444–6; 678–9)

> 'Don't expect me to return home by this street; under the circumstances I've decided to go through the back passage.' (*Pseudolus*, 1234–5)

In summarizing the evidence for stage structure provided by the texts of early Roman comedy, we find little to suggest that their stages deviated significantly from the model provided by the *phlyakes*, or what we think to have been the virtually identical platform stage of the *Atellanae*. There is no need to propose a borrowing of any of the characteristic elements of the Hellenistic stage itself (with one exception, discussed below), and no suggestion of a chorus and the area

61

allocated to it; the orchestra. Moreover, unlike the Greek-inspired practice of the peoples to the south of them, the Romans did not choose to erect their theatre in a permanent form. This initially close adherence to the format of the *phlyakes* and *Atellanae* is in fact what we might have assumed, in light of what we believe we know about the introduction and early history of drama at Rome. But in the course of time, both as theatre acquired an ever-larger role in the cultural life of the city through its increased presence at both regular and extraordinary festivals; and as the strong tide of Hellenization swept through Roman culture in the course of the second century BC, it seems altogether likely that alterations in the earliest rude stages would reflect these developments.

Perhaps in the suggestion already cited of the raised porch in front of the stage doors, we do already see the first such innovation – a deviation from the earliest format – particularly since it would seem to replicate the most characteristic feature of contemporaneous Greek-inspired theatre architecture (and the one most useful for staging works in the style of Hellenistic comedy): the *paraskenia*. Both Greek New Comedy and the plays adapted by the Roman comic writers require two, and sometimes three doors, each thought of as representing the entrance to a separate building. The *paraskenia* form, providing as it does three distinct structural elements prominently set off from the stage itself, is well suited to staging such plays, and may have been created for this purpose, following the demise of old comedy with its more generalized settings.[17] The Roman playwrights would have found it to be the most obvious and immediately useful element to be borrowed from Hellenistic architecture, and I believe that by Plautus' day it had indeed become part of their temporary stage structure.

In time we would expect further elements to have been introduced into Roman theatre architecture, in a process analogous to that we can trace in dramatic literature: an increasing tendency to assimilate Greek practice. The scant notices that survive documenting the construction of temporary theatres at Rome do tend to support this hypothesis. In 194 BC at the urging of the elder Scipio the aediles ordered that special seats at the scenic games be reserved for members of the Senate.[18] This indicates a new element of stratification in contrast to the earlier impression (gained in particular from the prologues of Plautus) of socially unselfconscious spectators. Such an altered audience would almost certainly exhibit tensions based on taste, education, and sophistication, and this could readily encourage innovation in the drama and its presentation such as is observed in the plays of Terence. Indeed the provision of special seats is an architectural feature frequently noted in the remains of the Hellenistic theatres south of Rome, from which perhaps, it was borrowed.[19] It has been suggested that these senatorial seats were located in an orchestral area between the stage and the wooden tiers of the auditorium.[20] The provision of such an orchestra would in all likelihood itself represent a further architectural innovation. Presumably it would normally have been occupied by privileged spectators but cleared when special events required it.

Just such exceptional occasions are known to have taken place at about this time. Greek *technitai* visited and performed at Rome for ten-day periods twice in 186 BC, and are recorded again for 167 BC.[21] The material presented by them, which they were accustomed to performing in a Hellenistic theatre, required the provision of an orchestral area. These performers were from the Greek east (which is why their visits were noted); tours by troupes from the Hellenistic south may have been relatively common. By this time Greek theatrical custom was sufficiently well known at Rome for Roman actors successfully to present Roman material in Latin, at a festival in Delos, in the heart of the old Hellenistic world.[22]

Stages were presumably erected periodically (in the Forum and the Circus) for the various annual scenic games. Since the historians recording the period (principally Livy) pass over such recurrent constructions, there are grounds for believing that the structures they specifically mention were in some way special. These include a stage and auditorium built near the temple of Apollo in 179 BC by order of the Censor M. Aemilius Lepidus, probably for the *Ludi Apollinares*.[23] In 174 the censors arranged for a stage to be constructed for games given by the aediles and praetors.[24] There is strong evidence that by this period the taste of the Roman theatre-going public for extravagance was already well established, and despite early documented attempts by the Senate to curb it, the tendency continued unabated. Just as the plays themselves may be seen to have offered temporary respite from the otherwise constant pressures of piety and propriety, so too the actual stage settings provided an opportunity to indulge vicariously in acceptable excess. As Cicero characterized it later, the Roman people appreciated public *magnificentia*, but hated private *luxuria*.[25] From the beginning of the second century BC, until the construction of the first permanent theatre, the temporary stages and the performances taking place in them were increasingly lavish; sometimes astonishingly so. As E. J. Jory notes,

> Theatrical activity was intimately connected with three interlocking facets of Roman life; worship of the Gods, the honouring of the dead, and individual self-glorification or, put another way, with religious ceremonial, eulogy of the family and vote-winning. All three aspects tend to stimulate and encourage extravagant display and excessive expenditure.[26]

In addition to a variety of plays and the use of large numbers of costumed performers, extravagance would be concentrated on the temporary theatre structures themselves, their decoration, and scenic elements. The impulse towards spectacle would itself engender experimentation and innovation; trends which inevitably would render the earlier stages obsolete, and encourage the use of architectural and scenic refinements such as might be found in Hellenistic examples. A hint of this may be found in an account of the show produced for the triumph of L. Anicius Gallus, in 167 BC, when, according to Polybius, a stage was erected in the Campus Martius, together with a 'very large *skene*', and an orchestra for dancers.[27] This was at a time when there was interest at Rome in developments in Hellenistic painting, encouraged by the presence there of Demetrius of Alexandria, a painter of scenes of townscapes, shrines, and the like. Such painting was used in the Hellenistic theatres, and it is perhaps not too far-fetched to suggest that the stage facade of 167 would have been enhanced by painted decoration. Polybius himself in another passage refers to such practice; 'the difference between history and declamatory writing is as great as the difference between real building and furniture and the views and composition we see in scene paintings'.[28]

The subject of painting in connection with the Roman temporary stages is most intriguing and suggestive. The earliest mention of theatrical painting is found in Aristotle's *Poetics* (1449a), where he credits Sophocles with having introduced scene painting; *skenographia*, in the middle of the fifth century BC. Having originated in a specifically theatrical context, the term came to be used in antiquity to refer to perspective painting in general. According to tradition, it was first developed by the Athenian Agatharchus (working with both Sophocles and Aeschylus), whose example inspired his contemporaries, Democritus and Anaxagoras, to develop the formal principles of perspective. If we may believe the later commentary of Vitruvius, written in the reign of Augustus, even at this early date such theory was employed, 'so that by this visual deception, a representation of the appearance of buildings can be conveyed in scenery, and what is depicted on a vertical and flat facade, may appear to recede in some places, and project in others'.[29]

Agatharchus is said to have been forced by Alcibiades to decorate the interior of his house is the new type of painting,[30] and if the story is true, it would seem to establish the first connection between theatrical and domestic painting, a subject which I take up later. The earliest and most common form of painted scenery consisted of simple flats decorated in *trompe-l'oeil* to give the impression of solid architectural forms; columns, pilasters, entablature, and the like. Having appeared in the fifth century, the use of some such painted scenery appears to have remained a feature of the Greek and Hellenistic theatre throughout its subsequent structural evolution. Its use is adequately documented in contemporary reference. Inscriptions relating to the theatre of Delos, for example, beginning in about 300 BC, trace the use of painted wooden panels, first to face the front of the stage itself level with the orchestra, and later, about 180 BC, as backdrops against the scene building behind the raised stage. In this and other eastern Greek theatres, the back wall contained large openings, *thyromata*, into which painted panels, curtains, or canvas screens could be inserted. In theatres of the *paraskenia* type, both the front facade of the stage and the flat back wall of the scene building are thought to have made use of painted effects.

It is difficult to suggest when or to what extent such customs, the general nature of which is reasonably clear, began to influence practice in the Roman theatre. For the period in question, the mid-second century BC, the introduction of some such painting would obviously have been an enhancement, and one likely to be welcomed both by ambitious and munificent patrons of the games and by an audience evidently fond of spectacular display.

In 154 BC an attempt was made to build a permanent theatre near the Palatine hill in Rome, placing it on a par with cities both in Campania and Samnium, as well as Latium itself, which acquired such theatres at about this time. Building materials were collected, and the project was evidently well advanced when, three years later, the former consul P. Cornelius Nasica, who had opposed the work from the start, persuaded the Senate to order the demolition of the structure on the grounds that it was 'useless and injurious to public morals'. It was pulled down, the materials were auctioned off, and a ban (subsequently lifted) was imposed on the provision of seating at games held within the city limits.[31]

It is useful to place this event, a milestone in theatrical history at Rome, within the larger context that determined it. Following the era of relative domestic harmony achieved in the course of the third century BC, Rome experienced extraordinary social change in the period after the end of the second Punic war (201 BC). Sudden and extensive expansion abroad had created unlimited opportunities for trade and commercial activity, which in turn had led to the restructuring of society and, inevitably, to grave new conflicts. An upper stratum consisting of the old senatorial aristocracy and landowners, now augmented by a large group of ambitious *nouveaux riches* merchants and entrepreneurs (the basis for the equestrian order) sought to maintain order and manage the affairs of state, while a huge and volatile proletarian mob swirled beneath them. As the Roman historian Sallust described it,

> affairs of state, in war and peace, were conducted through the arbitrary decisions of a few persons. State finances, the provinces, offices, honours and triumphs lay in their hands. The people, however, were oppressed by poverty and military service. While the generals and their cliques seized the spoils of war, their

soldiers' parents and children were driven from house and home if they had stronger neighbors.[32]

In the course of the second century, as exploitation, rents, and the cost of food increased, these desperate people would support any politician who helped them through handouts, or distracted them with entertainment. They were a highly explosive social and political force. After around 150 BC this situation resulted in periodic crisis and continuous tension, both between the patricians and equestrians and with the mob. The earlier cohesion of society, ensured by norms based on tradition, religion, and morality, was severely weakened and the system destabilized.

Strict traditionalists, epitomized by Marcus Porcius Cato, regarded intellectual and artistic innovations as dangerous and morally subversive. In 184 BC during his censorship, Cato had instituted a number of notoriously repressive puritanical measures, intended to halt the growth of foreign-inspired luxury, and other measures were enacted from time to time that reflected an ambivalence, now tolerant, now repressive, towards fashionable new ideas and practices, mostly Greek-inspired.[33] Obviously, the theatre was right in the midst of the battle, involving as it did foreign elements, extravagance, new modes of art and, of course, political catering to the mob and the threat of manipulation or riot. Following upon periodic attempts to curb the costs of the games, in 115 BC the censors took direct measures against the theatre itself, even expelling its practitioners from the city, although the extent and length of the ban is uncertain.[34]

The most obvious consequence of a divided attitude towards the theatre was the prolonged refusal by the authorities to allow the construction of one in stone, despite condoning (and financing) ever more elaborate temporary structures. Whatever innovations in theatre architecture and decoration at Rome might be inspired by the example of Hellenistic cities, their customary provision of a permanent structure was clearly unacceptable. Such antipathy, apart from reflecting a forlorn desire in some circles to limit the burgeoning growth in scenic holidays on moral and financial grounds, may have arisen from the danger to public order that such a building might have been thought to present. A permanent theatre represented a site where a large and unpredictable mass of people could assemble at any time, without warning and therefore, potentially, with no means at hand to control them. Theatres were, after all, purpose-built for mass communication. In the Greek world, including the Hellenized parts of Italy, they had long been used for all sorts of public meetings, including political assemblies and (at least in fifth-century Athens) the plays themselves frequently explored matters of direct public concern. In a period of social unrest and the ever-present threat of violent upheaval, it could certainly have been argued (particularly by those with little sympathy for the theatre in the first place) that this was unacceptably dangerous.[35]

In the absence of a permanent facility, the impulse towards the display of scenic and architectural virtuosity on the temporary stages appears to have become ever more pronounced. In 99 BC Claudius Pulcher created an elaborate, multi-coloured *scaena*, which attracted great admiration. It made such effective use of *trompe-l'oeil* technique to imitate architectural details that, according to Pliny the elder, 'crows were deceived into flying to the painted image of roof tiles'.[36] Thus by this time (if not, indeed considerably earlier), the Hellenistic practice of *skenographia* was being used to decorate the Roman stage.

The audience enjoyed further refinements, as patrons of the games produced new effects to please and dazzle them. At the shows given by Quintus Lutatius Catulus in 69 BC celebrating the dedication of the rebuilt temple of Jupiter on the Capitoline, he added an additional pleasure borrowed, according to the account, 'in imitation of Campanian luxury'.[37] This was the *vela*, or *velarium*, an awning or linen roof – the Greeks termed it *petasos;* a wide-brimmed hat – which could be stretched out over the auditorium. Brightly coloured, it both pleased the eye and protected the spectators from the sun. Such a device is known to have been used at Pompeii, and possibly at Capua as well.[38] An indication that at this time the theatre was by no means attended only by the lower orders, but also attracted members of a self-conscious elite (presumably concerned about the comfort and luxury provided for their enjoyment) is found in the legislation of 68 BC in which members of the equestrian order were ensured the right (previously reserved formally to senators), to occupy special seats of honour in the theatre: the first fourteen rows behind the orchestra.[39]

The innovation quickened and the shows became more ostentatious when, according to Valerius Maximus, in the course of the next decade 'C. Antonius decorated the stage entirely in silver, Petreius, in gold, and Q. Catulus with ivory . . . P. Lentulus ornamented it with scenic devices of silver.'[40] Finally, in 58 BC – three years before the dedicaton of Pompey's permanent theatre – the aedile M. Aemilius Scaurus produced what was literally the last word in scenic excess in the temporary theatres. According to Pliny, (whose account almost beggars belief), Scaurus

> constructed during his aedileship, (and merely for a few days' temporary use), the grandest edifice ever wrought by man, even when meant to be permanent. I refer to his theatre. The structure had three storeys, supported by three hundred and sixty columns. . . . The lowest level was marble; the next glass – a luxury never heard of since – and the top was fashioned from gilded boards. The lowest columns . . . were thirty-eight feet high, and between them

were placed three thousand bronze statues. . . . The rest of the
equipment, including cloth of gold, painted panels, and various
theatrical properties, was so lavish that when those remnants
suitable for everyday use were taken to Scaurus' Tusculam villa,
and the villa then burnt by angry servants, the loss was calculated
at 30,000,000 sesterces.[41]

This must be exaggerated, although the general suggestion of
a highly ornamented *scaena* is probably valid, and anticipates the
sumptuously decorated *scaenae frons* of the permanent theatres to
come, providing further grounds for believing that, by this time,
much of the formal evolution leading to it had indeed taken place
through architectural developments and experiments in the temporary
structures. That this process was heavily influenced by practice in the
Hellenistic world in which Rome was now deeply immersed is
suggested by Vitruvius' account of a theatre structure which echoes
and complements the description of Scaurus' contemporaneous stage.
Like it, which evidently incorporated painted effects (*tabulae pictae*)
into the facade of the *scaena*, the example described by Vitruvius
was composed of a mixture of actual, as well as fanciful, painted
architecture.

> At Tralles, Apaturius of Alabanda skilfully designed the stage of
> the small theatre . . . on which he depicted columns, statues, and
> centaurs holding up the architraves; rotundas with rounded
> domes; the angles of projecting pediments; and cornices formed of
> lions' heads to carry off rainwater from the roofs. Moreover, the
> storey above this had rotundas, porticoes, half pediments, and all
> types of painted embellishment displayed on a roof. When the
> appearance of this stage, by virtue of its high relief, pleased its
> viewers, Licymnius the mathematician came forward and said . . .
> let us take care lest this painted stage make Alabandines or
> Abderites of us [peoples renowned for, respectively, extravagance
> and stupidity]. For which of you could have buildings, or columns
> or elabourate pediments above the tiles of your roof? . . . If we
> approve of such pictures which can have no basis in reality, we
> shall, like those other communities, be deemed idiots, because of
> such faults.[42]

Earlier Vitruvius had described the way in which such perspective
painting when used in the theatre could indeed be deceptive;

> The eyes do not always convey an accurate impression, but
> sometimes cause the mind to deceive itself. For example, in stage
> paintings columns and mutules may appear to project, and statues
> stand out, even though the picture is undoubtedly a flat surface.[43]

Vitruvius approved of the use of perspective effect so long as the actual objects it depicted were drawn from reality. In the section just preceding his critical account of the impossible architecture depicted by Apaturius, he lays out this principle, and mentions by way of illustration a most intriguing example:

> Now painting makes an image of something which exists, or can exist, such as a person, a building, a ship or some other object, from whose fixed and definite forms its imitations are taken. Therefore the ancients who introduced polished finishes [to their walls] first imitated the various types of marble inlay, and then different combinations of festoons, mouldings and dividers. Later they proceeded to imitate also the contours of structures, and projecting elements of columns and gables. In open areas such as *exhedra*, because of the dimensions of their walls, they depicted the facades of stages [*scaenarum frontes*] of the tragic, comic or satyric type.[44]

Our attempt to build up a picture of the Roman temporary stage through the analysis of playtexts, together with frequently random and fragmentary historical references now turns to an entirely new and independent category of evidence: surviving Roman wall painting may actually preserve depictions of such stages! The possibility that such painting (much of which was preserved at Pompeii and Herculaneum by the eruption of Vesuvius in AD 79) may be used as evidence for the nature of Roman stage architecture and scenery has long been the subject of intense scholarly debate. Some authorities, taking Vitruvius at his word, have seen in many paintings accurate representations of actual theatre structures. Others, rejecting this, have argued that although wall painting and the *scaenae frons* may have evolved along stylistically similar lines, they did so quite independently of each other. The paintings may occasionally contain theatrical elements, such critics assert, but in no way take actual theatre architecture or scenery as a direct model.[45]

The wall paintings were the object of several extensive studies in the first decades of this century. These however, even when they were inclined to recognize some theatrical content in the frescoes, were hampered not only by the absence of several highly suggestive examples which have since been discovered, and which are of great help in interpreting the paintings generally, but also by an approach which frequently examined the works for the wrong kind of evidence. Scholars repeatedly looked in vain for images which could be seen to depict what was known to be the form of the Roman *permanent* stage facade: the *scaenae frons*. Failing for the most part to find such images, they concluded that such proximate and suggestive examples as there were owed their presence not to any attempt actually to represent stages in the paintings, but rather to some general stylistic tendencies common to both painting and architecture of the period. Had they given more weight to the possible (and probable) role of the temporary stages as appropriate subject matter, their conclusions might well have been different.

Roman wall painting is inherently illusionistic. It was conceived and executed as a means of conveying the spectator, often with great subtlety, from a real to an imaginary world. It developed to a high degree *trompe-l'oeil* techniques in order initially to create upon a real wall illusionistic structural elements dependent upon it, and in a later phase, to abolish the reality of the wall altogether, by 'opening it up' to depict doorways, windows, and distant vistas. Not only did it represent as a matter of course architecture not in fact real; it frequently created (particularly in its later period) an altogether impossible architecture which never was and never could be built.[46] But, significantly, if we believe the testimony of Vitruvius cited earlier, this is also precisely what theatrical scenery did.

The difficulty in correctly interpreting the possible theatrical evidence provided by such paintings can be better appreciated if we consider that even an exact and faithful representation of a decorated stage set would present the viewer with, in effect, an illusion within an illusion. The written evidence indicates that the stage background itself might well contain illusionistic perspective painting representing imaginary architecture as part of its décor, and then, in turn, this stage has itself been illusionistically rendered by the wall painter. Thus, even an accurate depiction (or for that matter, a photograph, if such existed!) of a theatrical set will present problems in discerning 'real' architecture from painted architecture, since the set is itself a combination of both. If we then take into account that the artist may choose *not* to depict the stage set accurately; may enliven it with non-existent elements or even use it merely as the point of departure for his own improvised rendering of imaginary architecture with very little basis in fact, then the problem of achieving any reliable analysis is truly daunting.

Even if we assume that painters did frequently take stage sets as their subject matter, they must have done so, not to depict such sets per se, but rather because they provided a starting point for organizing the space to be decorated and creating on it the illusion of unreal architecture. In particular, the tripartite division of the stage itself, with its three doorways, would have provided an obvious and ready-made formula for decorating the wall, and moreover, one based (as Vitruvius insisted it ought to be) on a model drawn from real life; from an actual object. The attraction of stage sets as subject matter would be that while allowing the artists to adhere to this important principle of verisimilitude, they simultaneously invited a large measure of fantasy and variety, both because of some variation in the actual stage architecture and, more importantly, because the stage itself used painted illusionistic scenery. Therefore, until the practice of depicting real objects was gradually displaced by tendencies which led in the later phases of Roman wall painting to pure fantasy, the stage would have provided the perfect compromise: an opportunity to maximize the illusionistic element, while still abiding by the fundamental principle of objective accuracy. We can see why (as Vitruvius asserted), stage sets would be popular subjects for depiction.

The paintings have to be viewed with a degree of caution and scepticism. Nevertheless, there are some works which, after all opposing arguments have been taken into account, still seem manifestly to depict stage sets. These sets, moreover, if sets they be, are ideally suited to those staging requirements of Roman theatrical fare independently determined on the basis of textual evidence alone. They also support (and extend) the knowledge already gleaned from historical accounts about the nature of the temporary stages.

In 1960 a room was discovered during the excavation of an area believed to be the house of Augustus, the first of the imperial residences on the Palatine hill in Rome.[47] The 'Room of the Masks', which takes its name from several unusual masks depicted within its decorative scheme, was found in a good state of preservation and, because it had been buried since antiquity and protected from moisture and erosion, the quality and freshness of the colours, and indeed, the condition of the painting generally is exceptional. The work is unusual too, not only in the artist's extremely skilful use of vanishing-point perspective, but also in his decision to depict a manifestly 'real' structure without the embellishment and imaginative fantasy which, as noted above, frequently make difficult any precise distinction among what is meant to represent actual architecture, what are perspective vistas placed within that architecture, and what is purely ornamental, fanciful architecture.

In this painting we find arranged all the elements which (on the basis of the textual evidence) were deemed essential to the comic stage, and much else besides. It depicts a brightly coloured wooden structure formed of a central pavilion connected by low, partitioning walls to two flanking apertures which are backed by folding wooden doors. Each of the three *vestibula* is covered by a low roof, supported on slender pillars. In the central opening these pillars are reinforced by lateral braces to connect them to pilasters to the rear, while the pillars at the side doors are joined to the facade by a slender half-wall which serves to create a small porch.

The structure of doorways and columns rests upon a low podium made up of projecting plinths, and this in turn rests upon a stage, whose

4 Painting in the 'Room of the Masks' in the House of Augustus at Rome which is
thought to depict a temporary stage.

depth has been foreshortened by perspective. At the extreme edges of
the composition, wings project from the scene building, which with its
coffered ceiling forms a shell to enclose from three sides and above the
stage constructed within it.

The ornamentation in this work is sparse when compared to other
Roman painted architectural representation, consisting only of two
masks resting on the low walls which flank the central pavilion,
festooned garlands, and small vases and figures placed on the pediments
of the roofs and connecting entablature. The picture in the central
recession, which represents a rural religious shrine and is sketchily
painted in lighter tones than the rest, is seen in the context of the
structure to be not a view behind the architecture, but rather a
painted panel or *pinax* positioned within it.

That the structure is wooden and temporary is indicated by the
slender columns (decorated with dies and bosses) which support the
roof of the central pavilion, by the small pillars at either porch, the
braces and narrow reinforcing walls, and by the thin, insubstantial
roofing. The artist has tried to show that the structure is meant to be

5 Painting in Room 23 of the Villa of Oplontis near Pompeii. Similar to the setting in the 'Room of the Masks', it shows additionally a receding colonnade behind the architectural facade.

real, and an important aspect of its reality is its temporary nature, which he has therefore been careful to record.

If, for the sake of argument, we assume that what is depicted here is indeed a stage set, we could then use its format as a model, a sort of visual 'Rosetta stone' to apply in identifying and interpreting other, less straightforward paintings. In fact, a good number of surviving examples of Roman wall painting provide further evidence when such an approach is used to analyse them. I will limit my discussion to just a few of them, returning to the topic in chapter 6 when I take up the subject of the use of movable scenery in the Roman theatre.

In the recent and continuing excavations at the imperial villa of Oplontis, beneath Torre Annunziata on the Bay of Naples, a painting has come to light which depicts a structure fulfilling the basic requirements of the Roman comic stage, and also bears a striking resemblance to the work from the 'Room of the Masks'. Although the artist has allowed himself somewhat greater freedom, primarily in the representation of an architectural background, the structure of the facade itself is virtually identical to that depicted in the House of Augustus.[48]

A central roofed alcove contains a monochrome panel representing a sacred shrine. Above the panel rests a large theatrical mask. Low partitioning walls similar to those seen in the Palatine structure extend to two side pavilions, which, unlike the former painting, are not roofed but, like it, are backed by folding wooden doors. Once again the entire structure is contained within a larger shell, with a coffered ceiling and projecting wings, the side walls of which are visible at the extreme edges of the composition and have windows inserted into them. The facade again rests upon a podium. The major difference between the two paintings, that the structure depicted at Oplontis displays behind the architectural framework (and partially masked by black, sagging curtains) a receding colonnade, is a subject I address later in my discussion of scenery. In both paintings, there is a suggestion of a passageway (the *angiportum*?) extending behind the stage facade into which the stage doors give access.

A further example is found in the House of the Gladiators at Pompeii. The structure represented in the painting is more elaborate architecturally than the Palatine or Oplontis works, although its basic format is very similar. It shares the same fundamental elements: doorways with folding doors, forming part of small *vestibula*, which are connected to one another by low flanking walls, and rest upon a continuous podium which in turn rests upon a stage narrowed by foreshortening. Its more highly ornamented structural elements can still be seen to be temporary in nature: the columns, doors, and walls would have been built of wood. Moreover, their particular arrangement directly anticipates that adopted for the permanent stages.

> In the foreground is a *pulpitum* with a curved niche flanked by two rectangular niches on each side. The *scaenae frons* behind this has three doors; the central one is set in a curved *exhedra*, and is flanked by four spirally fluted columns, while the two outer doors are set in rectangular *exhedrae*, and also flanked by projecting columns. This represents the scheme which was later to become common.[49]

Again, as in the example from Oplontis, this work displays behind the structural framework of the stage facade the suggestion of further architecture in the background.

In a number of other works the architecture depicted is sometimes subjected to such fantasy and elaboration, or alternatively, so reduced to designs whose lines merely hint at their formal inspiration that, were it not for the more explicit evidence of paintings such as these, any hypothetical model in real architecture would be difficult to discern.

6   Wall painting in the House of the Gladiators at Pompeii, depicting an elaborate
temporary facade resting upon a stage. The particular arrangement of doorways in
the facade, and niches along the front of the stage, corresponds to the architectural
pattern frequently found in the later permanent theatres.

However, having once recognized the basic model, one can readily
identify the variations which stylization has produced out of it.

The stage format suggested by the examples of paintings considered
thus far, in addition to confirming the various architectural elements
whose existence could be predicated on the basis of written evidence, may
also provide the answer to questions that scholars have raised on the basis
of such evidence. For example, although most of the plays which survive
wholly or in part require only two doors for their staging, several
require three. What became of the third door when a particular play did
not require it?[50] It is important to remember in this context that the
Roman stage almost certainly was never a stage of monoscenic illusion.
That is to say, there was no attempt to represent realistically a particular
location and environment. If scenic elements were employed, they were
used emblematically, to suggest or designate a place without attempting
to depict or represent it accurately. Given such conventions it is quite
unlikely that the continuous presence of a prominent central aperture
not actually required by the performance would cause the audience

7   Painting in the 'Room of the Masks' at Rome. The wall is not as wide as that illustrated in Fig. 4, and the painter therefore has concentrated on depicting the central section of the facade with its painted panel showing a sacred shrine.

much concern, although it has distressed some later commentators. The presence of similar static elements on the Elizabethan stage, which was also an emblematic theatre, does not seem in any way to have detracted from the audience's pleasure, their ability to understand the play, nor indeed, because it was an accepted convention of that theatre, to have been thought of as somehow intrusive or anachronistic.[51] Modern observers are sometimes too conditioned by their experience of theatrical realism, the particular set of conventions which still dominate our theatre, easily to imagine a radically different mode of production.

On the basis of the wall paintings, what seems likely is that, when not actually required in the staging of the play, this central aperture functioned scenically, either to denote a shrine or landmark peculiar to the play's locale, or perhaps the garden which is frequently thought of as being behind or adjoining the houses in the play. With the central panel in place (it may have been 'revealed' at the beginning of the performance by the removal of a curtain), an effective emblematic element existed which, although the relevant iconography is largely lost to us, could

8 Painting in the House of the Vettii at Pompeii. In the lower portion, dominated by a central decorative panel and fantasy architecture, the influence of a theatrical model is no longer obvious; in the section above however, the suggestion of a temporary stage format is easily recognizable.

have been useful in establishing the type of play and possibly its theme and subject matter. That the Roman stage used some painted scenery is certain[52] and the depiction of what are obviously meant to be painted panels in many of the paintings thought to represent stage sets would be an appropriate and altogether likely place for the display of such scenery. For the wall painter moreover, this aspect of the stage was very attractive, since it provided an ideal central area upon which purely decorative, non-architectural compositions could be rendered. In fact, in the course of the later phases of Roman wall painting, it was enormously expanded until it completely dominated the composition which, through the process, lost all resemblance to any real architecture, theatrical or otherwise.

A number of earlier paintings, however (when the compositions were more directly imitative of real objects), alternate the depiction of a central panel with a central doorway. This was often the case when the width of the actual wall did not allow the painter sufficient space to depict architecture derived from the full length of the tripartite stage facade. Then the painter might represent only the central section of the facade, usually in the form of a large doorway with the flanking pillars, roof, and other elements forming a *vestibulum*. This approach seems to

9 First-century BC painting from the *triclinium* of the Villa of P. Fannius Sinistor near Pompeii, now at the Museum of Mariemont, Belgium. A large central doorway is flanked by half-walls with receding colonnades depicted behind small black curtains. No side doors were represented, probably because this was not feasible given the scale of the composition relative to the width of the wall.

have been popular with painters of the earlier period because the central painted doorway was a most suggestive illusionistic device, providing visually and imaginatively a direct access in the centre of the composition between the real space of the room itself and the fictional spaces evoked on the wall. Scholars have frequently disputed the role of stage architecture in inspiring such compositions in part because the paintings failed to depict the full length of a stage structure, and, without the benefit of the model format (derived from paintings discovered subsequently) they failed to discern that only the central portion of a stage facade was being represented.

Such a central doorway is seen in a work from the House of Pinarius Cerialis at Pompeii. Here, however, because of the presence of performers, there can be little doubt that the work was inspired by stage architecture even though the width of the wall was not sufficient to show the doors at either side. It is one of several somewhat similar versions of the same scene found in both vases and paintings.[53] The general arrangement of the figures may go back to an original Greek version as early as the fourth century BC. The picture is probably based upon Euripides' *Iphigenia in Tauris*, although it is apparently meant to be a composite scene not corresponding to any particular moment in the extant play. The central figure of Iphigenia, accompanied by two female servants, is shown exiting from the Temple of Artemis, whose statuette she carries together with a laurel wreath. Framed on a panel behind the doorway is an image of the goddess within her circular temple or *tholos*. A vase stands on the steps in front of Iphigenia, and a sword leans against the base of the podium, to the right. In the right-hand portion of the painting stand the manacled figures of Orestes and Pylades, their heads garlanded. At the opposite side, King Thoas sits, accompanied by a guard in Scythian dress, who carries a shield.

Although conceived on a more elaborate scale than most, the actual architectural format of the background is similar to that found in other paintings thought to depict temporary stage sets. As in them, the central *vestibulum* and doorway has low flanking walls linking it with further structures at the edges of the composition. Close inspection of the architecture depicted reveals that, as in other examples, the structure is placed within a sort of shell, the coffered ceiling of which is clearly visible, particularly in the upper right portion of the picture. When viewed in colour, what emerges is that the architecture is in fact a mixture of 'real' and painted elements. The structures in the foreground are picked out in various colours, mostly shades of gold with some green. The architecture to the rear, however, is all of one colour; a uniform shade of red. It has been represented in *trompe-l'oeil* on what are probably meant to be painted panels, placed against a solid wall behind the protruding structure of the 'real' architecture in the foreground.

10 First-century AD painting in the House of Pinarius Cerialis, Pompeii, thought to
show a scene based on a version of *Iphigenia in Tauris* on a stage set.

Thus, if one looks closely at the upper portion of the columns and
pediments set back and forming the porches depicted at either side of
the central aedicule, and behind the draped garlands, one notes that they
terminate at the top in a slightly V-shaped line; the uppermost edge of a
panel, placed against a blank wall: a wall which, significantly, is of the
same golden colour as most of the rest of the 'real' architecture in the
foreground.

The basis for this in actual theatre structure would be either a
complex temporary stage, composed of a combination of plastic and
painted elements or, possibly, a very basic permanent stage consisting of
a solid architectural shell against the flat wall on which an arrangement
of painted panels and articulated wooden sets could be placed. This
subject arises in my discussion of permanent theatres in chapter 6, but it
is useful to note here that the *scaena* of the small permanent theatre at
Pompeii consists of just such a flat wall, and the large theatre there also
had a flat facade (probably in the time of Augustus; around the period in
which this painting was executed) before being converted to the typical
format of the Roman permanent *scaenae frons* (the earliest surviving
example) some time between AD 63 and the destruction of the city in 79.[54]

The paintings lend credence to the possibility, suggested on the basis of one or two direct references (and many inferred instances), in the comic texts and fragments that the early stages made use of a partially enclosed porch, or *vestibulum* in front of the stage doors. The frescoes repeatedly show such aedicules in a variety of formats. In most cases they are framed on either side by wooden panels, in a way which suggests a possible sounding box effect. Such porches were regularly a feature of the permanent Roman stage facade, and on the basis of the paintings it seems certain that they had evolved (possibly as early as Plautus) on the temporary stages. Vitruvius, in his discussion of theatrical acoustics, notes the particular characteristic of the wooden stages: 'One may object that many theatres are built every year at Rome without regard to these matters. But one would err, because all public wooden theatres have a great deal of boarding which resonates naturally.'

In the same passage, he describes a custom which may suggest that even the stone theatres still made use of wooden porches and doors. 'We can observe . . . those who . . . when they wish to sing with a louder tone, turn to the wooden doors, and with this help, gain resonance for their voice'.[55]

Yet another question seems resolved by the paintings. The permanent Roman theatres had a large, coffered ceiling which sloped out over the *scaenae frons* and stage, and scholars have tended, as Margarete Bieber does, to assume that it 'became probably a permanent feature only after permanent theaters were built'.[56] But a coffered ceiling is clearly evident in the wall paintings, and seems moreover a thoroughly logical element, necessary to protect the highly decorated temporary scenery forming the stage facade beneath it.

One of the most characteristic elements of the permanent stage was that the structural facade of the *scaenae frons* was supported on a continuous podium, or range of plinths which, in turn, rested upon the stage itself. This peculiar element is not known to have been a feature of the wall of the Hellenistic *skene*, and is first found in the remains of Roman theatres. But it is a prominent part of the scenic facade shown in many of the wall paintings, some of which also depict steps descending from it to the level of the stage. This seems to provide proof that this feature (which would remain part of the permanent stages throughout their long history) evolved in the temporary theatres. Moreover, if we compare the general form of the stage facade seen in the paintings with depictions on vases thought to show earlier temporary Hellenistic *paraskenia* stages, we see a startling resemblance. It actually appears as if such a structure (with its two flanking porches linked by continuous entablature and roof) has been placed within a larger shell formed of a second stage, back wall, and coffered ceiling. Or, expressed in terms of

81

11   Reconstruction of the format of a temporary *paraskenia* stage, based on a vase found at Tarentum, now in Würzburg.

ancient theatre architecture, a structure of the *paraskenia* type has been placed upon a basic *phlyakes* stage with its platform, rear wall, and ceiling.

Such a stage within a stage would account for several curious aspects of the structures represented in the wall paintings. It would explain the presence in effect of two ceilings; the one above the porches, the other over the entire stage. It would also justify the existence of two back walls, the one linking the three aedicules, and another behind it, which is shown bare in some examples, or faced with apparently painted panels of more distant architecture in others. Most significantly, if would also account for the podium upon which the entire structure of the facade rests, for what is this if not a stage upon a stage?

To summarize then: on the basis of textual, historical, and visual evidence, taken together we can trace, however dimly, the gradual evolution in the temporary stages of a hybrid form; a 'missing link' between earlier native and Hellenistic structures, and the permanent Roman theatre. Beginning perhaps with the simple format of the *phlyakes* (and its native equivalent, the stage of the *Atellanae*), other elements were gradually introduced. These include three doorways, *vestibula* (possibly derived from the *paraskenia*), painted panels, elaborately embellished temporary architecture, and a raised podium. A ceiling was evidently retained from the *phlyakes*, although unknown in formal Hellenistic structures. Possibly under the influence of visiting

Greek performers, an orchestral area was provided in front of the stage, although normally it was not used for Roman dramatic presentations. Following Hellenistic precedent, special seats were set aside for dignitaries, but, unlike the Greeks, the Romans did not use the theatre for political assemblies nor, until 55 BC, did they allow it in any permanent form.

The temporary stages had developed, possibly along the lines I have suggested, in order to meet the needs of the contemporary repertoire. The evidence indicates that this changed relatively little over a long period of time; although at different periods some authors or genres of theatre may have been more popular than others, the same *type* of entertainments (including even the primitive *Atellanae*) with the same basic staging requirements continued to be performed. There seems no persuasive reason to suppose that, once having achieved a workable form contingent upon the requirements of the dramatic performances, the structure of the temporary stage would thereafter have been altered in any fundamental way during the long period for which its presence is documented. Indeed, as we shall see in chapter 6, the subsequent permanent theatres of the imperial period, which certainly coexisted with the temporary stage, embodied nearly all of its essential characteristics.

These elements were eventually consolidated and incorporated into a single, autonomous theatre building, a type unknown in the Hellenistic world. As noted earlier, Greek-inspired theatres were not free-standing, but made use of a natural enclave, out of which the auditorium was formed. In marked contrast, the later Roman theatres were independent architecturally unified structures in which the separate elements of scene building, stage, orchestra, and auditorium were fused to form a single 'purpose-built' entity standing on level ground. This tendency may have been encouraged by the custom of erecting the earliest temporary stages (on a flat surface) in the Forum or Circus. In particular, in the case of the circus, we know that artificial raised seating had been constructed there at an early date,[57] and it would have been logical for the temporary theatres to have continued the custom of providing such seating, even when they were placed in locations other than the Circus.

In the ambivalence and suspicion which sometimes conditioned the attitude of the Roman authorities towards the theatre, we may discern one of the reasons why a self-contained building came to be favoured over the Hellenistic examples widely available. Access to, and order within such a building was far easier to control than in the more permeable Greek theatres. In the Roman theatre, as in modern outdoor theatres and stadia based in part on its example, spectators had to enter and exit through an external door or doors, where order and surveillance could be maintained, or indeed entry denied; they could not simply descend upon and invade the building from a variety of points as was often the case with Greek theatres.[58] With this final development the basic architectural form of the Roman theatre was complete.

After studying and analysing a large number of wall paintings, in 1984 I began a project based in part on the results of these investigations. Taking literally as a 'working' hypothesis the proposition that the stage suggested by the wall paintings was indeed the type used for staging Roman drama, I first constructed a small model, and then built a full-scale replica wooden stage at the Arts Centre of the University of Warwick.[59] Then, over several years, I staged a series of plays by Plautus upon it. Although the stage of Plautus may have been somewhat more austere than that suggested by the paintings, his plays, perennially popular, together with other works requiring the same format, continued to be performed on the temporary stages as they evolved.[60]

In the course of rehearsals, I tested my hypothesis by observing how well (or indeed, whether) the 'architecture' of a Roman play – its development, necessary actions, movements, and spatial demands – was

12   A replica temporary stage, based on the evidence of Roman wall painting, and built and used at the University of Warwick.

served by the actual architecture of the set. I was struck early on, once I got the actors onto the set, by how easily the play seemed to stage itself. Eliot described how, in reading ancient drama; 'behind the dialogue . . . we are always conscious of a concrete visual actuality'.[61] The sense that one frequently has of the physical presence of the stage architecture was readily realized in my set.

It was found that the arrangement of the stage effortlessly accommodated and incorporated the texts I chose (initially the *Miles Gloriosus* and *Casina*). The set met all the plays' basic staging requirements, and at the same time through its formal layout and the positioning of its performance areas *vis-à-vis* the audience, it provided the basis and suggestion for a style of presentation as well. Its colourful exuberance and frank theatricality supported the deliberate self-consciousness of Plautine farce, with its frank acknowledgement of its own conventional artificiality and the constant awareness of and reference to the participating presence of the audience. The appropriateness of the set derived from the wall paintings was further demonstrated by the manner in which various elements such a niches, stairs, doors, the side wall to either porch, and the continuous podium connecting them, proved very useful for various bits of comic business, and invited a lively 'collaboration' between the actors and the set. I also devised and successfully employed a system of movable painted scenery, according to the ancient visual and literary evidence, a subject taken up in chapter 6.

The critic for the *Times Educational Supplement* wrote of the first production:

> The audience found the set instantly appealing. Every part of the stage (except the upper level, which seemed to merge into the painted backcloth) was in use at points which required it naturally, throughout the play. The niches and steps and doors (and the indispensable unseen passageway between the houses), *must* have been used like this. The proportions of the set were elegantly convincing . . . but this street was not at all like a street in Rome, or even (though closer) like real Pompeii; its brilliance and symmetry belonged to the scenographic world, like its fantasy background of impossibly soaring columns. Most producers of Plautus (who has a lot to offer to schools and others) cannot do things on this scale. But if they saw this production they will be trying to create their own artificial framework for his perennial small-town comedy.

The replica set has been kept for use as a teaching resource and for future productions of other Roman plays.[62]

4

A FUNNY THING: PERFORMING A PLAY BY PLAUTUS

If, as I have claimed, Plautus was quintessentially a 'man of the theatre', whose work owed its immense popularity (and enduring influence) primarily to a talent for expressing funny things dramaturgically – creating comedies for the enjoyment of a theatrical audience – it follows that the proof of his pre-eminence must lie in performance itself. Of course, that cannot be *demonstrated* here, but it can be argued and indirectly illustrated with reference to a description of how elements of his work might be rendered on stage. However, the experience of a drama as an active art (and therefore its *existence*) in performance is both ephemeral and incremental. The play unfolds and simultaneously shapes and modifies the spectators' perception and reaction as they are involved in a continuing sequence of events. To attempt to explicate Plautus' theatrical talent through a selection of disparate examples – snapshots – taken variously from his plays, is not likely to convey a very comprehensive sense of his genius. I hope that a series of illustrations and sketches drawn from a single work may provide more suggestive insights, and help justify my assertions about his power as a *playwright* whose works require an audience and a theatre to give them life.

I have chosen his *Casina* for discussion on the grounds that it has a fair claim to be an excellent example of Plautus' particular qualities as a dramatist (which, the evidence indicates, made it greatly popular with its original audience), and also because I have had the useful experience both of translating and staging it before a modern audience. As with other surviving works of ancient drama totally lacking original stage directions, the text provides all the information necessary for an intelligible presentation – all essential action is signified – but Plautus' style of comedy often requires that a director and cast intuit plausible moments in which the dialogue and situation suggest particular bits of comic business.[1] A measure of Plautus' craft, and the confidence that producers can consequently place in him, is the uncanny ease with which such moments often emerge from the text, prompting the performers to 'flesh out' the suggestions they find there. As a playwright with a keen sense of theatricality, Plautus provides scenarios for performance that, 2,000 years later, readily respond to and reward sensitive analysis and trustful respect by a director and cast. The condescension frequently evident in the literary criticism of Plautus' works which so distorted their evaluation by earlier scholarship, seems entirely misplaced once the plays are allowed literally to 'take place' in the theatre.

The staging of the plays – their realization in time and space – is also greatly assisted by taking into account the plausible assumptions about the basic physical format of the Roman stage which I discussed in the previous chapter. With such a format firmly in mind (or ideally, working on a stage which replicates it), the essential stage picture and the lineaments of the actors' movements can be readily discerned from the text. The given conditions of the physical setting, the actions dictated by the text, and the language the characters speak in the evolving circumstances of the play: these taken together provide a practical dramaturgical framework within which further refinements of pacing, patterns of movement, characterization, and complementary business can be developed and integrated. The account that follows here is meant to illustrate how these elements might be brought together in a production of *Casina* and is intended only to suggest one way in which Plautus might effectively have been presented before an ancient audience, by drawing upon my direct experience in realizing his works for a contemporary one.

Of course, it would be naive to presume that an approach necessary to present the play successfully before today's spectators would be identical to that used in antiquity; the ancient audience, its expectations and response were subject to a vast array of local conditions: they lived in a different world. Even their reasons for being in the theatre differed greatly from those motivating modern theatre-goers. This is merely a particular instance of the general truth that 'those who study and teach the history of the ancient world suffer from a great disadvantage, which we find difficult to admit even to ourselves: in a perfectly literal sense we do not know what we are talking about'. What we have is 'accumulated knowledge *about* what we are talking about'.[2] Yet, in the example of a work intended for the theatre, our situation is somewhat improved; the playwright has left us not merely a text, but, through its careful reconstitution, the conditions for having a more particular and structured experience of a type with which (at least through analogy), we are familiar, and can 'know'. It is the nature of theatrical art that the playwright 'is not writing about something; he is writing something'.[3]

At a fundamental level, there is a considerable area of 'overlap' between what we know about – or rather may know *from* – the experience, and what an ancient audience knew. Plautus' characters, the situations in which he places them, and their consequent behaviour and language do in fact find a ready response in our theatre: they make us laugh.

Much laughter is nervous; the perception of incongruity sets it off and it often arises from such social and psychological tensions as those engendered by the relations between the sexes, class conflict, generational antagonisms, and reactions to disparities of power and authority. Because these are still felt by a modern audience, they empower the play to continue to function as a living act of comic theatre: to seem, in a word, 'funny'. Despite the denigration they have sometimes suffered as literature, and the challenge of attempting to understand the full resonance and subtlety of meaning they would have had for their original audience, Plautus' dramas can indeed work for us as *plays*, and this is strong empirical evidence suggesting that many of the factors determining the dramaturgy and effect of ancient Roman comedy in performance are not really foreign at all: they have become part of our theatrical tradition.

As its prologue makes clear, *Casina*, in the version preserved to us, was already part of theatrical heritage only a generation or so after Plautus composed it: the text derives from a revival. This means that the work (as the prologue emphasizes) had been popular, and therefore may be taken as a reliable example of an effective and successful play. It also raises the vexed question of how authentically Plautine our text is. The general (but not universal) consensus is that with the exception of some fifteen lines in the prologue which explicitly refer to its earlier history, the text has survived in the form in which Plautus composed it.[4]

We may conceive of the function of the performer presenting the prologue to this play as analogous to that of a fairground barker. As the other examples discussed in chapter 2 illustrate, Plautus in presenting a play in such festive and distracting circumstances frequently first sought to secure the attention and goodwill of the audience, while in the process arousing its interest and anticipation. This task is quickly assumed by the *Casina* prologue, who, unlike some others, is neither presented as a character in the play about to be performed, nor begins to induct the audience imaginatively into its aesthetic realm. Standing 'outside' the play, he describes its background to us, but only after first praising our good faith, and asking us to confirm his high opinion of us with an opening round of applause; 'if that seems fair then give a little sign, to show you'll hear us with an open mind'.[5] Thus both through flattery and by encouraging our immediate active participation, the prologue takes control. The flattery continues in the brief post-Plautine insertion while, at the same time, praising the play itself, comparing it to a vintage wine which wise men know how to value over inferior 'modern' plays. It concludes:

'we've duly taken note of what the people say:
you're longing to applaud a play by Plautus here today.
A titillating tale, to charm, amuse and move;
the sort of stuff the older crowd approve.
You younger folks who don't remember Plautus,
we'll also do our best to win your plaudits,
with such a play! The greatest glory of its age,
Once more before you on a modern stage!
Those dedicated, decorated, dear-departed souls
those ancient comic playwrights shall inspire our roles.' (11–20)

The Plautine text resumes with a persuasive call to the audience to join into the holiday spirit (and open itself to the play) by putting aside normal cares, and particularly anti-comic thoughts of finance and business, in order to give the 'company' of actors its very 'close attention./ Away with sorrowing, thoughts about your borrowing/ the games are underway, and even bankers get a holiday!/ The forum's peaceful, quiet, sunken in repose,/ the shops are shuttered, and the banks are closed' (22–6).[6] Having now put the audience into a receptive mood through flattery, the promise of a good play, and a reminder of its duty to enjoy itself, the prologue moves on to provide an account of the background to the play, first noting its Greek ancestry, and that Plautus has fashioned it anew.

After delivering these opening lines from the edge of the stage, immediately in front of the audience, the speaker would have turned or gestured back towards the upstage scenic facade, with its two projecting doorways; 'A married gentleman, somewhat past his prime/ together with his son lives *here*, and once upon a time . . . ' (35–6). The elements of the plot are familiar. A girl has been abandoned as a foundling, some sixteen years ago, then brought up by the old man's wife, who raised the child, though a slave, as her own. Now the son has fallen madly in love with her, but alas, so has his father. Plautus outlines the situation using one of his frequently occurring (and for his audience evidently effective) military metaphors; 'Now each prepares his forces, summoning all hands/ while knowing nothing of his rival's plans' (50–1).

Each protagonist hopes to have the girl marry his own slave, with whom he will then be able to share her. Then, introducing the first of several deviations from a well-worn pattern (and probably departing too from the plot of the original Greek play by Diphilus), one of these two protagonists (each having a slave surrogate), is replaced.

'The old man's wife has stumbled on the plot!
To thwart her husband, she would throw her lot
in with the son, but then, the secret's out!
Dad learns of son's infatuation, and – the lout! –

sends him abroad, while wily mother, still party to the plan,
determines to assist the son in every way she can.' (58–63)

The audience is instructed not to expect the presence of the
conventional *adulescens amans*, as the speaker – like many other Plautine
prologues – adroitly and self-consciously treads the line between art and
life, 'That son who went abroad won't make it back today./ Plautus
changed his mind and dropped him from the play,/ by washing out a
bridge that lay upon his way' (64–6). Having noted, on the one hand, an
unusual aspect of the plot as a work of *artifice*, the prologue then turns to
consider, on the other, the way in which some in the audience (speaking
amongst themselves), may think it departs from *reality*. They might ask,
' "since when can slaves propose, or marriages take place?/ Nowhere in
all the world, can such things be the case" '; to which the speaker
responds, (emphasizing that such indecorous things take place *elsewhere*). 'And yet, *it is*, in Carthage, and Apulia – and the Greeks/ are
prone, and have been known to celebrate for weeks/ when slaves get
wed' (69–74). He proposes a bet on his assertion with the winner
providing a drink, but then, finding no takers, gives it up, suggesting
that the audience has had enough to drink already.

The speaker then returns briefly to the plot, to promise the audience
that despite such irregularities, in the end both dramaturgical and moral
convention will be observed: the girl will prove to be a freeborn
Athenian, and won't be corrupted

> 'not in this play
> at any rate. But just you wait,
> till afterwards to date her.
> For a little money, she's anyone's honey,
> and the marriage can wait for later!' (83–6)

Irony and playfulness abound, as the world of the play and that of the
actors and audience are brought together in collusion and conclusion.
The girl, Casina, will not in fact appear in the *play* at all; if she did, she
would be portrayed on *stage* by a male actor. In the *plot* of the play, she is
impersonated by a male slave, whose virtue 'actually' is seriously (and
hilariously) assaulted. Metatheatrical ambiguities abound as the audience,
reassured (but feeling perhaps mildly and pleasurably compromised by
the verbal wink and nod of this last ribald remark), is nudged into the
play with a final stroke of flattery for its renowned military prowess. 'Be
strong and retain what through valor you gain, and win your way, as
ever' (87–8).[7]

In the course of the prologue a certain rapport has been established,
and sufficient background provided (intriguing in its suggestion of a
somewhat unorthodox treatment of familiar material) to render the
spectators well disposed towards the production and stimulate their

interest. But it has been done from the outside looking in – all talk and no activity – and what is required now is a fast, action-packed scene which will propel the audience into the heart of the play and its central conflict. With a deft theatrical sense, Plautus provides just this (a short scene of fifty lines), using the two broadly drawn characters of the rival servants to capture attention, present, and personify the conflict in first verbally and then physically violent terms.

Two slaves (in the middle of an animated conversation) come striding onto the stage, one following the other so closely that when the first suddenly halts, the other collides with him, thus immediately giving their confrontation a physically violent expression. These two, Olympio in the lead and Chalinus at his heels, as well as acting as surrogates for, respectively, the old man Lysidamus and his wife, Cleostrata, also present a contrast between rural and urban attributes. Olympio, a bumpkin fond of crude jests and prone to violence, serves as a country bailiff, while Chalinus, more diffident and plaintive, is a town slave. The same contrast arises elsewhere in Plautus; evidently appealing to the Roman audience both for its flattery of urban sophistication, and perhaps for providing an opportunity for the traditional farcical treatment of country life characteristic of the *Atellanae*. *Mostellaria* begins with a vivid scene of verbal abuse between a town and country slave, Tranio and Grumio which, in its use of imagery and insults appropriate to the contrast between urban and rural life, is markedly similar to the opening of *Casina*.[8]

Olympio rebukes Chalinus for following him to which he responds 'I'm resolved to go wherever you go. Just like your shadow, I'll follow. Even if you're strung up on the cross, I'll string along' (91–4). Told to mind his own business, Chalinus in turn orders the 'over-sized overseer' Olympio, to get back to the farm and his 'own turf'; leaving city affairs to city folks. Accusing him of planning to carry off Casina, he continues, 'Back to the farm! Get back to the outback!' (103)[9]. Olympio arrogantly replies that indeed he does intend to marry Casina, and once back on the farm, 'you can bet I'll bed down with my bride, on my "own turf!"' (110).

> *Chal.* 'You have her, you! Hang me, by Hercules, I'd sooner die than let you get her!'
> *Ol.* 'Hang on! She's mine, my booty, baby! So your neck's for the noose.'
> *Chal.* 'You, dug from a dungheap! She's your booty, booby?' (111–14)

These insulting exchanges should be underscored by a variety of escalating knock-about abuse; slaps, blows, trips, and the like. Chalinus' cry in the middle of line 115, '*Vae tibi*!' would serve to punctuate the moment in which Olympio grabs hold of him in some suitably cruel embrace prior to delivering an extended climactic description (interrupted only by Chalinus' two plaintive cries, 'what will you do to me?') of how he intends to torture Chalinus once he obtains Casina. Beginning with, 'Oh, how I'll needle you at my nuptials!' (116), he recites a rich catalogue of first physical and then mental torment which he promises to inflict upon his urban rival. He chooses an appropriately countrified means of punishing the household slave, Chalinus. He will force him to carry pitchers of water to fill eight immense vats; 'and fill you will, or you'll be well full of welts!' (123); until Chalinus is bent like a horse's crupper – the part positioned right under the tail. Next he will starve him; 'further, when you fancy some fodder, you'll eat dirt like a worm, compliments of the compost heap . . . you'll famish on the farm!' (126–7; 129).[10]

Olympio's abuse next turns sexual, as he describes how at night Chalinus will be fastened in the frame of a window – infenestration! –

13 Olimpio teases Chalinus with an account of the torture that awaits him 'fastened firmly in the frame of the window' (line 132). From a production of Plautus' *Casina*, University of Warwick Arts Centre, 1988.

and forced to listen while he makes love to Casina. This verbal violence, taken with that just preceding it, demands some physical correlation, with Olympio manhandling Chalinus throughout the sequence, while perhaps miming the sort of torments awaiting him. Thus, clasping him tightly from behind, and facing him directly towards the audience, he might now run his hand mockingly over Chalinus' body, as he describes how Casina will murmur to him,

> ' "Oh sweetie-pie, oh Olympio my darling, my little honey pot,[11] my joy, let me kiss those cute little eyes of yours, my precious! Oh, please please let me love you, light of my life, my little dickey-bird, my lovey dovey, my bunny-wunny!" ' (134–8)

As well as adding variety to the miseries suffered by Chalinus, this passage, particularly if physicalized in a mock-erotic manner, ironically foreshadows the form of Chalinus' subsequent revenge upon Olympio and, more generally, introduces the element of gross sexuality that characterizes the play. Olympio then returns to his more normal mode of abuse, probably concluding with some final physical assault on Chalinus.

> 'Well then, when she's cooing these things to me, you'll flutter, gallows bird, you'll shudder like a mouse shut up in the wall. And you can shut up now. I'm going in. I'm tired of talking to you.' (139–43)

Olympio struts up the stairs and into Lysidamus' house, closely followed by Chalinus, 'bloodied but unbowed' vowing to continue in hot pursuit, and in the course of this scene, likely to have secured a good measure of sympathy from the audience.

This attention-grabbing opening scene, delivered in spoken *senarii*, is now followed by one sung between Cleostrata and Myrrhina, the wives of respectively, Lysidamus and the next-door neighbour, Alcesimus. In a brief preface to this scene, Cleostrata enters onto the porch in front of the stage doors representing her house and, turning back inside, gives domestic orders to her servants, one of whom, Pardalisca, replies that the old man has ordered his dinner. In her impassioned response, Cleostrata initially reinforces the assumption that the audience might well have (prompted by her mask and the general circumstances) that she will present the role of the archetypal comic shrewish wife (the sort Plautus refers to elsewhere as a 'barking dog'),[12] while advancing the play's central metaphor comparing sexual appetite and its object with the craving for and consumption of food. She intends to deny her husband the satisfaction of either desire.

> 'I'll not do his dinner today! Not when he turns against his own dear son – and ME! – in order to appease his amorous appetite; that

93

monster of a man! I'll wrack that rake with hunger and thirst, curses and worse! By Pollux, I'll torture him with torment from my tongue, that dungheap dandy, the haughty debauchee, that sink of sin!' (148–59)

Although Cleostrata appears at first sight as an unattractive and (to put it mildly) 'unfestive' character likely to thwart the pleasure-seeking spirit appropriate to comedy, Plautus does contrive for her (both through robust language and the commands she delivers to her unseen servants) a strongly impressive entrance which is further enhanced by her physically elevated position on the stage. Just as she announces a desire to visit her next-door neighbour, Myrrhina herself appears on cue at the opposite porch as she too addresses servants concealed within and announces her intention in turn to visit Cleostrata. Thus the scene is nicely balanced, and this symmetry would be visually preserved as at the same moment each descends the steps of her house, and they sweep forward to meet at centre stage directly in front of the audience for their duet.

After assuring one another of their mutual devotion, Myrrhina, hungry for gossip, quickly draws from Cleostrata the reason for her evident unhappiness. In her reply, Cleostrata makes her first claim on the spectators' sympathy, although her complaint is jokingly undercut by Myrrhina.

> *Cleo.* 'My husband! It's perfectly scandalous how he treats me, and as for justice, well, I can just forget about that.'
> *Myrr.* 'If that's the case, it's very odd, since usually it's the men who don't get what they deserve from their wives.' (189–92)

Cleostrata ignores this, going on to reveal that she is aware of her husband's intrigue;[13] 'intending to give my maid to his foreman on the farm – the maid whom I've raised at my own expense – because *he* fancies her!' (193–6). Not only is Lysidamus attempting to be unfaithful to his wife, but the object he chooses right under her nose is particularly inappropriate; with even an unsavoury whiff of incest about it: a veritable member of the family and the special responsibility of his wife.

This first tentative encouragement of sympathy for Cleostrata's plight is then skilfully nurtured by Plautus when, in response, Myrrhina overstates the opposing argument;

> 'After all, a proper wife ought not to have any property apart from her husband. And if she does have things, in my opinion she got them improperly; she's guilty either of stealing or stealth or hanky-panky. In my opinion ALL that you have is your husband's.' (199–202)

94

The initially friendly and sympathetic exchange between the two women turns progressively nastier as, in response to Cleostrata's shrill protest, Myrrhina smugly concludes, 'Let him have his fling, and do what he wants, just so long as he looks after you properly at home' (205–6).

In the course of the scene, suspense is built from the antagonism growing between the two women, by references to the danger of being overheard, and now by Cleostrata's sudden announcement that she sees her husband approaching. Both women scurry away; Myrrhina exiting into her house, and Cleostrata withdrawing to the porch where she remains physically (and therefore mentally) in the eye of the spectators; an ironic presence. The audience is ready, and an open stage is waiting (after two successive scenes, each with two characters and each preparing for this moment) for the climactic solo entrance of the play's central figure: Lysidamus. For the occasion, Plautus composed a highly fanciful and revealing monologue through which this lively lecher first takes the stage, and employed a rollicking anapaestic tetrameter; the 'Gilbertian' meter.

> 'You can take it from me: not on land, or at sea
> is there anything finer than love.
> Nothing half so entrancing, every day life-enhancing;
> Not in earth, nor in heaven above.
> And I do think it odd, when a cook's at his job
> giving dishes the very best flavour,
> he can't use for a spice, what is ever so nice
> just a sprinkling of *Love* to add savour.
> Why, what more could you wish, a mouth-watering dish
> neither salty nor cloying? How handy!
> *Love* would transform it all, making honey from gall,
> and a dirty old man to a dandy!
> Now, I didn't just hear this; I speak from experience,
> for since Casina captured my heart,
> quite over-powered, I have utterly flowered;
> I've made nattiness into an art!
> To become more alluring, I'm even procuring
> the very best scent that's available.
> Just a touch of perfume to make her love bloom,
> for it does seem her virtue's assailable.' (217–27)

Accompanied by the *tibicen*, and with the whole stage open before him, it would be comically apt for Lysidamus, overdressed, full of himself (and also, as the subsequent scene reveals, with more than a bit of wine), to perform a little jig celebrating his delight in the anticipated success of his love affair. The spectators' enjoyment of the illicit

95

monologue confided to them would be increased by their awareness of Cleostrata's presence, unseen by Lysidamus until during his final lines he spots her; his song undergoes a sudden transition, and no doubt, his dance stutters to a halt. Then, changing tone once more while ceasing to address the audience, he greets her affectionately.

'Yet I am at a loss, there's that old rugged cross
that I bear, while she lives, called my wife.
And she's looking quite vile – soothing words – mustn't rile!
Ah! How goes it, sweet light of my life?' (227–9)

Lysidamus compares his married life to crucifixion, and implies a death wish (which in a few lines will be made explicit), upon his wife. As elsewhere in New Comedy,

the marital home is a battleground, and we recognize a classic situation of comic drama, versions of which fill many hours each day on modern television. The constant complaint of Plautus' errant and henpecked husbands is that they sold their freedom when they took a wife with a large dowry.[14]

In the farcical exchange that follows, Cleostrata gruffly brushes off her husband's attempts to 'sweet-talk' her, but Lysidamus persists. As the two engage in a veritable verbal game of tag, the physical depiction of his determined attempts to be winsome and her equally robust rebukes of his approaches make for a lively scene, which Plautus enhances both by the use of an unlikely simile comparing their marriage (hardly made in heaven!) to that of Jupiter and Juno, and by the device of the inadvertently overheard aside.

Cleo. 'You shall be the death of me!'
Lys. '(If only it were true!)'
Cleo. 'Now *that* I believe!' (233–4)[15]

The language of the scene as it builds is highly colloquial and energetic, punctuated by oaths and exclamations and coloured by suggestive imagery. Cleostrata compares her grey-haired husband to a white fly (the first example of the play's prevalent use of animal imagery to characterize sexuality), and imagines him wandering about town, wallowing in the fleshpots and soaking up wine. Finally Lysidamus proposes a truce; 'Oh now dear wife, *please*, that's enough! Get hold of yourself – and that tongue of yours! Save a bit of abuse for tomorrow's row!' (248–50).

After a series of quick responses and rising verbal violence, the scene moderates its rhythm as Lysidamus attempts to negotiate with his wife, suggesting in an innocent fashion that Casina ought to be married off to his slave, Olympio. Cleostrata is not taken in; 'By Castor, you disaster of

a man, you do amaze me! At your time of life, forgetting how to behave'
(259). She points out that the female slaves are her responsibility, and it
would be better to have the girl marry their son's slave, Chalinus. Her
assertion of her domestic rights (which the audience would probably
concede) unnerves Lysidamus, whose guilty motives cause him first to
suspect that his wife 'is on the scent', and then to stutter; an early hint of
the Freudian slips that will plague him throughout the play.

Building on his discomfiture, Cleostrata proposes that she persuade
Olympio to let Chalinus have the girl, which Lysidamus counters with
the idea that he persuade Chalinus to give her to Olympio; 'which I
believe I may just be able to do' (271). Cleostrata agrees, and exits into
her house to plead with Olympio while Lysidamus does the same with
Chalinus. As soon as she goes, Lysidamus again addresses the audience;
'By Hercules, I wish the gods would do something nasty to that woman!
Is that too much to ask?' (275), then frets that 'she's definitely got wind
of what I'm up to' (277).

Chalinus enters onto the porch, announcing that he comes at
Cleostrata's command, and rather insolently asks his master what he
wants. Lysidamus replies, 'Well, for starters, put on a happy face when
you speak with me; it's ridiculous for you to scowl like that when I'm
the one in charge here' (281–2). Plautus deftly makes a metatheatrical
joke (Chalinus cannot change his expression because he wears a mask),
and at the same time encourages the audience to question Lysidamus'
stature and the legitimacy of his authority, which have already been
undermined during his confrontation with Cleostrata. If his power is
suspect, his wits serve him no better: his attempt to bribe Chalinus with
an offer of freedom if he gives up Casina, fails. Losing his temper, and
taunted by Chalinus, Lysidamus dismisses the slave while angrily
announcing that the matter will be settled by drawing lots. Left alone,
he again turns to the audience in self-pity.

> 'Was ever anyone more wretched than I? How all things do
> conspire against me! Now I'm worried that my wife may have
> talked Olympio out of marrying Casina. If so, she's made an old
> man very unhappy. If not, there's still hope for me in the lots. If I
> lose the lots, I'll just lay my life down on my sword, and so,
> goodnight!' (303–7)

His morose soliloquy ends abruptly as Olympio enters onto the
porch, shouting back through the doors; 'By Pollux, Madam, you can
put me in the oven and turn me till I'm turned to toast, before I'd agree
to what you're asking!' (309–11). In response to Lysidamus' anxious
questioning, Olympio confirms that he has refused Cleostrata's request
to forgo Casina; 'I wouldn't give her up to Jupiter himself, not even if he
begged me!' (323). Nevertheless, he reveals that Cleostrata's anger and

the trouble Lysidamus' love affair is causing him with everyone in the household has weakened his resolve.[16] Lysidamus attempts to restore it by a show of bravado; 'So, what's your worry? As long as old Jupiter here is on your side . . .' (330–1).

Lysidamus' attempt to associate himself with Jupiter seems particularly inept not only because of the impotence he has just shown in dealing with his wife and Chalinus, but also because only moments before Olympio has explicitly ruled out any deal to share Casina (which is precisely what Lysidamus has in mind) with 'Jupiter himself'. Olympio tries to bring his aged master down to earth:

> 'That's a load of bull! Don't you know how suddenly these mortal Jupiters can shuffle off? Tell me this: if old Jupiter here snuffs it, and your kingdom falls to the small fry, who's going to save my hide and cover my backside?' (333–7)

Undaunted, Lysidamus replies that they can count on the lots. 'I trust in the gods. We'll just put our faith in heaven' (346); to which Olympio responds cynically; 'I wouldn't invest a penny up there. Why everyone alive trusts in heaven, but I've seen plenty of those faithful foolish folks flumoxed!' (347–9).[17]

Casting aside the conceit of divinity, Lysidamus next fancies himself as a military commander. Indeed, in the light of the domestic battle about to commence, their downstage conference is rather like a council of war. Lysidamus advises Olympio that 'the time has come that we must draw swords and fight it out' (344) and with the appearance of Cleostrata and Chalinus entering from the doors to his house, he suggests they 'close ranks and fight' (352), then a few moments later gives orders to 'lift our standards and charge' (357). This provides the key to staging the ensuing scene. Man and wife, each with a slave ally, form opposing camps centre stage; the hostile forces glaring at one another on either side of the urn where the outcome of their struggle must be decided. The importance of the lot-drawing sequence to the plot is obvious, but a reader might overlook how powerful it could be in performance

> This is one of the few scenes in Plautus where there is true suspense – not the common variety, exciting enough but rather vague, where the audience knows what is going to happen but not how or when, or where it has a shrewd suspicion that (for example) the slave's deceptions will be found out because slaves' deceptions always are; here the suspense is much more highly developed, in that the audience is aware that one specific action of crucial importance is about to take place . . . but does not know, because in the nature of things it simply cannot know, what the outcome of that action will be.[18]

14 *Cleostrata*: 'Now Chalinus, what is it my husband wishes me to do?'
Chalinus: 'Gee, what he'd most like is to see you going up in smoke out
beyond the gates!' (lines 353–4)

Plautus deftly extends the proceedings for over sixty lines with a
series of delays, interruptions, and diversions. In the course of the
conflict there are first threats and taunts, the ritual calling upon the gods,
then feints and sorties, and finally actual physical combat, with one side
fighting in the name of Jupiter, the other, Juno. Things start off badly
for Lysidamus, who, by an unfortunate slip of the tongue urges that
Casina be given to him (his actual wish), instead of to Olympio, which is
his 'official' position. Thoroughly discomfited by this, he then back-
tracks, attempting to avoid conflict at the last minute through a
negotiated settlement.

Lys. 'Both of us, recognizing your rights in the matter appeal to
you.'
Cleo. 'For what?'
Lys. 'Why just this my sweet. To do a little favour for our foreman
here in this Casina affair.'
Cleo. 'By Pollux, I won't! I wouldn't dream of it!' (371–3)

The lots are then distributed, with mutual accusations of bad faith, followed by Olympio's insolent insults to Cleostrata. He begins formally to invoke the gods, but each time the formula is interrupted by Chalinus.

> *Ol.* 'I pray the gods . . . '
> *Chal.* '. . . will fit you with a ball and chain . . .'
> *Ol.* '. . . that the lots will let me . . .'
> *Chal.* '. . . be hung up by your heels, by Hercules!' (389–90)

A few moments later the rite, which is meant to contain the conflict and avoid violence, breaks down altogether, and each side resorts to force. The actual physical violence (infrequent in Plautus), is in essence a punch-up between Lysidamus and Cleostrata, waged by their slave surrogates. Because Cleostrata is also fighting for her son Euthynicus, as rival to his father, it is also a conflict between generations. Moreover (and extending the comic to the cosmic), each is also associated with a god. This is, in effect, total war: resounding from the lowest social order of slaves, right up to heaven.[19] Lysidamus is the aggressor, but comes off worse.

> *Lys.* 'Shut that man's mouth this minute! Go on, what are you
>   waiting for?'
> *Cleo.* 'Don't you dare raise a hand!'
> *Ol.* 'Shall I sock him or slap him, Sir?'
> *Lys.* 'Whichever your prefer.'
> *Ol.* 'Take that!!'
> *Cleo.* 'How dare you strike that man?!'
> *Ol.* 'My Jupiter here gave orders.'
> *Cleo.* (to Chalinus) 'Well, you hit him right back!'
> *Ol.* 'OWWWW! He's pounding me to a pulp, Jupiter!'
> *Lys.* 'How dare you strike that man?!'
> *Chal.* 'My Juno here gave orders.'
> *Lys.* 'We'll just have to put up with it. My wife's already giving the
>   orders even though I'm still alive.' (404–9)

Lysidamus, despite his anxiety and the impatience of all to know the outcome, has drawn out the suspense by his ponderous handling of the procedure. Now he indulges in one more bit of bluster, before the lots are finally drawn; *Lys.* 'I warn you, Chalinus, keep an eye out for trouble', to which Chalinus responds, 'Oh, that's kind of you, after my eye's been blackened!' (411–12). To reinforce the suggestion of a schoolyard brawl, Chalinus' line, and that uttered a moment earlier by Olympio, 'Why did he have to go and spoil my omen?' (410) could each be allowed to end in a drawn-out whimpering whine. This in turn allows Lysidamus' and Olympio's rather pompous pronouncements a few seconds later, when they win the lots, to seem both incongruous as well as an indulgence of dangerous hubris in their evocation of the gods and the hallowed Roman concepts of *pietas* and of sacred custom, the *mos maiorum*.[20]

> *Lys.* 'The gods are smiling on us, Olympio, rejoice!'
> *Ol.* 'It's all due to the piety of me and my forefathers.' (417–18)

'Throughout the scene, tension has been mounting, and an atmosphere of such suspense is created that the eventual drawing of the lots comes as a relief.'[21] The action would have been played centre stage, down close to the audience. As the outcome is announced with Olympio's exultant cry, 'It's mine!!' (416), the tight knot of opposing forces would quickly unravel, Lysidamus and Olympio spinning off into a quick victory dance, while the unfortunate Chalinus withdraws back and to one side after his exclamation, 'Hell and damnation', and Cleostrata's line, 'You've lost, Chalinus!' (416–17). Lysidamus at once orders Cleostrata into the house to prepare for Olympio's wedding and his departure 'to that country villa where he's taking her' (420). A moment later he too goes indoors, together with Olympio, after a pointed reference to Chalinus who lingers in the background; 'I don't wish to say anything more in present company.'

This is a signal to the audience, alerting them that Lysidamus has interesting things to discuss with Olympio, which ought not to be (and therefore, on dramatic grounds *must be*), overheard by Chalinus. Together with the empty stage and a moment's silence, it 'sets up' Chalinus' monologue and the decisive scene that follows: the central, pivotal moments of the play. Up to now the spectators have had the elements of the conflict and the characters that embody it presented to them, and have seen the interests of one side advance. The time has come to turn both the audience and the course of the action decisively against them. Chalinus provides the means. In the opening scene he was abused by Olympio, and in the drawing of the lots was worsted again; this positions him to receive the sympathy which Plautus now focuses upon him. In contrast to the bravado and arrogance of his rivals, he delivers a short monologue in the 'minor key' which, because it can only be addressed to the audience, amounts to a direct plea for support.

> *Chal.* 'If I hanged myself now from a noose
> the effort would serve little use.
> Why pay out for a rope,
> and thus give my foes hope
> when I'm already dead from abuse?
>
> That I've lost the lots can't be denied.
> And Olympio's taken my bride.

101

But what rankles me so,
and I'd most like to know –
why was Master so keen on his side?

How it worried and wracked the old boy!
When he won, how he capered with joy!
Wait! They're coming outside;
from my kind friends I'll hide,
and learn what I can of their ploy.' (424–36)

As Lysidamus and Olympio re-enter from their house, Chalinus scampers upstage, concealing himself. Because his subsequent reactions and asides must be perceived by the audience while he remains conveniently unnoticed by the two characters on stage, it would make sense for him to be behind and above them, peeking out from the architectural elements which stand on the podium of the *scaenae frons*, while with their backs to him, they face the audience.[22] In the course of the scene, and to give emphasis and variety to his asides by physical action, Chalinus could move laterally ('like a crab' as he puts it) amongst the range of columns, darting behind one whenever either of the downstage characters grew suspicious or turned towards him.

Master and slave enter, gloating over their intention to 'give our fallen foe even more misery and woe' (441–2), as Olympio relishes putting into effect the tortures with which he threatened Chalinus in the opening scene. 'Just wait till he comes to the farm! I'll return him to you bent double like a coalman!' (437–8). This prompts Chalinus to protest agaist such 'double-trouble'; 'while one of them flails me, the other one nails me!' (445), and then, crucially, to resolve, 'That settles it. I'll postpone my passing: I won't perish till I've posted that pest off to purgatory!' (447–8).[23] Whether, as he claims, to express his gratitude, or simply because of his overstimulated state, Lysidamus now proceeds avidly to kiss and fondle *Olympio*, until the bemused foreman objects (in an apt line certain to have set the audience howling); 'Hey there lover boy! Get off my back' (459). Chalinus watches in amazement, concluding, 'I'm afraid, by Pollux, those two will soon be head over bollocks in bed! Actually the old boy always did go for anything with a beard' (465–6).[24]

Turning again to thoughts of Casina, and the deception he has in mind, Lysidamus exclaims, 'Ah how I'll kiss and cuddle Casina today! What a life, what a lark! And my wife in the dark!' (467–8), then relates his scheme to Olympio.

> *Lys.* 'It's neatly and completely arranged. My wife will invite Myrrhina over for the wedding where she can hang about, make herself useful, and stay the night. I've told my wife to do it, and she's agreed. So Myrrhina will sleep *here* [indicating his own

house], and I can promise you her husband won't be *there*! [indicating the house opposite] You'll take your bride off to the farm, but the farm will be right *here* where Casina and I will enjoy our wedding night. Tomorrow, before dawn, you'll take her away to the country. Pretty clever, huh?'

Ol. 'Brilliant!' (480–8)

While Lysidamus struts back and forth on stage, pointing to the houses, his movements provide the opportunity for some visual humour, as Chalinus deftly reacts with split-second timing to avoid detection, and then daringly exclaims to himself and the audience, 'Go right ahead and plot a lot! By Hercules, you two will be screwed for being so shrewd!' (488–9). Plautus now once again employs his culinary metaphor to characterize Lysidamus' lust, as Olympio is sent shopping for the wedding feast by his master with orders to 'get something sumptuous since she's so scrumptious' (492). He continues,

Lys. 'Get some cockles, some cuddly cuttlefish, some little octopussies . . . and some sole.'
Chal. [concealed] 'Sole? Why not get the whole damn shoe to smash your face with you odious old man?!'
Ol. 'How about a little snapper?'
Lys. 'Who needs a little snapper when we've got "jaws" that wife of mine at home, who never closes her mouth?' (493–8)[25]

After a final order to 'Hurry! But buy plenty; don't be selfish with the shellfish!' (500–1) Olympio runs offstage, and Lysidamus exits into his neighbour's house. The stage is again deserted for Chalinus to deliver a closing monologue neatly balancing that with which he opened this crucial scene, and announcing by its complete change of tone that the plot (precisely at the mid-point of the play) is now about to shift decisively against Lysidamus. With a nice touch of irony, this uncharacteristically dutiful slave continues the culinary metaphor to indicate how Cleostrata and he will now turn things to their advantage.

> *Chal.* 'You could offer me freedom, nay offer it thrice,
>   but you couldn't dissuade me, whatever your price,
>   from cooking those two in a stew – and how?
>   By spilling the beans to my Mistress right now.
>
> Our rivals are cornered, and caught in the act.
> If she plays her part, then we've won – that's a fact!
> We'll trap them but good; they won't get away.
> We victims are victors – it's our lucky day!
>
> How shameless our chef has cooked up his plan!
> It's flavoured and simmering inside, in the pan.

> But I'll lend a hand, and give things a stir;
> The seasoning I use won't satisfy Sir!
> The tables are turned, so ready or not,
> He'll get what I serve: thus thickens the plot!' (504–14)

He scampers off gleefully to inform his mistress of the dastardly deeds their rivals have planned.

The spectators now expect to see Cleostrata as she reacts to Chalinus' revelations, but Plautus skilfully exploits their anticipation by delaying her entry while he interposes a short scene between Lysidamus and his aged next-door neighbour, Alcesimus. The two enter from Alcesimus' house, already engaged in a conversation which indicates at once that Lysidamus has told the other of his plans, and recruited him as accomplice, while receiving from Alcesimus in exchange some unwelcome criticism of his unseemly conduct along the lines of 'a man of your age'; 'with your grey hair'; and '*you* a married man!' (518–19).[26] Lysidamus' stature is further diminished by his misplaced attempt to play at being a true lover – whom he conceives to be 'wise and witty' (529) – with two atrociously contrived puns[27] that merely make him appear silly, prompting Alcesimus to exclaim in Greek, '*Attatae!*' and then protest, 'you really ought to be suppressed' (528). Lysidamus hurdles off stage to attend to business in the forum; Alcesimus re-enters his house, and the stage is left entirely empty for a moment.

This dramaturgical holding of breath further sets off the delayed entrance of Cleostrata, who now appears, thunderously, on the porch in front of her house. Although in her first appearance she claimed to be aware (at least in general terms) of Lysidamus' designs on Casina (150 and 195–6), she evidently lacked details of his plans, and in particular the knowledge, which Chalinus has since shared with her, that her husband intends to accomplish the deed immediately and right next door.[28]

> *Cleo.* 'By Castor, now I know the reason why
> My husband's been so keen to have the neighbours by.
> With them all here, the house next door'd be free,
> Where they can carry off Casina, and cuckold me!
>
> Well now, I shan't invite them, nor provide a spot
> for amorous rams to rut, however hot
> they are. But wait! My neighbour's coming out.
> That Bastion of the Senate[29] and the state: the lout!;
> who panders to my husband's fatal fault.
> By Castor, men like he aren't worth a pinch of salt!' (531–8)

Cleostrata takes charge of the play and mounts her counter-attack by announcing that she – will do *nothing*! Alcesimus stands musing on the front steps to his house, and spotting Cleostrata opposite, assumes at once she must be coming to invite his own wife Myrrhina over according to the scenario outlined by Lysidamus. But now, despite Alcesimus' perplexed promptings, Cleostrata does *not* take the part her husband assigned her. She indicates complete indifference to the suggestion that Myrrhina help out at the wedding, then feigns an exit back into her house, mission accomplished: leaving Alcesimus thoroughly confused and angry – with Lysidamus!

'So what do I do now? What a dastardly deed I did! On account of that ruthless, toothless old goat, I'm offering my wife's services around like some sort of scullery maid. What a lying lout he is! Saying his wife's inviting her over, and then she says she doesn't want her!'

Cleostrata, who has remained in her doorway concealed from Alcesimus, views his departure with satisfaction, then addresses the audience as she plans the next scene of her plot, for which she requires only the presence of her husband, whom, obligingly, Plautus now produces. Lysidamus, in lyrically describing his irresponsible public behaviour (in the *Forum* of all places!) perfectly fits the character just assigned to him by Cleostrata.[30]

Cleo. 'Well, he's finely flumoxed! What a flutter the old fools are in! Now if only that worthless, washed-out wimp of a husband of mine would happen along, I could fix him just like I fooled the other one. I'd just love to stir up a quarrel between them! And here he comes, right on cue! Goodness! Look at that solemn face. You'd almost think he was an honest man.' [*Withdraws. Enter Lysidamus*]

Lys. 'Now it seems to my mind, really quite asinine,
when a lover's in service to Cupid,
with a sweetheart so pretty, to spend time in the city,
like I've done; why it's perfectly stupid!

For I've wasted my time on a kinsman of mine
who used ME as a character witness.
But I'm pleased to report, he was beaten in court.
Serves him right, bothering me with his business!

Now between me and you, it is patently true,
when a man asks a friend to bear witness,
It behoves him to find, if his friend's of sound mind;
send him home if the witness is witless!' (558–74)

Spying his wife, and worried that she may have overheard him, he ambles upstage and addresses her as she stands in an appropriately dominant position above him on the porch. He begins sweetly (calling her, 'mea festivitas'), but when (falsely) informed that Alcesimus refused to allow Myrrhina to accept her invitation to come over, he explodes in anger. Having once again effortlessly accomplished her purpose, Cleostrata retires into the house, pausing only to promise the audience more of the same. 'By Pollux, I'll give him a fright all right! I'll soon make this lover suffer!' (589–90).

In what became the tradition of 'revolving door' farce, when the comings and goings of the characters occur with mechanical precision and inevitability,[31] Cleostrata exits at precisely the same moment as Alcesimus enters onto the opposite porch, setting Lysidamus into a spin. The two fall at once into a violent row, each accusing the other of bad faith, without realizing that their confusion has been skilfully stage-managed by Cleostrata. The shocking spectacle of the two old men, bereft of all dignity, shouting, cursing, and flailing at each other would make for a lively scene, which Plautus caps with Lysidamus' final ironic line; 'Now there's a real friend!' (615), when Alcesimus finally submits and shuffles back into his house. Lysidamus then comes down to the audience, enquiring plaintively,

> 'I wonder what omen I omitted when I began this love affair? Or
> how I incurred such Venus-envy? Why, when I'm longing to get
> laid, am I constantly de-layed?!' (616–18)

Even as he speaks, fresh disasters commence with the sound of 'unholy hubbub' (620) in his house. Pardalisca, Cleostrata's servant, bursts through the doors and in a frantic, mock-tragic tirade pretends to report shocking events unfolding within. Switching at this point from a spoken to lyric meter, Plautus contrives for her song a piece of splendid parody, immediately evocative of high tragedy in its linguistic style, meter, and content.[32]

> 'I'm lost! Lost! Totally done for, and dead!
> My heart has stopped, my limbs are trembling with dread!
> Help! Safety! Shelter! Oh, where to turn for aid?
> Such things I saw inside, can scarcely be conveyed.
> Bold and brazen badness! Turmoil and alarm!
> Be careful, Cleostrata! Lest she do you harm!
> The woman's lost her senses – her mind has gone astray!
> For goodness' sake avoid her, but snatch the sword away!' (621–9)

In the ensuing scene, Pardalisca tells her increasingly terrified master how Casina has run amok, 'swearing by all the gods and goddesses, that the man she sleeps with tonight . . . she'll murder!' (670–1). This induces in Lysidamus another unfortunate slip of the tongue, quickly seized upon by Pardalisca to cause him even greater discomfort.

106

Lys. 'Murder ME?'
Pard. 'What's it got to do with you, Sir?'
Lys. 'Damn!'
Pard. 'Why should you be concerned about that?'
Lys. 'Why, I misspoke myself! I meant to say my foreman.' (672–4)

Pardalisca pushes her advantage relentlessly, asserting that Casina does indeed intend to kill them both. After a quick gleeful aside to the audience – 'What fabulous foolery! It's all fantasy from first to finish! Mistress and her neighbour set the trap, and I've been sent to spring it on him!' (685–8) – she raises the pressure further, claiming that Casina has *two* swords to murder the pair 'this very day!' Lysidamus is in despair; 'I'm the dead-deader-deadest man alive!' (693–4). Recovering slightly, he first proposes to don armour and confront Casina, but then, thinking better of it, suggests that his wife ought to be equal to that task. Told that the girl refuses to give up the swords so long as she has to marry Olympio, Lysidamus next reacts with guilty fury.

> *Lys.* 'Well, like it not, the ungrateful slut
>   will be given in marriage today.
>   I won't change what's planned: she'll give me her
>   hand . . .
>   To my *foreman*, I meant to say!'
> *Pard.* 'Seems you stumble a lot.'
> *Lys.* 'I'm so frightened, I'm not
>   giving thought to the words that I say.
>   But *please* beg my wife, if she values my life,
>   to get Casina out of the way!
>   And you beg her too.'
> *Pard.* 'And I'll beg for you.'
> *Lys.* 'Do your best, as you know how to do.
>   If you hush up these scandals, I'll buy you some sandals,
>   a gold ring, and some other treats too!' (700–9)

Pardalisca scurries inside, and, maintaining the pace of this sequence of scenes, Olympio at once enters, returning from the market together with several retainers weighed down with groceries. Anxious to get into the house and assuage his hunger, Olympio angers his master who threatens to punish him, upon which the slave in turn reacts violently; 'leave me alone, for the gods' sake. Do you want to make me retch, wretch?' (731). Lysidamus blusters, vainly attempting to remind Olympio of his subservient position, only in turn to be threatened with a reminder of their pact, and presumably, an unspoken physical threat to break it.

> *Ol.* 'Am I not a free man? You do remember, don't you? Don't you?'

Lys. 'Wait! Stop!'
Ol. 'Leave me alone!'
Lys. 'I'll be *your* slave!'
Ol. 'That's more like it.' (736–8)

The spectators now have a graphic demonstration (which would probably have been reflected in some knock-about domination of master by slave), of how Lysidamus has been brought low by his unseemly and brutalizing lust: social roles have been reversed, and moreover, the master has become a suppliant. This is further confirmed by Lysidamus' use of the formulaic language of submission, and compounded by Olympio's contemptuous evaluation of him, even as a slave.[33]

Lys. 'Dear, dear Olympio, my father, my patron, I beg . . .'
Ol. 'Now, you're talking sense.'
Lys. 'Yes, I'm yours. Indeed I am.'
Ol. 'What do I want with such a knave of a slave?'
Lys. 'Well then. How soon can you make me over?' (739–42)

The audience witness Lysidamus' degradation as Olympio, dressed in a little brief (and unearned) authority, takes charge and gives orders.

'Get on inside and hurry things along! Move! I'll be in a minute. And make sure it's a super-supper, with lots to drink. An elegant and dandy dinner; none of your rotten Romans slop![34] Well? What are you waiting for? Be off! What's keeping you?' (745–8)

Told of Casina's threats inside, Olympio at first arrogantly brushes these off, but then, thinking better of it, suggests that Lysidamus and he enter the house together, which eventually (after a bit of comic business as each endeavours to get the other to go first), they do, leaving the stage empty.

Although there is no indication in the manuscript of an interlude or break in the action at this point, it is possible that the *tibicen* remained on stage and continued to play following the departure of Lysidamus and Olympio, to suggest a passage of time. Pardalisca when she enters, gleefully relates the goings-on inside the house in the present tense, but to the extent that Plautus and his audience were concerned with verisimilitude, a brief interlude would have been appropriate. Her playful report is filled with theatrical allusions as she reviews the progress of Cleostrata's scenario.[35] The men's hunger and haste are being frustrated by the delay and denial which her mistress has decreed to thwart them. Pardalisca descends the stairs and approaches the audience to confide to them Cleostrata's supreme comic ploy: to substitute Chalinus for Casina with the male slave decked out as a bride! Meanwhile the servants employ diversionary tactics:

'The cooks in their cunning are conning their Master
by delaying his meal, and designing disaster;
overturning the pots right into the fire,
and contriving whatever the ladies desire!
They would like if they can, to deprive him of food,
and consume it themselves, once he's gone – very rude!
I confess that the ladies eat more than they should.
They would bloat on a boatload of food if they could!' (772–9)

Lysidamus now emerges onto the porch, where he stands and calls back into the house, telling the women to go ahead with the banquet; he's anxious, he claims, to depart for the country. Plautus once again uses the old man's shaky command of language to reveal his state of mind. Lysidamus starts a sentence, 'I want to escort our new bride and groom to the farm' – then interjects a revealing if unsyntactical thought – 'I know the disreputable ways of men'; before concluding; 'so no one will way-lay her' (782–4). Pardalisca, downstage, whispers to the audience, 'what did I tell you? The ladies are sending the old boy off, unfed!' (788–9). Catching sight of her, Lysidamus angrily orders her back inside, then descends to confide to the audience, in his turn, 'By Hercules, a fellow in love feels full even when he's famished' (795). Seeing Olympio enter from the house, he coins a new word to greet his 'co-husband', who summons the *tibicen* to make the stage sound with wedding music.

Lys. 'How are you my saviour?'
Ol. 'Hungry, by Hercules! And there's nothing around to savour.'
Lys. 'Yes, but I'm in love!'
Ol. 'I don't give a flying flogging! You can feast on love – as for me, my guts have been rumbling for hours!'[36]
Lys. 'What makes those laggards linger so long? The more I hurry them the slower they go. It almost seems on purpose!'
Ol. 'Well, suppose I sing the wedding song again, and see if that gets them going?'
Lys. 'Good idea! And I'll sing too, since its a twosome-screwsome!' (801–7)

Plautus again makes use of animal imagery to characterize the men's lust, as Olympio compares Lysidamus to a horse, 'Always champing at the bit!', to which his polymorphously perverse master responds, 'ever fancy trying a bit with me?' (812).[37] At this point the wedding procession commences with Chalinus entering onto the porch dressed as a bride, preceded by Pardalisca, and followed by Cleostrata and Myrrhina. Although the lines (an ironic parody of actual practice) indicating the ceremony are brief,[38] it seems likely that there would have been a good deal of mock ritual and comic business to round out the spectacle, as the procession descends and occupies centre stage, with the men standing to one side barely able to restrain themselves from seizing the 'bride'. Cleostrata, who has master-minded the scene, stands silently by watching with bemused satisfaction as the plot which she prepared 'back-stage' unfolds:

> *Pard.* 'Here we go, take it slow,
>   step over the threshold with care.
>   Safe by his side, blushing bride,
>   keep the upper hand always and dare,
>   to hold sway, night and day.
>   Make him pamper you as his task.
>   Never cease, him to fleece.
>   Just treat him like dirt's all I ask!'
>
> *Ol.* 'By Hercules, she'll get a whopping whipping if
>   she's guilty even of any mini-mischief!' (815–25)

Advising them to 'be kind to this innocent, unspoiled maiden' as 'Casina' simpers coyly beside them, the women draw out their departure as long as possible to frustrate their avid rivals, then slowly depart into the house. Lysidamus and Olympio immediately advance to take possession of their spoils. *Lys.* 'Almighty, mighty Aphrodite! What pleasure you gave me in giving me this treasure.' *Ol.* 'Oh, your iddy,

15   Lysidamus and Olimpio await the presentation of their 'bride' from Cleostrata, Myrrhina, and Pardalisca.

110

biddy, body, baby!' (841–4). The mock solemnity of the wedding ceremony is now crowned by a few moments of purest farce as the two men attempt to paw and pet their prize before carrying her bodily off the stage and up the steps into Alcesimus' house.

Ol. '. . . What the Hell!?'

Lys. 'What's wrong?'

Ol. 'She just stamped on my foot like an elephant!'

Lys. 'Hush up! Never a cloud was softer than this breast!'

Ol. 'By Pollux, what an iddy, biddy, pretty, titty! Ouch! Goodness me!'

Lys. 'What now?'

Ol. 'She hit me in the chest – it wasn't an elbow; it was a battering ram!'

Lys. 'Well, why are you handling her so roughly then? Look at me. Just treat her kind, and she doesn't mind!'

Ol. 'OWWWW!'

Lys. 'What's the matter now?'

Ol. 'Damnation! What a pint-sized power-house she is!! Her elbow almost laid me low!'

Lys. 'Maybe *she'd* like to be laid low – you know?'[39]

Ol. 'Let's go!'

Lys. 'Look lively, little, lovely, lady!' (844–54)

Again at this point, there is clearly meant to be a passage of time (possibly suggested by a musical interlude) while the men 'enjoy' Casina, and the women enjoy their banquet. Cleostrata, Myrrhina, and Pardalisca then emerge onto the porch, laughing; 'nicely wined and dined' inside, they've come to watch the 'wedding games', which are crowned by the play composed by Cleostrata. Myrrhina explicitly underscores the theatrical connection; 'No playwright ever conceived a plot cleverer than this masterpiece of ours!' (860–1).[40] Cleostrata, who scripted the scenario, hints at the scene to come: 'Now I'd like to see the old fool come out with his faced smashed!', then cues Pardalisca 'to stand watch here and have fun with the one who comes out' (862; 868). What ensues is indeed one of the funniest scenes in Plautus.

The doors to Alcesimus' house are flung open and Olympio hurtles out, howling, searching he says for a place to hide from the overwhelming shame and ridicule that he feels – 'for the first time!'. But, this being a comedy, the character's wish to share the joke with the audience overrides verisimilitude. Despite his distress, Olympio as a conscious performer in the play acknowledges that his plight will entertain the audience, whom he asks to[41]

'listen while I tell you all, and lend an ear.
It's worth the price; as comical to narrate as to hear

111

the quite appalling mess I've made of things inside.
The moment that we went in there, I took my bride
straight to a little bedroom which was dark as night.
Before the old man had arrived, I said, "All right,
get comfy on the couch". Then helped to smooth the bed,
and soon began to soothe her there, and said
a few kind words and some sweet nothings to her,
so prior to Master I could start to . . . *woo* her.

I start out slowly, but am filled with fear
lest turning round I find the old man there.
To get things going and begin her bliss,
I start by asking for a sloppy kiss.
She wouldn't kiss me; pushed my hand away.
That only stiffened my . . . *resolve*, which stayed that way.
I longed to taste in haste chaste Casina's embrace,
and let the old man come in second place!
And so, I closed the door to try and minimize
the chance that in the dark he'd take *me* by surprise.' (875–91)

The women suddenly reveal themselves, to Olympio's great chagrin, and proceed to tease and question him mercilessly, noting that 'It'll be a good lesson for our audience!' (902). The text in this scene and to the end of the play is very corrupt, but the general drift is clear, and highlighted by fragments which indicate its highly ribald nature. Olympio is interrogated by Cleostrata on what happened in the dark.

Cleo. 'Was it?'
Ol. 'Oh, it was just enormous! I was afraid she must still have a
    sword. So I started to investigate, and while I'm searching for
    the sword, checking to see if she's carrying one, I got hold of its
    hilt . . . On second thoughts, though, she couldn't have had a
    sword; the hilt would have felt cold . . . '
Cleo. 'Go on.'
Ol. 'I'm so embarrassed!'
Cleo. 'Let's see, was it a carrot?'
Ol. 'No.'
Cleo. 'A cucumber?!'
Ol. 'Heavens no, it wasn't any sort of vegetable. Or at least, if it
    was, it certainly was never nipped in the bud: whatever it was, it
    was full-grown!' (906-13)

Much of the humour of this scene in performance would derive from the physical antics on stage, as the women cluster around Olympio, assaulting him with questions (and perhaps simulating a game of charades in the matter of the vegetables) then reacting with shrieks and

laughter to his distressed responses. Myrrhina takes up the interroga-
tion, demanding further details. Olympio relates how he tried pleading
with 'Casina' to be more cooperative, but she only covered herself up
and turning her back to him frustrated his amorous pursuit.

> *Ol.* 'Since she's in that position, I ask her permission,
>   to attempt the alternative route!'
> *Myrr.* 'What a marvellous tale!'
> *Ol.* 'As I tried to prevail,
>   I leant over to snog with my sweet.
>   But something was weird: she'd a bristly beard!
>   Then she kicked me with both of her feet!
>   I fell flat on the ground, and she started to pound
>   and beat me just as you discern.
>   Without a word more, I ran straight out the door,
>   to let the old man have his turn.' (922–33)

At this point, on cue, the door is heard creaking, and all withdraw
upstage as Lysidamus stumbles out of the house and throws himself
down in front of the audience, in supplication. Confessing his disgrace
and fear of awful retribution from his wife, he asks in vain for someone
to take his place, and then, compounding and confirming his humiliation, decides to assume the most degraded of all social positions: that of
a fugitive slave.

> 'Is there no one out there who'd be wanting a share
> of the fate that awaits me inside?
> Then I think I'll behave like a runaway slave,
> since my back's for the rack in these parts.
> I got beat black and blue. You may laugh, but it's true!
> It's my folly, but by golly, it smarts!' (949–54)

If, as seems certain (despite the severely fragmented state of
Lysidamus' account), he has indeed been beaten up by Chalinus, it
marks the only occasion in Plautine drama when a master is physically
punished by his slave.[42]
Lysidamus says 'I'd better make a run for it right now!' and thereby
along with the particular role which his action would suggest in its
equivalent *real-life* situation, he also takes on the *dramaturgical* function
and persona of *servus currens*, the 'running slave' one of the most popular
characters in New Comedy, whose stereotypical behaviour Plautus
parodies both here and elsewhere.[43] One convention of the role, with
which the audience would be well acquainted and would enjoy seeing
fulfilled, is that once in motion, the slave is frequently stopped short by a
call from behind. Lysidamus is set to start, only to freeze at the 'starter's
block' when Chalinus' cry rings out from the porch of Alcesimus'

house; 'Hold it right there, lover boy!' (955). After first asking him if he
'yearns to return to the bedroom', the slave (still wearing his bridal
garb) threatens his master with further violence – a beating with a club –
whereupon Lysidamus, reflecting that 'it's either make tracks this way,
or break backs that way!' (968) again is poised for flight. 'Greetings!
Lover boy!' Cleostrata bellows from her place of concealment, causing
Lysidamus to stop again, and cry out in despair, 'Wolves to the right of
me, bitches to the left!' (970).[44]

The spatial arrangement on stage aptly depicts Lysidamus' predica-
ment as he stands stock still, centre stage; 'caught in the act'. On
one side his wife glowers at him from the door of their home, the
honourable head of which as pater familias he has rendered himself
unfit to fill; while, on the other, the mistaken object of his unseemly lust
and agent of his disgrace – a male slave – mocks and threatens him. All
the characters on stage now approach and surround him, firing
questions.

> *Myrr.* 'How's the second-hand husband?'
> *Cleo.* 'Why dear, why are you going about like this? What happened
>   to your cloak, and what ever did you do with your cane?'
> *Pard.* 'I think he lost them, conjugating with Casina!'
> *Lys.* 'I'm dead!'
> *Chal.* 'Don't you want to go back to bed again? I am *Casina*!'
> *Lys.* 'Go to Hell!'
> *Chal.* 'Don't you love me?' (973–8)

Lysidamus tries vainly to blame his circumstances on Bacchae, in a
reference which may have had a certain topicality for his original
audience, since only shortly before the play's performance the increasingly disruptive Bacchic rites had been banned by a Senate decree.[45]
Myrrhina will have none of it; 'That's rubbish and he knows it. There
aren't any Bacchae anymore!' (980). At this point, Lysidamus' former
ally and co-conspirator, Olympio turns against him; 'Congratulations!
You're the dirtiest old man that ever was! And he brought misery and
mockery on me because of his dastardly deeds! . . . Why you begged and
egged me on to marry Casina – on account of *your* love affair!' (990–1;
993–4).

Lysidamus stands totally isolated and humiliated, surrounded by a
circle of threatening accusers. Cleostrata advances grimly to deliver
sentence, taking him by the ear like a naughty child and ordering him to
'just march yourself right inside!' (998). Lysidamus capitulates. He begs
her to forgive him; begs Myrrhina to intercede; promises that if he
should ever make love to Casina again 'or even appear to want to do so –
let alone do it – if I ever again do such a thing – well then, dear wife, you
can just suspend me and skin me alive' (1001–3).

16   Cleostrata: 'Just march yourself right inside!' (line 998)

Cleostrata hesitates . . . Myrrhina urges clemency . . . all stand waiting
. . . and then – she relents with a nod to the audience 'in order to keep a
long play from running any longer' (1006). And so, even this rather dark
comedy ends in reconciliation;[46] but also in the punishment of
destructive excess, and the reward of domestic virtue, with the triumph
justly won for once by the women.[47]

Lys. 'You're really not angry?'
Cleo. 'No, I'm not really angry.'
Lys. 'Do you promise?'
Cleo. 'I do!'
Lys. 'There's not a living soul with a more loving and lovely wife
   than mine!' (1007–8)

As everyone gathers around the 'loving' couple, Chalinus, still
standing behind and above them on the porch, is told by Cleostrata to
restore to Lysidamus the symbols of his manly dignity; his cloak and

cane. Chalinus does so while delivering one final, and rather sophistic-ated joke to end the play with a laugh.

> *Chal.* '. . . Just consider my plight's all I ask.
> For I think it's a sin to be wed to *two* men,
> neither one of whom managed the task.' (1010–11)

All that remains to round off the performance is a brief epilogue, reminding the audience of the altogether conventional way in which the plot of the original Greek version of the work ended, before Plautus hi-jacked it, and introduced all those funny things on the way to the wedding.

> 'Now audience, wait, here's Casina's fate.
> We'll share what's discovered inside.
> A slave no more, she's the girl from next door!
> And soon, Euthynicus' bride!
> And now it's your right with all of your might
> to applaud till you bring down the house!
> If you do your part, you'll be given a tart,
> to enjoy while you cuckold your spouse!
> Yet listen, because, if you curb your applause,
> you'll live to regret it, please note:
> No Nooky! Instead, we'll send you to bed
> with a sodden and smelly old goat!'

5

TRAGEDY, MIME, AND PANTOMIME

Evidence can mislead. The survival of a generous sampling of works by Plautus, together with the complete output of Terence, colours our estimation of the Roman theatre and, if it does not entirely persuade us that the Roman playwrights and their audience had little interest in tragedy, it certainly distorts our estimation of its relative importance.[1] Yet the fact is that those in a much better position than we to assess the passing and past theatrical scene – the Roman scholars and critics active towards the end of the Republic – considered the Roman achievement in tragic writing to surpass by far that attained in comedy. Although eventually tragic writing lost its vitality, to become more an academic and aesthetic exercise than an expression of popular theatre, for several centuries the genre clearly attracted and held the Roman audience in thrall. Horace recalls the inspiration and early success of tragic playwrights.

> Not till late did the Roman turn his talent to Greek writings, and in the tranquil time which followed the Punic wars, he began to investigate what Sophocles, Thespis and Aeschylus might have to offer. He also undertook to see if he might render this in fitting style, and was pleased to find he could, imbued with spirit and with vigour: for he has the tragic sense and is fortunate in his ventures . . .[2]

Elsewhere Horace exhorts playwrights to 'work with Greek models by day; and work with them by night!'[3] and his advice had clearly been anticipated by Rome's first tragic writers beginning, as we saw, with Livius Andronicus. The titles and fragments of his tragedies confirm that they were derived from Greek myths and Greek models. Far less certain is the extent to which he and his early tragic successors based their work directly upon the 'Greats' of the classical Greek tragic theatre; Aeschylus, Sophocles, and Euripides (who had worked over two centuries before), or may have looked to contemporaneous Hellenistic tragedians for their inspiration and guidance. The question

117

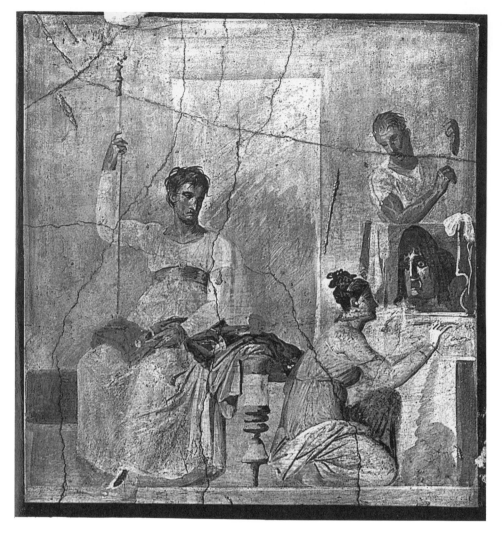

17 Depiction of a tragic actor in a first-century AD painting from Herculaneum,
now in the Naples Museum.

is vexed by the paucity of Roman textual evidence on which to base any
analysis, the almost complete absence of any Hellenistic tragic writing
and, coupled with this, a dearth of knowledge about Greek staging
conventions after the fifth century.

If we could believe with any confidence that Roman tragedy was
greatly similar to those thirty-two Greek works which survive to us, the
task of understanding it would be eased. But merely because these
works are accessible must not, for the sake of convenience, encourage us

to forget that undoubtedly the most immediate influence upon which the early Roman tragedians could draw was the contemporaneous Hellenistic repertoire, particularly as practised in southern Italy and Sicily. We can only therefore with prudence build on analogies derived from familiar fifth-century tragedies, while examining the few scraps of direct evidence to suggest whatever we can about the Roman plays and their staging. Broader assertions beyond the narrow range of such knowledge are highly speculative.

In this connection what can be determined about Andronicus' models is that a few of his plays dealt with material treated by Sophocles and Euripides, but that he may just as easily have taken these from subjects known to have been handled by several Hellenistic playwrights. His position as Rome's pre-eminent tragedian was next occupied by Quintus Ennius, who lived from 239 to 168 BC. Born in Calabria, an area suffused with Greek culture, he grew up in the city of Tarentum (from which Andronicus too had come), which, as noted earlier, was famed for its theatrical activity. He was fluent in Greek, Oscan, and Latin. Ennius fought with the Roman forces in Sardinia, and – possibly influenced by the plundering of Tarentum in 209 to punish its harbouring of Hannibal – he chose not to return there upon completing his military service at the age of thirty-five in 204. Instead he made his home in Rome where he enjoyed the patronage of Cato the elder,[4] and, living there in close contact both with other playwrights and leading citizens, became heavily involved in the cultural life of the city. In 189 he was the first poet to be invited to serve on the staff of a Roman general, accompanying the Consul Fulvius on his campaigns in the East. Inspired by his sense of Rome's past and destiny, Ennius wrote an epic poem on Roman history for which later generations venerated him. In 184 he was granted Roman citizenship for his service to the state.[5]

We have the titles of some twenty tragedies by Ennius, and 400 lines, which on the whole do indicate a pronounced Euripidean influence; a fact noted in antiquity.[6] About a dozen plays may be traced to an original by Euripides, but since his work exercised the greatest influence upon Hellenistic tragedy generally, Ennius' debt may be an indirect one. Among the plays in question are an *Andromeda*, a *Hecuba*, an *Iphigenia*, and a *Medea*. In addition we find a *Eumenides*, which if based on Aeschylus' version (the concluding part of the Oresteian trilogy), is likely to have involved substantial adaptation to make it intelligible on its own to a Roman audience. A comparison between what little we can garner from these works, and the surviving originals, suggests that in terms of overall concept, plot, and division into scenes, Ennius has tended to follow his Greek models. But in his use of language, metrical arrangement, the emphasis he gives to particular ideas or themes, and occasionally the introduction of thoughts not encompassed by the original text, he exercised considerable freedom. He is particularly fond of heightening the rhetorical effect by alliteration, assonance, word-play, antithesis, and repetition of particular words or phrases. This gives his work a certain self-consciousness, and occasionally the sense of striving after effect (not entirely unlike that found in the comedies of Plautus, although Ennius takes far fewer linguistic liberties), which suggest both the limits of his compositional skill and perhaps a taste on the part of his audience for somewhat unsubtle gratifications. Although Cicero greatly admired his oratorical skill, and quoted him often, Horace charged him with 'launching his verses ponderously onto the stage' and of 'either too hasty, and negligent work, or ignorance of the art'.[7]

In his *Iphigenia* (in Aulis) Ennius replaces the Euripidean chorus of Chalcean maidens with a male chorus of Achilles' soldiers, who (in a short excerpt preserved to us) ruminate on the boredom of military life: a subject that must have found some response in an audience at Rome where one third of the adult male population had been mobilized recently during the second Punic war.[8] In other instances Ennius replaces speech with song, or vice versa, and strives for a more stylized (occasionally overwrought) rhetorical display. In addition (and again reminiscent of Plautus) the action of his plays is occasionally interrupted by sententious asides, or extended passages explicating some moral insight or worthy precept.

> The dialogue . . . is sometimes expanded with treatments of everyday problems and ethical questions: the relations between slaves and masters, between upper and lower classes, the rich and the poor, the role of the tyrant, patriotic duties, the choice of work, the requirements of honour, manly virtue, courage and justice. These and similar subjects are handled often . . .[9]

Nearly half of Ennius' works are drawn from the myths involving the Trojan War; subject matter which we noted earlier was also used extensively by his predecessors, Andronicus and Naevius, and which evidently appealed to the Roman audience both for the relevance of its treatment of the emotions and fortunes of war, and because of the belief, already prevalent at Rome, that the city had been founded by Trojan refugees.

Ennius was succeeded as foremost tragedian by his student and nephew, Marcus Pacuvius, who was born in Brundisium in 220 BC. Like him, he migrated to Rome where he moved within a circle of influential aristocrats and lived during a period of extraordinary imperial expansion and a greatly accelerated espousal of Greek culture. He was befriended by the important politician, Gaius Laelius (himself a close friend of Scipio Aemilianus) who was remembered for his love of literature and philosophy, and whose name is also associated with

Terence and the poet Lucilius. Pacuvius was himself both a writer and renowned painter, and admired later as the most learned of Roman playwrights.[10]

He was the first Roman playwright to limit himself exclusively to tragedy, and his output too was limited: we have the titles of only a dozen works, and a remnant of some 400 lines. Since he lived to an advanced age, dying about 130 BC, and is thought to have presented his last play at the age of eighty, Pacuvius evidently was not dependent upon the theatre for his livelihood. That he could afford to take risks may be reflected in his choice of unusual subject matter, dealing with mythic material which was relatively unfamiliar to his audience and therefore might not have readily won its approval. Few of his works handled the stories commonly used by his Roman predecessors, who, as noted, mutually recycled their subjects. Only one of his works, the *Antiopa*, is related to a Euripidean original, with four (*Hermiona, Iliona, Medus,* and *Niptra*) based on Sophocles, and one (*Armorum Iudicium*) possibly on Aeschylus. Nor can several of his titles be traced to treatments by Hellenistic authors.

This originality of subject matter was complemented by innovative dramatic technique. Pacuvius used his language with close attention to sound effects, to the creation of moments of great pathos, and to the painting of evocative imagery. Cicero praised his 'finely wrought and elegant verses', and indeed his metrical arrangements, more than those of any other Roman playwright, approximated those of the Greek masters. He was fond of complex plots and intrigue, lofty sentiment, and the occasional flight of rhetorical fantasy. His plays offer examples of lively debate, and the discussion of moral conflicts and philosophical issues. More intellectual than his predecessors, he was long admired for 'the gravity of his insights, the weight of his language and the dignity of his characters'.[11]

In the light of this, we should note that Pacuvius' plays managed to attract and hold a Roman audience both during his lifetime and long afterwards. At least half of them are known to have been performed (up to a century after his death) in the time of Cicero, who, notwithstanding his profound admiration of Ennius, pronounced him the greatest Roman tragedian.[12] The audience presumably was equal to the challenge of Pacuvius' works, despite somewhat obscure subjects and elevated style, because he joined these with a deft understanding of dramaturgical technique. Suspense, pathos, startling revelations, moments of spirited rhetoric; Pacuvius evidently had a particular talent for forming and moulding such elements to create compelling theatre.

Lucius Accius was born in 170 BC in Umbria, the son of a freedman. In his thirtieth year he produced a tragedy at Rome, his work sharing the honour of the occasion with a play by Pacuvius, who was then very old.

According to an ancient anecdote, shortly thereafter he undertook an educational journey to Greece, pausing on the way to visit Pacuvius, in his retirement at Tarentum. Here the young and aspiring playwright was able to read his latest work, the *Atreus*, to the 'grand old man' of the Roman theatre.[13] Following the pattern of his playwriting predecessors, Accius soon attracted the attention and support of eminent and culturally enlightened Roman patricians, including the former Consul, D. Junius Brutus, then in his sixties, a distinguished orator and man of letters. By the age of thirty-four he was sufficiently prominent to be mentioned by name in a mime performance; an impropriety which prompted Accius to bring a successful lawsuit against the offending actor.[14]

Rome was now caught up in a quickening tide of Hellenistic influence, which everywhere was eroding conservative opposition, and leading to a profound and permanent transformation of Roman culture. Not only were Greek scholars, writers, and artisans flooding into the city, but the Romans themselves, including influential politicians and aristocrats, now avidly studied and imitated the intellectual and artistic achievements of Greece.

> Every aspect of Roman intellectual culture in this period can be seen undergoing confident reshaping in the light of growing acquaintance with Greek culture . . . Romans were more and more initiated, in a natural day-to-day way, into the Greek way of life, and many of them liked what they saw and adapted their own way of life accordingly – even to the extent of wearing Greek dress.[15]

Accius both benefited from and participated in this process. He was a man of great personal force and vitality; confident, ambitious, and curious. He pursued extensive study of literary history and published learned essays on aspects of composition and style. Perhaps in imitation of Ennius, who had published a military and political history of Rome – the *Annales* – Accius, (using the same title) composed a work chronicling cultural and artistic developments. In turn, he had the advantage of producing works before a more enlightened and sophisticated audience than his predecessors; an audience which expressed its esteem (and the status that a playwright might now enjoy at Rome) by erecting a colossal statue of the poet, who lived to an advanced age, dying around 86 BC.[16]

Although generally judged inferior to Pacuvius in the excellence and refinement of his works, Accius was Rome's most important and prolific tragic playwright. We have the titles of forty plays, and 700 lines. His subjects (about half of his tragedies can be traced to fifth-century examples) were extremely wide-ranging, spanning a vast body of myth, with comprehensive exploitation of the Trojan, Theban, and

18 A first-century BC relief from the monument of P. Numitorius Hilarus, now in the Museum of the Terme, Rome. It may depict a scene from the *Astyanax* of Accius, in which the boy Astyanax, his hand held by his mother Andromache, is about to be led away to his death by Odysseus. Note the *scaenae frons* in the background.

House of Atreus sagas. In addition, he drew upon the Argonaut myths, and the stories of Prometheus, Theseus, and Hercules. Several of his plays suggest the possibility that they were composed as a sequence, and may even have been intended for consecutive performance at the Roman games on the earlier Athenian model of linked trilogies. Sophocles (possibly as adapted by later Hellenistic authors) appears to have been his chief inspiration, with such works as *Antigona, Deiphobus, Astyanax,* and *Oenomaus* believed to derive from him. Aeschylus may have provided the source for Accius' *Telephus, Myrmidones,* and almost certainly for the *Prometheus.* The *Bacchae, Phoenissae, Meleager,* and possibly the *Alcestis* and *Minotaurus* may be based on Euripides. He also returned to subjects dealt with by the earlier Roman tragedians: an *Andromeda* and *Achilles* (which both Andronicus and Ennius had

123

handled); an *Aegisthus* and *Tereus* (Andronicus); a *Telephus, Hecuba*, and *Alcumeo* (Ennius); *Thyestes* (Ennius); and *Armorum Iudicium* (Pacuvius). For about a dozen of Accius' titles, no fifth-century, Hellenistic, or Roman antecedent is known.

Much of the material which Accius dramatized encompassed the military subjects and themes which from past example the Roman audience apparently found congenial; it is also tempting to think that the extraordinarily turbulent period during which he lived – marked by persistent warfare both within Italy and abroad, and intensive social struggle and political upheaval at Rome itself – was also reflected in his works as it must certainly have informed his audiences' perception and response. Accius' subjects include ample scope for the presentation of social conflict, factional intrigue, the perfidy and punishment of traitors, the downfall of tyrants and the death of kings; themes and events never far from removed from the memory or, at the least, the imagination of the individual spectator. In such circumstances, it is easier to explain the force of his style, the frequent excess of sentiment and emotion, the overheated, melodramatic quality of the characters and actions he presents: art was in competition with life for attention and intensity. There are moments of great and affecting drama, but there is also much bombast, hyperbole, and 'unearned' emotion.

In common with the other Roman tragedians (and some comic writers too) Accius was fond of rhetorical display and the sort of 'performing language' that calls attention to itself, sometimes inappropriately, through the devices of alliteration, word-play, and the deliberate use of archaic words and syntax. Although this can rise to moments of genuine emotion and high dignity, it can also plunge into bathos. But it was evidently no less popular for that. By way of analogy, to the modern ear the language and descriptions of nineteenth-century melodramas often seem ridiculous, but undeniably they held their vast audiences enthralled.

> Roman tragedy did not succeed in developing a style which was at once simple and dignified. That it did not do so is to be explained quite as much by popular taste in Rome as by the limitations of the writers of tragedy. The effects which to us seem forced may have appealed to the listeners for whom they were designed far more than would the artistic restraint of the Greek originals.[17]

Accius' plays were admired for their flamboyance and energy;[18] they also contained much verbal violence and descriptive gore: Thyestes dining upon his sons; Philomel raped by Tereus who cuts out her tongue to avoid detection; Medea's murder of her children. Accius probed his mythic material to bring forth its most intense pathos and horror. On the basis of the few examples where we can compare his treatment with the earlier Greek texts, he seems also to have heightened the dramatic effects through more sensational staging. For example, in his *Antigona*, he enacts Antigone's capture by the soldiers guarding the unburied body of Polyneices; an event which in Sophocles' work is merely reported. In this and in similar moments found in the work of other Roman tragedians, we detect a tendency towards greater *dramatization*, that is, greater realism through the actual depiction of events on stage rather than their description. The same trend can be broadly discerned in the evolution of classical tragedy during the fifth century, from Aeschylus through to Euripides, and it seems likely that the Roman writers are both reflecting and carrying forward a process that had continued in the works of the Hellenistic playwrights.

The analysis of tragic writing Horace provides in the *Ars Poetica*, composed perhaps some sixty years or so after Accius' death, casts some further light upon the characteristics which, ideally, Roman tragedy displayed. He stresses for example, that although some events are unsuitable for realization on stage (referring specifically to the cooking of Thyestes' sons and Medea's slaughter of her children), in general things should be enacted because 'the mind is less affected by what it perceives through the ears, than by that presented to the faithful eyes, and what the spectator can see for himself'. Elsewhere he again apparently endorses the trend towards greater realism, 'Fictions which find favour should be close to reality; a play may not demand belief for whatever it chooses.' In analysing the role of the chorus, Horace further strengthens the impression gained from the few fragments of Roman tragedy. These indicate that the chorus was also dramatized in a more realistic fashion than was customary in earlier Greek practice, taking an active role in the dramatic action, and not confined to providing mere commentary or poetic interludes. 'Let the chorus take on the part and active role of an actor, and interject nothing between the acts which does not advance and fit appropriately with the plot.'[19] The evidence is persuasive that all of the Roman tragedians made use of the chorus, although there is some suggestion that its songs may have devolved to individual soloists with the group as a whole tending to provide recitative.

The composition of tragedy – at least that intended for staging – apparently died out after Accius. A young contemporary, Julius Caesar Strabo – uncle of the famous Caesar – a prominent aristocratic politician and outstanding orator, who was caught up in factional strife, proscribed, and executed at the age of thirty-four in 87 BC, is known to have tried his hand at playwriting. On the basis of several works (three titles survive) he was admitted to the *Collegium*, of which Accius was then leading member. This, and one further reference, indicate that his works appeared on the stage, but Cicero thought little of them, evidently (and probably correctly) considering them an expression of dilettantism by a talented and versatile politician, to whom the stage provided desirable publicity. In marked contrast to Accius, Strabo's style (both in his tragedies and as an orator) was reputedly genial and urbane, yet also capable of effective and evocative dramatic expression.[20] In fact, Strabo's example may suggest a process of 'cross-fertilization' between oratory and theatrical rhetoric of the sort to which a number of Roman writers on the art of public speaking call attention, and may indirectly reflect the increasing importance of theatre as an extension of political activity and expression. There are several examples (to deem it a 'fashion' is perhaps excessive) of politicians in the late Republican and early imperial period who composed tragedies. Cicero undertook as stylistic exercises to translate passages from Greek tragedy, and his younger brother Quintus Tullius Cicero was an avid admirer of Sophocles, several of whose works he translated, or in some cases adapted.[21] As a young man, Julius Caesar composed an *Oedipus*, a subject which, surprisingly, no other Roman writer had yet handled. Almost a century later Augustus (no doubt mindful of the divine Julius' reputation – and, by extension, his own) ordered that it be suppressed. Augustus himself composed a tragedy, the *Ajax*, which he later destroyed.[22]

A member of Caesar's party, L. Cornelius Balbus, wrote a tragedy based on his own experience of contemporary Roman history, and staged it in Spain where he was serving, in 43 BC.[23] Thirty years later, under Augustus, Balbus sponsored and gave his name to Rome's second permanent theatre. L. Varius Rufus, a close friend of Vergil and Horace, wrote a single tragedy, *Thyestes*, which was staged for the celebrations of Augustus' victory at Actium in 29 BC. It survived to be read by Tacitus, who greatly admired it, and by Quintilian, who deemed it the equal of any Greek tragedy. They had similar praise for the *Medea* of Ovid. Still later in the mid-first century AD we find the Consul Publius Pomponius Secundus composing and staging tragedies, including another *Atreus* esteemed for its learning and polish – although some older critics evidently considered it rather lightweight in contrast to earlier Roman tragic fare. References occur to other tragic playwrights from time to time, extending into the second century AD, although it must be doubted that they wrote for full-scale performance; probably preferring publication and recitation.[24] The same is likely to have been true of the nine tragedies of Seneca, the only surviving examples of Roman tragedy, which are considered in a later section.

In addition to scripted comedy and tragedy, the Roman audience enjoyed certain other forms of theatrical entertainment which flourished during the Republic, and indeed, in the imperial period completely eclipsed these genres in popularity. As in the case of comedy, whose relative 'abundance' may cause us to underestimate the importance of tragedy, so too the literary evidence of comedy and tragedy which survives wholly or in fragments may prompt us to overestimate their relative importance to the Roman theatre and its audience not just for the period in which they were most frequently composed, but later as well. This evidence is particularly misleading if we simply assume that the dearth of new writing in the Empire reflects a general decline in theatrical activity.

Although there continue to be references to its performance, the composition of comedy seems virtually to have ceased after the end of the second century BC[25] and, like tragedy, it evidently lost its appeal as a subject for new writing for the stage. Although dramatic composition appears to have devolved to scholars and dilettantes, and away from professional playwrights, staged revivals of earlier works were abundant in the late Republic and well into the Empire. Cicero, for example, frequently records performances of tragedy, and refers to a production of Plautus' *Pseudolus* in the first quarter of the first century BC.[26] Later Horace indicates (in his epistle to Augustus written towards the end of the century) that the works of other Roman playwrights—including Ennius, Naevius, Pacuvius, Accius, Caecilius, and Terence—continue to hold the stage. These plays he claims 'mighty Rome learns by heart, and these she views packed into her crowded theatre'.[27] Still later Quintilian, in the first century AD, is well acquainted with contemporary performances of both comedy and tragedy, Juvenal attests to them in the second century, and as late as the fourth, Donatus in his commentary on Terence indicates that comic performances are still taking place.[28] The attribution of actors' roles in some manuscript copies of Plautus and Terence also suggests a continuing performance tradition during the Empire. Certainly too, the numerous examples of painted scenes from both comedy and tragedy found at Pompeii attest to continuing familiarity, at least within one level of society, for the period the paintings were executed: the decades prior to AD 79.

But alongside comedy and tragedy other genres sprang up or grew in popularity. On the basis of the literary evidence alone, we might presume that the virtual disappearance of playwriting dictated a commensurate decline in theatrical activity, or that such activity as continued was grossly inferior to what had taken place earlier, as the prologue to an early revival of Plautus' *Casina* expressed it, 'in that age when the flower of poets lived'. And yet, over a century later, in the period between 55 and 11 BC, Rome acquired three large and luxurious permanent theatres 'close together in what might be called the first "theatre district" in the Campus Martius'.[29] Although this may in part reflect the self-interest of individuals or factions vying for power and prominence in a period of political upheaval, it is certainly a measure too of the pressure of popular demand and enthusiasm for theatrical entertainment. As the great age of theatre construction during the Empire attests, this continued to intensify. Moreover,

> the number of days on which scenic entertainment was featured at the regular Roman festivals continuously increased throughout 700 years . . . the evidence of the literary texts is misleading. The heyday of the Roman theatre was not in the Republic but in the Empire.[30]

The venerable *Atellanae*, which had preceded Roman comedy, did not wither away after Roman comic writers borrowed and adapted some of their salient features and local colour for their own, more formal works. The factors which encouraged such concessions to established popular taste also ensured that the *Atellanae* themselves continued to hold the stage, and indeed, occasionally to satirize in turn the very comedies indebted to them. As the case of Terence may suggest, 'close imitation of humane and earnest Greek comedy would not hold a Roman audience'.[31] Prior to the construction of a permanent and enclosed theatre, spectators could freely move from one attraction to another, and the short sketches comprising the *Atellanae*, concentrating on the moment by moment entertainment, rather than the development and nuanced meaning of a longer plot, had a better chance of success under such conditions.

Perhaps by way of compromise, and an acknowledgment of the merits of a written script, the *Atellanae* are known to have acquired literary form early in the first century BC. At the time of Augustus they were still greatly in vogue and now widely performed in Latin, although at least occasionally in the original Oscan as well.[32] In AD 22 or 23 Tiberius tried without success to curb them because of their growing indecency.[33] A little later, in a passage which further suggests their continuing hold upon popular taste, Petronius, in his *Satyricon*, has his character Trimalchio (a parvenu of the worst sort), point out that although he employs a troupe of comedians, he in fact prefers them to perform *Atellanae*.[34]

As described earlier, it seems clear that the staging requirements of such archaic farces were minimal, and demanded little or nothing in the way of scenery. Given their rural origin and subject matter, it is probably safe to assume that they were widely played on simple, easily erected temporary stages, even after the appearance of more elaborate permanent theatre buildings. Indeed, Cicero, in a letter describing the inauguration of Pompey's theatre, when the *Atellanae* were included amongst the extensive presentations, suggests that they may have suffered from a more sumptuous format. 'They did not even have the sprightliness which one usually finds in ordinary shows – one lost all sense of gaiety in watching the extravagant productions.'[35]

Juvenal provides a glimpse of performance in a more appropriate setting.

> There is much of Italy, if we admit it, where no one dresses in togas unless they're dead, and where even at festive days, honoured, if at all, in a grassy theatre, where the familiar farce [*exodium*] returns to the stage, and the mouth of the pale mask frightens the rustic child in its mother's lap, you will see that both those in the orchestra, and the general crowd wear much the same clothing.[36]

Despite their heartiness, in time the *Atellanae* appear to have been usurped by a related, but even more formless and diverse species of popular entertainment, the mime. After the second century AD, no direct references to Atellane farces appear, although a notice of their death by then might well be premature; perhaps they were in essence subsumed into the mime, thereafter providing one further variant amongst its diverse examples. The mime (which it is important to emphasize was *not*, like the modern form bearing its name, mute) originated in Greece, where it had long been popular, particularly amongst the Dorians who brought it with them to their colonies in *Magna Graecia*. Performed by *autokabdaloi*, 'improvisers', initially it was not even essentially dramatic: acrobatics, song and dance, jokes, conjuring – every type of broad entertainment in fact – were grafted onto the flimsiest of impromptu scenarios to create a kind of variety show. According to Plutarch (who held it in low esteem), it was so formless that even a dog could perform in it, and indeed at times animals, including even elephants, did![37]

The Romans were probably familiar with the mime from an early date, certainly before the introduction of scripted comedy, and it may well have exercised a formative influence on their own emerging theatrical fare of music, songs, jests, dance, and buffoonery.[38] Together with such entertainment it was formally incorporated into the Roman holiday calendar and, from at least as early as 173 BC, provided the chief ornament of the *Floralia*; festivities noted for their licence and merriment, and in particular, for naked female performers.[39] However, it could be presented at any time on its own, as an interlude or afterpiece with other drama, or in conjunction with any other form of public or private entertainment. As wealth accumulated in the long period of expansion during the second and first centuries BC, well-to-do Romans began to lay on lavish cabaret-style entertainment at their grand dinner-parties (often a cosmopolitan collection of poets, politicians, wits, and the like), to which the style and content of the mime might well have been particularly appropriate; in fact, it became the custom for well-established households to include such performers amongst their staff.[40] Undoubtedly its adaptability and minimal staging requirements help to explain its striking popularity and longevity.

The performers, who could be men or, significantly, women, were maskless, unlike the players of *Atellanae* or scripted drama. Performing barefoot,[41] their grimacing, gesticulation, and general expressiveness were an essential part of the performance. The subject matter was generally coarse and frequently obscene, with the emphasis firmly on sex, parody of town and city life, and general buffoonery. A notable feature was the absence of stock characters. The artistes were quintessentially entertainers, play was the thing, and although beyond titles and descriptions little indication of the substance of their work survives, their improvisation, anarchic humour, and horseplay undoubtedly influenced Roman comic writers, and decisively conditioned the taste of their audience. The versatility of the mimes (the term used for both the performers and performances) is suggested by the epitaph of one Vitalis, a virtuoso from the imperial period, which records

> At sight of me wild frenzy met relief;
> My entrance changed to laughter poignant grief . . .
> An hour with me was ever happiness,
> In tragic role my word and act could please,
> Cheering in myriad ways hearts ill at ease:
> Through change in look, mien, voice I so could run
> That many seemed to use the lips of one.
> The man whose double on the stage I seemed
> Shrank, as my looks his very own he deemed.
> How oft a woman whom my gestures played
> Saw herself, blushed, and held her peace dismayed!
> So parts which I made live by mimicry
> Dark death hath hurried to the grave with me.[42]

The performance was frequently preceded by a brief prologue, and the mime itself was short, largely improvised, and often delivered in unliterary language (including much slang) which the performer was quick to adapt to the mood and response of the audience. Although undoubtedly low-brow jokes, banter, and ribaldry were their stock-in-trade, the mimes directed their comments not only at the *Vulgus* in 'the upper part of the auditorium', but at the better educated and sophisticated spectators as well, including the leading citizens in the seats reserved for them at the front. But one such viewer, Cicero, noted with disdain how a mime purporting to present 'a symposium of poets and philosophers', anachronistically included at a single gathering Euripides, Socrates, Menander, and Epicurus, and that, worse still, the audience loudly applauded it in their ignorance.[43] Seneca the younger was more generous in his assessment of the mimes' claim to be taken seriously, recording that at times 'the whole theatre would resound' with approval when some particular words of wisdom or insight 'were acknowledged by general agreement to be true'.[44]

The audience was quick too to recognize the frequent topical and satirical allusions, or veiled political comment. Cicero expected to gauge from comments at the mimes the popular reaction to Caesar's death, and on another occasion warned a friend temporarily absent in Gaul, not to remain away from Rome too long lest he become the object of the mimes, 'A Britannic counsellor would make a marvelous figure of fun!'[45] But, for the most part, the presenters concerned themselves with caricature, sensationalized enactments from everyday life (the bawdier the better, with adultery a favourite theme) as well as more exotic subjects such as kidnappings, shipwrecks and, occasionally, plots drawn from mythology. Escapist treatments of tormented love, sudden changes in fortune, bizarre coincidences, unlikely impersonations, lovers hidden in chests and, above all, titillating tales of sexual derring-do far outweighed the mimes' occasionally more serious content. The Roman audience, obsessed as Tacitus noted by its 'characteristic and peculiar vice' – its love of virtuoso acting – found in the methods and material of the mimes a source of enormous interest and diversion.[46]

Despite such support and, not infrequently, adulation, the mime artists' social status was lower even than that of dramatic actors. Some nevertheless became close friends with prominent Romans. Sulla was much given to consorting with mimes; particularly fond of one Sorex, the leader of a troupe, and rather more than fond of another, Metrobius, who specialized in some refinement of female impersonation. Mark Antony too, enjoyed their companionship, and even Cicero upon occasion (and with reservations) dined in their company.[47] But by and large they were held in contempt – certainly by 'polite' society – and their low morals became in a literal sense, proverbial. References abound to the performers' shocking behaviour both onstage and off, and the disgrace of associating with them, while commentators frequently lumped them together with other low-life denizens; whores, pimps, parasites, and the like.[48]

In 115 BC, the censors L. Metellus and Gnaeus Domitius had ordered all theatrical personnel (including presumably, the mimes) from Rome,[49] but the ban if enforced at all was short-lived. Later, during the Empire, they suffered similar banishment from time to time, but the populace never endured their absence for long. Nevertheless, the mimes' life was a precarious one, and although popular individuals might amass considerable wealth (one Dionysia earned 200,000 sesterces a year in the later Republic),[50] most were slaves, and those who were not eked out a dubious living; greatly dependent on the largess and indulgence of patrons, the taste of the public, and the availability of suitable opportunities for performance. Surviving by their wits, and unable to afford respectability, they practised a 'rough and ready' but lively art whose very adaptability and tenuousness contributed to its extraordinary popular appeal as well as its lengthy survival.

The variety and versatility of the mime's subject matter was reflected in the actors who presented it; ranging from the individual itinerant performer presenting a one-man show to large troupes (with up to sixty members) offering a full bill of diverse entertainments. Some artists specialized in afterpieces, others in interludes, still others in such non-dramatic material as conjuring, juggling, and singing. Their adaptability enabled them to perform in the orchestra when the stage was set for other presentations; alternatively they may have used a small curtain to designate their playing space within the vast stages of the permanent theatres, or in any area (a market-place or public square) where an audience could gather.[51]

Generally the mime used a small cast of two or three actors or actresses; Ovid speaks of a serviceable three-actor cast consisting of an old man, shrewish wife, and vapid lover.[52] The lesser actors served as foils to the *archimimus* who perhaps functioned somewhat like the 'top banana' of vaudeville. As well as managing the presentation – a sort of master of ceremonies – he might summarize and comment on the plot, and instigate the actions, jokes, and intrigues, while the second actor, often representing a fool or parasite, played off, comically misinterpreted, and reacted to him.[53] The second actor sometimes had a shaven head, and might be endowed with a prominent phallus. Although a variety of costumes could be worn, those most directly associated with the mime were the *centunculus*, a colourful patchwork tunic, and the *ricinium*, a cloak with a square hood sometimes used to conceal the head.

In the years of relentless expansion and vast social and economic change following Rome's final victory over Carthage, the political constitution appropriate to a city-state proved incapable of providing stable government to a growing empire. After the middle of the second century BC, Roman society was in a state of almost constant upheaval, culminating finally in the civil strife and warfare of the next century. Although initially the conflict had been drawn between, broadly speaking, those purporting to champion the interests of the mass of people (the *populares*) on the one hand, and those protecting oligarchic privilege (the *optimates*), on the other, in time, 'the social substance of the conflicts . . . was thrust ever further into the background, while the quest for political power became ever more important until, finally, the issue became simply the predominance of particular political groupings and, especially, of their leaders'.[54] These became adept at manipulating the proletariat masses at Rome by demagogy and largesse, the latter made possible by the huge increase in public and private wealth brought about by expansion, entrepreneurial activity, and confiscations.[55]

During the last tumultuous decades of the Republic in the first century BC Roman political life was dominated by competing factions led by powerful individuals, and heading inevitably towards the rule of one man. Such men, and particularly Sulla and his successors, Pompey, and Caesar, perceived the potential usefulness as well as the danger of theatre. It was in this period that the mime appears greatly to have increased its popularity. Sulla, as noted, enjoyed the company of its actors, and his patronage may have encouraged its rise now. A canny politician, he recognized the value of the games for promoting his career, and indeed at a crucial stage had been elected praetor in 97 BC partly on the promise of spectacular celebrations following a period of relative neglect. Thereafter he used such shows as an instrument of power, personal prestige, and popularity. Claiming that his own celebrations, the *Ludi Victoriae Sullanae* were deserved by the people after their privations, he further indulged his audience by loosening previous restraints on private spending during the games to allow more sumptuous feasting.[56]

In addition to his own personal taste for the mimes (he even tried composing them himself)[57] Sulla and his successors may have favoured them as less potentially subversive than tragedy. The Roman public was always quick to note inconvenient passages that could be construed to suggest parallels between stage tyrants (and their fates) and those who might be sitting in the audience. Cicero for example records that in 59 BC, the Roman mob, which only two years earlier at his triumph had praised Pompey to the skies, now in his absence applauded an actor who pointedly delivered lines from a play 'that might have been written especially for Pompey'. Such phrases as 'by our misfortunes are you great', and 'in time to come you will lament your boldness' were encored and wildly applauded, until Caesar entered the theatre, and the audience, wary of offending him by such effrontery, fell silent. Later, at the performance of Pacuvius' tragedy *Armorum Iudicium* given for Caesar's funeral games, the crowd's fury was fuelled by the line 'Why did I spare these men that they might murder me?'. The Emperor Tiberius ordered a playwright to commit suicide because of an unflattering verse in his *Atreus*.[58] The mime, though not entirely adverse to making such personal allusions, was unlikely to do so in a context so resonant as those encountered in tragedy.[59]

At the end of the Republic, the mimes' popularity led to their becoming an object of literary endeavour, as writers began to compose them in comic meters. Two such writers, Decimus Laberius and Publilius Syrus, are associated with Caesar. Laberius, a Roman knight, wrote pungent pieces noted for their obscenity, and true-to-life diction.

133

Some of his forty-two surviving titles suggest subject matter akin to that of comedy e.g.; 'Pot of Gold', 'Twins', 'Fisherman', and 'Saturnalia', while others evoke more exotic subject matter. One fragment mentions the philosopher Democritus, while others appear to take Pythagoreanism as a subject for satire; requiring a level of knowledge and sophistication in the Roman audience considerably above that evident in the days of Plautus or Terence. In additon to ribaldry, Laberius was also admired for his 'elegant and finished verses', the freedom with which he coined new words,[60] and for his ready wit. In his 'Descent into the Underworld', a number of characters come forward who have witnessed strange portents and wonders. One had seen a husband with two wives, whereupon Laberius has a second character exclaim that this is even more remarkable than the recent dream of a certain soothsayer about six aediles. Caesar had in fact nominated six aediles instead of the usual four, and was rumoured to favour polygamy. As Mommsen observes 'One sees from this that Laberius understood how to exercise the fool's privilege and Caesar how to permit the fool's freedom.'[61]

At his games of 46 BC given to celebrate his victory over the remnants of Pompey's forces in Africa, Caesar may have taken his revenge when he challenged Laberius (then aged sixty) to perform in a competitive presentation of one of his own mimes. Laberius (as he noted wryly) could hardly 'deny anything to a being to whom the gods have granted everything', although by appearing on the professional stage he sacrificed both his dignity and his formal status as a knight. He redeemed the former, however, by uttering the lines, 'thus O Romans do we lose our liberties!', and 'many must he fear whom many fear'; the latter was restored to him by Caesar with a gold ring (the formal mark of equestrian rank) and half a million sesterces.[62] Suetonius notes that this enabled Laberius 'to walk directly from the stage to the orchestra, where fourteen rows of seats were reserved for his order'.[63] When his fellow knights were reluctant to let him resume his place, Cicero (in an exchange which conveys something of the flavour of the occasion) called out in a barbed reference to Caesar having packed the Senate with his supporters, 'I would offer you a seat, were I not so short of space myself!' Laberius scored a hit with his reply, 'It's surprising you lack for space, since you generally perch upon two at the same time!'

Laberius' rival (to whom Caesar awarded the prize) at this lively occasion was a former slave, Publilius Syrus. Probably born in Antioch, he had been brought to Italy and subsequently obtained his freedom. Well educated, he composed his own mimes, and had toured them widely in the Italian provinces before challenging other performers to compete with him at Rome.[64] Although only two titles survive, his works were valued in antiquity for their well-wrought sentiments and phrases expressed in refined Latin. Seneca the elder thought his epigrams often superior to the sentiments of tragic writers, and Gellius, who was an indefatigable collector of apt quotes, preserved a number of maxims excerpted from his mimes. Together with a great many more these were gathered together into an anthology and widely circulated in the Empire for their moral edification.[65] Of these, some 700 have come down to us. Such nuggets as 'O life, so long for the wretched, so short for the happy'; 'what can't be cured must be endured'; 'patience too oft provoked is turned to rage'; and 'mid too much wrangling truth is often lost' are typical. Many of his proverbs are purely platitudes, but pithy and, as time has proved, memorable. 'There is honour even among thieves'; 'the end justifies the means'; 'do unto others as you would have them do unto you': Syrus the one-time slave and actor was surely not the first to say such things, but he *did* say them and was remembered and honoured to the end of antiquity and beyond for having done so.

It may have been the growing popularity of the mime in the last days of the Republic that encouraged the establishment at this time of a school for mime artists in Rome. Its founder, Tigellius Hermogenes, was characterized at his death by Horace in terms which indicate that despite his efforts mimes had not entirely succeeded in becoming respectable.

> The guilds of flute girls, the drug-quacks, beggars, mimes, jesters, and all that sort are in grief and mourning over the death of the singer Tigellius. He was, forsooth, so kind.[66]

Nevertheless, Cicero was not above quoting from or using mimes as examples in his speeches (and was on friendly terms with one Valerius, who composed them); Pompey did not disdain to present them at the inauguration of his theatre; Mark Antony enjoyed associating with and assisted their artistes; and Octavian, fond of attending their performances, also employed them as entertainment at his private banquets.[67]

The development of literary mimes must have further obscured the distinction between them and traditional comedy, if not for contemporaries then certainly for later commentators. Not infrequently the word 'mime' was used indiscriminately to designate 'players', or 'stage-folk'. The salient difference between the two was the mime's maskless performance, but undoubtedly there was rich stylistic interchange between the genres, and even perhaps some movement by performers from one type of 'show business' to another. Writing in the mid-first century AD, when the mimes had achieved enormous popularity, Quintilian gave an eyewitness account of the work of 'the greatest of comic actors, Demetrius and Stratocles', which conveys some slight impression of mimetic skills and 'tricks of the trade'. Demetrius had the gift of charm, a pleasing voice, and great good looks. He was 'best in the roles of gods, young men, good fathers and slaves, matrons and respectable old women'. His particular talents extended to the subtle

> movement of his hands, his ability to delight spectators with the languid sweetness of his statements, the way he made his dress seem to flow in the wind as he moved, and occasionally the expressive movement of his right side.

Stratocles by contrast was praised for his stronger voice, and for his portrayals of 'nasty old men, clever slaves, parasites, pimps, and all the livelier characters'. He was noted too for 'agility and quickness of movement, his laugh which, even when inappropriate to the character, he consciously used for the crowd's benefit, and finally for the way he sank his neck into his shoulders'.

Quintilian concludes his sketch by remarking that had either actor affected the other's routine, the attempt would have been disastrous.[68]

Although the popularity of the mimes continued unabated into the Empire, the general standard (which probably had always fluctuated considerably) appears now to have declined, as greater liberty was condoned in the choice and depiction of subject matter. Their very popularity may have encouraged presenters to take liberties; improvising to suit the mood of the crowd, pushing licence to its limits – and beyond. At times respectable knights and matrons took the stage (a practice which had been outlawed under Augustus), and Nero encouraged noble patricians to take part as well.[69] The most popular mime of the first and second centuries AD, was the *Laureolus* of Catullus. It enacted the sensational story of a robber who was crucified and torn to pieces by wild beasts. Suetonius records a performance of around AD 40 under Caligula; 'At the close of which the leading character, a brigand, had to die while escaping, and vomit blood.' He notes that it was 'immediately followed by a humorous afterpiece – the comedians were so anxious to display their proficiency at dying that they flooded the stage with blood'.[70]

Early in the second century, Juvenal recalled the portrayal of the same role by one Lentulus, uncharitably adding that in his judgment, the disgrace was such he should have been crucified in fact.[71] Indeed, according to Martial, such horror had already taken place in the reign of Titus when a criminal was forced to take the part – and was subsequently taken apart – 'by a Caledonian bear . . . his mangled limbs quivering and dripping gore, the form of his body entirely disformed'. In the same account (written to celebrate the construction of the Colosseum), Martial mentions that the myth of Pasiphae (who concealed herself in an artificial cow in order to be mounted by the object of her lust, a bull) was 'faithfully enacted'. 'Whatever Fame sings of, is realised in the arena'. Elsewhere he admires an actual re-enactment of the legend of Mucius Scaevola, who heroically plunged his hand into a burning brazier. The early third-century writer Tertullian recalls the *Laureolus*, and similarly degraded works including a depiction of the death of Hercules, whose presenter was burned on a funeral pyre.[72]

From the beginning the mimes had encompassed indecent display and unedifying and indulgent subject matter within the broad scope of their repertoire. But in addition, much of their appeal had doubtless been that they undertook to portray the rich variety and quirkiness of everyday life and manners. This they did with a frankness that entertained not only their most fervent audience drawn from the lower orders (whose affection and support they helped to secure for those sponsoring the performances) but, for a time, spectators from the upper strata as well. Augustus himself recognized both their usefulness, supporting the mimes with hospitality and money and, apparently, their relevance, asking at his death 'have I played the mime of life believably?'[73] In the Empire, however, although their popularity evidently continued, their quality declined, together it seems with the taste of their audience.

Domitian employed two prominent mimes at his court, Panniculus and Latinus (using the latter as an informant), but executed another, Helvidius Priscus the younger, for writing a mime that alluded to the Emperor's divorce.[74] A little later Dio Chrysostomos, the stoic moralist and orator, denounced the decadence of the mimes, and the hold it had upon an adoring audience.[75] In the next century Marcus Aurelius tolerated them, and showed favour to a mime writer, Marullus. His co-ruler, Lucius Verus, brought back a number of mimes from Syria and Alexandria (a frequent source of supply) on his return from his command in the East in AD 166, together with actors, jesters, and magicians. By contrast, Marcus Aurelius' son and successor, Commodus, attacked the mimes for their immorality, and had the performers exiled for a time from Rome.[76]

Two decades later, however, in the third century, further references indicate the mimes were still flourishing. Elagabalus ordered that sexual scenes should be actually enacted, not feigned, and Maximinus was admonished by a mime to 'beware the many if you fear not individuals'. But the verse was in Greek; the Emperor, a former peasant, failed to understand, and was duly murdered together with his son, by the army.[77] A few years later when Gallienus entered into Rome, his baggage wagons were loaded with 'mimes and all sorts of actors', and he was reported later to consort only with 'pimps, mimes and prostitutes'. His example was continued under Aurelian who was greatly attached to the mimes, and then by Carinus, who in AD 283–4 collected them from all over the Empire and 'filled the Palatine with mimes, whores, pantomimes, singers and pimps'.[78]

In the course of the third and fourth centuries AD, the mime earned the enduring hatred of the Christian church, whose leaders attacked all aspects of the scenic spectacles as expressions of paganism, while reserving a special hostility for mimes and their performers. The mime frequently satirized Christianity and its practices, parodying its most sacred rituals (such as communion) and beliefs (including the trinity, the divinity, the virgin birth of Christ, and reincarnation): this caused it to be fiercely denounced in such extravagant terms that it becomes difficult to separate fact from hyperbolic rhetoric. Tiberius Donatus, writing in the fourth century, lends some support to such criticism by noting that the mimes are pleasing only to disreputable people and adulterers, and his low estimation is confirmed by a contemporary, Euanthius, who describes them as 'frivolous', and 'always representing base subjects and trivial people'.[79]

The Christian emperors tended on the whole to oppose or restrict the mime, but some were neutral or even lent their support. Theodosius I took steps to ensure that the mimes were properly regulated, and severely curtailed their rights, e.g. forbidding actresses to leave the profession once they had taken it up. But a little earlier the Emperor Julian, as part of his espousal of paganism and his attempts if not to 'roll back' Christianity, at least to contain its power, had evidently supported the mimes, and took a troupe of mime artists with him on his final campaign in AD 363. Later Stilicho too employed them to entertain his army, and was reported to have been so absorbed in enjoying their performances that he wasted the chance to defeat Alaric the Visigoth at Corinth in 397![80]

The hostility of the Church had so strengthened in the course of the fifth century (when there are innumerable notices of opposition) that the mime artists were excommunicated in 452. Perhaps reflecting the fact that he had married a former mime actress (and a particularly scandalous one at that), Theodora, Justinian improved the legal status of the mimes, but closed down all the theatres (for an undetermined period) around 526. However, in 692 the Trullan Council had specifically to ban the mimes yet again. In the West the mime survived at least into the reign of Theodoric, the Ostrogoth king of Italy, who died in 526. Under his administration mime performances were authorized in order to keep the population content.[81] After that, the mime dwindles from the historical record, although undoubtedly much of its material informed popular modes of entertainment for centuries. When, a millennium later, *commedia dell'arte* emerged, its characters, plots, and theatrical form bore such striking resemblance to much that we discerned in the mime, and before it the *Atellanae*, that it is tempting (and not altogether whimsical) to believe if not in a continuing traditon, then in some process of transmission – a dramaturgical 'laying on of hands' –

recurring during the long period when the mime left no trace of its survival.

Although in the first centuries of the Christian era the mime had a decidedly 'bad press' from its opponents (who may have exaggerated its lurid and disreputable character), and the word itself was used imprecisely by commentators to designate a very diverse range of activity, it is important to note that at least some examples of it were admired by men of critical discernment and these presumably appealed to a more sophisticated audience than that which mobbed its less refined enactments.

Mimes often drew heavily on Greek sources for both their subject matter and form (as well as their performers),[82] and some scripted versions (probably intended for recitation) were actually composed in Greek. In the late first century AD, Pliny the younger considered the work of one such author, Vergilius Romanus, who wrote mimes, as well as comedies in the style of Menander, to be equal to the best of Plautus and Terence. He praised Arrius Antoninus (who was twice consul) even more extravagantly for his erotic epigrams and mimes. 'What sensitivity, what grace! How delightful they are, so full of love, and how humourous and tasteful!' Pliny compared them to the work of the ancient Athenian authors, and was greatly impressed (and altogether approved) that a Roman could write such elegant Greek.[83] It seems likely too that the mimes significantly influenced the composition and content of other literary genres such as elegy, satire, and the novel.[84]

The capacity of the mime to achieve a higher level of sophistication than that usually ascribed to it and, in particular, its synthesis of traditional Roman elements and materials derived from Greek culture is one part of the evidence suggesting that it is misleading to characterize the Roman theatre as 'going from bad to worse' or the Roman audience as invariably 'low-brow' and loutish by the end of the Republic. As E. J. Jory has noted, quite apart from the mime,

> There are a number of references to audience reactions in the theatrical productions of the Republic which point to keen attention to the detail of both play and acting on the part of some of the spectators of Roman drama. 'If an actor makes a movement that is a little out of time with the music or recites a verse that is one syllable too short or too long is hissed and hooted off the stage', says Cicero. Furthermore the strict training in gesture and voice production undergone by the actors would have been unnecessary unless the audience could appreciate the results. Precise delivery was demanded of the actor and movement of the dancer, [and] casting had to be appropriate.[85]

Along with such subtlety of critical reaction, performance was further conditioned by the presence in the audience of many who were now widely travelled in the eastern centres of learning and culture, were particularly well acquainted with Greek literature, and indeed eager to emulate and adapt much of what they admired. Although no section of Roman society was untouched by the pervasive influence of the Greeks (many thousands of whom now lived in Rome), the upper and most influential strata were particularly enthusiastic in their espousal of Greek custom, not merely because it had become decidedly fashionable to do so, but also out of an ever-deeper and better informed respect for its intellectual and artistic achievements. Interest was not confined as earlier primarily to self-conscious circles of intellectuals (although scholarship flourished in the late Republic and early Empire) or expressed in piecemeal adaption of one custom or refinement or another. It was, in contrast to the earlier period, far more broadly disseminated as, in effect, Roman and Greek culture merged.[86]

This process quickened under the new political conditions in effect after the final civil wars and the establishment of a stable system under the Principate of Augustus. The Emperor was himself an avid admirer of Greek culture and used his authority and patronage extensively to encourage artistic activity modelled upon Greek example and precedent, and in particular upon the achievements of the more distant 'classical' past of the fifth century BC. 'A stylistic change embodies a moral one. The discordant images of the Republic, the shocking excesses of Hellenistic luxury and manners . . . have been rejected in favour of a new language of classicism.'[87] The effects of this were soon widely evident in all aspects of Roman artistic expression, including the theatre.[88]

Although, as noted earlier, there were some attempts to revive tragic writing (August himself had composed an *Ajax*), the genre was evidently too antiquated – its practice and conventions too drained of vitality – to again hold the popular stage. The practice of composing in archaic styles and genres, which was employed by many writers at this time and brought praise and reward within the circle of their peers and patrons, was not likely to be successful under the conditions prevailing in the theatre. Instead, a new type of theatrical entertainment, *pantomime*, appeared which drew on the same mythological sources as tragedy (and may have appealed to similar emotions), but embodied these in an altogether different mode of performance.

Just as some 'Roman poets in the period invented ways of using Greek mythology that had no parallel among the Greek poets since the fifth century',[89] so too in the theatre old wine found its way into new skins. Pantomime had its roots in the venerable tradition of mimetic dance from which earliest dramatic forms of tragedy and comedy probably evolved, and which continued to hold a central place in Greek education, religion, and forms of artistic expression. Such dance had been prevalent too at Rome from an early date. Livy records that performers who danced, but did not sing, were summoned from Etruria in 363 BC to help in exorcizing a plague.[90] By the time of the second Punic war dance was a well established feature of Roman life, performed not just by professionals but by members of the aristocracy as well, who evidently took it up with what some saw as unseemly enthusiasm. Scipio Aemilianus condemned the mania of young people for dance, recording the dispiriting sight of some 500 boys and girls in a school performance; including even a twelve-year-old son of a noble house, dancing with castanets like some disreputable slave.[91]

Although dancers had been expelled for a time in 115 BC along with other theatrical personnel (only the performers of the decorous Roman robed dance, presented at the *Ludus Talarius* were exempted),[92] the upper echelon continued to cultivate dancing and dancers. Sulla merrily consorted with them, and the wife, Sempronia, of an early first-century BC consul was remembered for dancing 'rather more elegantly than propriety required'.[93] Afranius, the consul for 60 BC, was judged by malicious opinion to have been a more accomplished dancer than politician. Cicero frequently condemned the dance for its excesses (particularly that of nude performance) and its aristocratic practitioners for their immodesty.[94] Nevertheless, in the age of Augustus, the taste for dance increased. Horace notes that its performance was, regrettably, both a popular practice and subject of conversation, and Ovid assures his readers 'that I would have a woman know how to dance, so when the wine is laid out she may, when asked, move her arms'.[95]

The dance was continuously informed by foreign example and influence. Anicius Gallus had celebrated his triumph in 167 BC with imported Greek dancers and musicians. In the next century Caesar gave a festival marking the conclusion of his Spanish campaign at which high-born children from Asia Minor and Bithynia performed a mimetic war dance. Performers from such diverse realms as Syria and Spain were commonly seen at Rome.[96] Pantomime was itself an expression of this tradition of foreign influence although it may have been modified in the process of assimilation.[97] Certainly the Greeks record mimetic performances in which mythological material was enacted in dumb show by dancers accompanied by musicians:[98] the essential elements of the new genre.

Pantomime sought to present characterization, emotion, and narrative entirely through the movements and gestures of the body, or parts of the body, of an individual performer who neither sang nor spoke. Its introduction into Italy took place (according to later tradition), in 22 BC.[99]

It was said to have been fashioned by Pylades from Cilicia, and Bathyllus from Alexandria, each of whom was a superb dancer as well as, apparently, a theoretician of considerable force and sensitivity. Although the elements of their art must have developed and been perfected in the East, Pylades and Bathyllus evidently established it at Rome by virtue of their own particular skills and personality. Both achieved enormous personal renown and success, which enabled them to found schools that preserved their name and promulgated their art long after their deaths.

Bathyllus was the freedman and darling of that close companion of Augustus and patron of legendary wealth, Maecenas.[100] He is credited with developing the comic pantomime, which was fairly simple in composition, often lascivious and droll, and evolved its subject matter as witty travesties of the more salacious Greek myths, or burlesques of well-known ancient tragedies. He was remembered for playing such roles as Echo and Pan or an Eros and satyr, presenting these *dramatis personae* simultaneously. Horace may have had his protean skill in mind when he formulated his descriptive analogy of one 'who wears the look of being at play and yet is on the rack, like a dancer who plays now a satyr and now a clownish cyclops'.[101] Such mythic sources of inspiration were somewhat limited however, and pantomime does not seem to have been drawn to the more mundane narratives of everyday life dealt with by New Comedy.

The comic pantomime was much in vogue during Bathyllus' lifetime but appears later to have faded away, displaced in popularity by the much more extravagant form first practised by Pylades, a freedman of Augustus. This, the tragic pantomime, was evidently contrived of sensational moments from Greek mythology generally, and from the great tragedies in particular,[102] the scenes linked as lyrical solos, and all performed by a single actor who was usually but not always male. This individual, silent performer was backed by musicians and either a single actor or a chorus which sang the part and provided the narrative continuity, during which he impersonated all the characters, male and female, sequentially, in a series of interlinked solo scenes consecutively arranged. His task was to give an impression of the whole ensemble and the relationship of one character to another while preserving the sense of the plot, and creating graceful and expressive movements and gestures.

Clearly, this was a formidable challenge requiring enormous skill and imagination from the performer, who underwent extensive training to be able to depict both the actions as well as, simultaneously, the emotional state of the several characters. He was aided in this daunting task by appropriate masks and often elaborate costumes (which he would change in the course of performance), and by the conventional nature of the most prominent of the many roles he was expected to learn: the movements of which (a sort of gestic vocabulary) were 'set' by firm tradition from which the actor strayed at his peril. The most important element was the complex and subtle movement of the hands and arms, which one observer likened to the creation of pictures as though using the letters of the alphabet.[103] Even so, it is baffling to contemplate how such recorded subjects as Pythagorean philosophy or the dialogues of Plato could be intelligibly rendered in performance.[104]

Lucian, who left an extensive commentary on pantomime, details the glories and pitfalls of performance.[105]

> In general, the dancer undertakes to present and enact characters and emotions, introducing now a lover and now an angry person, one man afflicted with madness, another with grief, and all this within fixed bounds . . . within the selfsame day at one moment we are shown Athamas in a frenzy, at another Ino in terror; presently the same person is Atreus, and after a little, Thyestes; then Aegisthus, or Aerope; yet they all are but a single man. . . . The dancer should be perfect in every point, so as to be wholly rhythmical, graceful, symmetrical, consistent, unexceptionable, impeccable, not wanting in any way, blent of the highest qualities, keen in his ideas, profound in his culture, and above all, human in his sentiments.

He notes the disgrace of a performer who, while dancing Chronos in the act of devouring his children, inadvertently slipped into the role of Thyestes committing the same act. 'And another, trying to enact Semele stricken by the thunderbolt, assimilated her to Glauce, who was of a later generation.' Evidently the audience was familiar with the different myths, and, moreover, (rather like contemporary devotees of the ballet), the precise way in which they were to be danced.

Lucian records how one pantomime in presenting the madness of Ajax became so overwrought in the role that he snatched the *tibia* from one of the musicians and gave such a blow to the dancer portraying Odysseus that only his helmet saved him. Lucian's account provides an intriguing glimpse of the Roman audience.

> The pit, however, all went mad with Ajax, leaping and shouting and flinging up their garments; for the riff-raff, the absolutely unenlightened, took no thought for propriety and could not perceive what was good or what was bad . . . while the politer sort understood, to be sure, and were ashamed of what was going on, but instead of censuring the thing by silence, they applauded to cover the absurdity of the dancing.

When the actor returned to his senses later he was mortified by his unseemly indulgence, and refused thereafter to repeat the role.

> What irked him most was that his antagonist and rival, when cast for Ajax in the same role, enacted his madness so discreetly and

sanely as to win praise, since he kept within the bounds of the dance and did not debauch the histrionic art.[106]

This suggestion that the audience was composed of spectators of diverse taste and refinement agrees with other evidence, discussed in the next chapter. One segment (probably a minority) were keenly sensitive to the subtleties and nuance of the performance, were responsive to the profounder ideas and emotions informing the story, and most significantly perhaps, could follow the libretto (often in Greek) which was sung while the dancer rendered his detailed interpretation. It was said of Pylades' exquisite depiction of the god Dionysus that if he appeared on Olympus, Hera would claim that she, and not the mortal Semele, had borne him.[107] Lucian repeatedly emphasizes the importance of restraint, decorum, and artistry, while acknowledging that the pantomime was open to abuse and could lapse into bad taste. It was often lascivious and sensual. Juvenal notes the effect of this upon susceptible members of the audience;

> When the soft Bathyllus[108] dances the role of the gesticulating Leda, Tuccia cannot constrain herself; your Apulian maiden raises a sudden and longing cry of ecstasy, as though she were embraced by a man; the rustic Thymele is rapt: now is the time that she learns her lessons.[109]

Ovid had warned of the same effects in the Augustan theatre, advising the lovelorn not to

> indulge in theatres until love has quite deserted your empty heart; zithers, flutes and lyres weaken the resolve, and voices and arms swaying in rhythm. Fictive lovers are constantly danced: the actor by his craft teaches you what to avoid and what pleases you.[110]

It was probably the potential for sensationalism together with the extraordinary notoriety of some 'stars' that provided the basis for the pantomimes' enormous popularity with the masses. The less restrained element in the audience was at times highly volatile and quick to voice its criticism or approval. On one occasion when Pylades was performing the role of the 'Mad Hercules', the audience began to mock and taunt him for not (in their opinion) observing a dancer's proper movements and rhythms; he appeared uncertain, or possibly inebriated. In a fury, Pylades threw off his mask and upbraided the audience. 'Fools! I *am* dancing the role of a madman!'[111] On another occasion 'when a spectator began to hiss, he pointed him out to the entire audience with an obscene gesture of his middle finger'.[112]

Although Augustus himself supported and enjoyed the new art of the pantomime (and thought his patronage of the people's pastime a democratic gesture),[113] only a few years after its introduction he found it necessary to curb the 'pantomania' it had engendered in the Roman audience. Rivalries between different performers led to outbreaks of violence among their supporters; a pattern that prevailed for centuries. On one occasion Augustus ordered that Pylades' former student and chief rival, Hylas, be publicly whipped. However, on another, he indicated his favour by amending the law which allowed public officials to beat performers whenever they wished: henceforth they could do so only for offences committed during the games or other public performances. Together with other stage performers, the pantomimes (the great majority of whom were foreigners; many of them slaves or freedmen) were subject to severe restrictions. They were denied Roman citizenship, their descendants were banned unto the fourth generation from marrying into the senatorial class, and if caught in adultery, they could be killed with impunity. On the other hand, from time to time as a public gesture, the Emperor would bestow freedom on a performer who had won the crowd's support,[114] and a successful pantomime could earn substantial sums of money.

Pantomimes were frequently attached to particular patrons, many of whom kept their own troupes. Although such support was an indication of the esteem in which their art might be held by leading members of society, the moral repute of the dancers was generally low, and their behaviour frequently caused scandal.[115] Under Tiberius (who is reported to have been generally hostile to the theatre but was reluctant to offend popular taste) senators were forbidden in AD 15 to enter the home of a pantomime, and members of the equestrian order were banned from escorting them in public. At the same time performances were ordered to be confined to the theatre, and rowdy spectators were subject to exile.[116] Eventually after further rioting between factions supporting rival performers, in AD 23 'Tiberius spoke to the Senate concerning the misbehaviour of the pantomimes and their offences against public order and private morality. . . . The dancers were then ejected from Italy'.[117]

In time they returned to the stage in response to public demand, and the express will of Tiberius' successor, Caligula, who had a passion both for the genre and for some of its performers. His favourite was Mnester, with whom he indulged a scandalous liaison, publicly 'smooching' with him in the theatre, and ordering that any spectator who interrupted his performance be dragged before the Emperor for a personal whipping. On one occasion Caligula challenged Jupiter to single combat for disrupting a pantomime presentation with thunder and lightning. He himself gave private performances, and was believed to have been on the verge of his public stage début as a pantomime at the time of his murder.[118]

The case of Mnester is a graphic example of a recurring phenomenon; pantomimes were frequently prominent in the imperial household and often figured in its intrigues. No doubt they were in demand in part because of their physical beauty complemented by the gifts of intelligence and subtle psychology which their art demanded. Moreover, prominent performers were often figures of great public acclaim and interest, with whom emperors and their courtiers were, not surprisingly, pleased to consort. This no doubt won for the art of pantomime a certain prestige and patronage (and increased its appeal to the public), but often proved perilous to its performers, as Mnester's subsequent history illustrates.

Early in the reign of the next emperor, Claudius, in AD 47 he entered into an adulterous affair with the wealthy and beautiful Poppaea Sabina who had attracted the jealousy of Claudius' third wife, the venomous Messalina. Although Poppaea soon committed suicide (charged with having consorted with the former consul, Asiaticus, another of Messalina's victims), Mnester was spared, even though two other prominent Romans, thought to have lent him their house for his assignations with Poppaea, were executed. In fact, Messalina had herself conceived a passion for Mnester, who, however, rebuffed her advances. Claudius was unaware (or feigned ignorance) of the situation, and out of shame for her, and respect for Mnester's artistry, no one called his attention to it. But when Messalina's unbridled debauchery and audacity led her actually to marry the Consul-designate Gaius Silius, acting (according to Tacitus) out of 'sheer outrageousness – a sensualist's ultimate satisfaction',

> The imperial household shuddered – particularly those in power, with everything to fear from the new Emperor. There were secret conferences. Then outrage was no longer hidden. 'When a pantomime dancer violated the Emperor's bedroom' they said, 'it was disgraceful enough. Yet it did not threaten Claudius' life'

Claudius was informed. In due course Messalina, her lover, and accomplices were condemned to death.

> Only Mnester caused hesitation. Rending his garments, he begged Claudius to view his whip-marks and remember that he had been placed in Messalina's power. Others, he pleaded, had sinned for ambition or greed, he only from compulsion . . . Claudius had a sympathetic nature, and was moved by this. But the other freedmen persuaded the Emperor, after condemning so many prominent men, not to spare a pantomime.[119]

Mnester was executed.

Theatrical activity, and particularly the pantomimes, became even more popular and controversial in the reign of Nero, who was uniquely and memorably associated with it. His grandfather, Lucius Domitius, had made himself notorious as Praetor and again as Consul for requiring certain members of the equestrian order, as well as high-born women, to take roles in pantomime performances. His father having died when Nero was three, and his mother having been banished by Caligula, Nero himself was brought up by an aunt with a pantomime as his tutor. As a child he danced in the Circus; shortly after becoming Emperor in AD 54 at seventeen, he recited his own poetry in the theatre; and to celebrate his coming of age, he instituted a lavish dramatic festival at which men and women of the upper orders were encouraged to perform, and young Greek pantomimes were given Roman citizenship to reward their artistry. Nero himself sang and played the lyre, while his sycophants 'maintained a din of applause day and night, showering sacred epithets on his beauty and voice'.[120]

Although Nero banished the pantomimes and some of their supporters from Italy in AD 56 (following more rivalries and consequent acts of violence which the Emperor was rumoured to have encouraged),[121] he summoned them back around AD 59. The following year he established a new religious festival, the *Neronia*, devoted to music and gymnastics, to be held every five years, in imitation of Greek practice. Nero presided over events from a private box, but later descended into the orchestra to be awarded prizes for his own recitation and lyre playing. Following Greek example, these games were financed directly by the state, with the purpose (it was claimed) of encouraging talent and raising the level of public taste. Tacitus records the objections raised by traditionalists to such an innovation:

> As for the games, they should be given in the old Roman way, whenever the praetors are to present them, and provided that no citizen is expected to perform. Traditional morality, already slowly declining, has been totally destroyed by such foreign laxity! . . . now they are compelling the Roman elite to disgrace themselves as orators or stage singers . . . does informed attention to effeminate music and songs contribute to justice?[122]

Perhaps as a concession to conventional opinion, pantomimes, although allowed to perform again, were banned from these sacred games.

The most prominent pantomime during Nero's reign was Paris, who was a freedman of Domitia, Nero's aunt. In AD 56 she involved him in an intrigue against Nero's mother, Agrippina. Paris was sent to Nero (with whom he customarily engaged in late-night debaucheries) to accuse Agrippina of conspiracy. However, she managed both to defend herself against the charges and to exact revenge on several of her accusers, although 'Paris played too important a part in the Emperor's vices to be punished.'[123] But ten years later, Paris fell from grace and was executed by Nero, in whose maniacal imagination he loomed as an artistic rival.

Nero's art was undoubtedly inferior to that of Paris, who was recalled a century later by Lucian as a man 'who was no fool, and excelled if ever a man did, in remembrance of legends and beauty of movement'. He recounted an anecdote in which Paris was challenged by Demetrius the Cynic (who had a low opinion of pantomime) to perform without benefit of musical or choral accompaniment. This Paris did, dancing a complex sequence from Homer's *Odyssey*, depicting the tale in which Aphrodite and Ares are entrapped by Hephaestus in a net while making love, and then humiliatingly displayed to all the other gods. He enacted the entire story with all its characters so vividly that Demetrius was utterly enthralled, and in the end exclaimed in a great shout, 'I *hear* the story that you are acting, man, I do not just see it; you seem to me to be talking with your very hands!'[124]

At the second celebration of the *Neronia*, in AD 65, Nero again took the stage, both as a poet and musician, and was wildly acclaimed by his Roman audience. Tacitus suggests that this meant little, since their taste was corrupted and indeed, Nero had arranged for huge claques (up to 5,000) to provide thunderous applause whenever he appeared. He sang an entire tragedy, the *Niobe*, and any who hesitated to applaud or showed any sign of displeasure were punished on the spot by soldiers posted in the theatre: a veritable captive audience. On other occasions, according to Suetonius, Nero 'actually performed in tragedies, taking the roles of gods and heroes, and even heroines and goddesses, wearing masks modelled on his own face, or on that of whomever happened to be his current mistress'. His performances (probably of dramatic solos adapted from the original tragedies) included 'Orestes the Matricide', 'The Blind Oedipus', and 'The Mad Hercules'. These could be so tedious and long that people feigned death in order to be carried from the theatre!'[125] Like a modern prima donna, 'he always kept a voice master at hand telling him when to save his voice, or protect his mouth with a handkerchief'.[126]

Not content with such acclaim at Rome, he toured Greece as well, spending eighteen months in AD 66 to 68 garnering prizes at all the great festivals which were re-scheduled as necessary to accommodate him. Acting with apparent modesty and according to the rules, but lavishing gifts on the judges and, on one famous occasion, rewarding the audience by declaring the entire province of Achaea free from direct rule and tribute,[127] he was, not surprisingly, invariably successful.

> Once, while acting in a tragedy, his sceptre fell, and although he recovered it quickly, he feared being disqualified. His accompanist however, who played the *aulos* and enacted the silent mime illustrating his words, swore that the error had been missed since the audience were so enthralled listening to him.[128]

Upon returning to Italy he repeated his performances in a triumphal progress from Naples up to Rome, which he entered with lavish display of his prizes and trophies together with placards identifying the songs and plays he had performed to win them. Statues were set up showing him playing the lyre. Naturally, such display attracted a good deal of satiric comment in secret, with lampoons posted on walls, or passed about by word of mouth. He was even the object of thinly-veiled subversive comment in the theatre.

> The comic actor Datus, performing in an Atellan farce, illustrated the opening line of the song 'Goodbye Father, goodbye Mother' with gestures of drinking and swimming – Claudius had been poisoned, and Agrippina nearly drowned – and the last line, 'Hell guides your feet' was directed with a wave of his hand towards the senators whom Nero intended to murder.[129]

Some in the audience regarded it as an auspicious omen when Nero (in what proved to be his farewell performance) sang the role of 'Oedipus in Exile' which concluded with the suggestive line, 'wife, mother, father, all do urge my death'. At about this time, Nero took an oath that if he survived the uprising against him, and held his throne, he would produce yet another festival, where, after performing on various instruments, he would dance the role of Turnus in a pantomime based on Vergil's *Aeneid*. He never had the chance. Trapped and forced to commit suicide, he first struck histrionic poses and muttered various theatrical quotes, 'uttering through his tears, "What an artist dies in me!" '.[130] He is reported to have been widely and sincerely mourned in Greece.

Even a brief account of Nero's involvement with the theatre (to which much further evidence could be added) implies a good deal about the condition of the Roman theatre and its audience in the imperial period. Just as earlier the theatre had provided ambitious politicians with invaluable opportunities for propaganda, so too it could contribute mightily to the image and prestige of an emperor. Merely by initiating and being present at theatrical entertainments, the ruler could impress the public and attract its favour. But beyond that, if he chose, an emperor by virtue of the *auctoritas* and *dignitas* of his position, as well as through vast patronage and personal charisma, could create awesome spectacles of mass appeal and engage in acts of potent demagoguery whose influence might be exercised far beyond Rome itself. Nero, with his narcissism and megalomania, is an example of the phenomenon which is extreme in degree but not in substance. Inevitably such imperial interest and manipulation of the theatre had a powerful effect on its form and practice as well as on the taste and expectations of its audience. This influence was most direct and immediate at Rome itself, but undoubtedly was felt much more widely as well.

As detailed in the next chapter, the theatre buildings of the Empire were built to impress, the entertainments which filled them (particularly those associated with an imperial occasion) were likely to be lavish and spectacular, with, it seems fair to infer, relatively little concern for intellectual content or subtlety and still less for the exploration of controversial subjects. The place in such a theatre for writers and poets of genius is limited; indeed, serious authors turned their attention to other genres, and in time many of the more erudite members of the public viewed the theatre with contempt. It is, however, very difficult in evaluating such distaste to determine the degree to which it represents a thoughtful critique of the theatrical fare per se, or simple snobbery: the distain of a self-conscious elite for a popular pastime which was distained simply because it was popular. In fact literature itself, which might otherwise have indirectly nurtured theatrical art, had lost much of its former vitality to

> become an innocent source of diversion for the bored upper classes; it no longer took a passionate interest in political and social problems that could be embarrassing or even dangerous to authority, and imperial interests saw it as mere entertainment.[131]

It is, I think, misleading to characterize the imperial audience as invariably unsophisticated and corrupt in its taste, or to believe that all its entertainments were entirely decadent and devoid of merit. Despite the castigations of its Christian critics, there are too many trustworthy witnesses – Lucian is an excellent example – prepared to defend the theatre (as opposed to the diversions of the circus or amphitheatre) and praise its accomplishments, for us simply to dismiss it as a monstrosity.

Even in the case of Tacitus, who is frequently a severe critic of 'the degraded populace, frequenters of the arena and the theatre', we may detect a contradictory note. He is compromised certainly by an anecdote related by his friend Pliny the younger in a letter of around AD 100, in which Pliny records

> I never was more pleased than I was lately by a remark by Cornelius Tacitus. He told me that at the last games in the Circus there sat next to him a Roman knight. After much learned talk his neighbour asked him, 'are you of Italy, or from the provinces?' Tacitus replied, 'you know me, and that from your reading.' Then said the other 'Are you Tacitus or Pliny?'

The incident reveals both that Tacitus himself might upon occasion attend the games, and that he could find himself there in the most learned company.[132]

Roman theatre, unlike that of classical Greece, had never been one in which the exploration of public issues was of central importance, or poets sought to instruct their audience. Later it ceased, certainly, to be a place where an elevated *dramatic* art could flourish, as comedy and tragedy dwindled into rare revivals, if they did not vanish altogether. Their place was usurped by the virtuosity and titillation of the mime, and the visual grace or splendour of the pantomime. The theatre may have become ever more a medium of sensation than of thought; its achievements dazzling or seductive to the eyes, delightful to listen to, and even profoundly moving, but rarely probing or provocative. The audience may well have been capable of sensitive and critical appreciation; their theatre did not, however, appeal to or stimulate them very profoundly on an intellectual level.

The Roman audience had from earliest times been a lively and responsive one, often highly perceptive and quick to be roused to enthusiasm, but always volatile and prone to self-indulgence. These qualities (which the conditions governing theatrical production had from the first encouraged) were amongst the most characteristic and enduring features of the Roman theatre. Polybius recorded that a refined performance by visiting Greek artists in 167 BC had degenerated into farce when the audience boisterously forced the performers to extemporize a mock battle out of their more elevated mimic dance; Terence lost his audience to a side-show entertainment; a century and a half later Horace complains of much the same thing: elements in the crowd would break into angry rows over the merit of a performance, or interrupt a play with demands for an animal show or boxers. Yet the same audience knew some of the great tragedies by heart, were tuned to the subtlest nuance of the mime's wit or the pantomime's gesture, and could on hearing a quotation from Vergil, spontaneously arise *en masse* to pay homage to the poet in their midst.[133] Following the demise of tragedy and comedy the theatre in its basest expressions (which might encompass the mime and pantomime alongside the gladiatorial shows and animal fights) undoubtedly appealed to the most sordid and depraved instincts; but it was capable too of achieving at times a high and edifying art, and its audience of rising to it.

Pantomime held the stage until the end of antiquity, its character and the responses to it displaying remarkable continuity. Even the names were recycled: another Paris and Bathyllus under Domitian; another Pylades famous in the reign of Trajan. Their performances onstage and off were much the same too. Paris had an elicit affair with Domitian's wife, Domitia, and exercised such pervasive influence in the imperial court that Juvenal cited him later in one of his satires. He claimed that his friend, P. Papinius Statius (a distinguished poet 'whose verses brought down the house' when he recited them in the theatre), would have starved unless he managed to sell his pantomime, the *Agave*, to Paris.

For it is Paris who appoints many to military commands, Paris who puts the golden ring [signifying elevation to the equestrian order] around the poet's finger after six months' service. You can get from a stage performer what no great man will give you.[134]

Domitian took steps to curb the pantomimes, banishing them from the public stage (for a while they could only perform at private functions), and forbidding theatre managers to allow the ordinary members of the audience to encroach upon the seating areas reserved for knights. He also tried to limit the practice of satirizing prominent men and women in the theatre; setting an example by executing Helvidius Priscus the younger for his mime that touched too closely upon the affair between the Empress and Paris. Paris himself was eventually executed by Domitian around AD 87. His tomb was decorated and venerated by his devotees, and the poet Martial dedicated an epitaph to him.[135]

Trajan allowed the pantomimes back on the stage around AD 100, and his successor, Hadrian, who was particularly fond of the theatre and its artists, took all the pantomimes associated with the court into state ownership. They were favoured under the next emperor, Antoninus Pius, as well, but their pay was curbed and their performances limited by Marcus Aurelius, who was perhaps ill-disposed to pantomimes because of the rumour that the Empress, Faustina, consorted with them.[136] The pattern of periodic espousal and repression continued throughout the imperial period. Occasionally emperors – Commodus and Elagabalus, for example – followed Nero's precedent and took to the stage themselves as singers or dancers. Others such as Severus Alexander and Carinus were renowned for the extravagance of the pantomimic shows that they sponsored. Individual performers came in and out of favour at court, the public rioted from time to time at presentations of rival artists, and Christian writers and preachers railed at the scandal and immorality of it all. In AD 353 there were some 3,000 female dancers active in Rome, augmented by innumerable musicians and choruses. The male dancers probably were even more numerous. Elsewhere in the same period, the pantomime continued to flourish, and was practised with particular enthusiasm in the coastal cities of Asia Minor and in Egypt.[137]

Even the pagan Emperor Julian was moved (around AD 360) to forbid his priests to attend the theatre or indulge in the company of pantomimes, while a little later the devout Christian Theodosius I was compelled to ban their performances altogether, for a while.[138] Over a century later, after the last emperor in the West had been deposed and Italy was ruled by the Ostrogoths, Cassiodorus, the Roman chancellor of King Theodoric, continued to be troubled by public disturbances arising from the pantomimes and their supporters, and took measures to control and regulate the performances, which, however, continued. In the East, Justinian closed the Hippodrome, a major venue for pantomimes in AD 526. Nevertheless, sufficient activity continued for the Trullan Council, held at Constantinople in 692, to ban it yet again. Although it seems likely that in some form 'the dance went on', perhaps for centuries, nothing further is heard of pantomime until the word was adopted early in the eighteenth century to describe a very distantly related hybrid form of theatrical entertainment.

6

LATER STAGES AND STAGINGS

By the end of the first century BC, the composition of new plays for the theatre had virtually ceased, as alternative forms of scenic entertainment gradually displaced scripted comedy and tragedy. The theatre itself, however, thrived, and steadily increased in popularity and importance. Old plays were occasionally revived, while mime and pantomime (often in spectacular and lavish stagings) attracted huge and enthusiastic audiences. Throughout the Empire vast, new, permanent theatres were constructed, as the opportunities for different types of performance burgeoned, and public demand for entertainment encouraged prudent politicians and rulers as well as ambitious patrons to provide generous sponsorship and support. The picture we can build up of the Roman theatre in its later stages is diverse and incomplete, but impressive.

The last decades of the Republic were a period of virtuoso acting. The Roman tragedies with their depictions of hyper-dramatic conflicts between larger-than-life heroes and monsters of iniquity, all revelling in their rhetoric, demanded a high degree of histrionic skill, and the very familiarity of the many roles and stories that the playwrights recycled must have encouraged ambitious actors to heighten and enhance their portrayals to hold audience interest. Cicero (always keenly observant of audience response and quick to appreciate the art and artifice of performance) provides a few revealing references to effective acting. In the *Iliona* of Pacuvius, the tragedy opened with Iliona, wife of the King of Thrace, asleep on stage. Her son Deiphilus had been murdered by his father who had been tricked by Iliona into believing the boy to be the son of his defeated enemy, King Priam of Troy. She had hoped by this deception to save Priam's actual son, who had been entrusted to her care, but instead unwittingly lost her own. As the play opened, the ghost of Deiphilus materialized in the shadows calling out to his mother for burial. The audience wept, overwhelmed it would seem more by the skill of the actor than the pathos of the scene, which they knew by heart. On another occasion, the actor playing Iliona was *actually* asleep and after failing to be awakened by the plaintive call of the actor, was only

154

finally roused when 1,200 members of the audience shouted the line, '*Mater, te apello!*'; 'Mother, I call to thee!'[1]

In Pacuvius' *Chryses*, Orestes and Pylades have been captured in Tauris, and brought before its king, Thoas, who determines to kill Orestes. The two friends then each claim to be Orestes; an example of devotion and virtue so skilfully enacted by the performers that according to Cicero the whole audience acclaimed them with a standing ovation. In another play by Pacuvius, *Teucer*, he recalls that the actor playing the part of Telamo was so inspired when delivering a tirade that his eyes seemed to be on fire behind the mask. Elsewhere Cicero makes general critical points, observing for example that the actor had to depict his character not just with his head and voice but with his whole body. Each word should be accompanied and underscored by an appropriate stance or gesture. In Ennius' *Medea,* the actor portraying her should win over the chorus of Corinthian women by the expressiveness of his hands. Cicero notes that the slightest failure by the actor to observe the metrical form of his speech, or to move in the proper rhythm, would be hissed and booed by the audience, and the same would occur if the chorus missed a note. The audience was so sensitive that it could determine which character was about to speak from the first note played by the *tibicen*.[2]

Cicero was a close friend and great admirer of one of the leading actors of the day, Quintus Roscius Gallus, who specialized in comic parts, although he also played in tragedies. He was particularly noted for his impersonation of parasites, and famous for the perfection of his realization of Ballio, the maniacal pimp in Plautus' *Pseudolus.* Born around 131 BC he was admitted in 82 BC to the equestrian order by Sulla, who greatly admired his art. Roscius enjoyed a long and highly successful career, and by the time of his death, around 63 BC, his name had become proverbial for excellence and popularity. At the height of his fame he was able to earn up to 600,000 sesterces a year, a princely sum.[3]

A dedicated and immensely talented and inventive artist, Roscius could convey the spirit and vitality of his characters, while preserving a sense of grace and style, the product of meticulous observation and care. He was said never to have used a gesture on stage which he had not rehearsed and tested at home, and according to an anecdote would contest with Cicero to see which could best express the same thought with greatest variety; Cicero through his language, or Roscius through his movements.[4] Indeed Cicero cited (as an example of how meaning is a synthesis of both words and action) his skilful use of gesture and nuance to give a ribald and hilarious interpretation to a line from a comedy by Turpilius in which the character laments that he has been abandoned (in his hour of need) by a prostitute: '*Ita me destituit nudum*'; ('thus she left me bare!')[5]

155

Sharing public acclaim with Roscius was his younger contemporary, Clodius Aesopus. Both men were said avidly to have attended the speeches of Q. Hortensius Hortalus who as orator and lawyer was famous both for his somewhat mannered delivery and for the studied perfection of his gestures and movements. Once again, we should note a connection between the political and histrionic arts; a symbiosis in which theatrical performance drew upon the style and sentiments informing political oratory, while in turn politicians looked to the theatre as a platform both for impressive display and for mass communication and manipulation of popular feeling. Aesopus even gave Cicero lessons in elocution.[6]

Aesopus' great speciality was tragedy – although he also appeared in comic parts – which he performed with a powerful voice, while reserving a more subtle talent for conveying heart-rending pathos and touching sensitivity. He was renowned for the gravity and strength of his characterization and for so immersing himself in a role that he lost touch with everything else about him.[7] Aesopus was remembered for his embodiment of the titanic and monstrous tyrant Atreus in Accius' version of the tragedy and, by way of a total contrast, the gentle and sensitive character, Teucer in *Eurysaces* (also by Accius), in which he enjoyed tremendous success in 57 BC. Two years later Cicero was saddened to record in a letter that when Aesopus returned to the stage for the dedication of Pompey's theatre, he was only a shadow of his former self and, alas, had lost the strength of his once mighty voice.[8]

Cicero mentions other actors of his day, some of them with approval, but also records his dismay that the work of such individual artists was overshadowed by the display of empty spectacle, the worst example of which (up to then) was witnessed at that same inauguration of Pompey's new theatre in 55. In the *Clytaemestra* of Accius, a parade of 600 mules carried the plunder of Agamemnon as he returned from Troy and, amidst hundreds of performers, some 3,000 bowls were used in the *Equos Troianus* (of Naevius?) to display booty upon the stage. The public, he remarked, loved it.[9] Later, towards the end of the century, Horace indicates that the taste for the 'vain delights' of spectacle was well established. Echoing Cicero, who made a distinction between refined taste (his own, and that of the recipient of his letter) Horace laments the fickleness of fashion, and how readily the more cultured sections of the audience, whom he identifies as the equestrian order (in the front rows of the auditorium), could be overwhelmed by the 'stupid and ill-educated' – the 'rabble' – that greatly outnumbered them.

> For four hours and more . . . cavalry and infantry sweep past; soon kings are dragged in with bound hands . . . hastening along come chariots, carts, wagons and ships, with spoils of ivory and

Corinthian bronze carried in triumph. . . . What voices have ever been heard above the din to which our theatres resound? . . . Amidst such clamour and works of art and foreign luxury, the play is seen, when, buried beneath this, the actor steps onto the stage to the crash of applause. 'Has he said anything?' 'Not a word.' 'Why then the uproar?' 'It's his woollen robe, dyed in violent violet in the Tarentine fashion!'[10]

A similar sentiment was expressed at about the same time by the historian Livy who condemned the gross lavishness of theatrical art, 'the insanity of which is now almost beyond the means of wealthy kingdoms'.[11]

The Romans' inherent love of theatrical display had been obvious earlier in the ever more opulent decoration of the temporary theatres (which I considered in chapter 3), and undoubtedly it had both encouraged the provision of a permanent theatre and, in turn, became more pronounced after its construction. But the basis for the marked (and evidently increased) emphasis on spectacle lay as much in social and political events as in matters of taste and aesthetics.

In 61 BC Pompey the Great celebrated the most magnificent triumph ever seen at Rome. 'Others may have celebrated three triumphs before him', wrote Plutarch, 'but Pompey was the first to celebrate his third triumph over the third continent, for having celebrated his first over Africa and his second over Europe, he was now triumphing over Asia . . . the three divisions of the world had become so many monuments to his greatness.' Preparations had begun some ten months earlier when Pompey returned from his victories in the east. He was determined to provide a spectacle so dazzling that it would totally eclipse both he memory of his predecessors and the prestige of his rivals; setting him in the public imagination on the level of the fabulous Alexander the Great.

The spectacle lasted two days. In the procession marched hundreds of captives representing the fourteen nations and nine hundred cities which Pompey had defeated, together with the families and generals of the conquered kings; placards identified them, and paintings accompanied their train illustrating all the major events of the campaigns. A vast amount of plunder – innumerable wagonloads of it – was carried along in a glittering stream, above which towered the twelve-foot statue of Pompey's most formidable adversary, Mithridates, King of Pontus, made of solid gold. Behind it came Pompey himself magnificently costumed and carried in a great bejewelled chariot drawn by four white horses.

The event was a consummate piece of propaganda, meticulously stage-managed to record indelibly in the imagination of its Roman audience an image of Pompey's power and majesty. Moreover,

Pompey had the satisfaction of knowing that Rome would have more permanent reminders of his achievements. Greatest among these was to be a new theatre which he was planning for the Campus Martius, a palace of entertainment which would associate his name permanently with pleasure and detract from the glory of whoever happened to put on a show there. For the beauty of a theatre was that it could bear his own name.[12]

Thus the theatre could in effect provide Pompey with a continuous 'triumph'. The stagings, as Cicero's account quoted above of the style of the two inaugural tragedies suggests, could be used deliberately to remind an audience of Pompey's own spectacular triumph, and the building itself, which he dedicated to Venus the Victorious, was used to display his trophies permanently.[13]

A further attraction of the theatre to Pompey (and his successors) was its provision of a convenient site where he could appear before a huge crowd to in effect display and validate the popular basis of his authority. Under the new political conditions of the late Republic, which disrupted earlier constitutional limits on the exercise and duration of public office, powerful leaders now might expect to hold power for an extended period. It was expedient and efficient to be able to make use of a permanent site for presenting a portion of their scenic games, displacing the traditional dependence upon temporary provision either by the responsible magistrates or (for the ever-increasing number of 'extra-ordinary' occasions), by the individual politician.[14]

Both the method of provision for the *ludi*, and the nature of the occasion when they took place had changed, albeit gradually, in the first and second centuries BC. From the beginning, the responsible aediles and praetors had received a fixed sum from the treasury but this was quite inadequate, and to ensure splendour and win popularity, officials had happily supplemented state funds with their own resources. Such benefaction had become an indispensable instrument for a successful political career: from the early second century a man who had not had an opportunity to serve as aedile (and thus provide games) had little chance of achieving higher office; Sulla himself had been defeated for the praetorship when he attempted to forgo serving as aedile. In addition to increasing their sumptuousness, one way of augmenting the success of the games (without further burdening the treasury) and attracting prestige to their producer was to extend them in length. The religious requirement of 'instauration' – repetition if any aspect of the *ludi* had been incorrectly performed – provided a convenient excuse for such prolongation. Thus, within limits, magistrates had manipulated the religious basis of the shows for their own benefit, so that they came increasingly to be seen not just as public ceremonies, but as gifts from the responsible official, with the effect that 'during the last two centuries of the Republic and even more under the Empire, the games lost their religious dimension in the minds of their organizers and of all their spectators'.[15]

Earlier Roman statesmen had resisted the creation of a permanent theatre, perceiving a potential danger to public order and the possibility of political abuse; now as the Republican government and its institutions collapsed into factional struggles from which one demagogue after another emerged to exercise supreme power, what had been feared as perilous was seen as desirable by men who knew how to benefit from it. Indeed, for leaders whose power derived in part from their control of militia personally loyal to themselves, one of the attractions of a permanent theatre as a place for display and celebration (instead of conducting such things in the streets and open places of the city) was that it could both be 'stage-managed' and more easily controlled in any volatile situation. Because the theatres were located outside the boundaries of the city, in the Campus Martius, proconsuls and other officials holding military authority could attend while retaining their *imperium*; their formal right of command.[16]

In the period following Pompey's triumph and before the completion of his theatre in 55 BC, a most striking demonstration of the political potential inherent in theatrical occasions was witnessed at Rome. In 58 BC under threat from his mortal enemy Publius Clodius, Cicero had fled the country. Clodius then (illegally) had him declared an exile and employed hooligans to destroy or vandalize much of his property. At gladiatorial shows given in the Forum the following year, 'the type of spectacle attended by crowds from all classes, and which are particularly enjoyed by the masses', one of Cicero's defenders, the Tribune Publius Sestius, deliberately attended to test and demonstrate the degree of public support Cicero enjoyed. 'At once from all the spectators . . . was heard such applause that it was said the entire Roman people had never demonstrated greater or more obvious unanimity for any cause'. By contrast, Clodius' brother Appius Claudius, who was Praetor at the time, attempted to skulk in unseen to avoid popular condemnation; when the crowd spotted him the hisses were so strong that it 'alarmed the gladiators and frightened the horses'!

Even more graphic scenes took place in the temporary theatre. During a production of the *Brutus* of Accius, a line referring to the sixth-century king, Servius Tullius – 'Tullius, who secured the people's freedom' – was deemed by the crowd to be a reference to Cicero (whose middle name was Tullius) and 'encored a thousand times'. Subsequently in July of 57 BC the Senate passed resolutions favouring Cicero, which were vehemently opposed by Clodius. This occurred during the celebrations of the *Ludi Apollinares*, and once again the people seized the opportunity to demonstrate their feelings. When the news of the

Senate's actions came, Aesopus, who was performing in Accius' *Eurysaces*, repeatedly 'pointed' whatever passages could be fashioned to apply to Cicero, even interpolating appropriate lines from another play (the *Andromacha* of Ennius), and as he did so was wildly encored by the audience. Cicero later asserted that 'he pleaded my cause before the Roman people with far weightier words than I could have done myself', and described

> How [Aesopus] wept as he spoke of the burning and destruction of my house . . . his acting was such that after describing his former happiness, when he turned to utter the line 'all these things I have seen in flames' it drew tears even from my enemies and my rivals!

The audience was so worked up by this that a little later, when the senators entered the theatre, they were roundly applauded, and as the Consul P. Lentulus Spinther arrived he was given a standing ovation by a crowd 'weeping with joy'. When Clodius entered he had first to endure the 'clamour of cries, threats, and curses' which rained down upon him, and then sat totally dispirited during a performance of the comedy *Simulans*, 'The Pretender', by Afranius, every possible passage of which was construed by the entire audience to compound his humiliation. At one point the entire cast 'leaning forward threateningly, and staring right at the foul creature, chanted in unison the line "This Titus is the sequel, the end of your vicious life!" '. Shortly thereafter, the Senate passed a resolution enabling Cicero's recall, with only one dissenting vote: that of Clodius.

In reflecting upon this episode, Cicero noted that there were 'three venues where the opinion and feeling of the Roman people could be most directly expressed about public affairs: at a meeting, at the Assembly, and at a gathering for plays and gladiatorial shows'. Exactly two years after this episode, the Roman people acquired a permanent facility where the latter could take place.[17]

Pompey's theatre probably held around 17,500 spectators, although some estimates are much higher. The diameter of the auditorium was over 500 feet, while the stage itself was some 300 feet in width; the length of a football field. Behind it the *scaenae frons* probably rose to the full height of the upper tiers of the auditorium opposite: three storeys. The outer semi-circular wall was composed of three tiers of engaged columns carved from red granite. Although nothing of the external facade of Pompey's theatre remains visible, the theatre of Marcellus erected by Augustus forty-four years later probably resembled it. If so, then the columns on the first (ground) level were Doric, the second Ionic, and the third Corinthian. This impressive facade was adorned with stone and stucco and embellished with numerous statues of stone and bronze. Hinting at the sumptuous architecture and spectacle within, it formed a series of huge vaulted arches at street level, from which a system of passages and staircases efficiently conducted spectators to their seats inside. Examples of tickets found at Rome, Pompeii, and elsewhere indicate that seats were precisely designated according to entrance, section, level, etc. – very similar to modern practice at theatres and sports stadia – and this helped to ensure public order since there was no competition for seats or confusion about their location.

The most striking element in Pompey's edifice was the provision of a temple to *Venus Victrix* at the top and rear of the auditorium placed directly *vis-à-vis* the stage and *scaenae frons*. Apparently this was constructed in such a way that the monumental ramp of steps leading up to it formed the central bank of seats in the auditorium. It was said that when Pompey's political rivals objected to a permanent theatre, he claimed that in fact he was building a temple beneath which steps would be provided for watching the games. Allowing for the sophistry which was the privilege of a powerful man, the circumstances do indicate the continuing integration of theatrical performance and religious rites, and the custom of close physical proximity between theatre buildings and religious shrines, which can be traced throughout the history of the Roman theatre.[18]

Pompey however, went beyond this custom. By law, *triumphatores* (such as Pompey) were only allowed to construct monuments of a religious character; most had found that entertainments, provision of public banquets on a religious pretext, and distributions of gifts were more useful to their careers. Wishing to provide a theatre to ensure present popularity and lasting glory, Pompey circumvented the restriction by amalgamating and crowning it with a temple.

Curving outward from either side of the temple was a covered and colonnaded gallery that extended around the top of the auditorium to connect with the two large lateral wings of the scene building, the *versurae*, which formed the recess for the scenic facade and framed the stage. Around the external perimeter of this colonnade were located the masts used to anchor the huge, brightly coloured linen awning; the *vela*, that shaded the auditorium.[19]

In addition to the theatre itself, the complex included an assembly room or *curia*; a new meeting place for the Senate which was dominated by a statue of Pompey himself, at the foot of which Caesar was murdered a decade later.[20] Its prominent position was an unsubtle reminder of Pompey's own political eminence, which was further suggested by the provision of Pompey's new residence conveniently at hand a short distance away. The *curia* was located within a large park stretching for 600 feet behind the *scaena*; the *Porticus Pompeii*, also known as the 'Hall of the Hundred Pillars'. Within were rows of trees, shaded streams and numerous fountains. The great colonnade itself was festooned with golden curtains, and displayed a collection of statues and paintings; all works of outstanding merit and elegance. This feature (which is found at Pompeii and in many of the imperial theatres) was probably based on Greek practice. It was useful on the days of performance as a place for the audience to stroll between the entertainments without leaving the theatre complex or causing disruption in the streets, while at other times it provided a splendid amenity for the Roman citizenry to enjoy whether for relaxation and escape from the summer heat or for amorous assignation.[21]

The theatre was dedicated – probably in September 55 BC – with what Cicero (despite his private strictures) praised publicly as the most magnificent and munificent games ever given or ever to be given in the future.[22] In addition to a variety of (albeit over-long and over-sumptuous) dramatic performances, there were athletic contests, music, gladiators, races, and the hunting of wild beasts. Together with 600 lions, 150 leopards, and 18 elephants, Pompey delighted the public by displaying even more exotic beasts: baboons, lynx, and, for the first time on any stage, a rhinoceros![23] Although Pompey's popularity and acclaim undoubtedly soared with the mass of spectators whose favour and taste were his chief concern, Cicero's more fastidious opinion must have been shared by a portion of the audience.

> As for the Greek and Oscan plays, I don't suppose you were sad to miss them . . . and, as for the athletes – I can't conceive you regret forgoing them – you who scorned the gladiators . . . all that's left is the hunts; twice a day over five days. Magnificent to be sure; who can deny it? But what pleasure can a man of culture derive from seeing some poor mortal torn to pieces by a mighty beast, or some fine animal impaled on a spear? And even if such things were worth seeing, you've seen it all before. I certainly saw nothing new.[24]

With the establishment of his splendid theatre (its permanence placed beyond the reach of envy), Pompey, like the Hellenistic monarchs he wished to emulate, could now regularly enjoy (and employ) the demonstration of the public's homage and their visible support in the appropriate ambience of Rome's most magnificent building.[25] Prior to his theatre the monuments of patrons or *triumphatores* were usually modest; now 'by raising national monuments and giving national festivals the magnates showed that theirs was a national destiny which was based on their personal prestige or which consisted in their personal power'.[26] Pompey's example, which in this and much else, anticipated the pattern of imperial practice, was soon followed by others, beginning ironically with Caesar, who in 46 BC lavishly celebrated the final defeat of Pompey's forces with the *Ludi Victoriae Caesaris*.[27] He placed a raised couch for himself in the orchestra and a golden throne in the tribunal (a place of honour to the right of the stage over the entrance) reserved for the patron of the games, and later for the emperor. As Cicero observed afterwards, 'by shows, buildings, benefactions, and banquets [Caesar] charmed the ignorant multitude'. To further mark his success, Caesar planned and began to construct his own theatre,[28] but was assassinated in Pompey's edifice before the project was completed.

Caesar's successors in turn benefited from his example, beginning with Octavian who, as Ronald Syme noted, 'acquired a mastery of the demagogic arts . . . the heir of Caesar at once devoted himself to Caesarian propaganda. Games and festivals were customary devices for the organization of popular sentiment.' Later, when emperor, 'as a showman, none could compete with Augustus in material resources, skill of organization and sense of the dramatic. . . . Each and every festival was an occasion for sharpening the loyalty of the people and inculcating a suitable lesson.'[29] To mark the beginning of the new age by way of exorcizing the evils of the past, and sanctifying the reforms and ideals of his regime, Augustus held the *Ludi Saeculares* in 17 BC. These encompassed every variety of theatrical entertainment, including the performance of Greek plays in Pompey's theatre. For such events a permanent theatre was an invaluable resource (supplemented on this occasion by the erection of a temporary one as well), and early in his reign Augustus acquired two more such splendid edifices (those of Balbus in 13 BC, and Marcellus in 11 BC) to complement that provided by Pompey and bequeath to his imperial successors.

These theatres ultimately became the prototypes of the buildings so widely constructed during the subsequent centuries of the imperial period. They were free-standing, architecturally unified structures consisting of a large auditorium, a semi-circular orchestral area, and a wide raised stage, backed by the solid facade of a *scaenae frons*, which had doorways giving access onto the stage. Probably in its earliest form, Pompey's theatre employed a straight facade, relatively free of the articulated architectural pattern of aedicules, columns, and niches which characterized the later *scaenae frons*. It was, however, decorated with a huge variety of sculpture and paintings depicting marvellous and fantastic objects and scenes.[30]

In common with the other earliest Roman stone theatres (notably those at Ostia and Pompeii) it is likely that Pompey's scenic facade was initially decorated not with solid architectural embellishment, but with painted panels. It may well have been entirely of wood, or perhaps had wooden boarding or other structures facing it since, according to Tacitus, it was damaged by fire in the reign of Tiberius, whom he credits with rebuilding it, and specifically with replacing the stage.[31] The flat facade could have used perspective painting – with little plastic decoration, perhaps only columns on either side of the three doorways – rendered in such a way as to suggest the type of architectural elements which we saw in the painted depictions of the temporary stages. In fact, the representation on a flat wall of solid, elaborate structures was precisely the achievement of the early second-style artists who were active at the time these early facade stages appeared in the second half of the first century BC. Gradually these painted *trompe-l'oeil* elements were displaced by real architecture until the ornate, highly articulated facade of the *scaenae frons* (as seen in surviving structures) finally appeared. Initially this emerging architecture may have been comprised of wooden sets projecting outward from the flat facade, which was later transformed completely into stone ornamentation. Vitruvius, writing his book on architectural practice after the construction of Pompey's theatre, and while Rome's two subsequent theatres were being built, may indicate such sets when he notes 'we can observe . . . those who . . . when they wish to sing with a louder tone, turn to the wooden scenery, and with this help, gain resonance for their voice'.[32]

The earliest surviving example of the final format of this *scaenae frons* type of theatre is that at Pompeii, which was converted into that form about AD 65. Its architecture had passed successively through various phases. It began in the early second century BC, like most other theatres in southern Italy and Sicily, as a Greek *paraskenia* stage with projecting wings. Shortly after Sulla established a colony of Roman veterans at Pompeii in 80 BC, the *scaena* of the theatre was remodelled to form a straight facade which was probably decorated with painted flats and possibly some wooden structure projecting outwards from it. Then in the imperial period it was converted again to incorporate the elaborate doorways, niches, columns, and entablature characteristic of later Roman theatres. But this form had probably been prefigured in the increasingly decorated *temporary* theatres of the previous century. The impressive theatre of Scaurus (which we considered earlier) constructed in 58 BC with a three-storey facade, and itself a mixture of extravagant architecture and *tabulae pictae*, may well have resembled the *scaenae frons* form ultimately achieved by the permanent theatres, the first of which, built by Pompey only three years later, may already have begun to render some of its temporary architectural effects in more permanent form.[33]

In the long subsequent history of the Roman form of theatre building, various minor changes appeared in the arrangement of the scenic facade. Sometimes the plastic elements were heavily emphasized, with the columns, *vestibula*, and podium significantly projected out from the surface of the wall. In other cases these structures tended to fade back into the facade, but without ever disappearing entirely. Similarly, at times the forms of the three separate pavilions framing the main doors stood out sharply along the lateral facade. This was particularly true in Italy and North Africa where the Roman theatres generally displayed three large and well-defined aedicules, which contrasted sharply with

19 The remains of the *scaenae frons* of the Roman theatre at Sabratha in North Africa built in the imperial period.

the line of the wall itself. In the East, and especially in the case of remodelled Hellenistic stages, there was usually less articulation, less pronounced niches, frequently five doors, and the whole tended to form a more flattened and continuous line of columns and porches. In this we are probably justified in seeing additional evidence of the relationship between the temporary Italian stages and the permanent Roman theatre. The earlier 'purpose-built' theatres, including the three built at Rome, conformed to the essential model derived as I suggest from the coexistent temporary stage. In the East this influence was less immediate and to fully incorporate it would have involved more substantial alteration of the existing Hellenistic structures than was actually necessary.[34]

The new social and political conditions of the Empire encouraged the building of theatres, and largely determined the nature of the performances taking place within them. The most important new factor was the establishment of the imperial monarchy both as the basis for the administration and governing of Rome and its provinces, and as the head of a new and more clearly defined social hierarchy. The Principate of Augustus and a new system of imperial government (facilitated by predominantly peaceful conditions) assisted the integration of the provinces and their population into the Roman state and Roman society and, crucially, led to their cultural development and urbanization. In the Empire there were close to a thousand cities, and although many of these had relatively small populations of under 15,000 inhabitants, by the end of the first century AD frequently even the smallest towns had acquired a collection of monumental public buildings, including a theatre.

The social supremacy of the emperor and his family, which displaced from their former pre-eminence the circles of oligarchic families who had so often been engaged in prolonged and disruptive rivalry, encouraged patronage on a vast scale, both in terms of its largesse and its geographic distribution. The emperor was personally responsible through his officials for the administration of the provinces, with whose population he enjoyed privileges and in turn exercised the responsibility of a ruler and patron. The new pattern was established by Augustus.

> When Augustus took the title *pater patriae* [father of the country] in 2 BC the whole empire became almost clients under his 'fatherly' protection. Social connections of this sort might assume a concrete form, particularly in the close relationship between the ruler and urban communities, regions, provinces, and other organized groups in the population. Thus the emperor was also the *defensor plebis* who bestowed upon the *plebs* of the city of Rome largesse of grain and money and public games, too.[35]

Often the emperor was given the top magistracy in cities throughout the Empire, which he in turn delegated to an official representative.

During his year in office, the emperor could appropriately lavish gifts upon the city and sponsor festivals.

During a long, peaceful, and prosperous reign (31 BC to 14 AD) Augustus reconstituted and regulated the different social orders and the relations between them, and defined the social hierarchy more precisely than before. This process was, incidentally, formally extended to the allocation of seats within the theatre. Under the *Lex Julia Theatralis*, he consolidated and extended earlier regulations, to determine far more precisely how the different social groupings were arranged so that the auditorium came to resemble a microcosm of society itself.[36]

The class which most directly benefited from these reforms was that of the well-to-do *equites*, who under the Republican oligarchy had remained at the margins of much public life. The majority of these citizens (whose ranks had been greatly expanded) now came not from Rome but from the towns and cities of Italy, and similar propertied individuals were numerous throughout the Empire. With the spread of Roman authority, quickening urbanization, and the wealth and culture generated by prosperity and security, such men now became enthusiastic supporters of the ethos and ideals of Roman government and society. Within the new conditions governing status and position, one effective way for a provincial worthy to distinguish himself and attract favour was through public patronage and benefaction.[37]

The four annually elected town officials (the *duoviri* and aediles) were obliged by law to provide expenditure for games, or, exceptionally, for the provision or maintenance of buildings where they took place. In addition the ordinary members of a town council, the *decurions* were also expected to sponsor public celebrations when they first entered into their duties and privileges.[38] Complementing such formal requirements there was, during the first three centuries of the imperial period, extensive informal benefaction from prominent and wealthy citizens who in effect bought status by building or refurbishing provincial buildings and monuments, often including theatres. Indeed, Plutarch, while exhorting such generosity in the wealthy, felt it prudent to warn that less well-off aspiring patrons 'must not produce races, theatrical games, and banquets in competition with the rich for reputation and power'.[39]

One to whom money was no object, Maecenas, was said to have advised Augustus to 'adorn this capital with utter disregard for expense and make it magnificent with festivals of every kind'. Augustus could afford to. He controlled huge personal wealth − quite apart from the state treasury − which he used extensively for benefaction, (some 600 million sesterces in the course of his reign) and bequeathed to his successors. This enabled subsequent emperors to draw freely upon a private fortune, which vastly enhanced their capacity to secure and hold popular support.[40] Augustus had himself set the example at Rome, which he systematically transformed through the provision of elegant new public buildings. These were intended not only to impress, but to make an important moral and political statement as well.

> The magnificence of the new marble architecture is simultaneously a rejection of the old private *luxuria*; public parks, baths, galleries, libraries and theatres make the culture of the rich directly accessible to the poor of the city. Materials and forms of the monuments may be Greek, but they express a Roman message, a revival of the *mores maiorum*.[41]

The last building erected in Rome by anyone other than the emperor or Senate (often on his behalf) until the city ceased to be an imperial capital, was the theatre which Augustus deigned to let Balbus provide in 13 BC. Emperors were exclusively responsible for the provision of municipal buildings, and, moreover, reserved for themselves alone the right to present any extraordinary shows, while sharing the customary ones with the responsible officials. In quite a literal sense, the emperors were unwilling to let any potential rivals 'in on the act'. It is in this context that between 13 and 11 BC, two new theatres were built which effectively doubled the total provision of seats at Rome to over 38,000.[42] During the same period, Vitruvius wrote his great work on architecture, and the section detailing theatre construction is incontrovertible evidence that – in addition to 'many [wooden] theatres built every year at Rome' – the erection elsewhere of new stone theatres along these lines was anticipated.[43]

All the indications are that under Augustus (through his own initiative or that of wealthy benefactors) numerous theatres were indeed provided (and older ones were renovated), including examples at Arles in Gaul, Merida in Spain, Leptis Magna in North Africa, and within Italy itself at, *inter alia*, Fiesole, Milan, Turin, Aosta, Herculaneum, Ostia, and Minturnae. Under subsequent rulers new theatres continued to be built throughout the Empire during the first and second centuries AD, provided either directly by the emperor himself, or through the patronage of prominent and often local, officials.[44] The audiences in these theatres were catered for by members of a thriving acting profession which under Augustus and his successors had been organized along more efficient lines into an Empire-wide guild that probably had its headquarters at Rome.[45]

The conditions favouring the provision of theatres also tended to encourage opulence and grandeur in their entertainments. The place and occasion were symbolic of Roman prestige and imperial glory, and an important expression of the official ideology which justified, gave meaning to, and secured public support for the operation of the

Principate. Inside Rome's imperial theatres the audience often was presented with dazzling spectacles calculated to impress and to cast reflected glory upon the rulers and patrons (or their representatives) whose presence frequently added to the excitement and splendour of the occasion and ceremony. The emperor attended his own games, and often presided at those given by the responsible officials. Eventually the *ludi* were so frequent that ordinary life at Rome was overshadowed by festivity; the emperor and his people might spend as much as a third of the year together at shows. Rome in effect became, like Versailles later, a 'court city' obsessed with the ruler and his affairs. The emperor was himself the star of the shows. They began with ritual homage to him – the different sections of the crowd chanted rhythmic acclamations which were gradually codified and accompanied by music – and all that followed was expected to be worthy of his magnificence.[46] In part this was accomplished by the sheer massed cohorts of actors, musicians, and supernumeraries, and (in the case of both mime and pantomime) by the diversion, artifice, and intensity of their performances. In addition however, there was undoubtedly a great deal of scenic embellishment, although its more precise nature and modes of operation is obscure.

Just as an understanding of the architecture of the permanent theatres is greatly enhanced by reference to the temporary stage structures which were in use in the period before (and indeed, after) 55 BC, so too our perception of later Roman scenery benefits by examining the scant but intriguing evidence of earlier scenic practice. The permanent theatres of the Empire clearly drew upon an architectural tradition, and are likely to have made use of the scenic one as well. In the third *Georgic* of Vergil (composed during the reign of Augustus), lines 22–4 state

> Even now it pleases to lead the solemn procession to the shrine, and view the sacrifice of the steers; or to watch how the scene divides as the panels turn . . .

In his commentary on this passage, the fourth-century grammarian Marius Servius explained,

> Amongst out ancestors theatres were merely a structure of steps. For at that time the *scaena* was made of wood. . . . Now the scenery which existed then could either be turned or drawn; it was turned when it was entirely revolved by a certain contrivance, and displayed another form of picture. It was drawn, when, with panels pulled to one side and the other, a painted scene was revealed behind. Whence [Vergil] skilfully includes both when he says, it 'divides as the panels turn': with each expression encompassing each function.

Servius may not be correctly interpreting the sense of Vergil's phrase,

169

20   Detail from a painting in Room 15, the Villa of Oplontis, thought to depict
scenic panels behind small drapes (*siparia*).

which is ambiguous, but even so, he appears to have a clear picture in his own mind of two specific systems of movable scenery. Leaving aside for the moment the 'turned' scenery, the second type, that which is 'drawn'; the *scaenae ductiles* – also mentioned by the first century BC historian Varro[47] – may be clarified by reference to the type of wall paintings considered earlier in chapter 3. In the example from the Villa of Oplontis, we noted behind the low partitioning walls which connected the two doors and the central aperture, the depiction of a receding colonnade. A similar depiction occurs in another painting from the same villa, a detail of which shows a two-storeyed colonnade, once again located behind a low wall flanking at either side a large central doorway. In both of these paintings we note running along the top of the walls a dark sagging curtain which has a rope attached along its upper edge.

With minor variations, the same format is used in a great many paintings, including examples from the House of the Cryptoporticus, the House of Obellius Firmus, and the House of Livia. In each case the architectural background, sometimes on two levels in the form of a receding colonnade, or a distant cityscape, is clearly depicted as being at some remove to the rear of the structure of the actual stage facade. Almost invariably there are curtains attached to this stage structure which partly obscure the painted architecture laid out behind them. If we suppose, as we did earlier in analysing the wall paintings for evidence of temporary theatres, that the painters are depicting something close to the actual format of the stage, then we must imagine a scenic facade that had an open area behind it; a sort of passage into which the stage doors gave access. In this passage could be placed flats or panels, painted in perspective (*skenographia*), which would then be visible above and behind the half walls of the structural facade. Such a passage would correspond to the *angiportum*, the area referred to by Plautus as allowing unseen passage 'backstage' from one doorway to the other, which I discussed in chapter 3.

If the flats operated as Servius described the *scaenae ductiles*, to effect a change of scenery, then the function of the curtains might be to mask that operation; the transition from the display of one picture to another. They would be raised while the 'scene divides' and the panels are 'pulled to one side and the other', and then lowered to fold up in the position shown in the paintings so that another 'painted scene was revealed behind'. Such an hypothesis is consistent with the evidence of the paintings themselves – it satisfactorily explains what seems to be represented in them – and, in addition to Servius' statement, there is some further evidence independent of the paintings, to support it.

The Roman theatre used two types of curtains: the *aulaeum*, a large drop-curtain, and a smaller one, apparently used to conceal portions of the stage facade, called a *siparium*. Both are believed to have been in use in Republican times, and indeed, Cicero used the phrase 'post *siparium*' to mean 'behind the scenes'.[48] It appears that the smaller curtains, the *siparia*, were involved somehow in a change of acts, and thus, presumably, in a change of scenery. What the evidence suggests is that whereas the large *aulaeum*, which concealed the entire stage, was used only at the beginning and end of the presentation, the smaller *siparia* could be used between acts or interludes to mark a transition, which logically would have been accompanied by some change in décor.

The most revealing reference is found in the *Metamorphoses* by the second-century AD writer, Apuleius. In chapter 10, following a mimic dance which may have taken place in the orchestra, an elaborate scene is presented on the stage: 'aulaeo subducto et complicitis sipariis scaena disponitur'; 'The curtain is removed, the *siparia* fold up, the scene is revealed.' The same process was alluded to earlier by Apuleius in chapter 1: 'aulaeum tragicum dimoveto et siparium scaenicum complicato': 'having removed the tragic curtain, and having folded up the scenic *siparium*', once again, to reveal the stage. The word *siparium* is a variant of *supparum*, which means a topsail or the upper portion of a woman's garment; both uses remind us graphically of the type of sagging curtain seen in the paintings, its upper curve reminiscent of the neckline of a loose garment hanging over and concealing the breasts, or of a sail which could be raised or lowered by ropes attached to its upper edge. The evidence for the *siparia* is meagre, but in accord with both the appearance and the use which I presume for the curtains observed in the wall paintings.

As part of the experimental project detailed in chapter 3, I devised and set up a scenic system of *scaenae ductiles*, sliding panels, and operated it using *siparia* in the manner indicated above. To effect a change of scenery, all the curtains rose in unison (a simple matter of rigging them together by joining up the cords along their top edges), using a single stagehand stationed behind the scenic facade. This 'blacked out' the openings in the facade through which, as in the wall paintings, architectural vistas had been visible. The panels upon which these had been painted were then shifted to either side, to uncover a second set behind them. The curtains were allowed to fold up, revealing the new background. The operation was simple and effective, took only a few seconds, and, above all *made sense* of the meagre evidence that survives from antiquity.

In the same passage quoted earlier concerning the *scaenae ductiles*, Servius observes that the *pegma* (a scenic device which I discuss below), that was perhaps used primarily in the circus and amphitheatre, in his day is still by custom operated by the personnel who are normally responsible for theatrical productions. He evidently considers this the

21   General view of the Warwick University replica temporary stage, showing the format of the *scaenae ductiles* and *siparia*. The backdrop is changed when 'blacked out' by the raised *siparia*.

22 Detail of the Warwick set.

consequence of a tradition that began in the temporary theatres. A system of sliding panels of the type I have suggested – partially visible behind the half walls of the scenic facade – might have been adapted for use on the earliest permanent stage when the facade was, as suggested, a flat wall against which flats could be placed. It would, however, have been inappropriate in the later, elaborately decorated *scaenae frons* stages once solid architectural ornamentation had replaced painted effects. In describing the scenic elements of such permanent theatres, Vitruvius makes no mention of it.

23 A relief panel, now in the Naples Museum, depicting a scene from New Comedy. An apparently inebriated young man, holding his festive fillets in his right hand, is assisted by a slave. He is accompanied by a young female musician playing the double pipe or *tibia*. To the left, an older man bearing a staff is restrained by another.

A relief panel now in the Naples Museum depicting a theatrical scene has not been reliably dated, but clearly represents a situation from New Comedy, and the stage facade behind the actors suggests Roman theatre architecture. The elaborate decorated doorway is similar to those seen in such wall paintings as those discussed earlier which are thought to represent temporary stage facades. The architectural background, to the right of the door, which is partly concealed by the curtain, also resembles the depiction of similar architecture, similarly placed, in a

175

number of paintings where it was suggested that such backgrounds were painted panels used as stage scenery. One interesting difference, however, is that the curtain shown in the relief does not appear to be placed behind a low flanking wall as seen in the paintings. If, as I have argued, the existence of such a wall were indeed an element in the function of the movable *scaenae ductiles*, its absence here may indicate that the relief depicts a scene taking place on a stage with a permanent flat facade, against which scenic panels or wooden sets could be placed: a transitional form before the construction of highly decorated *scaenarum frontes*.

The scenic content of such panels (cityscapes, colonnades, and houses), may have remained the same, although once in place in the larger permanent theatres, they may no longer have been shifted during or between performances; if so, the only way to conceal and display them would have been by using the *siparia*. There is evidence that these drapes continued to be used in the later theatres as part of the scenic display. An inscription relating to a theatre constructed in the mid-second century at Dugga in North Africa records that its benefactor, the priest P. Marcius Quadratus (serving the cult of Augustus), erected 'the stage with *siparia* and all its decoration, the auditorium as well as the halls, colonnades and walks'.[49]

Although Vitruvius does not refer to *scaenae ductiles*, he does mention different, possibly alternative devices; the *periaktoi*. The *periaktoi* are probably the same as the system of 'turned' scenery, the *scaenae versatiles* mentioned by Servius in the passage quoted earlier. The earliest reference to its use may be found in the notice that the aediles L. and M. Licinius Lucullus made the *scaena* 'revolving' in 79 BC.[50] This would indicate that *both* methods of scenic change were used in the temporary theatres, and the context of Vitruvius' description strongly suggests that the *periaktoi*, at least, continued to be employed in permanent theatres as well. Probable corroboration for this is found in the description given of them in the second century AD by Pollux, writing when such theatres were common. It seems plausible that once the permanent scenic facade had acquired elaborate stone decoration, sliding panels were no longer appropriate or feasible, and were displaced by the revolving mechanism of the *periaktoi*.

Unfortunately neither Vitruvius' nor Pollux's account of the *periaktoi* is entirely clear. The word may be translated literally as merely 'things which move', although there is an implication of rotary motion, and this is clearly what Vitruvius takes it to mean. He writes,

> Now the scenery is so arranged that the middle entrances have the decoration of a royal door, the ordinary doors are to the left and right. Adjacent are spaces prepared for decoration, which areas the Greeks call *periaktoi* from the fact that in these areas are revolving

prismatic machines each having three types of decoration, which when there is an imminent change of plays or the arrival of gods with sudden thunder, are turned and change the type of decoration on their panels.[51]

Like Vitruvius, Pollux evidently conceives of the *periaktoi* as rotating devices, located to either side of the central door of the *scaena*, close to the two side doors. They are decorated with some sort of presumably emblematic scenery. In a second reference to them, Pollux associates their decoration with the *katablemata*; painted curtains or panels, apparently (as etymologically the word implies) 'let down' upon them. He states,

> By each of the two doors to either side of the centre are . . . the location of the *periaktoi*. . . . A *periaktos* can present sea-gods and anything too heavy to be flown in on the crane [*mechane*]. When the *periaktoi* are revolved, the right hand one can change anything; both together alter location. . . . As for the lightning and thunder machines, the one is a high swivelling *periaktos* . . .
>
> *Katablemata* are curtains or panels with decoration appropriate to the play's requirements. On the *periaktoi* the background could be a mountain, sea, river or some such.[52]

Unfortunately the somewhat imprecise accounts by these two authors cannot be complemented by any obvious visual evidence from wall paintings, vases, reliefs, or elsewhere. Nor is there any certain archaeological proof although in several Hellenistic theatres holes have been found, appropriately located, which may have held the axis for a hypothetical revolving prismatic device. It is impossible to say how widely they were employed in the Roman theatre. Perhaps the most significant fact to emerge from otherwise inconclusive evidence is that both authors undoubtedly conceived of scenic decoration which was both movable and could be changed in the course of performance. In terms of theatrical convention this is an significant concept, with broad implications for stage practice. It is also important to note that neither writer limits scenery to the *periaktoi*, with both indicating that other scenic devices were employed.[53]

In a passage which was greatly to influence the work of Renaissance scenic artists, who sought to interpret it for the scenery used in their own productions, Vitruvius writes,

> Now there are three styles of scenery [*scaenae*]: one which is called tragic, another comic, a third satyric. The decoration of these are dissimilar and of different arrangement one from another, because the tragic settings are designed with columns and pediments, statues, and other royal things; the comic, however, have the type

177

and appearance of private buildings and balconies, and projections
with windows arranged in a manner imitating ordinary buildings;
the satyric are decorated with trees, caves, mountains, and other
country things, designed in the manner of a landscape.[54]

He refers to three types of *scaena*. As noted earlier in the discussion of
temporary stages, the use of the word here and elsewhere is ambiguous:
it may mean 'scenery', 'stage', or the 'stage house' and its facade.
Perhaps Vitruvius means to indicate that several different modes of
scenic design could be used – whether painted or constructed –
according to the theatrical genre, when he refers to the scenery as being
both 'dissimilar and of different arrangement'.

This apparently superfluous repetition seems curious in an otherwise
compact section by an author noted for his succinctness, unless Vitruvius'
actual meaning is that the three scenic genres differ not only in the content
of their subject matter, but also in the form in which each represents it.
Some such distinction may be further inferred from the different words
used immediately thereafter to describe the method of arrangement: the
tragic scenes are designed (*deformantur*); the comic have the appearance
(*habent speciem*); and the satyric are decorated (*ornantur*). One possible
interpretation might be that tragic scenery consisted of a stage facade of
formal, ornamental architecture (similar to the décor of the permanent
scaenae frons); comic settings had aedicules opening onto the stage, with
painted panels in the background depicting houses or cityscapes (such
as are seen in wall paintings); and the satyric stage was set with trees,
rocks, and so on, either painted or constructed as free-standing pieces; a
format (as we shall see) very like one described by Apuleius.

In addition to the paintings already considered, an example (dated
about 40 BC) from the Villa of Fannius Sinistor near Pompeii, now in the
Metropolitan Museum, New York may be compared to the comic relief
panel.[55] Its ornamented doorway is similar, and its architectural
background may provide a fuller picture of a scenic cityscape only
glimpsed behind the curtain in the relief. However, the presence of the
flanking wall, and the extension of the cityscape behind the doorway,
resembles the format which I suggested for the scenic display in the
temporary, rather than in the early permanent theatres. If the
background is indeed meant to depict a scenic panel, it closely follows
Vitruvius' description of comic scenery: 'private buildings and balconies, and projections with windows . . .'.

There are a number of literary references from the imperial period
which, although they fail to provide any comprehensive account of later
Roman scenic practice, do certainly confirm that its was capable of
complex and impressive effects. Seneca the younger refers to the scenic
virtuosity of the 'arts of entertainment which give amusement to the eye
and ear';

24 First-century BC painting from a bedroom in the Villa of P. Fannius Sinistor at Boscoreal, near Pompeii, now in the Metropolitan Museum, New York. Its scenic background echoes Vitruvius' description of comic scenery; 'private buildings and balconies, and projections with windows'.

Amongst these you may count the engineers [*machinatores*] who contrive a structure that soars up by itself, or wooden panels that rise silently aloft, and many other unexpected devices such as objects fit together which come apart, or things separate which automatically join together, or objects which stand erect, then slowly collapse. The eyes of the ignorant are astonished by such things.[56]

The theatre was a place of spectacle, and although eventually the spectacle outgrew the theatre to be presented elsewhere, very considerable effects were almost certainly achieved, first on the temporary, and later on the permanent stages. The dedication of Pompey's theatre encompassed, as we noted, in addition to the dramatic and musical contests, gymnastic events and the 'hunting' of vast numbers of animals.[57] Even when the context of a reference makes it certain that the event described occurred in the circus or amphitheatre, it may plausibly suggest theatrical practice as well, since from earliest times the distinction between activities appropriate to each venue does not appear to have been rigidly defined by the Romans, and, as Servius suggests later, the same personnel were customarily responsible for scenic spectacle wherever it took place.

The soaring 'structure' that Seneca refers to was the *pegma*; some sort of flying device which apparently originated in the theatre and was later used in scenic entertainments generally; there are with references to it from the late first century BC, through the late fourth century AD. It could exhibit performers as well as scenic displays which may have divided laterally (like the *scaenae ductiles*), and certainly could be borne aloft. It was sometimes elaborately decorated and could consist of several storeys. Phaedrus recounts an anecdote from the reign of Augustus during a performance by the famous comic pantomime Bathyllus

Princeps, the flute player, was rather well known, since he usually accompanied Bathyllus with his music on the stage. It happened at one of the shows . . . that as the *pegma* was being whirled through the air he accidentally had a bad fall, and broke his left shin bone . . . then the curtain went down, the sound of thunder rolled through the theatre, and the gods spoke in the traditional way. Thereupon the chorus struck up a song.[58]

A far more serious accident occurred under the reign of Nero when an actor, making his premier flight in an enactment of the Daedalus and Icarus myth – playing Icarus – came hurtling down to land so close to the Emperor's couch that he was splattered with blood. The use of the *pegma* for such aerial displays is confirmed by Juvenal who mentions that its could 'waft boys away, up into the awning' which covered the theatre. In order to discourage untoward events and concentrate the minds of the theatrical 'builders, assistants and others of that type', Claudius ordered that 'if any automatic device or *pegma*, or the like had not functioned well' those responsible would be sent into combat as impromptu gladiators.[59]

Strabo records the use of a collapsible *pegma*, to stage the execution of a notorious Sicilian brigand. It was decorated to represent Mount Aetna, the area in which he had operated.

> I saw him [the criminal, Selurus] torn to pieces by wild beasts at an appointed combat of gladiators in the Forum; for he was placed on a lofty scaffold [*pegma*], as though on Aetna, and the scaffold was made suddenly to break up and collapse, and he himself was carried down with it into cages of wild beasts – fragile cages that had been prepared beneath the scaffold for that purpose.[60]

In a different context, the Jewish historian Josephus notes the sensation caused by a series of huge scenic *pegmata*, used to display *tableaux vivants* during the triumph of Titus (following the sack of Jerusalem) in AD 71.

> Nothing in the procession excited so much astonishment as the structure of the moving stages; indeed, their massiveness afforded ground for alarm and misgiving as to their stability, many of them being three or four storeys high, while the magnificence of the fabric was a source at once of delight and amazement. For many were enveloped in tapestries interwoven with gold, and all had a framework of gold and wrought ivory. The war was shown by numerous representations, in separate sections, affording a very vivid picture of its episodes . . . temples set on fire, houses pulled down over their owners' heads . . . and the art and magnificent workmanship of these structures now portrayed the incidents to those who had not witnessed them, as though they were happening before their eyes. On each of the stages was stationed the general of one of the captured cities in the attitude in which he was taken.[61]

Later accounts echo Josephus, emphasizing the sumptuous decoration of the *pegmata*, which could be gilded with gold or silver; Pliny the elder claims that Caligula displayed one in the circus that had been ornamented with 124,000 pounds weight of silver.[62]

According to the somewhat garbled account left by Pollux, the theatre made use of a great many other scenic devices in addition to those already considered. He has to be read with some caution, both because his descriptions lack clarity, and because it is not always evident whether his references are to contemporaneous (second-century AD) practice in the Roman theatre, or possibly to earlier Greek or Hellenistic practice.[63] On the whole, however, the general picture he provides of scenic variety and extravagance is consistent with that derived piecemeal from other sources.

Amongst the many devices he lists are the *ekkuklema* (which is thought to have been used as early as the fifth century BC), a platform which could be wheeled out from within the scene building for the discovery of the results of actions which are conceived as having taken place within; i.e. the display of murder victims. He suggests that these were 'available at every door and every house'. He mentions the *mechane*, a crane-like device known to have been used on the Greek stage to fly in 'gods and heroes in mid-air – Bellerophons and Perseuses', and stipulates its use in both tragedy and comedy. Mention is made of a *distegia*:

> an upper storey of a palace like the one in *Phoenician Women* from which Antigone surveys the army, or it can on another occasion be made of tiles which can be used for pelting. In comedy prostitutes solicit from it, or any old hag can keep an eye on things from up there.

Pollux goes on to mention a thunder machine made of stones rolled into copper pots; and two further flying devices: the *geranos*, a 'contrivance let down from above for raising up a body', and *aorai*, 'ropes hung down to raise up heroes and gods into the air'. He mentions trapdoors in the stage floor for the appearance of the furies or, enigmatically, 'for the rising of a river or some similar manifestation', and 'Charon's steps' for 'removing ghosts'.[64] The use of some sort of scenic *tableaux* is implied by his references to two further devices: the *hemikuklion*, 'semi-circle', located 'by the orchestra, its function to show some part of the city far off or people swimming in the sea; and the *stropheion*, a "reveal" which has heroes translated to divinity or those who have died at sea or in battle'.[65]

The impression that we derive from Pollux of a theatre equipped for scenic ostentation and sensational effects is lent substance by an account written at about the same time by Apuleius. He describes a spectacular representation (which he places in the amphitheatre at Corinth) of the 'Judgment of Paris'.

> There was a hill of wood, similar to that famous mountain which the poet Homer called Ida. It was fashioned as a lofty structure, planted with foliage and live trees, from the highest peak of which, a flowing stream ran from an artificial fountain. A few goats grazed upon the grass. . . . Then from the summit of the hill through a concealed pipe, there burst on high saffron mixed with wine, which, falling in a perfumed rain upon the goats, changed their white hair to a fairer shade of yellow. And now with the entire

theatre sweetly scented, an opening in the ground swallowed up the wooden hill.[66]

The description occurs in a fictional context, but its details are supported by the allusions noted above by Seneca the younger and Strabo to collapsible sets, and by frequent references to the use of scented sprays and saffron mists to cool and perfume the theatre.[67] Apuleius states that the hill-like structure is made of wood, and its sudden removal subsequently, evidently through traps in the stage floor, implies (to prevent the operation from becoming unwieldy) that it was composed in part of flats, painted in perspective, which could fold up or telescope into one another and sink beneath the stage. Although the coordination of both solid and painted elements (and indeed, the plumbing!) to realize Apuleius' impressive description must have required considerable engineering skill, it was certainly feasible. And it would, as Seneca noted, 'astonish the eyes of the ignorant'.

A less sophisticated way of delighting the spectators (but evidently very effective), was through the use of lavish costumes. As Horace noted (not, I think entirely facetiously) in the passage quoted earlier about tumult in the theatre, a novel colour or unusual type of cloth could win a round of applause. In this we are probably correct in discerning further evidence of a growing taste for spectacle which characterized imperial entertainments. The balance of evidence for the earlier Republican theatre, at least that derived from playtexts, suggests by contrast that no very great emphasis had been placed upon costuming.

Literary comedies based upon Greek models, or derived from Hellenistic New Comedy texts, were notionally set in Greek locations, and this conceit extended to conventions of dress; hence the generic term for such plays amongst the Romans: *fabula palliata*; plays in Greek garb. The typical costume used in such comedies (and in somewhat different form by characters of either sex) was the Greek *chiton*, a tunic over which a long cloak or *himation* was worn, which the Romans called a *pallium*, or when worn by women, a *palla*. Occasionally characters wore a shorter cloak, the *chlamys* instead of the *pallium*. This basic costume was supplemented whenever appropriate to the character or plot by military or nautical dress, foreign (non-Greek) elements, or clothes peculiar to a particular trade (such as a cook), or circumstances (such as a wedding). Despite an attempt by the fourth-century AD commentator, Aelius Donatus, to codify comic costumes according to character type, neither the plays nor the visual evidence lends much support to this, and it seems likely that his description owes more to a somewhat muddled attempt to catalogue earlier practice than to record custom in his own day.[68]

The use of masks in the Roman theatre is a much-debated subject, focusing on the question of when they were first used in comedy, and

25 Painting in the House of Casca Longus, Pompeii, depicting masked, costumed actors in a comic scene. The woman wears a full-length violet coloured tunic (the Greek *chiton*), which has a yellow *palla* (or *himation*) wrapped about it. She has bright red slippers. The young man behind her wears a white tunic and a brown *pallium*. The slave has a short fringed but sleeveless tunic and a short cloak over his left shoulder; both garments are yellow.

therefore whether the earliest comic playwrights wrote for masked actors. Certainly the pre-Roman *phlyakes* employed masks, as did the performers in the *Atellanae*. Greek actors had routinely worn them (so far as we can determine from the available evidence) from earliest times. Despite some contradictory comments by Latin writers, which are difficult to reconcile, on balance, it seem to me likely that masks were used in Roman comedy at an early date, and quite possibly from the beginning.[69]

The most complete written evidence for the nature of theatrical masks is that given by Pollux. He catalogues forty-four masks in all, ranging over comedy, tragedy, and satyr play, to provide a repertoire fully adequate for staging the plays and portions of plays which have come down to us. Although his list is thought to derive in part from a third-century BC source,[70] the masks it describes are with few exceptions comprehensively illustrated and substantiated by abundant visual evidence. Such evidence is found in artifacts ranging over several centuries from the early Hellenistic to late imperial period, and, if it indeed reflects actual stage practice, would indicate extraordinary continuity, both in the use of fixed character types and in their theatrical representation. In the case of comedy, such external evidence is supported by the plays themselves; the *dramatis personae* which are with very few exceptions recycled from play to play.

There is relatively less evidence for the costuming of tragedy in the Roman theatre. The literary references are sparse, but the possibility of greater stylization than the essentially realistic bias evident in comic costume must be allowed, particularly in light of some visual evidence. Roman tragedy seems, possibly from its beginning, to have affected an archaic and rather self-consciously 'grand' style, and this was probably extended to the stage dress. Certainly the tragedies or tragic excerpts which were performed in the imperial period appear to have been viewed as esoteric and potentially an object of ridicule. Both the manner of delivery and the costume itself were deemed grotesque by several late commentators.

From perhaps as early as the mid-fourth century BC, the tragic mask (which earlier was fashioned in a broadly realistic mien) had acquired its elongated forehead; the *onkos*, that together with its gaping mouth, gave it a decidedly unnatural aspect. What was to become the other characteristic element of tragic costume, the high platform shoe, or *cothurnus*, also appears to have been in use on the Hellenistic stage by the late second century BC, although it is not certain whether it was used by Roman actors of the Republican period.[71] The word had not originally connoted an elevated shoe per se, but only a type of footwear associated with tragedy, for which it became a synonym, as did the light slipper, *soccus*, for comedy.[72] But for the imperial period there is ample evidence, literary and visual, to indicate the use both of greatly heightened shoes and of padding, the effect of which must have been to transmogrify the form of the tragic actor into an overgrown *simulacrum* of a man, tending rather to stumble than to strut upon the stage.

26　A mosaic from Pompeii, now in the Naples Museum, depicting a typical tragic mask, with its elongated forehead, the *onkos*.

Lucian, in his mid-second century AD essay on dance, characterizes the appearance of the contemporaneous tragic actor as

A dreadful, hideous sight! A man out of all proportion, perched on platform soles, mask stretching far over his head with a great gaping mouth fit to swallow the audience. Not to mention all that padding for chest and stomach so as not to betray a slender figure. And inside, the man himself, howling away, rocking back and forth as he chants out his lines and – how awful can you get – making a song out of his disasters.

His description is echoed by an account early in the next century of the effect the tragic actor's appearance had upon an unsophisticated audience.

When the actor was silent walking on high stilts which made him over life-sized, and with a wide open mouth, they were already fearful. But when he lifted his voice, the spectators fled from the theatre as if persecuted by a demon.[73]

In the conventional nature of their costumes and the limited scope for innovation we are probably right in perceiving another reason why comedy and tragedy were relegated by the imperial theatre, with its bias towards spectacle, to infrequent revivals; their presence on stage was largely displaced by a repertoire of pantomime, mime, and various scenic extravaganzas. Indeed, Lucian himself makes an invidious comparison between earlier dramatic forms which no longer enjoyed any real vitality in the theatre, and the expressive potential of pantomime, including its visual appeal.

The aspect of a dancer now is decent and fitting, I need hardly tell you, as it is clear enough to any but the blind. The mask is as handsome as possible, suitable for the character in question, mouth closed not open, because the dancer has others to do his shouting for him.[74]

Apuleius, in his description of the ballet-like presentation of the 'Judgment of Paris' gives a vivid impression of the variety and visual splendour of the sort of costumes used in pantomime and other scenic entertainments of the imperial period. His account also suggests that the costumes and props could have a strongly emblematic quality; conveying information about the characters and plot to complement and extend that communicated through action and language:

A young man in the manner of Paris as a Phrygian shepherd, richly dressed with a barbarian cloak flowing from his shoulders, and a golden mitre on his head, pretended to tend the goats. Next to him was a fair boy, naked except for the ephebe's cloak covering his left

27 An ivory statuette of a tragic figure, found at Rieti, now in the Petit Palais Museum, Paris. The figure, thought to date from the late second century AD, depicts a female character. It has been painted blue, and the full-length belted *chiton* has patterned stripes, picked out in blue and yellow. The extensions to the feet may be pegs for mounting it to a base, or perhaps *cothurni* concealed beneath the hem of the robe.

shoulder; he had radiant blond hair, and amongst his locks were visible on either side a pair of golden wings; his caduceus and wand showed he was Mercury . . . then followed a girl with a noble countenance in the likeness of Juno; for her head was bound with a white diadem, and she carried a sceptre. Another sprang forward, whom one took for Minerva (for her head bore a shining helmet which was wreathed with a garland of olive leaves), carrying a shield and brandishing a spear as when she fights. After these there came another of surpassing beauty, representing Venus in the glory of her ambrosial colour . . . naked . . . except that a cloak of sheerest silk veiled her lovely waist . . . the colour of the goddess was of two sorts: her body was white since it had descended from heaven; her cloak was blue, since it rose from the sea . . . Castor and Pollux were boy actors, who followed Juno, their heads bearing pointed helmets covered with stars . . . the other maiden, whose armour showed her to be Minerva, was accompanied by two boys; those armed escorts of the goddess of battle, 'Terror' and 'Fear', dancing with their naked swords.'[75]

It is easy to understand how the sumptuous costumes and fanciful mythological setting conjured up by the type of scenery Apuleius describes would have appealed to a popular audience, many of whom lived otherwise drab and economically precarious existences. People who were close to starvation at home demanded and delighted in the gorgeous and gaudy pomp of the performers.[76] The provision of such entertainments was at the most basic level a manifestation of the 'bread and the circus' approach to social control, but it went beyond that to enable the audience to participate, however marginally, in imperial grandeur. The theatre buildings themselves with their imposing architecture and décor were not only places of performance and religious shrines; they were also *public monuments*, meant to awe the viewer with the power of the state and its august ruler, but simultaneously to allow him his 'moment of glory': a share in the pride and prestige of imperial achievement.[77] Thus the theatre and its entertainments provided both an opiate and a form of highly persuasive propaganda.

Writing at about the same time as Apuleius (the mid-second century AD) the politician and rhetorician Fronto observed that

The Roman people are held fast by two things above all; the corn-dole and the shows . . . the success of the government depends on amusements as much as more serious things . . . by gifts of food only those on the corn-register are humoured singly and individually, whereas through the shows the entire population is kept in good spirits.[78]

189

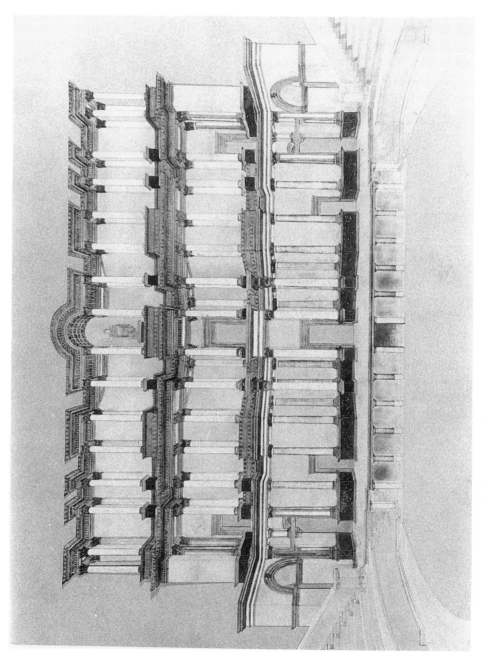

28 Reconstruction of a typical imperial theatre, that at Miletus.

Clearly the shows had an important political dimension. They were public and official ceremonies as well as still (theoretically at least), an expression of the state religion. As earlier in the Republican period, they provided an important opportunity too for the large mass of the Roman population to express its opinion if only at the most basic level of granting or withholding visible signs of its approval of the responsible public officials. The spectators also had the right to criticize the show itself. Even the emperor, having placed himself in the role of providing a service to the people when he sponsored games for their entertainment, was thereby subject to the people's traditional right to express themselves freely at the games.[79]

Of course, the emperor was particularly concerned to court popular approval through the public spectacles. Those who were anxious to maintain some constitutional or conventional limit on his power, particularly members of the Senate, tended by contrast to disparage the games and regret their excesses, even while feeling obliged to attend them. The potential for unbridled demagoguery was great. Ancient commentators frequently viewed with contempt – and identified as the most degraded elements of the population – those who did little else but frequent the shows. Such idle and marginal people were judged 'available' to whatever politician sought to mobilize them by pandering to their pleasures. Normally the emperor ensured that he was there first, with the most to offer. In the Empire private citizens were no longer allowed to give shows; the right was restricted to the emperor and the magistrates, who were tightly under his thumb. Emperors used their virtual monopoly to demonstrate that they shared popular feelings and enthusiasms, for which gesture in turn, the lower orders who comprised the greater part of the audience expressed their affection. Tacitus notes a typical example of such reciprocity in Vitellius who 'by showing himself as a spectator in the theatre, and as a partisan in the circus, courted every breath of applause from the lowest rabble'.[80]

Some emperors flattered the spectators by referring to them as 'my masters' at such events, while frequently receiving and responding favourably to special requests and petitions presented during them. Even those who disliked the games, or found them a distraction from the serious business of state, neglected them at the risk of incurring public disapproval. A portion of the population jealously guarded their right to be entertained in the approving presence of their emperor, viewed the theatres as their own, and were keenly aware of the political nature of the occasion. Indeed, in times of civil strife or political agitation, crowds surged to the theatres and circuses as the natural venues to demonstrate their power and vent their feelings.[81]

Undoubtedly the audience at the shows included disreputable and violence-prone hooligans – just as contemporary football matches are apt to do – and in the large cities of the Empire such as Rome (with a population approaching a million), Alexandria, and Antioch, these could be very numerous and troublesome. From time to time serious outbreaks of civil disorder and consequent carnage took place. But the shows' inherently political nature means that we may not always take at face value – without regard for their political position – the criticisms levelled at them by ancient observers. In so far as the emperor was subject to political opposition, it resided in the Senate, whose membership was for the most part socially conservative, jealous of their ancient privileges and honours, and hostile to any emperor who sought to limit or compromise them. Senators felt particulary threatened by a tyrannical alliance between the emperor and the plebs, which sometimes resulted in humiliation (or far worse) being inflicted upon them. The 'worst' emperors such as Caligula, Nero, Domitian, and Commodus, all persecuted the Senate while courting the adoration of the mob by providing the most memorable of lavish entertainments. Nero's reign was viewed with horror by Roman historians, but he had been intensely popular with the general populace who revered him centuries after his death.[82]

Under such circumstances it is easy to see that senators and the upper echelon of Roman society centred on them were likely to resent the games as the most public expression of rights and power being conferred upon their social inferiors and political rivals by potentially hostile emperors. The special relationship engendered by such occasions between the ruler and his most humble subjects was viewed with deep suspicion and even alarm by those who at best felt snubbed, and at worse directly endangered by it. Certain emperors in turn were quick to exploit senatorial discomfort. Occasionally they inflicted the ultimate disgrace of forcing senators to perform in shows or combats, at others they might content themselves with more subtle humiliations. Caligula provided a private theatre that had 'no seats set apart either for the Senate or for the knights, so that the seating was a jumble; men and women mixed together, and free men with slaves'. In the public theatre he exercised the same offensive disregard for social hierarchy and tradition by distributing vouchers to the mob, thereby tempting them to take over the sections reserved for the knights.[83]

Despite their undoubted importance, in time the means to provide great public spectacles suffered severely. By the third century much of imperial society was in permanent crisis: wracked by famine, devastated by the consequences of continuous wars and political upheaval, crippled by the burden of taxation, and afflicted with severe economic dislocation. After 300 AD private benefaction, except in Rome itself, had almost entirely ceased. No longer were a large body of provincial citizens able or willing to finance the entertainments or to provide for maintaining their venues. The social mobility, so marked in the first centuries of the Empire, had ceased as wealth, no longer newly accumulating from expansive wars, had now instead to be expended for defence. Trade and commerce declined, and with it prosperity and, inevitably, patronage. Changes in imperial administration, and in particular greater centralization meant that local office was now more often viewed as a burdensome responsibiity than a source of real power and prestige. With the decline of autonomy and control, local pride plummeted. The municipal councillors, the *decurions*, who had been made personally responsible for the collection (and liable for payment) of taxes, often complained bitterly of their lot, while seeking to avoid what were now seen as onerous duties with little benefit to those bearing them.[84]

Provincial support for traditional games was further eroded by the disapproval of the Church, which saw little merit in entertainments associated by venerable tradition with paganism, and considered some of them an abomination. Imperial interests could to a considerable degree ignore or at least moderate such opposition, but were only inclined to do so for their own games or those taking place at the seat of government in Rome. Tertullian had railed against the spectacles early in the third century and the theme was pursued energetically by others. In the course of the fourth century condemnation on moral grounds was joined by pragmatic economic arguments. As Ambrose warned, 'It is prodigal to waste one's wealth for the sake of popular fame. This is what is done by those who ruin their inheritance by giving circus games, or even theatrical displays, gladiatorial shows, or beast-fights.'[85]

As a consequence of such factors, by around AD 400 provincial games, which earlier had flourished throughout Italy, were infrequent and restricted to a few towns. Fifty years later the Christian polemicist Salvianus noted (evidently with mixed feelings) that despite the public's lingering desire for them, 'such shows no longer can take place because of the misery and poverty of the present age'. In 425 the Church had succeeded in having games banned on Sundays and Christian holidays.[86]

At Rome, however, the situation was fundamentaly different. Here both private and, most significantly, imperial patronage remained very strong. At the end of the Republic, the number of days set aside for *ludi* featuring scenic entertainment had been about fifty-five, having risen from around a dozen two centuries earlier in the time of Plautus. But by 354 AD some one hundred days a year were devoted to such spectacles, and this would normally have been increased further by special votive and funeral games, as well as the obligatory repetitions ('instaurations') consequent upon mishaps in any aspect of rite or presentation.[87] A law passed that same year compelling provincial senators to attend the games at Rome indicates the significance the state attached to them, while a revolt in AD 356, sparked off by the arrest of a popular charioteer, suggests their importance to the general populace.[88] Three years earlier, when Rome had been wracked by famine, vast numbers of people deemed idlers were expelled from the city (including 'professors of the liberal arts'!), but 3,000 dancing girls together with their teachers and choral accompanists were allowed to remain.[89]

If anything, in the later Roman Empire when the political ethic and imperial cult of the Principate set up by Augustus could no longer fulfil the intellectual, spiritual, or moral needs of its peoples, officials at Rome resorted ever more frequently to games, spectacles, and the debased pastimes of the circus and arena to divert an increasing troubled and restive urban population. As the alienation of society (particularly its most desperate and oppressed elements) from the Roman state increased, the games functioned as an important, if sometimes volatile means of releasing tensions. Moreover, in contrast to the decline in importance of provincial adminstrative posts, the concentration of power at Rome continued to encourage wealthy residents to seek official positions. As in centuries past, huge amounts were still spent voluntarily on games by aspiring candidates, as well as by those who having achieved office were legally obliged to provide them.[90] Even after membership in the Senate and the position of consul had become an honour empty of power, prestige lingered about them and their attendant pomp and ceremony. Moreover, after Rome ceased to be an imperial residence in the fourth century, it again became possible for local officials to enhance their prestige by providing and refurbishing public buildings, including the theatres; a privilege previously reserved to the emperors.[91]

Christian polemicists saw both in the attitude of the rulers that at all costs the shows must go on, and in the veritable obsession with such diversions by the general population, irrefutable evidence of the moral collapse of paganism and its approaching destruction. Yet even in the Christian community, when the games were on the churches were deserted. Later, with barbarians literally at their gates, the public still mobbed the spectacles.[92] In its resentment the Church conceived a hatred and horror of the theatre which endured for centuries, was reactivated in the Renaissance, and indeed, in some circles is still evident today.

For Christian leaders the games were an affront and annoyance, and morally repugnant; the pagan religion, however, was a present danger, even potentially a threat to survival. In the course of the fourth century, under pressure from the Church measures of increasing severity were taken to suppress pagan cults and practices. Imperial decrees banned public worship of the pagan deities in AD 346, and a decade later, the temples were closed. The temple revenues were confiscated in 364, and those supporting the pagan cults in 382. In 391 the cults themselves were totally banned, and four years later the great Roman families were forced to convert (some with great reluctance) to Christianity. In 408 the temples and other buildings associated with the old religion were ordered to be put to secular use; many of them were already badly deteriorated from neglect. Nevertheless, between 393 and 402, under the Emperors Honorius and Arcadius, the theatre of Pompey (which was in a dangerous condition) was comprehensively restored and refurbished. In 404 Honorius was able to use it for games celebrating a consulate and victory over the Goths.[93]

Despite the systematic suppression of paganism, throughout the fourth and fifth centuries AD the spectacles continued, their variety and scale still impressive. In 342 Constantius II, though a Christian, ordered that certain pagan temples be restored so that the spectacles traditionally associated with them could be maintained.[94] At a time when imperial coffers were depleted by the refusal of the senatorial class to bear its share of financial obligations, its members were still content to expend vast sums on public games. In 384 a law was passed to prevent senators of modest means from bankrupting themselves in imitation of wealthier colleagues. Nevertheless, the former Consul (and prominent pagan scholar) Symmachus gave 2,000 pounds of gold for his son's games of 401, and another senator, Maximus, spent double that sum a few years later.[95]

Although extensive descriptions and details of performances are lacking, the general state of play is tolerably clear. What it conveys is a picture not of decisive change but rather of remarkable continuity from earlier epochs. Despite the ascendancy of a new religion, and massive social and political upheaval, at the end of antiquity we find similar genres, the same mixture of sophistication and vulgarity, and the same conjunction of diverse entertainments which were first evident in Roman theatrical practice seven centuries before. In the first century AD Apuleius listed mimes and dancers, comic and tragic performers, tightrope-walkers and magicians; the same variety of holiday entertainments which first shaped the taste of the Roman audience and gave form to its theatre when Plautus and Terence (and their predecessors) had produced their plays in the midst of competing fairground entertainments.[96]

Much later, at the beginning of the fifth century, Claudian describes scenic celebrations which provide a veritable playbill of traditional Roman theatrical fare.

[Following an account of wild beast hunts] . . . Nor let gentler games lack in our delights: the jester who makes us laugh with his happy wit; the mime whose language is in his nods and gestures; the musician who sets the *tibia* pulsating with his breath, and the lyre, with his fingers; the slippered comedian with whom the stage

echoes; or the tragedian raised on his loftier boots . . . or acrobats
who throw themselves like birds through the air and build a
swiftly rising pyramid with their entwined bodies.

And, lest we think that the scenic display and technical virtuosity
referred to by Seneca centuries earlier has lapsed, he continues,

> Let the counterweights be removed and the mobile *pegma* descend,
> and on the lofty stage let men circle like a chorus, scattering flames;
> let Vulcan mould balls of flame to roll harmlessly over the panels
> and swift flames play about the painted beams, and a tame fire, not
> allowed to rest, roam amongst the untouched towers . . .[97]

In AD 410, a decade after the festivities described by Claudian, Rome
was attacked by a raiding party of Visigoths under Alaric, and sacked
for three days. Despite widespread looting, there was no massacre and
only limited damage to the fabric of the city. But the shock reverberated
throughout the Empire, East and West, with the awesome realization
that Rome, which 'for more than a thousand years had been – and still
was – the head of the civilized world and its cultural capital . . . had
fallen to a horde of illiterate barbarians from the back of beyond'.[98] With
the capital of the Western Empire located in Ravenna after AD 404,
Rome came to be dominated for many years by a small circle of
senatorial families who took the initiative in maintaining the great civic
institutions, restoring public monuments, and asserting their position as
public patrons and benefactors by sponsoring spectacles.[99]

In 476 the last Roman Emperor of the West, Romulus Augustulus,
was deposed by the German mercenary leader Odoacer, who pro-
claimed himself King of Italy, sent Romulus to live on a pension in
Campania, and proceeded to stage a great variety of entertainments at
Rome. Under his successor (and murderer) Theodoric the Ostrogoth,
who ruled from AD 493, the supremacy of the Eastern emperor was
recognized and strenuous attempts were made to preserve imperial
administration, practices, and institutions, including the customary
scenic entertainments. Although for a period under Odoacer the office of
consul had lapsed, it was eventually renewed and continued under
Theodoric, probably at the insistence of a few Roman aristocratic
families for whom its only remaining official duty, that of providing
lavish games, was essential to maintain their prestige in the traditional
manner. With the king and court at Ravenna, the old patrician order
continued to enjoy considerable autonomy at Rome. Indeed, the state
seems to have encouraged competitive personal patronage among the
aristocracy.[100]

The tradition of private sponsorship for building and repairs,
however, appears now to have dwindled, and its burden fell predominantly upon the central administration, which also provided its

own games from time to time. The last case on record of private benefaction for a public building is the comprehensive repair of Pompey's theatre carried out by a member of an old senatorial family around AD 500. In that year Theodoric gave lavish games at Rome to celebrate the anniversary of his rule, and further games took place thereafter with some frequency, notable examples occurring in 519 and 522.[101]

Theodoric and his administrators were concerned (so far as their means allowed) to show themselves worthy of the classical legacy for which they had now become the responsible – if somewhat unlikely – heirs. In addition to a programme of structural repairs to the great antique edifices, their sponsorship of games served (as they had under the emperors before them) both as useful diversion and as an important ceremonial display of power and prestige. Theodoric's chancellor, the Roman Senator Cassiodorus, used public funds to sponsor the mimes and pantomimes while (also traditionally) attempting to curb the violent disorders which broke out from time to time among their partisan supporters. He recorded with pride that the opulence of the official games amazed even the ambassador from the Byzantine court of Constantinople. Early in the sixth century AD, Cassiodorus visited the theatre of Pompey, which had now been standing for over half a millennium, and described with admiration its 'caves vaulted with hanging stones, so cleverly joined into beautiful shapes that they resemble more the grottoes of a huge mountain than anything wrought by human hand'.[102]

The Ostrogoths were not alone amongst the barbarians in continuing to favour traditional Roman entertainments. During the century in which the Vandals ruled North Africa before it was reconquered by the Byzantine forces in 533, the population was able, as before, 'to pass their time . . . in theatres and hippodromes' and in the amphitheatres as well.[103] Meanwhile in the East, the games continued to fulfil their pragmatic and ceremonial function, although they were increasingly subject to careful regulation, particularly under Justinian. By as early as AD 400 gladiatorial shows seem to have disappeared throughout the Empire (probably due in large part to Christian opposition), and the animal hunts, if not wholly eliminated, were certainly rare after 500.[104] Moreover,

> it was not prudent for a private citizen, however rich, to make the same sort of bid for popular favour in Constantinople as was customary in Rome. No emperor would tolerate that sort of competition . . . unlike the Ostrogothic kings, successive eastern governments did their best to discourage lavish private expenditure on public entertainments.[105]

The last consul in the West served in 534, when the office was suspended by Justinian. The last citizen consul in the East held office in

541, and thereafter, during the remaining twenty-five years of Justinian's reign, no further consuls were appointed, nor did he again take the office himself. Consequently there were no consular games; indeed, continuous warfare on all fronts left less money for games of any type. In fact, Justinian had ordered the public theatres closed in 526, although this may have been only a temporary measure, and would have been valid in Italy only after most of it was reconquered by him in the Gothic wars between 535 and 540.[106]

This struggle (which was not finally resolved until 553) greatly impoverished Italy, and destroyed the wealth of its great landowning families. Thereafter the ancient senatorial class of Rome disappears from history, together we surmise with the last of its festive patronage.[107] The last recorded games at Rome were given in 549 by King Totila to celebrate his brief success in restoring Ostrogothic power in the city after it had earlier fallen to Justinian's forces, who in turn retook it in 552. Subsequently, during its brief authority,

> the Byzantine administration based in Ravenna, seems to have been very little interested in providing spectacles for the people of Italy, which for the first time since the establishment of the Empire was treated by emperors as a mere province, and a beleaguered one at that.[108]

In any case, at Rome the formal presentation of theatre appears certainly to have ceased – just short of a thousand years from the date recorded for its birth – with the occupation of Italy by the Lombards from 568 and the final fading of Byzantine power in the West.

In the Eastern Empire, following Justinian's death in 565, the new Emperor, Justin II, immediately revived the consularship as an office held by himself, a practice which was followed by his successors until 642. This evidently was a deeply popular measure, perhaps in large part because it may have allowed the vestiges of traditional games to continue. In general, however, formal theatrical activity, including the mimes and pantomimes, appears to have withered, and was officially banned by the Trullan Council in 692.[109]

POSTLUDE

A THEATRE IN SEARCH OF AN AUDIENCE

The legacy of the Roman theatre is a subject worthy in itself of several extensive studies. The sketch appended here is intended only to indicate its significance and point to some of its ramifications. Although as in so many areas, the heritage of the Greeks has tended to overshadow – at least in the popular conception of things – that of the Romans, in fact the modern theatre as formulated and practised since the Renaissance owes far more in virtually all its manifestations to Roman custom and achievement than to Greek. Our critical theory, our drama, and our physical theatre are hugely in its debt.

During the period of broad cultural decline and economic and political disruption which characterized the early medieval period, theatre, in the forms which had been so popular in antiquity, withered away. There were no new theatre buildings, and the great edifices surviving from antiquity were despoiled, or put to other uses; adapted as shops and dwellings or occasionally, churches.[1]

These impressive physical remnants embodied a type of theatrical presentation which no longer took place, and thus isolated, in time their original function was all but forgotten, together with any true understanding of the nature and different varieties of dramatic art itself. Of course in an abstract sense the ancient theatre survived. The remnant of its aesthetic theory and a sampling of its drama existed in written form, and once recovered and reconstituted could provide the basis for a renewed stagecraft. But the vital element of a living art – the audience itself – had first through a lengthy and convoluted process to be identified, attracted back, and conditioned to perform its essential function; to prompt and respond once again to the particular methods of an ancient art: to invigorate and in turn be stimulated by a revitalized theatre.

The end of the tradition of great public entertainments did not mean that theatrical art, particularly in its more humble forms, vanished entirely. The same innate human impulse towards mimetic expression which had originally engendered the Roman theatre continued to find

199

an outlet in the activity of strolling players, jesters, mimes, and mountebanks, whose existence in the early medieval period is documented throughout Europe. Italy seems in particular to have been noted for its mimes and actors, which impressionable students from the north were warned to avoid.[2]

By its nature, such activity left little concrete evidence behind, although in the mid-fifteenth century when *commedia dell'arte* first emerges from the mists (already it seems in a fairly well-developed form) its striking resemblance to earlier popular drama makes it difficult indeed to doubt the survival of an ancient craft. The masked *commedia* performers presented unscripted farces whose stock characters, type of humour, dramatic form, and style of presentation are all vividly reminiscent both of Roman plays themselves and their Atellane precursors. As noted earlier, the *Atellanae* undoubtedly survived well into the imperial period, when they may have merged into or become one category of mime. As the most 'rough and ready' of entertainments, they were ideally suited to survive as hardy perennials when more formal and sumptuous types of theatre withered and died. Alternatively, they may have been transplanted back into Italy by migrating mime actors after the fall of Constantinople in 1453. In any case by the seventeenth century *commedia* had spread throughout much of Europe (where it would flourish in its own right for almost two centuries), and thereafter was grafted by playwrights into comic works which would preserve many of its characteristics in permanent form.

The marked affinity between *commedia* and ancient farce may indicate (not illogically) that medieval subject matter and performance was directly nourished by a centuries-old tradition of popular theatre as actors pragmatically drew upon the material they knew and which audiences had long enjoyed. A related possibility is that *commedia* evolved early in the Renaissance from a more erudite and self-conscious attempt to revive the plays of Plautus and Terence, which eventually devolved into improvisation and in turn generated a great many *scenari* still stylistically similar to Roman comedy, but newly created to supply a more varied repertoire.[3] Manuscripts of Terence were known (however obscurely) throughout the Middle Ages, and continued to be copied and read. In 1429 twelve newly discovered plays by Plautus were brought to Rome, and between 1470 and 1518 printed editions – some of them illustrated – were published of all the extant Roman drama. By 1600 Terence alone had appeared in almost 450 complete editions throughout Europe.

By 1500 several academic societies existed in Italy which were devoted to the production of plays and to scholarly investigation of staging technique and theatre architecture. The most important of these was the Roman Academy founded by Julius Pomponius Laetus; a circle

29 Illumination from the fourteenth-century *Térence des Ducs* in the Bibliothèque de
l'Arsenal, Paris. The actors (*joculatores*) are dressed like medieval mimes, the figure
reading the text resembles the stage manager of contemporaneous religious plays,
and the booth in which he sits is like a medieval 'mansion'. The spectators (*populus
Romanus*) cluster about in an architecturally undefined circle, the *theatrum*.

201

of learned and aristocratic humanists who (though engulfed from time to time in controversy) enjoyed influential patronage, and undertook to determine an authentic method of staging. Their chief authority in this was Vitruvius' architectural handbook, *De Architectura*, which had been rediscovered in 1414, and was first published in 1486 with the assistance of Laetus and the Academy. The Roman academy took care to establish good critical texts, and in their Latin productions of Plautus, Terence, and Seneca drew upon the best scholarship of the day.[4] Comedies were also regularly performed in Latin at such Italian courts as Ferrara, Florence, Mantua, and Urbino during the fifteenth century. A significant milestone was the first presentation of a Roman comedy in translation, the *Menaechmi* of Plautus performed in Italian in 1486 at the ducal court of Ercole I D'Este at Ferrara. Whereas previously the study and presentation of Roman drama had been the elitist preserve of scholars, the way was now open for its exploitation as vernacular entertainment. An audience of over 10,000 attended the *Menaechmi* production, which was presented as a great popular celebration. Thus two vital elements – the identification of drama as a independent type of literature, and the appreciation of it as a form of art and of entertainment – were directly derived from Roman theatrical heritage. Further productions followed, both of Plautus and Terence. By 1500 several plays were being performed each year, and the custom continued under Alfonso, who became Duke in 1505.[5]

Three years later, a second milestone was passed at Ferrara with the first documented production of an original comedy in Italian. Encouraged by the Duke's brother, Ippolito, Lodovico Ariosto wrote and produced *La Cassaria*, set in contemporary Italy, but with a plot modelled generally on Plautus and Terence, and including such figures as servants, old men, and a pimp; all direct descendants of Roman comic characters. Ariosto soon followed it with similarly indebted works such as *I Suppositi* and *La Lena*. The rebirth of dramatic composition in Italy is directly based on Roman precedent and models. The ancient theatre was nurturing a new audience for dramatic art.[6]

While theatrical content – the plays themselves – were being reconstituted in the Italian courts, elsewhere scholars were at work on form; trying to determine an authentic format for presenting the plays. In the preface to the 1486 edition of Vitruvius, dedicated to the Roman Cardinal Riario who had served as patron to their activities, the Roman Academy appealed to the Cardinal to crown his career with the construction of a permanent theatre in Rome; the first since antiquity.[7] Although the invitation was not acted upon, it indicates the keen scholarly interest which Vitruvius' written descriptions of ancient theatre architecture had engendered. Illustrated editions of Terence published at the same time, the end of the fifteenth century, may reflect

the increased understanding that grew out of the practical experiments
which Laetus in Rome and the humanists at the Ferrara court
conducted. A series of woodcuts printed in 1493 were used to illustrate
the Terentian texts, and were commissioned by a scholar, Jodocus
Badius Ascensius, who is thought to have been directly acquainted with
the Ferrara productions, and possibly with those at Rome as well.[8] They
show a platform stage, in front of a continuous facade arcaded to form
doors with signs above them indicating to which character each 'house'
belongs. In contrast to the medieval practice of using free-standing and
separate scenic mansions, these designs clearly evoke the unified
architectural setting used by the Romans.

Illustrated editions of Vitruvius were published in 1511, 1521, and
subsequently, and these allow us to chart the process by which,
gradually, scholars pieced together a tentative understanding of Roman

30 One of the extensive series of woodcuts illustrating the edition of Terence
published at Lyon in 1493. The scene (lines 787–854 from the *Adelphoe*), is shown
taking place in front of a continuous scenic facade with signs over the doors to
indicate the houses of Micio, Demea, Hegio, Sostrata, and Sannio.

203

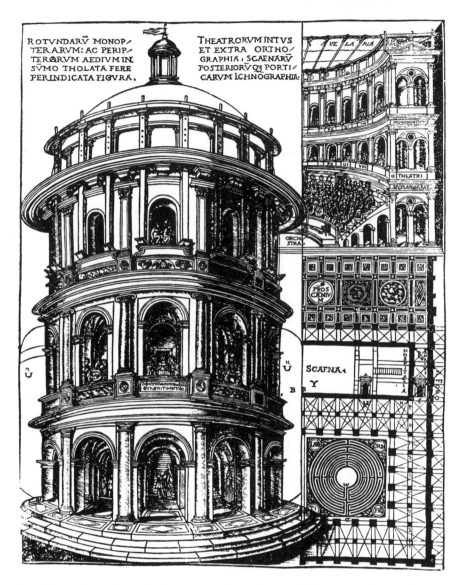

31 Illustration from the first vernacular edition of Vitruvius' *De Architectura*, published by Cesare Cesariano in 1521. Although he uses much Roman theatrical terminology (*orchestra, velaria, podium, scaena*, etc.) Cesariano's commentary betrays a very limited understanding of actual practice.

theatre architecture and stagecraft. By the end of the seventeenth century more than thirty editions had appeared in Europe, together with extensive commentaries, interpretations, and treatises based on the work. The problem of understanding and reconciling Vitruvius' references to stage architecture and scene design (which was never fully resolved) became the subject of extensive speculation and practical investigation which were to dominate the European theatre for many years and, to a great extent, determine its future. Two examples may serve to illustrate each of the major areas – architectural and scenic – in which such work took place.

In 1513 the Roman Academy was responsible for the construction of a theatre on the Campidoglio in Rome, the site of the Ancient Capitol. It was built as part of the elaborate festivities to celebrate the granting of Roman citizenship to Giuliano and Lorenzo de'Medici, the brother and nephew of the recently elected Pope Leo X; the event symbolically conceived as a marriage between Florence and Rome. Plautus' *Poenulus* was exquisitely performed in Latin by the Academy's pupils, and was preceded by extensive allegorical presentations employed to highlight the symbolic significance of the occasion. The festival was heralded as marking the rebirth of a golden age and, significantly, its patrons saw the presentation of classical Roman drama as an integral part of an essentially political celebration: the ancient *ludi theatrales* were to live again. Aware of the splendour associated with such occasions in antiquity, the sponsors deliberately undertook to create a sumptuous reconstruction of a Roman theatre, drawing upon such factual evidence as they could, to build a 'great wooden theatre which contemporaries regard as the eighth wonder of the world'.[9]

The building was similar to the depictions seen in the Terence illustrations and, like them, probably was inspired by the Academy's practical experiments and scrutiny of Vitruvius. The rectangular structure, approximately 38 metres long and 31 metres wide, had seven tiers of seats on three sides, while on the fourth was located a scenic facade decorated with architectural and painted embellishment, and broken by five doors. In front of it was a raised stage with an adjacent area set aside for dignitaries, and called an 'orchestra'. The open area in the middle of the structure was occupied by benches; the building (covered by a blue, white, and green *velarium*) accommodated some 3,000 spectators. In all this we can discern a thoroughgoing attempt to recreate ancient theatre architecture as accurately as possible, while evoking as well something of the political and celebratory qualities of Roman practice.[10]

A very different approach had been taken only shortly before, in the 1508 production of Ariosto's *La Cassaria* at Ferrara. For the first time, we have a record of the use of a *perspective* stage setting, created by the painter Pellegrino da Udine. Using the combination of a painted backdrop together with flats set up as angle wings to suggest three-dimensional buildings, the stage was arranged with great skill to depict a cityscape. Its designer had adapted to theatrical use the illusionistic perspective technique which painters had been investigating since Brunelleschi and others laid out its theoretical basis in the previous century. This innovation marked an entirely new era in theatre history, the modern illusionistic stage, yet at the same time was a further expression of the desire to understand Vitruvius – in particular his description of the three types of scenery used on the Roman stage – and to apply this to contemporary practice.

The fascination with perspective settings was so great that soon noble courts everywhere demanded them from the artists in their service, together, of course, with the plays which they illustrated. Theatrical activity flourished, but it was fundamentally altered from previous experiments by being in the thrall now of pictorial illusion. Following (whether consciously or not) in the tradition of its Roman ancestors, as far as the courtly audience was concerned, the bigger the spectacle, the better the 'show'. As one artist, Sebastiano Serlio described it,

> Among all things made by the hand of man, few in my opinion bring greater satisfaction to the spirit than the unveiling to our view of a stage setting. There the art of perspective gives a thousand marvels.

In Book Two (1545) of his work, *De Architettura*, which he conceived as an elaboration of Vitruvius, Serlio, who had worked as a court painter, scenic artist, and archaeologist, provided in effect a practical handbook of stagecraft which summed up contemporaneous Italian scenic activity. It proved immensely popular and influential, helping promote and establish practices which were to dominate scenic design throughout Europe for two centuries.

In its text and illustrations Serlio described and showed how to set up perspective flats; angle wings, on a raked stage so as to create an illusionistic setting. Because no permanent theatres had yet been built, he assumed that a temporary stage would be erected in a rectangular hall, yet he imitated ancient practice by placing a semi-circular orchestra and auditorium within such a hall, even though this arrangement was not the best for appreciating the optical illusion of the perspective flats.[11] Taking his cue again from Vitruvius, Serlio produced illustrations for his own versions of the three types of scenery: comic, tragic, and satyric, formed of sets of angle wings and a backdrop, and these (with usually only variations in detail) provided for decades the standard subjects and format for most theatrical scenery.

The courtly entertainments emphasized illusionistic spectacle, which foreshadowed the stage as a three-dimensional *picture*, subject to the rules of painting. The actual Roman theatre had been quite different: an open stage, placed in front of the elaborately ornamented facade of the *scaenae frons* with its doors. Thus the Roman theatre had, paradoxically,

32   The *Teatro Olimpico*, Vicenza, designed by Andrea Palladio, completed in 1584. A wide stage extends before the ornate *scaenae frons*. In front is an elliptical orchestral area and tiered seats forming an auditorium. Although Palladio, who had studied Roman theatre remains, had to place his structure within a rectangular building, this is disguised by the curved loggia.

inspired two initially incompatible lines of development. While the impulse towards ever greater spectacle dominated stage practice in the courts, elsewhere scholars had continued to follow a different route: trying to determine what ancient theatre architecture had actually been like.

In fact 'Renaissance theorists and architects were never able to determine the relationship between the *scaenae frons* and the perspective set, and instead chose to develop one or the other'.[12] In 1585 the *Teatro Olimpico* at Vicenza, which had been designed by Andrea Palladio and completed after his death by Vincenzo Scamozzi, was opened with a lavish production of Sophocles' *Oedipus Rex*. The theatre survives to this day. Its stage and auditorium, which closely approximated actual Roman practice, particularly in the creation of an ornamental *scaenae frons*, represents the final achievement of the attempts begun a century earlier to recreate Roman theatrical architecture.[13] Palladio had himself carried out extensive archaeological investigations of Roman theatre sites and, based on such work, provided the illustrations for the most scholarly edition yet of Vitruvius, published by Daniel Barbaro in 1556. But his theatre also attests to the confusion that existed in the minds of those trying to understand Roman architectural and scenic practice. Within its five doorways (three in the middle of the facade, and one located in the walls at either side) and largely obscured by the *scaenae frons*, Scamozzi had rather incongruously placed perspective vistas (formed of Serlian angle wings) on a steeply raked stage. Although the audience can see them, the sightlines make them completely impractical areas of performance. Instead of creating a truly illusionistic three-dimensional setting, they serve as a sort of secondary backdrop to that provided by the architectural facade itself.[14] The *Teatro Olimpio* is, therefore, something of a hybrid; a curious combination of a Roman non-illusionistic architectural format and the Serlian theatre of pictorial representation.

A solution to the impasse between the conflicting demands of perspective scenery and architecture, each claiming authentic Roman antecedents, finally came with an ingenious compromise first realized in permanent form at the beginning of the seventeenth century, and firmly establishing the shape of things to come, theatrically speaking, virtually to the present day. In the surviving *Teatro Farnese* of Parma, built for Duke Ranuccio I in 1618, the architect and engineer Giovanni Aleotti in effect took the large central doorway of Palladio's *Olimpico* facade, and *opened it up* to reveal the scenery behind it. The proscenium arch, the modern picture-frame theatre, was the result. Like most such frames to be built over the next three and a half centuries, it was embellished on either side with ornamentation (columns and statues) that recall both Palladio's facade and, in turn his model, the Roman *scaenae frons*.

33 The *scaenae frons* of the *Teatro Olimpico*, showing the original Serlian style angle wings placed within the doorways by Vicenzo Scamozzi who completed the theatre. The opening of the central doorway is an architectural precursor of the proscenium arch.

34   The *Teatro Farnese*, Parma, completed by Giovanni Aleotti in 1618. With its 'picture frame' scenic stage and horseshoe-shaped auditorium (both derived, albeit indirectly, from ancient Roman practice) it is the earliest example of the basic architectural form of the modern theatre.

Henceforth (until the reforms of the twentieth century) the scenery and most of the stage action are confined behind the frame, separated from the audience, to create a world of scenic fantasy and imagination. To further enhance the illusion Aleotti is credited with introducing a system of flat wings which slid on and off the stage in grooves. Simply by placing successive flats in the grooves, the setting could be changed as often as desired, the whole operation effectively masked by the proscenium arch. This final innovation, which dominated European and later American stage practice until the modern era, was itself based upon an interpretation of Servius' somewhat obscure description of Roman sliding panels, the *scaenae ductiles*.[15] Thus, through a process of research, experiment, misunderstanding, and compromise, Roman theatrical remnants were painstakingly reassembled to create a curious amalgamation: the architecture and scenic practice of the post-Renaissance theatre. Once reconstituted, they attracted and held an audience enthralled.

A somewhat similar process determined the nature of dramatic theory. As noted earlier, the very idea of drama was inspired by the Roman legacy, and this extended to considerations of length, the division into acts, the use of a chorus, the conception of character, the structure of dramatic action, and the use of such devices as prologues, asides, and soliloquies. Classical critical theory was dominated at first not by Aristotle but by the Roman, Horace, with such early works as Marco Girolamo Vida's *De Arte Poetica* of 1527 and Bernardino Daniello's *La Poetica* ten years later greatly in his debt. Later, after Aristotle's *Poetics* was published in Latin, and followed by a critical edition in 1548, the precepts of Horace and Aristotle were 'systematically compared and combined until they were, in the popular mind at least, virtually indistinguishable'.[16] It is arguable that in time the impulse toward independent dramatic creation suffered under the continuing prescriptive pressure of a critical theory derived from a distant theatre; initially however, such theory, and the ancient plays themselves, were invaluable in engendering dramatic composition.

As noted, it was above all the Roman drama which inspired first presentation, and later emulation, in a pattern that was first seen in Italy but repeated later throughout Europe. Polonius in *Hamlet* (Act 2, Scene 2) notes that 'Seneca cannot be too heavy nor Plautus too light' for the players, and indeed, just as much Renaissance comedy took its model from Plautus, so Seneca provided the example and stimulus for tragedy. About twenty years after the first production of Plautus in Italian at Ferarra in 1486 we hear of vernacular performances of Seneca; similarly, the 1508 *La Cassaria* of Ariosto, modelled on Plautus, is followed in 1541 by the Seneca-based *Orbecche* of Giraldi Cinthio; the first production of an Italian tragedy. The same progression occurs slightly

211

later in France and in Britain: Nicholas Udall's *Ralph Roister-Doister*, of 1553, inspired by Plautus and the first full-scale comedy in English, is followed in 1561 by the earliest English tragedy, Sackville and Norton's *Gorboduc*, heavily influenced by Seneca.[17]

As early as the beginning of the fourteenth century a commentary had been written on Seneca by Nicolas Treveth; after the appearance of Greek plays late in the next century, controversy raged for a while over whether tragedy should be modelled on Greek or Roman example; the choice eventually fell decisively on Seneca. On first consideration this may seem odd. The nine tragedies of Seneca, based loosely on Greek orginals, date from the first half of the first century AD.[18] The general consensus of scholars (which is however hotly debated) is that they were written for recitation and not intended to be staged.[19] Although such problematic elements as unannounced changes of setting, sudden entries and exits, dumb-shows, and the like do not absolutely preclude ancient staging (the plays have, after all been presented in the modern period, and with considerable success) they do argue against it. Unlike surviving specimens of Greek tragedy, and fragments of earlier Roman works, there are no implicit stage directions, and very little felt sense of practical dramaturgy. 'Among the binding forces are the complex systems of imagery that pervade the plays, the recurrent patterns of behaviour and character, the ironic interplay between the audience's knowledge and the chorus's half-knowledge of what is happening.'[20] Seneca aims not at subtle (or consistent) character delineation and still less at effective stage action, but at immediate (sometimes overheated or forced) rhetorical impact, and the excitement of raw emotion through lurid descriptive passages. As Eliot observes, 'In the plays of Seneca, the drama is all in the word, and the word has no further reality behind it. His characters all seem to speak with the same voice, and at the top of it'.[21]

And yet, these and other qualities evidently appealed to Renaissance audiences having little theatrical experience to temper their assessment. Indeed, no Latin author was more highly esteemed. The sensational violence and melodramatic horror, the prevalence of ghosts and black magic, the evocation of direst woe and catastrophe, and even the recourse to rant and bombast; these elements compelled attention and excited first admiration and then widespread imitation. Moreover, the dark mixture of court intrigue, deception, and pervasive anxiety which Seneca's troubled works distil from the age of Nero[22] was not altogether foreign nor too exotic for contemporary Renaissance taste. His themes and philosophy were readily intelligible; 'there are no conflicts, except the conflict of passion, temper, or appetite with the external duties';[23] while at times he rises to moments of genuine emotion, poetic beauty, or thrilling drama. Moreover he wrote in accessible Latin and followed a straightforward five-act format which was easy to emulate.

The first English translation of Seneca apppeared in 1559, and the Elizabethan stage was soon strewn with his demons, tyrants, fustian, and corpses. If Seneca-inspired 'revenge tragedy' spawned such flawed offspring as *Titus Andronicus*, it also deeply influenced *Richard III* and left more than its mark on *Hamlet*.[24] Nor was his influence felt only in 'blood and thunder', in violent action and passionate rhetoric; his ideas absolutely permeate Elizabethan drama and decisively colour its mood and morality. His impact on the great dramatic works of that age was fundamental and, through it, has never ceased to influence our own.

Amongst the greatest ironies of a theatrical history fraught with paradox are these: that modern comedy was fashioned in the image of the earliest of all Latin authors, the primitive play-maker Plautus; that modern theatre architecture arose from attempts to copy Roman practice but resulted in a form quite unknown in antiquity; and that the most profound influence upon modern tragedy was exercised by works which were probably never performed on the ancient stage.

NOTES

Except as indicated, all references to ancient authors are based on the standard editions of individual works, or collections of fragments. Readers unfamiliar with the titles of ancient works indicated in abbreviated form in the notes may readily identify them by referring to the list of authors and their extant writings found at the beginning of the *Oxford Classical Dictionary* (2nd edn, 1970).

1 AN AUDIENCE IN SEARCH OF A THEATRE

1 Livy, *Ab Urbe Condita*, 7.2. records the event for the year 364–3 BC The passage is discussed below.
2 Aristotle, *Poetics*, 4 (1448 b).
3 Horace, *Epist.* 2.1.139 ff. The law forbidding libel was included in the Twelve Tables; cf. Cicero, *De Rep.*, 4.10.12.
4 Livy, 7.2.4–8.
5 Tibullus, 2.1.50–6.
6 Vergil, *Georg.*, 2.380.
7 Aristotle, *Poetics*, 4. (1449 a).
8 See M. Bieber, *History of the Greek and Roman Theatre*, 2nd edn (Princeton, 1961) p. 38 ff. for a discussion of the early form and evolution of Greek comedy.
9 Livy, 7.2.
10 The scholiast to Juvenal, *Satires*, 3.174 ff. notes the practice. 'Amongst the ancients, an afterpiece was introduced at the end of the play which was amusing, and the laughter of this entertainment expunged the sadness and tears caused by the tragedy.'
  Cicero refers to the habit in his own day of introducing a mime at the end of the performance, whereas earlier, the *Atellanae* served the same purpose. Cicero, *Epist. ad Fam.*, 9.16.7; 'After the *Oenomaus* of Accius you have introduced not, as was the custom, an Atellan farce, but, as it is now done, a mime.' There are a number of other references to the practice, e.g. Suetonius, *Tiberius*, 45; *Domitianus*, 10.
11 The information we have about these characters is derived for the most part from descriptions of the later literary *Atellanae*, as well as titles and a few framents from some of them. There is a graphic reference to Manducus in Plautus' *Rudens*, 535–6, when Labrax, soaked to the skin, jokes about 'hiring myself out to a fair as Manducus . . . because of the marvellous way I gnash my teeth'.
12 See Gordon Williams on this vast topic in, *Change and Decline* (Berkeley, 1978) particularly chapter 3, 'The Dominance of Greek Culture'.

13 The theatrical activity in southern Italy is documented and discussed *inter alia* in T. B. L. Webster, *Greek Theatre Production* (London, 1970) G. Sifakis, *Studies in the History of Hellenistic Drama*. (London, 1967) and M. Gigante, *Rintone e il Teatro in Magna Graecia* (Naples, 1971). For an excellent recent survey of the archaeological evidence of southern Italian theatres, see K. Mitens, *Teatri Greci e Teatri Ispirati all' Architettura Greca in Sicilia e nell'Italia Meridionale c. 350–50 a.c.* (Rome, 1988). The examples of depictions of Greek drama found on southern Italian vases are included in A. D. Trendall and T. B. L. Webster, *Illustrations of Greek Drama* (London, 1971).

14 The vases are illustrated and their subject matter discussed at length in Bieber, *op. cit.*, chapter 10. A comprehensive treatment is provided by A. D. Trendall, *Phlyax Vases* (London, 1967). Oliver Taplin has suggested that the subject matter depicted on some of the vases may actually be directly based on Athenian fifth-century Old Comedy, and 'that Aristophanes' plays . . . were being performed in Apulia 50 years and more after the first performance'. 'Phallology, Phlyakes, Iconography and Aristophanes', *Cambridge Philological Society Proceedings*, 33 (1987), 96–104.

15 Varro, LL 5,55.

16 Janos Szilágyi has written a very persuasive article arguing for the existence of Etruscan satyric drama, and for linking it with a later tradition of Roman satire. 'Impletae modis saturae', *Prospettiva* 24 (1981), 2–23.

17 'Impletas modis saturas descripto iam ad tibicinem cantu, motuque cogruenti peragebant.' An emendation of *saturas* to *saturae* is sometimes suggested. For a fuller discussion see the article cited in the previous note.

18 Diomedes, *Ars Gramm.* 3 (GL 1.485K); Evanthius, *de Fabula*, 2.5. The translations are from W. Beare, *The Roman Stage*, 3rd edn (London, 1968), who discusses the problem, (reaching a different conclusion), pp. 17–19.

19 Appian, *Pun.*, 66.; Dionysius Halicarnassus 7.70–3, in C. Jacoby, *Fragmente der griechischen Historiker*, 3 C (1969), 865–9 which contains both Fabius' account and Dionysius' commentary. An account of the evidence and argument for a satyr drama derived from Etruscan practice, is in T. P. Wiseman, 'Satyrs in Rome?', *Journal of Roman Studies* 78 (1988), 1–13. Wiseman also makes use of the article by Szilágyi, already noted.

20 Livy, 7.2.

21 *ibid.*

22 *ibid.*, 1.56.1; Pliny, *Nat. Hist.*, 35.154. See also the fine discussion of this subject by G. Alföldy, *The Social History of Rome*, rev. edn, trans. D. Braund and F. Pollock (London, 1988), pp. 5–19.

23 Alföldy, *op. cit.*, p. 28.

24 Williams, *Change and Decline*, p. 103.

25 In 307 BC, 7,000 Samnites were sold as a single group (Livy, *op. cit.*, 9.42.8); in 262 some 25,000 inhabitants of Agrigentum, and in 254, 13,000 prisoners at Panormus came onto the market (Diodorus Siculus 23.9.11 and 18.5).

26 For a provocative discussion of the nature of political life at this time, and particularly the extent of 'democratic' elements, see Fergus Millar 'The Political Character of the Classical Republic, 200–151 B.C.', *The Journal of Roman Studies* 74 (1984), 1–19. Each year there were twenty-four military tribunes, ten *tribuni plebis*, two curule and two plebeian aediles, probably ten quaestors, six praetors, two consuls, and a number of lesser officials.

27 For the penalty against bribery; Polybius, 6.56.4. As Millar notes,

the giving of elaborate shows was becoming regularly associated with office – for instance, the first *ludi scaenici* to be put on at the Megalesia, in

194 (Livy, 34.54.3), or the sixty-three *Africanae* and forty bears and elephants shown at the *ludi circenses* in 169 (Livy, 44.18.8). It is impossible not to see these as competitive gestures designed to win popular favour and enhance future electoral prospects. Like funeral orations and games, and like triumphs . . . these displays were directed to the public at large – not to defined groups of supporters, but to whatever section of the populace happened to turn up. 'Political Character', p. 12.

28 Suetonius, *Gramm*. 1.
29 Cassius Dio, *Frags.* 39.5 and 39.6; Plutarch, *Pyrrhus*, 16.
30 Horace, *Epist.*, 2.1.156–7; 161.
31 It was set up by the plebeian aediles (the *Publicii,*) who had recently taken action against certain aristocratic landowners illegally using public land. Ovid, *Fasti*, 5.277–94. See also, Wiseman, *op. cit.*, p. 4.
32 An excellent account and analysis of Andronicus' style is provided by J. Wright, *Dancing in Chains: the Stylistic Unity of the Comoedia Palliata* (Rome, 1974), chapter 2.
33 H. Bulle, 'Von griechischen Schauspielern und Vasenmalern', in *Festschrift für James Loeb* (Munich, 1930), pp. 33–7.
34 Beare, *Roman Stage*, pp. 336, 356; Bieber, *op. cit.*, pp. 129–32. The literary fragments of these works are found in A. Olivieri, *Frammenti della Commedia greca e del mimo nella Sicilia e nella Magna Grecia*, 2nd edn (Naples, 1946–7).
35 Horace, *Epist.*, 2.1.69.; Cicero, *Brut.*, 18.72.
36 Livy 27.37.7; Festus, 446.32–448.1–4 L. For Andronicus' association with the powerful Livius family, see Jerome's account of the year 187 BC.
37 Valerius Maximus, 3.7.11; Cicero, *2 Verr.*, 3.184. For the *Collegium*, see E. G. Sihler, 'The Collegium Poetarum at Rome', *American Journal of Philology* 26 (1905), 1–21, or for a recent treatment, N. M. Horsfall, 'The Collegium Poetarum', *Bulletin of the Institute of Classical Studies of the University of London* 79 (1976).
38 Polybius, 6.56.6 ff.
39 Livy records several cases of such instauration between 216 and 179, and the cases in which it must be applied (if the dancer stumbled, or an official misspoke his lines etc.) are briefly listed by Cicero, *De Har. Resp.*, 2.23. The games could even be ruled invalid if the place of performance had previously been defiled and not sanctified, e.g. Livy, 7.2.
40 The fourth century AD grammarian Marius Servius provides a hint of the traditional involvement of such personnel in other aspects of the games. In his commentary on Vergil's *Georgics*, 3.24, he notes 'amongst our ancestors theatres were merely a structure of steps. For at that time the *scaena* was made of wood, whence to this day it remains the custom that the *pegmata* are operated by the producers of theatrical games.' The *pegmata* were movable scenic devices, which are discussed in chapter 6 of this book.
41 Polybius, 31.25.4.
42 A. Gratwick has suggested that 'by the 180s Rome, unlike any one Greek city, was maintaining her own internal and self-sufficient "circuit" '. *Cambridge History of Classical Literature*, vol. 2 (Cambridge, 1982), p. 82. On the general question, see too, L. R. Taylor, 'The Opportunities for Dramatic Performance in the Time of Plautus and Terence', *Transactions of the American Philological Society* 68 (1937), 284–304.
43 Aulus Gellius *Noctes Atticae* 1.1.24.2.
44 Terence, *Andria*, 18–21.
45 C. Garton makes this suggestion regarding similar titles by Plautus in *Personal*

Aspects of the Roman Theatre (Toronto, 1972), p. 121.

46 The translation is by Beare, *op. cit.*, p. 37.

47 Horace, *Epist.*, 2.1.55–6.

48 Cicero, *De Republica*, 4.

49 Plutarch, *Marcellus*, 6–8; Polybius, 2.34.

50 See, for example, G. Williams, 'Phases in Political Patronage of Literature in Rome', in B. Gold, ed., *Literary and Artistic Patronage in Ancient Rome* (Texas, 1982), pp. 4–5.

51 Polybius, 6.54.2.

52 The record of the offending line and the response is from the fifth century AD writer, Pseudo-Asconius, *Ad. Cic. Verr.*, 1.29. Aulus Gellius suggests Naevius gave offence to the powerful family of Scipio as well, and that he was put into prison, *Noct. Atti.*, 7.8.5. Cicero puts Naevius' death at 204, *Brut.*, 15.60. Q. Caecilius Metellus had given a funeral oration in 221 on the death of his father, L. Caecilius Metellus, consul in 251 and 247. As summarized by Pliny the Elder (*Nat. Hist.* 7.139–41), it indicates the pride, prestige, and popularity of the family. L. Caecilius had a statue recording his services erected on the Capitol, and was uniquely honoured by vote of the *populus Romanus* with the right to use a chariot to ride to the Senate house. Clearly, the family were not to be trifled with by a playwright.

53 The Senate passed a decree in 182 BC attempting to curb excessive expenditure, but ambitious men continued to see such largesse as a prudent investment, knowing that once they had been given provinces to govern (and exploit) they would recover their outlay, and indeed would probably have substantial sums left over to sponsor further shows on their return.

54 Plautus, *Miles Gloriosus*, 210–11. The scholium by Festus says that the reference is to Naevius, 36.2.

2 THE FAMOUS COMIC PLAYWRIGHTS OF ROME

1 For a succinct appreciation of Plautus' popularity, see Erich Segal's introduction to *Roman Laughter* (Cambridge, Mass., 1968).

2 See Bruno Gentili, *Theatrical Performances in the Ancient World* (Amsterdam, 1979), pp. 91–7, for an assessment of the nature of such contact, and its influence upon the earliest Latin literature. He notes, (p. 95) 'the first manifestation of this decisive encounter between Rome and Greece was the practice of translation, a literary phenomenon with its own well-defined *raison d'être*.'

3 *ibid.* p. 96.

4 This was Cato's advice to his son, as quoted by Pliny, *Nat. Hist.*, 29.7.14.

5 G. Alföldy, *The Social History of Rome*. rev. edn, trans. D. Braund and F. Pollock (London, 1988), p. 62.

6 See H. D. Jocelyn, *Ennius* (Cambridge, 1967), pp. 12–23.

7 The few details are recorded in W. Beare, *The Roman Stage*, 3rd edn (London, 1968), p. 45, and their ancient sources on p. 360, note 1.

8 Horace, whose standards were offended by Plautus, condemned him for allowing desire for material gain to override artistic integrity. 'He's only concerned to add a coin to his cashbox, and after that is indifferent whether his play stands tall or falls flat.' *Epist.*, 2.1.175–6.

9 See A. S. Gratwick, 'Drama' in *Cambridge History of Classical Literature*, vol. 2, *Latin Literature*, ed. E. J. Kenney (Cambridge, 1982), pp. 77–85; 96–7, for a discussion of the influence of Hellenistic companies on Plautus' models.

10 The prologue to *Trinummus* states (line 19), 'Philemo scripsit, Plautus vortit

barbare' ('Philemon composed it, Plautus transformed it into a barbarian version'). Elsewhere Plautus refers to Italy itself as *'barbaria'*; and its towns as *'barbaricae urbes'*; *Poenulus* (598); *Captivi* (884).

11 Victor Castellani, 'Plautus versus *Komoidia*: Popular Farce at Rome', in *Themes in Drama: Farce*, 10 (Cambridge, 1988), pp. 53–82, p. 54.

12 The standard work on the subject remains that by Eduard Fraenkel, *Plautinisches im Plauto* (Berlin, 1922), trans. and rev. by Franco Munari as *Elementi Plautini in Plauto* (Florence, 1960). There have been numerous other commentaries and articles in its wake.

13 George E. Duckworth, *The Nature of Roman Comedy* (Princeton, 1952), p. 385.

14 Fraenkel suggests (*op. cit.*, p. 223 ff.) that such passages are Plautine insertions, and the same conclusion was reached by K. M. Westaway, *The Original Element in Plautus* (Cambridge, 1917), p. 49 ff. Castellani notes, 'There is not a single play in which we do not find actual or at least threatened violence of a sort we believe to be alien to all or most of New Comedy' (*op. cit.*, p. 65).

15 As evidence for this we have the testimony of Cato the elder who counted his slaves as farm equipment, alongside livestock. Enforcing the most severe discipline, he kept them working without respite, deliberately undernourished, subject to extreme punishments – if his slaves prepared a meal which displeased him he had them flogged – and when they could no longer work because of age or illness, he sold them off. Cato, *De Agri Cultura*, 2.1 ff., 56–7.

16 Walter R. Chalmers, 'Plautus and his Audience', in T. A. Dorley and Donald R. Dudley eds, *Roman Drama* (London, 1965) pp. 21–50; p. 28. Gladiatorial combats were first recorded at funeral games in 264 BC; Valerius Maximus, 2.4.7. In 160 the public deserted the theatre during a performance of Terence's *Hecyra* (see 'Prologue 2', lines 31–4) in order to attend such displays.

17 For the nature of popular forms of drama at Rome, and their possible influence upon Plautus, see Alan McN. Little, 'Plautus and Popular Drama', *Harvard Studies in Classical Philology*, 49 (1938), 205–28. The *saturae* were recorded by Livy, 7.2, and by Valerius Maximus, 2.4. The *Atellanae* were given literary form by Pomponius and Novius, and their fragments exhibit some marked similarities to Plautus. See O. Ribbeck, *Scaenicae Romanorum Poesis Fragmenta II, Comicorum Romanorum Fragmenta* (Leipzig, 1873), pp. 223–72.

18 For a discussion of biographical details, and the derivation of Plautus' name, see A. D. Gratwick, 'Titus Maccius Plautus', *Classical Quarterly* 23 (1973), 78–84. For the *Atellanae*, see P. Frassinetti, *Fabula atellana: Sagio sul teatro popolare latino* (Genova, 1953), and D. Romano, *Atellana fabula* (Palermo, 1953) for details of the *Atellanae*, and discussion of their possible influence upon scripted Roman comedy.

19 Introduction to Plautus' *Casina*, ed. W. T. MacCary and M. M. Willcock (Cambridge, 1976), p. 35.

20 C. Garton, *Personal Aspects of the Roman Theatre* (Toronto, 1972), p. 67.

21 See Donatus, *Ad Ter. Adelphoe* Praef. 4., in P. Wessner, *Aeli Donati quod fertur commentum Terenti*, vols 1–3 (repr, Stuttgart, 1966).

22 Niall Slater provides a superb alternative to such an approach in *Plautus in Performance* (Princeton, 1985). His introduction, 'The Performance Dimension', ably corrects such misguided critiques.

23 G. Norwood, *Plautus and Terence* (New York, 1932), p. 19.

24 Although clearly its master, Plautus was working within a firmly established dramatic style, shared with his predecessors. John Wright identifies the elements of this style, and traces them in examples of the work of other early Roman playwrights in *Dancing in Chains: The Stylistic Unity of the Comoedia*

Palliata (Rome, 1974). In my discussion of Plautus' synthesis of scripted and popular forms of drama, I assume that his approach was conditioned by the taste and expectations of his audience, and that these also influenced the work of the other playwrights of the period.

25 The sheer manic pleasure of an anarchic performance can be observed – and experienced – today; even occasionally in material directly derived from Plautus himself. In reviewing Zero Mostel's performance in *A Funny Thing Happened on the Way to the Forum*, Richard Gilman wrote, in *Common and Uncommon Masks* (New York, 1971), p. 209,

> 'Hide the girl on the roof', Zero tells someone, who replies 'Why?' 'Why not?' Mostel answers, tiny hands trilling in the air, foot kicking backwards in that gesture whose only rivals are some of Chaplin's. Why not throw away the plot, the logic, the surrenders to expectation, and really have a ball? Whose approval do we have to have?

26 Norwood, *op. cit.*, p. 28.
27 Slater, *op. cit.*, pp. 17–18.
28 For the relationship between farce and freedom, Eric Bentley's analysis remains unsurpassed. 'Farce', in *The Life of the Drama* (New York, 1964), pp. 219–56. He notes (p. 255), that comic cartharsis and the release it provides is motivated not by the 'impulse to flee (or Fear), but the impulse to attack (or Hostility) . . . in farce hostility enjoys itself'. For Plautus' puritanical warrior audience, farce would seem a most apt form of popular entertainment, providing release from normal repressions, and an outlet for aggression.
29 J. C. Frazer, *The Golden Bough* (London, 1914), vol. 9, p. 306. Erich Segal's *Roman Laughter*, *op. cit.*, explores the implications of this attitude with great skill, and very persuasive insights.
30 The tension resulting from the necessity of reconciling two different types of theatre, and in particular, of incorporating popular elements into works derived from New Comedy models, was aptly characterized by John Wright in the book cited in note 24, as 'Dancing in Chains'. He borrowed the expression from Nietzsche's description of similar constraints upon Greek artists. His study is a very informative and astute analysis of the way in which such tension is reflected in a great many stylistic elements evident in most of the surviving examples of Roman playwrights, with the important and instructive exception of Terence.
31 Slater skilfully develops this analysis in his introduction, 'The Performance Dimension', *op. cit.*, pp. 3–18. In fact, this aspect of the performance could itself subtly contribute to the 'saturnalian' sense as well. 'Just as comedy is the critic and opponent of rigid social order, so too it becomes the opponent of its own artistic order', p. 15.
32 A. McN. Little, *op. cit.*, p. 227.
33 Periplectomenus even lapses into Greek in his excitement. The translation is by Erich Segal, *Plautus: Three Comedies* (New York, 1969).
34 It also 'sets up' the comic play between some of Plautus' most prominent character types. As Eric Bentley notes, 'One of the oldest relationships in the comic drama is that between the ironical man and the impostor. These are the comedian and the straight man, one a knave, the other a fool, the fun resulting from the interaction between the two' (*op. cit.*, p. 249).
35 Cf the epilogue of *Asinaria*, in which the audience is asked to applaud in order to save one of the dramatic characters, Demaenetus, from the whipping which his wife will otherwise give him. 'The epilogue stands with one foot in the world of the play and one foot in the world of the spectators. . . . The audience is thus an

essential participant in the play. Its response will determine old Demaenetus' fate' (Slater, *op. cit.*, p. 68). Shakespeare uses a similar technique with Prospero's plea to be set free by applause at the conclusion of *The Tempest*.

36 See, e.g. Fraenkel, *op. cit.*, p. 175 ff.

37 See, for example, *Curculio*, 288–95.

> Those cloaked Greeks, wandering about with covered heads, stuffed full with books and baskets, runaway slaves standing around to chatter and block the path, or amble along with their philosophising; the types you can always see drinking away in a bar when the've stolen something – heads covered and guzzling hot wine, then walking along dreary and drunk – if I come upon any of them, I'll knock the barley brew belches out of every one.

38 Slater, *op. cit.*, p. 167.

39 The texts contain abundant references to the play-making process e.g. *Persa*, 'Have you learned your parts? No tragic or comic actors ever had them better' (465–6); or *Pseudolus*, 'The man who comes on stage ought to bring some new idea, newly fashioned . . . ' (568–70).

40 Donatus, *Ad Eunuchum*, 57., in Wessner, *op. cit.*

41 In the *Asinaria* such a slave, Libanus, speaks for them all;

> We give our great and grateful thanks to Holy Trickery,
> for by our shrewdness, wiles, deceits, and clever machinations,
> our shoulders bold displaying courage in the face of rods,
> we've just defied hot-iron tortures, crucifixion, chains,
> strappadoes, fetters, dungeons, locking, stocking, manacles,
> and harsh persuasive whippers well-acquainted with our backs! (545–51)

Trans. Segal, *op. cit.*, p. 145.

42 A. Watson, *The Law of the Ancient Romans* (Princeton, 1970), pp. 37–8.

43 The old man as lover is found in *Bacchides, Casina, Menaechmi* and *Mercator*, and somewhat less prominently, in *Asinaria, Aulularia, Cistellaria, Rudens, Stichus,* and *Vidularia*.

44 In addition to the works already cited by N. Slater and Segal, the nature of the fantasy world evoked by Plautus' comedies is discussed by Konrad Gaiser in his contribution 'Zur Eigenart der römischen Komödie', in H. Temporini, *Aufstieg und Niedergang der antiken Welt*, vol. I (Berlin, 1972), pp. 1027–113.

45 The manner in which the architecture of the theatre and its location within a city contribute to the meaning of the event are the subject of a recent study by Marvin Carlson, *Places of Performance, The Semiotics of Theatre Architecture* (Ithaca, New York, 1989).

46 Segal's translation. Plautus employs the device of the delayed prologue, following an attention-grabbing opening scene of bombast and repartee between the soldier and his servant.

47 *Lictores* attending the magistrate presiding over the games were charged with helping to keep order.

48 The prologue to the *Amphitruo* (spoken by Mercury) includes an extended excursus on theatrical claques, calling for inspectors to go through the audience to prevent hired partisans from unfairly favouring some performers over others, by taking their togas as security. This by order of his master, Jupiter, who will himself be appearing in the play.

49 This is itself a subtle joke, since Casina does not appear in the play at all, and indecency abounds; it is also at once undercut by an explicit joke pointing out

that after the play, 'for a little money, she's anyone's honey, and the marriage can wait till later!' (85–6).

50 The joke reminds one of a music hall jest; Plautus himself used exactly the same line in the prologue to *Poenulus* (81–2) with regard to a visit to Carthage.

51 This prologue, and in particular, the Greek antecedents (which it may parody) is discussed by E. W. Handley in his article, 'Plautus and his Public: Some Thoughts on New Comedy in Latin', *Dioniso* 46 (1975), 117–32; see 117–22.

52 Cf. Seneca, *Epist.* 80. 7–8, quoted in Garton, *op. cit.*, p. 32.

> Look at the actor who sweeps grandly across the stage and says with head thrown back, 'Lo, I rule in Argos: my kingdom I have from Pelops . . .'. He is a slave; he gets his five measures of grain and five denarii. And look at the actor who with such pride and abandon and confidence in his power swellingly proclaims, 'And if you hold not your peace, Menelaus, this right hand will fell you.' He gets his daily wage and sleeps under a patch coat.

53 The early first century BC grammarian and commentator Aelius Stilo suggested that if the muses spoke Latin, it would be in the language of Plautus, and a little later Varro quoted with approval the epigram concerning Plautus' death:

> When the playwright Plautus' died,
> Comedy broke down and cried.
> Then the stage was empty, then all Laughter, Games and Fun
> And all his boundless bouncy rhythms – wept as one.

Quintilian 10.1.99; Aulus Gellius *Noctes Atticae*, 1.24.3. The translation is by Erich Segal, *Plautus: Three Comedies* (New York, 1963), introduction to the 1985 Bantam edition, p. xvii. Aulus Gellius, writing in the second century AD, judged Plautus' style 'the glory of the Latin tongue', *Noct. Atti.*, 19.8.6, and Cicero thought him 'graceful, civilised, inventive and charming', *De Officiis* 1.29.104. A dissenting opinion is given by Horace, *Ars Poetica* (270–2); 'Your ancestors praised the meters and wit of Plautus. Too tolerant, not to say, stupid, their admiration of both.' Quintilian too is sceptical, noting in the passage cited above that 'we still scarcely reproduce even a faint shadow' of Greek comedy's charm.

54 Wright, *op. cit.*, p. 191.

55 Cicero, *De Optimo Genere Oratorum*, 6.19; *De Finibus*, 1.2.41.; Horace, *Epist.*, 2.1.59. Earlier, in the second century BC, Volcacius Sedigitus in his *De Poetis* also placed Caecilius first amongst outstanding Roman comic poets. His list is preserved by Aulus Gellius, *Noct. Atti.*, 15.24.

56 Jerome, *Ad Ann. 1838* (179 BC); Aulus Gellius, *Noct. Atti.* 4.20.13.

57 The anecdote is somewhat doubtful. The *Andria* was not performed until 166, which would have been some two years after the date given by Jerome for the death of Caecilius. See Beare's analysis, *op. cit.*, p. 91.

58 Terence, *Hecyra*, Prologue Two, 21–3; 15. The prologue is spoken by Turpio.

59 As Elizabeth Rawson notes, the *Collegium* was 'the only cultural institution at Rome not connected with a private patron – in a sense the only cultural institution at Rome . . . ' (*Intellectual Life in the Late Roman Republic*, Baltimore, 1985, p. 39).

60 An alternative interpretation is that Caecilius followed the Plautine approach too closely, and that Ambivius Turpio encouraged him towards at least a superficial Hellenizing. Although not agreeing very well with the impression of Caecilius which I detail below, this notion does possibly lend somewhat greater

221

consistency to Turpio's critical stance, since clearly in producing Terence's plays Turpio must not have fundamentally opposed his espousal of closer adherence to Greek originals. But I suspect that as an actor manager, Turpio was less concerned with questions of composition and authenticity than of presentation, seeing potential (but perhaps certain inadequacies in theatrical realization) in the work of each playwright, he assisted each in 'getting it right'. In both cases his patience paid off. The problem is discussed by Garton, *op. cit.*, pp. 62–72.

61 Varro considered Caecilius superior in plot, Terence in character, and Plautus in dialogue; *Sat. Menipp. 399B*. The high opinion cited earlier of Volcacius Sedigitus and Cicero may also reflect their admiration of this aspect of Caecilius' work, although the former placed Terence only sixth.

62 The passage is from *Noct. Atti.* 2.23.

63 Segal's translation, *op. cit.*, p. 24.

64 B. Gentili, *op. cit.*, p. 53. Gentili presents a cogent analysis of the contrasting passages.

65 A similar comparison can be made between a Menander fragment and the equivalent scene in Plautus' *Bacchides*. One finds Plautus exercising the same freedom in cutting, augmenting, and drastically altering the tone of the original. See E. W. Handley, *Menander and Plautus: A Study in Comparison* (London, 1968); shorter treatments are in Sandbach, *The Comic Theatre of Greece and Rome* (London, 1977), pp. 128–34, and Gentili, *op. cit.*, pp. 54–62.

66 See Gentili, *op. cit.*, pp. 50–1 for a discussion of Latin texts in which the word occurs.

67 The account is from the life of Terence composed by Suetonius (*c.* AD 69–140) which was attached to the fourth-century commentary to Terence's works attributed to Donatus.

68 Of Scipio, more later. Laelius, who was consul in 140 BC, was mentioned by Cicero as having been thought to have been the author of Terence's works. *Ad Atticum* 7.3.10

69 Wright, *op. cit.*, p. 127.

70 Cato, during his famous censorship of 184 BC, had passed austerity measures which attempted to halt what he deemed the moral decline of Roman society, and its indulgence of foreign tastes. A similar concern may be seen in the senatorial decree of 186 against the cult of Bacchus at Rome. Cato clung to the old virtues of moderation and frugality, and thought Greek culture incompatible with Roman ideals. See A. E. Astin, *Cato the Censor* (Oxford, 1978). For the divisions and crisis of Roman society in the aftermath of the second Punic war, see Alföldy, *op. cit.*, chapter 3, 'The Structural Change of the Second Century BC'.

71 Rawson, *op. cit.*, p. 40. For the lifes of the Scipios see H. H. Scullard, *Scipio Africanus: Soldier and Politician* (Bristol, 1970), and A. E. Astin, *Scipio Aemilianus* (Oxford, 1967).

72 Scipio's enlightened attitude to Greek culture is discussed in its larger context by R. H. Barrow, *The Romans* (London, 1949), chapter 3.

73 Livy 34.44 and 54; Valerius Maximus 2.4.3.

74 Following the Punic wars, the population of Rome had been swollen by a vast mob composed of ex-slaves, displaced peasants, and former prisoners of war. As early as 213 BC attempts were made to pacify this urban population, and obtain its support through handouts (*congiaria*) as well as increased public entertainments. Cf. Livy, 37.57.11.

75 Polybius, who accompanied the younger Scipio on his own campaigns, records

this and the disturbances which took place at the games, in his history; 30.22.12.

76 The mime is discussed in detail in chapter 5.

77 Beare, *op. cit.*, p. 154.

78 Cicero suggested that 'because of their elegance the plays were thought to have been written by C. Laelius', *Ad Atticum* 7.3.10; while Quintilian tentatively ascribes them to Scipio, 10.1.99.

79 For a full and very perceptive discussion of Lanuvinus' work and his rivalry with Terence, see Garton, *op. cit.*, pp. 41–139.

80 Beare, *op. cit.*, discusses this and related charges at length, pp. 96–109. The fourth-century AD grammarian Donatus studied the plays by Menander which Terence was accused of combining, and could find little evidence for such amalgamation.

81 However, there is controversy concerning this word (line 9). The manuscript reads '*nunc nuper dedit*'; 'has recently presented'. This has conjecturally been amended to '*nunc nuper perdidit*'; 'has recently ruined', because it thus logically provides an example for the assertion of the previous line. See P. Fabia, *P. Terenti Afri Eunuchus* (Paris, 1895), p. 79, and E. Fraenkel, 'Zum Prolog des terenzischen Eunuchus', *Sokrates* (1918), 305. Garton discusses the problem in *op. cit.*, p. 128.

82 F. H. Sandbach succinctly analyses the alterations made by Terence in composing the *Eunuchus* in *The Comic Theatre of Greece and Rome*, pp. 142–6. Beare suggests (*op. cit.*, pp. 104–5) that Terence did not in fact borrow characters from the *Kolax*, per se (since after all, as Terence observes, they are essentially 'stock') but only 'certain touches which characterized the captain and parasite' of that play. To explain this to an audience would have required him to go into technical matters; instead he provided a brief and plausible answer to Lanuvinus' charge.

83 It is unclear whether the reference is to the disruption of the first performance of the *Hecyra* five years earlier, or to some other production.

84 R. H. Martin, introduction to his edition of the *Phormio* (London, 1959), p. 3.

85 D. Konstan, *Roman Comedy* (Ithaca, NY, 1983), p. 140.

86 R. L. Hunter, *The New Comedy of Greece and Rome* (Cambridge, 1985), p. 74.

87 For a discussion of the relationship between New Comedy and philosophy, see Hunter, *op. cit.*, pp. 147–51.

88 Wright has a very useful discussion of the differences in moral outlook between the two playwrights in *Dancing in Chains*, *op. cit.*, pp. 135–8.

89 Cf. for example, Plautus' treatment of such characters in his *Bacchides*, or *Miles Gloriosus*, with that of Terence in the *Hecyra*.

90 Cf. *Mostellaria*, 233–4 with *Adelphoe*, 519–20.

91 Donatus, preface to *Ad Hecyra*, 1.9.

92 D. Konstan, *op. cit.*, p. 129.

93 Beare, *op. cit.*, p. 111.

94 Suetonius records in his 'Life' that Terence was paid a large and unprecedented sum, 8,000 sesterces for his *Eunuchus*, which enjoyed two presentations. *Vita Ter.*, 2.

3 EARLY ROMAN STAGES

1 Vitruvius, *De Architectura*, ed. V. Rose (Leipzig, 1899), 5.5.7. References to ancient temporary stages are relatively abundant. For a discussion of the evidence see A. Rumpf, 'Die Entstehung des Römischen Theaters', *Mitteilungen des Deutschen Archäologischen Instituts* 3 (1950), 40–50.

2 The evolution of the Hellenistic theatre architecture and its possible relationship to the *scaenae frons* is summarized, *inter alia* in W. B. Dinmoor's *The Architecture of Ancient Greece*, 3rd edn (London, 1950), pp. 297–319.

3 See e.g. D. S. Robertson,

> nowhere do we find any real transition . . . the solution to the problem must be sought in the long period when Roman theatres were built only of wood, and in the influence on stage construction of the farces popular in South Italy, the Greek *Phlyakes*, and the Oscan *Atellanae*, much played at Rome. (*Handbook of Greek and Roman Architecture*, Cambridge, 1943).

4 Examples from the fourth century have been found at Herakleia Minoa, Iaitas, Morgantina, Solus, and probably Tyndaris. Probable third-century structures have been identified at Akrai, Segesta, Syracuse, and Taormina. The most recent survey and analysis of the archaeological evidence is K. Mitens, *Teatri Greci e Teatri Ispirati all' Architettura Greca in Sicilia e nell' Italia Meridionale c. 350–50 a.c.* (Rome, 1988) to whom my discussion is greatly indebted.

5 Castiglione di Paludi, Cossa, Elea, Gioiosa Ionicas, Lokroi Epizephyrioi, Metapontion and Rhegion.

6 Remains of theatres are located at Cales, Nuceria Alfaterna, Pietrabbondante, Pompeii, Sarno, and Teanum Sidicinum. There is literary proof of a theatre at Capua.

7 Valerius Maximus, 2.4.2. See also C. Garton, *Personal Aspects of the Roman Theatre,* (Toronto, 1972), pp. 56–7. For Gabii, M. Almagro-Gortbea, ed., *El Santuario de Juno en Gabii* (Rome, 1982), 61, 610 ff. For Lanuvium; F. Coarelli, *Dintorni di Roma: Guida archeologica Laterza* (Tome-Bari, 1981), p. 110.

8 Mitens, *op. cit.*, p. 31.

9 N. Slater, 'Transformations of Space in New Comedy', in J. Redmond, ed., *Themes in Drama: Space*, vol. 9 (Cambridge, 1987), pp. 1–10, p. 4.

10 I do not wish to suggest that the Romans had a sort of 'shopping list' from which they deliberately selected suitable architectural elements in order to achieve a preconceived type of theatre; rather that as their theatrical practices evolved, they found it expedient to use or adapt certain elements with which they had become familiar, while passing over others. Formal scripted drama was, after all, an innovation at Rome, and one decisively influenced by 'foreign' practice, and it is only logical to assume that the same would be true for its staging.

11 For an interesting discussion of the possible meanings of *proscaenium*, see G. M. Sifakis, *Studies in the History of Hellenistic Drama* (London, 1967), pp. 126–30.

12 Other examples include, Plautus, *Amphitruo* (91), 'Why only last year, didn't Jove appear on this very stage [*proscaenium*] . . . ?'; and *Pseudolus* (568), 'Now one who goes onto the stage [*scaena*], ought to bring something novel, newly fashioned.'

13 E.g. *Aulularia* (103), 'And shut the door with both bolts!'; *Menaechmi* (351; 362), 'Leave the door as it is, and go. I don't want it closed'; 'It surprises me, dear boy, that you stand here outdoors, when the doors stand open.'; and *Stichus* (87), 'I'll go inside. But the door is open.'

14 In *Rudens* 85–7 there appears to be a reference to a damaged roof, 'The wind blew the roof off the house . . . it stripped every single tile off.' However, this may only have been a suggestion to the audience to imagine such a roof. In *Amphitruo*, the roof is undoubtedly real and necessary to the action.

15 However, a second is probably to be found in the fragment no. 26–7 included on p. 364 of the Loeb edition of Plautus, vol. 5. Lindsay, frag. 146. See too the

discussion of stage structure in V. Castellani, 'Plautus versus *Komoidia*: Popular Farce at Rome', *Themes in Drama: Farce*, 10 (Cambridge, 1988), pp. 68–73.

16 See P. W. Harsh, 'Angiportum, Platea and Vicus', *Classical Philology* 32 (1937), 44–58.

17 For a discussion of the production of Greek plays in Italy, and of the relationship between New Comedy and the *paraskenia* stage, see amongst others, T. B. L. Webster's introduction to *Illustrations of Greek Drama* (London, 1971).

18 See Livy, 34.44 and 54; and Valerius Maximus 2.4.3.

19 K. Mitens (*op. cit.*) records examples in both Sicily and *Magna Graecia* of the front rows (*prohedria*) of the auditoria being distinguished either by larger seats or arm rests.

20 Garton, *op. cit.*, p. 53.

21 Livy records the earlier visits, 39.22.2. and 39.22.10. One group of Greek actors performed at the games celebrated in honour of M. Fulvius who had conquered the cities of Aetolia, and vowed the games to Jupiter Optimus Maximus. M. Fulvius was, perhaps significantly, a patron of the poet Ennius, who had accompanied him on the campaign, and a work by Ennius may have been performed at the games. Polybius gives an account of that taking place in 167 BC, 30.22.12. The mêlée that resulted when the Roman audience failed to understand the nature of the Greek performances is mentioned in my previous chapter.

22 The names of two such peformers at Delos, (*c.* 172 BC), possibly leaders of troupes of Roman actors, are known; Agathodoros and Antipatros. See G. Sifakis, *op. cit.*, p. 20; and Garton's list of Republican actors, *op. cit.*, Appendix I, entries 1 and 47.

23 Livy, 40.51.3. The sites for early scenic performances is a matter of some conjecture. E. J. Jory notes,

> It is clear that in some funeral games the *forum* was the site of both dramatic and gladiatorial presentations (Livy, 31.50.4. 200 BC). Gladiatorial games were first introduced in Rome as part of *Ludi Funebres* in 264 BC (Livy *Ep.* 16; Val. Max., 2.4.7.) and since the forum was the focal point for honouring the dead in distinguished families (Polybius, 6.53.) this may have been a regular site for such games before the building of amphitheatres. . . . That on occasion scenic performances were presented in the Circus Maximus is clear from Athenaeus XIV 615 = Polybius 30.22.1 . . . . For possible use of the Circus on another occasion see Livy, 41.27. ('Continuity and Change in the Roman Theatre', in Betts, Hooker, and Oren, eds, *Studies in Honour of T. B. L. Webster*, Bristol, 1986, pp. 143–52, note 14.

The question of the early performance sites is also discussed in J. A. Hanson, *Roman Theater-temples* (Princeton, 1959), pp. 9–26.

24 Livy, 41.27.5.

25 Cicero, *Pro. Mur.* 76. At first the state had paid the sums necessary for games directly to the responsible magistrates. It was known as *lucar*, possibly because it came from revenues accruing from the sacred groves (*luci*). Until 200 BC the sum was fixed by the Senate in advance, the amount for the *Ludi Romani*, for example, set at some 200,000 sesterces. But after that date, games were decreed without stipulating the amount, and magistrates, especially ambitious aediles, supplemented the state contribution from other sources. In 186 expenditure was limited for the games of M. Fulvius, and a similar curb was in force for those in honour of Q. Fulvius in 179 who had sought to lavish on the games money

which had been raised in Spain. In 182 the Senate forbade the attempt to raise money through exccessive collection from Roman subjects to finance the games of Tiberius Gracchus, and this would have had the effect of limiting the money available for the regular festivals as well. Livy, 39.5.6–12.; 39.22.1–3.; 40.44.8–12. Nevertheless, the sums continued to grow enormously. By 54 BC the state grant alone amounted to 760,000 sesterces for the *Ludi Romani*, 380,000 for the *Ludi Apollinares*, and 600,000 for the *Ludi Plebeii*. Livy, 32.12. At the time of Augustus, an ordinary legionary soldier was paid just under 1,000 sesterces a year. The annual income of a well-placed government offical might be around 100,000 sesterces; an estate of 400,000 sesterces qualified a Roman citizen to become a member of the equestrian order. Pliny, *Nat. Hist.*, 33.32.

26 Jory, *op. cit.*, p. 146.

27 Polybius, 30.22.12. Garton discusses the stage, *op. cit.*, pp. 55–6.

28 Polybius, 12.28. For Demetrius, see Garton, *op. cit.*, pp. 55–6.

29 Vitruvius, *De Arch.*, 7. Preface. 11. Although Aristotle credits Sophocles with introducing scene painting, while Vitruvius says that Agathargus worked for Aeschylus, there need be no contradiction, since Sophocles produced plays well before Aeschylus ceased doing so. For ancient perspective see A. M. G. Little, 'Perspective and Scene Painting', *Art Bulletin* 19 (1937), 487 ff.; G. M. A. Richter, *Perspective in Greek and Roman Art* (London, 1970); and J. White, *Perspective in Ancient Drawing and Painting* (London, 1956).

30 Plutarch, *Vitae*, 'Alcibiades', 16; Demosthenes, *Against Meidias*, 147.

31 Livy, *Epit.*, 48.; Valerius Maximus, 2.4.2. The destruction was dated to 151 by E. T. Salmon, *Athenaeum* 41 (1963), 5–9. In 145 BC, Lucius Mummius, the destroyer of Corinth, again erected seating for the plays given at his triumph, to which he had invited Greek actors. Tacitus, *Annales*, 14.20.

32 Sallust, *Bell. Jug.*, 63.6 ff.

33 The causes and effects of the second-century social upheaval is comprehensively presented and discussed by G. Alföldy, *The Social History of Rome*, rev. edn, trans. D. Braund and F. Pollock (London, 1988), chapter 3.

34 Cassiodorus, *Chron.* ad. 115 BC in J. P. Migne, *Patrologiae Cursus Completus . . .* 69 (Paris, 1865), col. 1224.

35 It has sometimes been suggested that no seats were ever provided in the temporary Roman theatres. This notion has been authoritatively demolished by W. Beare, *The Roman Stage*, 3rd edn (London, 1968), pp. 171–2, and 241–7. Tacitus reports the claim put about in the time of Nero that once upon a time 'in the remoter past' prior to the provision of temporary stage and auditorium 'spectators had stood since seats, it was feared would keep them idle for days on end'. But he does not suggest that the temporary stages lacked seats (*Annales*, 14.20). In Rome and her colonies political meetings took place in the *Comitium*, without seats.

For meetings in Greek theatres, see J. Colin, 'Apulée en Thessalie; fiction ou vérité?', *Latomus* 24 (1965), 342, note 3; and *idem, Les villes libres del'Orient gréco-romain et l'envoi au supplice par acclamations populaires* (Paris, 1965), chapter 3.

36 Pliny, *Nat. Hist.*, 35.23. Valerius Maximus also notes the theatre, 2.4.6.

37 Valerius Maximus, 2.4.6. Cf. Pliny, *Nat. Hist.*, 19.23.

38 D. S. Robertson describes the contrivance for supporting and operating these awnings in *op. cit.*, p. 279 ff. The use of such a device at Pompeii is illustrated in a wall painting (now in the Naples museum), showing its operation in the amphitheatre, and corbels survive in the large theatre in which masts were placed to hold the awning taut. M. Bieber records other examples of its use later in the permanent theatres; *History of the Greek and Roman Theatre* (Princeton,

1961), p. 179. Lucretius described (*De Re. Nat.*, 4.75–83) how it created a multi-coloured effect, as the light played through it onto the auditorium. For Capua, see Elizabeth Rawson, 'Theatrical Life in Republican Rome and Italy', *Proceedings of the British School at Rome* 53 (1985), 97–113; p. 104 and note 40.

39 The *Lex Roscia Theatralis*, put forward by the Tribune L. Roscius Otho to curry favour with the knights. Apparently they had previously enjoyed reserved seats, but the right had been so eroded that it was necessary to reaffirm it. See my chapter 6, note 16. and Garton, *op. cit.*, p. 144, and p. 303, note 14. For the importance of such status symbols in consolidating the position of the *equites*, see Alföldy, *op. cit.*, pp. 49–50.

40 Valerius Maximus, 2.4.6. For Antonius see also Pliny, *Nat. Hist.*, 33.53.

41 Pliny, *Nat. Hist.*, 36.114–15. Perhaps Scaurus was atoning for his father, under whose consulship in 115 BC, theatre personnel had been expelled from Rome.

42 Vitruvius, *De Arch.*, 7.5.5. The description occurs at a point in Vitruvius' discussion of wall painting where he asserts that such painting has become decadent in his own day, since it no longer represents actual architecture, but tends instead to depict bizarre and fanciful structures as part of its decorative scheme. The example he cites suggests that such fantastic *trompe-l'oeil* effects were introduced by means of painted flats into the fabric of the actual structure of the stage facade. The evidence of surviving wall painting supports the same conclusion.

43 *ibid.*, 6.2.2.

44 *ibid.*, 7.5.1–2.

45 The first scholar to claim to have identified in the surviving paintings examples derived from the stage was O. Puchstein in *Die griechische Bühne* (Berlin, 1901), p. 35 ff. He was supported in this view by A. Ippel, *Der dritte pompejanische Stil* (Berlin, 1910), p. 26 ff., who developed a theory of theatrical influence in Roman painting which was repeated by other writers on the ancient theatre, including E. Fiechter, *Die baugeschichtliche Entwicklung des antiken Theaters* (Munich, 1914), p. 42 ff.; H. Bulle, *Untersuchungen an griechischen Theatern* (Munich, 1928), p. 273 ff.; and M. Bieber, *Die Denkmäler zum Theaterwesen im Altertum* (Berlin, 1920), p. 42 ff. Others repeated or modified it, in their work on Roman paintings: e.g. E. Pfuhl, *Malerei und Zeichnung der Griechen, II* (Munich, 1923), p. 810 ff., 886; and G. E. Rizzo, *La pittura Ellenistico-Romano* (Milan, 1929), pp. 1–8.

The most extensive presentation of a theory of theatrical influence was given by H. G. Beyen in his massive work, *Die pompejanische Wanddekoration vom II bis zum IV Stil I* (The Hague, 1938), pp. 141–208. More recently it has been supported by A. G. M. Little in two booklets published in 1971 and 1977, (Star Press, Kennebunk, Maine), *Roman Perspective Painting and the Ancient Stage*, and *Decor, Drama and Design in Roman Painting*.

The majority of scholars, however, have rejected the theory of theatrical influence wholly or in part. L. Curtius in *Die Wandmalerei Pompejis* (Leipzig, 1929), pp. 121–2, 130–9, 174, 178–87, argued that wall painting and stage decoration developed along lines which sometimes may have run parallel to one another but were essentially independent. K. Schefold, in *Pompejanische Malerei, Sinn und Ideengeschichte* (Basle, 1952), found much religious symbolism and evidence of mystery cults, but little of the theatre in the paintings, and P. L. Lehmann in *Roman Wall Paintings from Boscoreale* (Cambridge, Mass., 1952), vigorously rejected assertions that these paintings were specific examples of Hellenistic or Roman stage settings. This view was supported by A. Pickard-Cambridge, *The Theatre of Dionysus in Athens* (Oxford, 1946), who maintained that neither the Boscoreal paintings, nor Roman painting generally, could provide reliable evidence about ancient theatre architecture. A more recent critic of the theory of theatrical influence, who rejects it entirely, is J. Engemann, 'Architekturdarstellungen des frühen zweiten Stils', in *Mitteilungen des deutschen archäologischen Instituts, römische Abteilung, zwölftes Ergänzungsheft* (Heidelberg, 1967).

46 Elaborate systems have been suggested for delineating and dating the evolution in Italy of such wall painting; this begins with August Mau in the 1880s who suggested four phases. In the first, (dated at the early first century BC) the painter simply embellished the flat wall of the room to suggest additional architectural elements such as marble inlay, friezes, and simple entablature. Not content with such basic articulation, the painters of the second phase (*c.* 80–15 BC) attempted to 'open up' the wall both by depicting imaginary apertures in it, and by representing projecting and receding elements; columns, plinths, and the like. In the third and fourth phases, down to the destruction of Pompeii in AD 79, further refinement took place, which involved abandoning the practice of thinking of the wall as an architectural entity capable of being subject to various embellishments and imaginary elements, and considering it instead purely as a decorative field, a sort of blank canvas, suitable for purely ornamental decoration which had no direct relationship to the actual architecture. Complex patterns and designs were executed on the wall, rather in the way in which wallpaper might be used today. But in the so-called fourth phase (from perhaps the middle of the first century AD) architectural improvisation and fantasy returns, with new exuberance and fanciful effects. Most recent opinion is divided about the chronology and even the definition of these four phases, and specifically, it is now widely felt that the fourth phase should be thought of as a chronological rather than a stylistic category, and even that a distinction between the third and fourth phases is impossible, so complex is the web of borrowed characteristics, overlapping influences, and re-emerging motifs in examples of painting after the full development of the second style.

47 The excavation was directed by Gianfilippo Carettoni, and discussed in his article, 'Due Nuovi Ambienti Dipinti Sul Palatino', *Bolletino d'Arte* 46 (1961), 189–99. The painting is believed to date from the late first century BC. The painting is illustrated in colour in plate 33 of *The Art of Rome* (London, 1978) by B. Andreae, who dates it 40–30 BC and considers it (p. 104) to be a depiction of a *scaenae frons*.

48 This painting, in a room off the large south atrium of the villa, is discussed briefly in A. de Franciscis' *Pompeian Wallpaintings in the Roman Villa of Oplontis* (Recklinghausen, 1975). Franciscis, who directed the excavations, is reluctant to date the paintings precisely. However, in any case, it almost certainly belongs to the late second style, and thus is generally contemporaneous with the work from the 'Room of the Masks'. See also C. Malandrino, *Oplontis* (Naples, 1977), pp. 63–80, and B. Andreae and H. Kyrieleis, *Neue Forschungen in Pompeji* (Recklinghausen, 1975), pp. 9–36.

49 Margaret Lyttelton, *Baroque Architecture in Classical Antiquity* (London, 1974), p. 202. In each of the cases considered so far, if the artist had chosen to depict a stage of greater depth, this would necessarily have 'pushed back' visually his main subject, the architectural facade, and by diminishing its size (while having the foreground of his picture dominated by the depiction of an uninteresting, bare stage) made for a less effective composition. In the example discussed later from the House of Pinarius Cerealis, the artist *has* shown a deeper stage, but it is enlivened by the depiction of figures upon it.

50 Beare suggests (*op. cit.*, p. 181) that possibly a curtain was hung in front of it. Elsewhere he raises the question in considering whether the stage made use of

small porches in front of the doorways; 'if three porches formed part of the background, it is not easy to see how plays were staged in which only one or two houses are mentioned. It is one thing to ignore a plain door set unobtrusively in a flat wall: it is another matter to pretend that a visible pillared and roofed porch does not exist' (pp. 281–2). He fails, I think, fully to appreciate how a non-illusionistic dramaturgy uses its scenic elements; not primarily as pretence, or to resemble actual objects, but to serve as functional emblems as and when needed. The Elizabethan stage also had permanent elements which were incompatible with any notion of versimilitude; they functioned when and if the dramatist (working through the actors) required them, and at other times they ceased, dramaturgically speaking, to exist.

51 The emblematic nature of the Elizabethan stage is now generally accepted, and production methods inspired by its example have helped to familiarize audiences and scholars with the conventions of a non-realistic dramaturgy. A concise discussion of this aspect is found in Glynne Wickham's *Shakespeare's Dramatic Heritage* (London, 1969), essay 8, 'Shakespeare's Stage'.

52 See Vitruvius, *De Arch.*, 5.6.8, and Pollux, *Onomasticon*, 4.124–32.

53 The several versions of the scene are described and discussed by E. Lowry, 'Iphigenee in Taurien', *Jahrbuch des deutschen archäologischen Instituts* 44 (1929), 87–103. See also Curtius, *op. cit.*, pp. 244–8, figs. 142–6; A. W. Pickard-Cambridge, *op. cit.*, p. 232, figs. 111–15.

54 Bieber describes the two Pompeian theatres (*History of the Greek and Roman Theater*, pp.172–9), and notes that the flat facade of the smaller one was decorated with architectural painting.

55 Vitruvius, *De Arch.*, 5.5.7. It is not entirely clear whether Vitruvius excludes permanent theatres from this effect or not. He begins the passage by speaking specifically of wooden stages, then mentions wooden doors, then notes that theatres built of solid materials 'which cannot be resonant' must use other means to secure good acoustics.

56 Bieber, *History of the Greek and Roman Theater*, p. 180.

57 Livy, 1.35.8., wrote, 'then a place was first provided for the circus, now called Maximus. Here separate seats were constructed for the patricians and knights; called platforms, they were supported on forked poles some twelve feet above the ground.'

58 Even so, as accounts of disturbances in the circus and amphitheatre show, things could still get out of hand. A famous example occurred at Pompeii in AD 59, in which bloody rioting broke out between rival factions in the amphitheatre. Tacitus records (*Annales*, 14.17.) that as a consequence the Senate forbade its use for ten years.

59 This project is the subject of a documentary video, 'Pompeian Painting and Plautus: Staging Roman Comedy', available (together with extensive notes) in North America from Films for the Humanities, Princeton, New Jersey, and in Britain from the Audio Visual Centre, University of Warwick.

60 The last recorded revival of a play by Plautus, his *Pseudolus*, took place at the time of Cicero (*Pro Rosc. Com.*, 20.), but they may well have been done subsequently. There is good evidence that Terence, at any rate, continued to be performed in the imperial period. Quintilian (11.3.178–82) writing about AD 90, refers to contemporary performances of Roman comedy, and appears to include Terence as an example. See my discussion of this question in chapter 5.

61 T. S. Eliot, 'Seneca in Elizabethan Translation', in *Selected Essays*, rev. edn (London, 1958), p. 68. Although he is referring to Greek tragedy, Eliot's description applies equally well to the 'acted and felt' physicality of Roman

comedy. 'Behind the drama of words is the drama of action, the timbre of voice and voice, the uplifted hand or tense muscle, and the particular emotion.'
62 Elizabeth Henry in *The Times Educational Supplement*, 20 April, 1984.

4 A FUNNY THING: PERFORMING A PLAY BY PLAUTUS

1 For a comprehensive discussion of this aspect of ancient tragedy, see Oliver Taplin's excellent treatment in *Greek Tragedy in Action* (Berkeley, 1978). It also informs the approach taken by Niall Slater to Plautus in his superb book (to which I am greatly indebted), *Plautus in Performance* (Princeton, 1985).
2 Fergus Millar, 'The World of the *Golden Ass*', *Journal of Roman Studies* 71 (1981), 63–75, p. 63.
3 The phrase was used by Samuel Beckett to describe James Joyce's work. Quoted and discussed by Richard Gilman, 'Art and History', pp. 157–71 in his collection of essays, *The Confusion of Realms* (New York, 1963).
4 With regard to the most worrying portion of the play, the prologue itself, Friedrich Leo, who was at pains to identify original material from later additions, concluded that 'if we disregard the specific revisions, that is, remove verses 5–20, we can consider the entire prologue as Plautine'. *Plautinische Forschungen*, 2nd edn, (Berlin, 1912), p. 207, note 2.
5 All quotations are from my own translation, which attempts to convey the sense, imagery, playfulness, and theatrical efficacy of Plautus' language; an undertaking which sometimes precludes rendering it word for word into English. Plautus is both idiomatic and inventive, and often the vitality and originality of his language, as well as the meaning it would have conveyed to his Roman audience, requires that a translation find an equivalent rather than identical turn of phrase.
6 Erich Segal discusses this prologue in his analysis of the importance of the festive occasion to understanding Plautine comedy. *Roman Laughter* (Cambridge, Mass., 1968), p. 52 ff.
7 The same line is repeated in the prologue to *Cistellaria*, then expanded with more specific advice for dealing with allies, enemies, and the conquered Carthaginians (197–202). A similar tag praising Roman military strength concludes the *Rudens* (82), and the *Captivi* (67–8).
8 John Wright provides an illuminating close analysis of the exchange between Grumio and Trania in the introduction to *Dancing in Chains: the Stylistic Unity of the Comoedia Palliata* (Rome, 1974), pp.1–13.
9 Chalinus uses the word, *provincia*, to characterize Olympio's rural realm. R. L. Hunter notes that 'this establishes the contest for the hand of Casina as a clash between these two spheres. . . . This feature gives concrete expression to the fact that [Olympio's and Lysidamus'] designs on Casina are offensive to the bourgeois decency of comedy'. Hunter points out too that the conflict given comic treatment here had a basis in developments in Hellenistic social conditions. 'Residence in the city away from one's landholdings seems to have become more and more regular in the fourth century; this is reflected in a large number of plays, both Greek and Roman' (*The New Comedy of Greece and Rome*, Cambridge, 1985), pp. 112, 110.
10 Wright observes that in the opening scene of the *Mostellaria*, the town slave is similarly threatened with punishment appropriate to the country; at line 16–19, Grumio predicts that Tranio will be forced to work on the farm in a mill (*op. cit.*, p. 7).
11 In their introduction to the text (Cambridge, 1976) W. T. MacCary and M. M.

Willcock note that this reference to honey marks the first connection between food and sex which is so prominent in the imagery of the play.

12 Cf. *Miles Gloriosus*, 680 ff. or *Menaechmi*, 569.

13 But see note 28 below.

14 Hunter, *op. cit.*, p. 90. As Hunter explains, in Greece the wife's dowry was intended to ensure that she would be well treated by her husband, since if the marriage was dissolved, the husband was deprived of it. The Romans had two forms of marriage; one in which the dowry became the property of the husband, and the other when it remained under the control of the wife's family. But in either case, a wife with a dowry was a peril for her husband, or at least this is how the comic poets chose to portray the situation. Either she expected to be extravagantly pampered because of the wealth she had brought into the marriage, or else she was able directly to threaten her husband with its loss. 'Roman dowries were, on the whole, larger than Attic ones, and this helped to emphasise the discomfort of comic husbands locked in a private, married hell' (p. 92).

15 Lysidamus wishes his wife dead a third time at the beginning of the lot-casting scene.

> *Cleo.* 'Now Chalinus, what is it my husband wants me to do?'
> *Chal.* 'Gee, what he'd most like is to see you going up in smoke out beyond the gates!'
> *Cleo.* 'Goodness, I think you're right.'
> *Chal.* 'By golly, I don't think, I *know*!'
> *Lys.* 'It appears I have more servants than I thought: we seem to have a mind-reader on the staff.' (353–6)

This is a good example of a favourite Plautine comic device; *para prosdokian*, the question which meets with a completely unexpected reply.

16 Olympio strengthens the impression which the audience would have begun to form earlier that he is a pretty unsavoury and foul-mouthed character. Just as earlier this would tend to develop sympathy for his antagonist, Chalinus, so now it would rebound in Cleostrata's favour, whom Olympio describes as a 'dog' and abuses with one of the crudest jokes found in Plautus. '*Ol.* Nunc in fermento totast, ita turget mihi. *Lys.* Ego edepol illam mediam diruptam velim. *Ol.* Credo edepol esse, siquidem tu frugi bonae es.' ('*Ol.* She's really on the boil now; about to explode in my face! *Lys.* By Pollux, if only she'd a split right down the middle! *Ol.* Well, gee! I suppose she does if you're any good at your job!' (325–7)).

17 Such apparently blasphemous jokes (taking place at a religious occasion) seem remarkable, particularly in light of the notorious Roman preoccupation with piety. As Segal notes, 'the very foundation of Roman morality is attacked in word and deed on the Plautine stage' (*op. cit.*, p. 31) which he explains in terms of the saturnalian impulse and its licence. The audience needs to escape briefly from normal strictures, even to mock their own morality, while employing the self-exonerating excuse that after all, everything is happening in Greece, where as one Plautine characer puts it, 'everyday morals get worse and worse' (*Mercator*, 838).

18 R. M. Pinkerton, in a review article in the *Journal of Roman Studies* 70 (1980), 240–1.

19 As Segal deftly points out,

> Husband and wife pummel each other by proxy, and it is well worth noting whose slave gets the worst of it; Juno beats Jupiter. This bellicose behaviour is completely at odds with the ideal of *obsequentia*, these barking

dogs so unlike the celebrated 'silent women of Rome'. (*op. cit.*, p. 25)

Segal's reference is to an article by Moses Finley, 'The Silent Women of Rome', *Horizon* 7 (1965), 56–64. The implicit conflict between the generations, was earlier highlighted by the prologue which stated literally, 'now the pair of them, father and son, prepare their opposing legions' (50–1).

MacCary and Willcock in the introduction to their edition of the text (*op. cit.*, p. 30) point out that the running Jupiter-Juno joke

> helps establish the relations among the characters . . . and a certain mock-heroic tone which persists throughout: just as Jupiter's philandering and lying is a contradiction of the dignity and power of his position as father of gods and men, so Lysidamus' role of *pater familias* is undercut by the shabby tricks he resorts to in order to get hold of a slave girl.

20 Of course, characters in Plautus, particularly his mischievous clever slaves, are often guilty of a form of comic hubris; exalting in their own ability to break the rules and come out smiling. Their triumphant capacity to 'beat the odds' lends to the comedy much of its regenerative force. But Lysidamus' case is different. Here and elsewhere he sets himself up in advance for the correction which follows, and which, as his subsequent conduct shows, he thoroughly deserves. As the audience will observe, his misbehaviour lacks the positive exuberance and life-affirming potential of Plautus' comic heroes: his lust is inhumane, selfishly destructive of others' happiness, and, above all, it causes him to abuse those over whom he holds superior power. Moreover, Lysidamus, unlike the characters whom Plautus expects his audience to admire (or, at the least, condone out of respect for their wit and wiles), is not in fact strong and capable, but weak and servile: his lust is uncontrolled, and, as later scenes show, largely undirected.

21 Pinkerton, *op. cit.*, p. 241.

22 Indeed, Chalinus' next line contains a stage direction which indicates his position against the scenic facade as well as his subsequent movements sideways along it; 'I'll just creep back against this wall like a crab, and listen to what they're saying' (443).

23 This is an instance where the Latin can be translated literally into English, whose meaning is very close to it (instead of resorting to equivalent English expressions), while also echoing the alliteration of the original: 'nam illorum me alter cruciat, alter macerat . . . protollo mortem mihi; certus est, hunc Aceruntem praemittam prius'.

24 Lysidamus is demeaned by his uncontrollable lust, which again in this scene and subsequently is characterized as animalistic; Chalinus exclaims, 'what fun to capture two boars in one bush!' (476).

25 Plautus' pun on 'sole' works well in English. 'Snapper', however, is not an exact translation but preserves the joke. The fish Plautus refers to is *lungulaca*; 'chatterer'. The literal rendering would be,

> *Ol.* 'How about a little chatterer?'
> *Lys.* 'What for when the wife is at home? She's our chatterer, since she's never quiet.'

26 Niall Slater astutely points out *Plautus in Performance* (Princeton, 1985, p. 84)

> Lysidamus is not a light-hearted old man whose fancy has turned to love, a sympathetic Plautine reveller with whom our loyalties should lie. . . . He will have from his friend none of the reprimands and advice appropriate to aply to a *senex amator* . . . in rejecting these admonitions, he rejects the

sympathetic role that goes with them. Lysidamus' sin is not sex; it is obsession.

27 Not really translatable, of course, but more or less, that any servants sent to assist in the wedding should bring their own provisions, 'just like in the birdies song: "to eat! to eat! to eat! to eat! to eat!" '. Plautus plays with the bird-song sound of the Latin; 'cum cibo cum quiqui'. The second pun is for specialists.

28 Slater op. cit., offers a very persuasive argument explaining why Plautus earlier allowed her apparently to possess information which, logically, she ought not to have until now. He suggests that Cleostrata's previous statement is not in fact meant to indicate the actual extent of her knowledge, but to serve as an early demonstration to the audience of her *situation*.

> Plautus is already demanding that we choose sides, and he wants to make it clear that, somewhat atypically for Roman comedy, the side to choose is that of the *matrona*. She is taking the absent son's part, of course, and with him we naturally sympathize. With her we need more reason to sympathize, and the dramatically anachronistic knowledge of her husband's illicit passion supplies that motivation for us. (p. 75)

As so often with Plautus, realism counts less than dramaturgy.

29 Plautus' reference to, literally, 'that column of the senate and bulwark of the people' is a good example of his use for deliberate comic effect of an anachronistic reference to Roman practice in an ostensibly Greek context, as was the reference a few lines earlier by Lysidamus to going to the 'Forum'. A similar usage (and the same phrase, 'senati columen') is found in *Epidicus* (189), when the slave Epidicus expresses contempt for the elderly Athenian gentlemen who are his opponents; 'Now to turn myself into a leech and suck the blood out of these so-called pillars of the senate.'

30 Segal points out (op. cit., pp. 88–9) that the same disreputable attitude is prevalent in other Plautine characters. In *Persa*, the same word used by Lysidamus ('stultitia'); 'asinine', to describe his official business is used in a similar context. 'No folly could be greater to litigate instead of live it up when you have got the chance. Wait and do this business later' (799–801).

31 Henri Bergson in his essay on 'Laughter' of 1900, suggests that our perception of the comic arises from situations in which humans are seen to behave with a certain mechanical rigidity, making them seem more like objects than persons. His insight is particularly relevant to farce.

> We gather that the usual devices of comedy, the periodic repetition of a word or a scene, the systematic reversals of roles, the geometric progression of blunder, and many other stage tricks may derive their comic thrust from the same source – the art of the vaudeville writer perhaps being to show us a visibly mechanical articulation of human events, all the while preserving the outward aspect of probability, that is to say, the apparent elasticity of life . . .

(Bergson, 'Laughter', excerpted in B. Dukore, *Dramatic Theory and Criticism*, New York, 1974, pp. 737–45).

32 The Latin, which Plautus has changed for emotional effect at this point from Lysidamus' *senarii* (a spoken metre) to sung *cretics*, rewards examination.

> Nulla sum, nulla sum; tota, tota occidi,
> cor metu mortuomst, membra miserae tremunt.
> nescio unde auxili, praesidi, perfugi,

mi aut opum copiam comparem aut expetam.
tanta factu modo mira miris modis
intus vidi, novam atque integram audaciam. (621–6)

MacCary and Willcock (*op. cit.*, p. 27) note the abundance of alliteration, assonance, repetition, and (somewhat rare in Plautus) end-rhyme, which taken together give 'a jingling quality to the whole which makes it appropriate for musical rendering'. They also point out (p. 36) that her lament is reminiscent of the story, dramatized by Aeschylus, of the daughters of Danaus forced into marriage with husbands whom they then murdered on their wedding night. Leo observed that Pardalisca's report of domestic mayhem was closely similar to the account given by the Phrygian slave in Euripides' *Orestes* (*Plautinische Forschungen*, Berlin, 1912, p. 133). Hunter records (*op. cit.*, p. 122) its close echo of a fragment from Ennius' *Andromache*; 'What protection can I seek or follow? What help in exile or flight can I find? No more do I have citadel or city. Where shall I go? To whom shall I turn?'.

33 Hunter (*op. cit.*, p. 169, note 8.) quotes the formula from *Captivi*, 444; 'You are now my master, you my patron, you my father', and cites other examples in Terence: (*Andria* 295; *Phormio*, 496; and *Adelphoe*, 456). Segal discusses the frequent occurrences of the master-as-suppliant motif in Plautus (*op. cit.*, p. 119 ff.), and devotes a chapter, 'From Slavery to Freedom' to the general topic of the reversal of status and transfer of authority which is so much a part of Plautine comic technique, and epitomized when the slave enslaves his master.

34 As elsewhere, Plautus uses the word, '*barbarus*', as did the Greeks, to mean 'Roman'. Cf. *Captivi*, 884; *Poenulus*, 598; *Trinummus*, 19; *Mostelaria* 828; *Miles Gloriosus*, 211; etc. As W. R. Chalmers noted, 'The Elder Cato specifically objects to the Greeks referring to the Romans as *barbari*, a practice which was a source of amusement to Plautus and his audience.' He sees this as evidence of the sophistication and robust sense of humour of the Roman spectators. W. R. Chalmers, 'Plautus and his Audience', in T. A. Dorey and D. R. Dudley eds, *Roman Drama* (London, 1965), pp. 21–50, p. 47. Cato's stricture is recorded in Pliny, *Nat. Hist.*, 39.7.

Segal points out (*op. cit.*, p. 36); 'In a Plautine context, the adjective *barbarus* means not only "Roman", but "unfestive" as well. The words of Olympio suggest that *Romanitas* and *festivitas* are incompatible. Paradoxical as it may sound, Greece must be the scene of a Roman holiday.

35 These are discussed in W. E. Forehand, 'Plautus' *Casina*: An Explication', *Arethusa* 6 (1973), 233–56, p. 246.

36 In this scene the audience see the most explicit expression of the food/sex metaphor, and can enjoy their awareness that the women, having successfully deprived the men of the one, are now likely to deny them the other as well. Evidently such knowing anticipation was a more effective means of pleasing the spectators than building upon elements of suspense or surprise; if not, why would Plautus give them advance knowledge of the trick the women plan through their disguise of Chalinus? An experienced (and rather sophisticated) audience would enjoy seeing what variations and refinements the playwright could introduce in working through basic and recurrent comic formulae within an established genre of well-worked plots and familiar character types.

37 Or words to that effect! The literal exchange is

Ol. 'By Pollux if you were a horse, you'd be untamable.'
Lys. 'On what grounds?'
Ol. 'You are so hard to hold.'
Lys. 'You've never tried me out have you?'

38 Gordon Williams has written of the scene,

> The solemn ritual language of Roman religious institutions is parodied with its pleonasm and parallelism, archaism and alliteration. . . . The advice here given . . . is also the reverse of normal and ordinary life. . . . The humour, in fact, is that here convention is stood on its head

'Some Aspects of Roman Marriage Ceremonies and Ideals', *Journal of Roman Studies*, vol. 48 (1958), 16–29, p. 18.

39 Plautus is making a pun on the words for elbow and going to bed. The earlier reference to an elephant would be readily appreciated by the audience to whom they were well known, having first been exhibited at Rome at the triumph of L. Caecilius Metellus who had captured them from the Carthaginians in 250 BC; Dionysius, 2.66.4.

40 Slater, whose discussion of the function of the *matrona* as playwright is excellent throughout, states 'One wonders whether she is praising Cleostrata or Plautus – or if it really matters. It is the ladies' matinee today, and they sit back with their popcorn to watch the show' (*op. cit.*, p. 88).

41 Slater notes (*op. cit.*, p. 88) that both Olympio and Lysidamus 'make rather direct appeals to the audience for help and sympathy. Olympio begs for the audience's attention in the second person much as a prologue asks for attention and indulgence for *his* play – one more way in which Cleostrata's fiction is structured as a play-within-the-play.'

42 See Segal, *op. cit.*, pp. 152–4.

43 E.g. Mercury in *Amphitruo* (984–7), who runs on stage claiming the right to do so like 'paltry slaves in comedy'; or *Captivi* (778–9), when the parasite Ergasilus states, 'Just like slaves in comedies, I'll bundle my cloak around my neck and run . . .'. Hunter points out (*op. cit.*, pp. 81–2) that 'a common feature of such scenes, [is] the fact that the running slave is normally hailed by someone behind his back', and suggests that 'Roman poets, building upon a Greek foundation, elaborated the "running slave" into a cherished part of the comic apparatus'. He sees in this a self-conscious awareness by poet and public of the established conventions of the genre.

44 A reference to the proverb, 'Inter lupos et canes nullam salutem esse' ('there's no safety twixt wolves and dogs'). Lysidamus says he will 'try to change the proverb, by Hercules, and head this way; I'll hope for the best with the dog omen' (971–2): in effect attempting (unsuccessfuly as it turns out), to 'teach his old dog a new trick'.

45 The *senatus consultum de Bacchanalibus* of 186 BC. Plautus' apparent reference in the play to the suppression of the cult is usually cited as evidence for it having been written in 185 BC, a year before his death. W. T. MacCary sees the evocation of the Bacchic cult as indicating that Plautus wanted his audience to see Lysidamus' excuse for his conduct in the context of the sexual misbehaviour (and in particular, homosexual abuse of initiates) in which members of the cult were commonly thought to indulge. Lysidamus attempts to explain away his assault upon Chalinus by blaming the Bacchae. 'The Bacchae in Plautus' *Casina*', *Hermes* 103 (1975), 459–63.

46 Slater (*op. cit.*, pp. 92–3) sees the reference as providing the crucial focal point for a pattern of role reversal which permeates the play. 'Lysidamus' lust is not human, not a straying within the limits that society and comedy can tolerate, but animalistic, frenzied, Bacchic.' A discussion of this pattern, and particularly that of sexual role change, is developed at length by G. Chiarini, 'Casina o della metamorfosi', *Latomus* 37 (1978), 105–20.

47 But not restoration. Lysidamus does not return to his position as head of the household, since henceforth, as the terms of his surrender stipulate, Cleostrata can exact punishment upon him at any time. See Slater, *op. cit.*, p. 90.

48 Although always ready to poke fun at a shrew, and sympathetic to licentiousness – within limits! – Plautus generally treats married women with respect. In *Mercator*, 817–29 he has Syra, an aged slave, state their case:

> 'By Castor, women have a wretched life, much worse, poor dears, than men. After all, if a man secretly brings home some tart, he gets away with it; but let a woman so much as step outside the house without his knowledge, and the man has grounds for divorce! If only there were the same rule for both man and wife! A wife – a good one at any rate – is content with her husband; why should he be less satisfied with her alone? By Castor, if men were punished for their secret wenching, just as guilty wives are divorced, you can bet there'd now be more single men around than women!'

5 TRAGEDY, MIME, AND PANTOMIME

1 We have the titles of some one hundred comedies in addition to the works of Plautus and Terence, and the names of about twenty comic playwrights. Although we know of somewhat fewer composers of tragedy, close to the same number of titles survive, and the plays themselves do not seem to have fared less well than comedy on the stage – revivals were probably a regular occurrence at least until the first century AD.

2 Horace, *Epist.*, 2.1.161–6. Horace qualifies his praise by noting that Roman tragic writing was marred by a disinclination to 'blot', i.e. a tendency to overwrite and under-edit.

3 Horace, *Ars Poet.*, 268–9.

4 Jerome, *Ad Ann.*, 240 BC. Gellius, *Noct. Atti.*, 17.21.43; 17.17.1. Cornelius Nepos, *Cato*, 1.4.

5 Cicero, *Brut.*, 20.79, De Orat., 2.63.256; *Pro Arch.*, 9.22.

6 *Glossae Salomonis*, 5.250, which notes that 'Ennius adapted all of his tragedies from the Greeks, mostly from Euripides.'

7 Cicero, *De Off.*, 1.31.114. Horace, *Ars Poet.*, 259–62.

8 Cf. Claude Nicolet, *The World of the Citizen in Republican Rome* (London, 1980), especially 104 ff., 111 ff., and 123 ff.

9 Otto Ribbeck, *Die Römische Tragoedia im Zeitalter der Republik* (Leipzig, 1875), p. 214.

10 Pliny, *Nat. Hist.*, 35.4.19; Jerome, *Ad. Ann.* 154; Cicero, *Brut.*, 64.229; *De Amic.*, 7.24. Quintilian, *Inst. Orat.*, 10.1.98, noted that 'those who lay claim to learning consider Pacuvius as the more learned' [in comparison to Accius]. Horace expressed the same opinion (*Epist.*, 2.1.55), noting that 'Pacuvius claims fame as the learned old writer.'

11 Cicero, *De Orat.*, 11.36; Quintilian, *Inst. Orat.*, 10.1.97, following Ribbeck's reading (*op. cit.*, p. 337, note 3) that the phrases apply to Pacuvius and not to both him *and* Accius. Varro expressed similar praise, as recorded by Gellius in *Noct. Atti.*, 6.14.

12 Cicero, *De Opt. Gen. Or.*, 1.2. He considered Ennius the greatest Roman epic poet, and Caecilius 'possibly' the best comedian.

13 Jerome, *Ad Ann.* 139; Velleius, 1.15.2; Cicero, *Brut.*, 64.229; Gellius, *Noct. Atti.*, 13.2.2.

14 Cicero, *Brut.*, 28.107; *Pro Arch.*, 11.27; Cornificius, *Ad Herenn.*, 1.14.24; 2.13.19.

15 Gordon Williams, *Change and Decline* (Berkeley, 1978), p. 112, who notes Polybius' statement (30.32.10) that by 166 BC, Greeks were pouring into Rome.

16 Cicero records that as a young man he discussed literature with him. *Brut.*, 28.107. Pliny mentions the statue, *Nat. Hist.*, 34.5.19.

17 W. Beare, *The Roman Stage*, 3rd edn (London, 1968), p. 78.

18 Velleius (2.9.5) admired his intensity; Vitruvius (*De Arch.*, 9.3.16), his evocative powers; Horace (*Epist.*, 2.1.56) his elevation; Ovid (*Amor.*, 1.15.19) his spirited rhetoric; Quintilian (10.1.97) his vigour; and Cicero (*Pro Sest.*, 56.120; *Pro Planc.*, 24.59) deemed him a 'great poet'; 'a grave and inventive poet'.

19 Horace, *Ars. Poet.*, 180–2; 338–9; 193–5.

20 Valerius Maximus, 5.3.3.; 3.7.11; Marius Victorinus, 6.8.8, in *Grammatici Latini*, ed. H. Keil (Berlin, 1855–1923); Cicero, *Brut.* 48.177.; *De Orat.*, 3.8.30.

21 Cf. Cicero, *Tusc. Disp.*, *De Fin.*, 5.1.3; *Epist. Ad Quintum*; 2.15.3; 3.1.13; 3.6.7; 3.9.6.

22 Suetonius, *Caes.*, 56.; *Aug.*, 85.

23 Asinius Pollio to Cicero, *Ad Fam.*, 10.32.3.

24 For Pomponius Secundus, see Quintilian, 10.1.98; Tacitus, *Dial.*, 12. At *Ann.*, 11.13 Tacitus records that the ex-Consul and playwright had been subject to insults in the theatre, which prompted Claudius to issue edicts strongly condemning public disorder at performances. Seneca is clearly familiar with tragic performance, *Epist.*, 80.7–8, and in addition to scattered references in Suetonius and Tacitus, *Hist. Aug.*, *Hadrian*, 19.6 records continuing theatrical performances of tragedy and comedy, as apparently too does Claudian at the very end of the fifth century AD; *Panegy. Man. Theo.*, 323 ff.

25 Later there are still occasional references to contemporaneous comic playwrights. Horace, for example, mentions Fundanius who 'alone of living poets can charm us with the chatter of comedies, where the sly courtesan and Davus trick old Chremes' (*Sat.*, 1.10.40–2). We do have a curious late survival in the form of the anonymous *Querolus*, or 'Grumbler' which is filled with echoes of Plautus and Terence, and written around AD 400. It is perhaps significant that the work is dedicated to Rutilius Namatianus, a spirited defender of paganism, whose own writing indicates close, even affectionate study of earlier classics.

26 Cicero, *Pro Rosc. Com.*, 20, a speech given about 76 BC. See C. Garton, *Personal Aspects of the Roman Theatre* (Toronto, 1972), chapter 7, 'How Roscius Acted Ballio', for an intriguing discussion based in part upon Cicero's evidence. See too the evidence of Cicero on tragic performance which I cite in chapter 6.

27 Horace, *Epist.*, 2.1. 50–61. Augustus may even have been responsible for rivivals of Greek Old Comedy. Suetonius (*Aug.*, 89) records that he 'was a good judge of poetry, and took pleasure in the early comedy which he frequently put on at public entertainments'.

28 Quintilian, *Inst. Orat.*, 11.3.73–4 discusses the relative qualities needed by actors of tragedy and comedy 'in plays composed for the stage', and later (11.3.178–82) explicitly compares the techniques of two recently active comic actors, Demetrius and Stratocles (cf. my reference in chapter 6). It is also clear at 11.3.4 that he is well acquainted with contemporary performance by 'actors in the theatre [who] add so much to the charm even of the best poets, that they please us far more when heard than when read, while they secure a hearing even for the most worthless authors, so that often what is ignored in the library, is welcome in the theatre'. At 11.3.112 he notes that 'on the stage young men and old soldiers and married women all walk with dignity, while slaves, maidservants,

parasites and fishermen are more lively in their movements'. Donatus mentions contemporary performances of the *Andria*, in which actresses presented the female roles. *Ad Andr.* 716.1.

Juvenal records the 'off-stage' performances of comic and tragic actors in *Sat.*, 6.73–4; 'Other women pay enormous sums for the favours of a comedian . . . Hispulla fancies tragedians'.

29 M. Carlson, *Places of Performance, The Semiotics of Theatre Architecture* (Ithaca, New York, 1989), p. 67.

30 E. J. Jory, 'Continuity and Change in the Roman Theatre', in Betts, Hooker, and Oren, eds, *Studies in Honour of T. B. L. Webster* (Bristol, 1986), p. 144. *Instaurationes* refers to the religious requirement, often evoked, to repeat the games if anything untoward had occurred to mar them. It seems likely that in practice this could greatly increase the frequency of theatrical presentations. See L. R. Taylor, 'The Opportunities for Dramatic Performances in the Time of Plautus and Terence', *Transactions of the American Philological Association* 68 (1937), p. 284–304.

31 Victor Castellani, 'Plautus versus *Komoidia*: Popular Farce at Rome', in *Themes in Drama: Farce*, 10 (Cambridge, 1988), p. 57.

32 Two composers of literary *Atellanae* are known to have been active about the time of Sulla: L. Pomponius, and Novius, from whom we have altogether over 100 titles and some 300 lines. They appear to have continued to use the stock figures, crude slapstick, coarse language, and rural settings characteristic of the unscripted tradition, but, in addition, to have introduced parodies of tragic and mythological subject matter, as well as elements, including character types, borrowed from New Comedy. Cicero quotes Novius in *De Orat.*, 2.255,279,285. Although frequently referred to as 'Oscan' farces by ancient commentators, it is unclear whether they continued to be performed at Rome in Oscan, and, if so, whether the language was intelligible to a popular audience. Strabo notes (*Geog.*, 5.3.6.) that by his time (the early first century AD), the Oscans had disappeared, but that the dialect survived and was used at Rome for a festival and the 'staging and miming of poems'. Suetonius (*Caes.*, 39.1; *Aug.* 43.1) mentions performances sponsored by Caesar and Augustus by 'actors of all languages', which implies at least Greek, Latin, and Oscan. See E. Rawson, 'Theatrical Life in Republican Rome and Italy', *Proceedings of the British School at Rome* 53 (1985) pp. 101–4.

33 Tacitus, *Ann.*, 4.14. Tiberius, in condemning the pantomime dancers, noted that the *Atellanae* too had become so degraded and influential that steps were needed to suppress it.

34 Petronius, *Satyricon*, 53.13, ' "Now I own some comedians", he said, "but I prefer them to play Atellane farces, and I have ordered my choralists to sing in Latin".' For further discussion of the *Atellanae*, see P. Frassinetti, *Fabula Atellana* (Genoa, 1953), and Beare, *op. cit.*, pp.145–6; 148–50; 159–60, and 247–8.

35 Cicero, *Ad Fam.*, 7.1.

36 Juvenal, *Sat.*, 3.174 ff. The scholiast notes the use of such farces as *exodia*: 'Amongst the ancients, an afterpiece was introduced at the end of the play which was amusing, and the laughter of this entertainment expunged the sadness and tears caused by the tragedy.' At *Sat.*, 6.71, he again refers to an 'Atellane afterpiece'.

37 Plutarch, *De Sollert. Anim.*,19. Suetonius records (*Galba*, 6) that Galba, as praetor in charge of the *Floralia*, had introduced the novelty of tightrope-walking elephants. Nero had done much the same, giving shows at which a prominent *eques* had ridden an elephant down a sloping tightrope.

38 The *phlyakes* of *Magna Graecia* may have been a variety of mime; within such a diverse genre, strict demarcations are difficult to determine. However, the use of masks and of predominantly mythological subject matter indicated by the vases, would appear to distinguish the *phlyakes* from the generally accepted definition of the dramatic mime. Certainly the Romans themselves recognized a distinction between masked *Atellanae* and the mime, despite similar subject matter. cf. Cicero, *Ad Fam.*, 9.16.7.

39 Pliny, *Nat. Hist.*, 18.286. Valerius Maximus, 2.20.8. The earliest actor found recorded on a Roman inscription was a mime; Protogenes, slave of Cloulius, who was noted for amusing 'the people' with his 'merry trifles' and was active *c.* 210–160 BC. See Rawson 'Theatrical Life', p. 111. For the character of the *Floralia*, cf. Ovid, *Fasti*, 5.329 ff.

40 Cf. Polybius, 31.25.4, or Sallust, *Bell. Jurg.*, 85.39. Later Pliny the younger records that although he prefers to divert himself and his guests with the more refined fare of readers, musicians, and comedians, many others favour at dinner the antics and coarse humour of clowns and buffoons from the mime. *Epist.*, 1.36; 9.17; 9.36.

41 It is possible that Plautus' name, which can be translated 'flatfoot', may indicate that at an earlier stage of his career he performed in mimes, whose presenters were also known as *planipes*; 'barefoot performers'. As noted earlier, his other name, Maccius, may suggest an association with the character Maccus featured in the *Atellanae*.

42 The translation, by J. W. Duff and A. M. Duff is from their Loeb edition of *Minor Latin Poets* (London, 1934), repr. 1961, pp. 637–9.

43 Cicero, *Pro. Gall.*, frag. 2.

44 Seneca the younger, *Dial.*, 9.11.8; *Epist.*, 108.8.

45 Cicero *Ad Attic.*, 14.3.3; *Ad Fam.*, 7.11.2.

46 Tacitus, *Dial.*, 29.

47 Plutarch, *Sulla*, 2.4;36. See also, Garton, *op. cit.*, pp. 147–8. *Anton.* 21. For Octavian, Ovid. *Trist.*, 2.507 ff. Cicero reports a dinner party, given by the knight, P. Volumnius Eutrapelus at which the famous female mime, Cytheris, was present (*Ad Fam.*, 9.26). Also known as Volumnia, she was the mistress of Brutus, Mark Antony, and allegedly the Lycoris to whom Vergil's friend Cornelius Gallus addressed his love poems, the *Amores*. She is also said to have performed a version of Vergil's *Eclogues* (Servius, *Ad Ecl.* 6.11). Cicero was rather sniffy about her presence; 'I assure you I had no idea *she* would be there . . . for my part, even when I was young I never had a taste for anything of that sort; less so now that I'm old. It's the party I enjoy.'

48 Cf. *inter alia*, Horace, *Sat.*, 1.2.57; Quintilian, *Inst. Orat.*, 6.3.8; 6.47; Juvenal, *Sat.*, 8.187 ff.; Martial, 3.86.; Valerius Maximus, 2.10.8.

49 Cassiodorus, *Chron.*, ad. 115 BC.

50 Cicero, *Pro Rosc. Com.*, 23. Until amended by Augustus, the law empowered magistrates to punish actors whenever they liked; although quick to condemn their misbehaviour himself, Augustus changed the law to allow officials to inflict penalties upon them only for misdemeanours committed during the games or at theatrical performances. Suetonius, *Aug.*, 45.

51 The mime appears to have been associated with the smaller curtain or *siparium* (as opposed to the large stage curtain, the *aulaeum*) and indeed Seneca uses it to designate mime in contrast to tragedy (*Dial.*, 9.11.8). Juvenal (*Sat.*, 8.185) writes of an impoverished noble forced to hire out his voice 'to the *siparium*', and the scholiast notes that this 'is a small curtain behind which the jesters hide until they come onto the stage, or [it provides] an entrance for the mimes'. Cicero uses the

term, 'post siparium' (De Prov. Cons., 14) to mean 'behind the scenes' See also Beare, op. cit., pp. 270–2, and my discussion in connection with movable scenery in chapter 6.

52 Ovid, Trist., 2.497–500.

53 Cf. Horace, Epist., 1.18.10–14, 'A man, overgiven to servility, a jokester of the basest sort, so trembles at the rich man's nod, so echoes his voice and picks up his words as they drop, that you might suppose a schoolboy were reciting before a stern teacher, or a mime acting the second part.'

54 G. Alföldy, The Social History of Rome, rev. edn, trans. D. Braund and F. Pollock (London, 1988), p. 66.

55 Pompey's conquests in the East, culminating in his third triumph which took place in September 61 BC, had trebled the annual income of the Roman Empire, as well as rewarding both him and many of his associates with vast personal fortunes. See Peter Greenhalgh, Pompey, The Roman Alexander (London, 1980), pp. 168 ff.

56 Appian, Bell. Civ., 1.99.464; Aulus Gellius, Noct. Atti., 2.24.14. See also Garton's excellent discussion, 'The Theatrical Interests of Sulla', op. cit., pp. 141–67. Cicero claimed in a letter of 53 BC to Gaius Scribonius Curio (who was himself to give games of memorable splendour), that 'fortune will count for more in gaining you the highest political awards than will shows. Nobody admires the capacity to give shows, which is a function of wealth, not personal ability; and everybody is sick and tired of them'. But Cicero appears to have been indulging in wishful thinking. Ad Fam., 2.3.

57 Athenaeus, 6.261C.

58 Cicero, Ad. Attic., 2.19.; Suetonius, Caes., 84; Tiber., 61. The playwright was Mamercus Aemilius Scaurus; Cassius Dio, 58.24.3 ff.

59 The public was prone to create its own satire; officials were teased with the names of actors whose traits were thought to resemble them. Thus such prominent officials of the period as C. Scribonius Curio; Q. Caecilius Metellus Nepos; P. Cornelius Lentulus, and Q. Hortensius Hortalus were popularly called by the names of the popular performers Burbuleius, Pamphilus, Spinther, and Dionysia. Cf. Cicero, Brut., 216; Valerius Maximus, 9.14.5; Pliny, Nat. Hist., 7.55. When speaking, Curio had a curious way of swaying, and acquired his nickname from a theatrical contortionist. Sextus Titius, Tribune of 99 BC, was so effeminate in giving his speeches that a dance was named after him. Cicero, Brut., 225. Aulus Gellius records (Noct. Atti.,1.5) that

> Hortensius, quite the most famous orator of his time . . . because he dressed with extreme foppishness . . . and in talking used his hands excessively in lively gestures, was attacked with jests . . . and taunts . . . for appearing like an actor . . . when, [in front of a jury] he was termed a poser and a Dionysia – the name of a notorious dancing girl – Hortensius replied in a soft and gentle voice: 'I would rather be a Dionysia . . . yes, a Dionysia, than like you, a stranger to the muse, to Venus and to Dionysus.'

Suetonius notes that the Emperor Tiberius was also popularly compared to a mime actor. In the first two years of his reign, although he announced his intention from time to time to leave Rome to tour the provinces, in fact he never set foot outside the city. This won him the nickname 'Callipedes' after an actor famous for a hilarious routine in which he imitated a long-distance runner, while remaining in one spot (Tib., 38). Caligula ordered the author of an Atellane farce burned in the amphitheatre because of a single ambiguous line, thought to refer to the Emperor (Calig., 27). Similar disfavour fell upon the ex-Consul Helvidius

Priscus under Domitian for composing an Atellane farce which was thought to comment upon the Emperor's divorce (*Dom.*, 10). Suetonius also records how – at the beginning of his brief reign – the Emperor Galba (who was a provincial commander before claiming the throne) observed the Roman audience's taste for satire. An Atellane farce was performed at the first show he attended 'in which occurred the well-known song "here comes Onesimus, down from the farm . . .". The whole audience took up the chorus enthusiastically, repeating that line again and again.' (*Galba.*, 13).

60 Laberius frags. 72, 36, 17. Aulus Gellius, *Noct. Atti.*, 10.17, comments upon and quotes Laberius' 'Ropemaker', which concerns a miser who claims that he would rather blind himself from viewing the splendour of his gold, than have to see his profligate son enjoy good fortune. At 16.7 Gellius provides extensive examples of Laberius' original use of language. Horace, although indicating a somewhat grudging respect for Laberius' satiric force, evidently considered the verse in his mimes uncouth (*Sat.*, 1.10.6).

61 Theodor Mommsen, *The History of Rome*, trans., W. Dickson (London, 1880), vol. 4, p. 581.

62 The account is from Macrobius, *Sat.*, 2.7.2; 2.7.6–7. Cicero was present, and reported afterwards to his colleague Q. Cornificius, how 'I have grown so thick a skin that at our friend Caesar's show . . . I heard Laberius' and Publilius' verses with perfect composure' (*Ad Fam.*, 12.18). To have left, risked offending Caesar.

63 Suetonius, *Caes.*, 39.

64 Pliny, *Nat. Hist.*, 35.199.

65 Seneca the Elder, *Controv.*, 7.3; Aulus Gellius, *Noct. Atti.*, 17.14.

66 Horace, *Sat.*, 1.2.1–4.

67 For Cicero, cf. Cicero, *De Orat.*, 2.242,259,274; *Ad Fam.*, 7.11.2. For Antony, see Plutarch, *Anton.*, 21 and Cicero, *Phil.*, 2.101. For Octavian, see e.g. Suetonius, *Aug.*, 43; 74.

68 Quintilian, *Inst. Orat.*, 11.3.178–80. A little later Quintilian (taking an example from the *Eunuchus* of Terence), describes how an actor might deliver certain lines, and elsewhere (11.3.89) he contrasts oratory with speaking for the stage, noting that 'the orator should be as unlike a dancer as possible, and his gesture should suit the thought rather than the actual words, as once was even practised by the more serious actors'.

69 Suetonius, *Aug.*, 43; *Nero*, 11; Tacitus, *Ann.*, 14.14. Tacitus, noting that those nobles thus disgraced were now dead, avoids humiliating the descendants of their ancient families by naming them. Tacitus notes elsewhere (*Hist.*, 2.62), that one of the first official acts of Vitellius when he became Emperor briefly in AD 69, (even before he had entered Rome) was to 'forbid the Roman knights, under severe penalties, to degrade themselves by appearing in public entertainments or in the arena'.

70 Suetonius, *Calig.*, 57. Juvenal, writing early in the next century, recalled (in a passage on the disgrace of respectable people associating with the stage) how 'the agile Lentulus acted well in the *Laureolus*, deserving in my opinion to have been actually crucified' *Sat.*, 8.187–8.

71 Juvenal, *Sat.*, 8.187–8.

72 Martial, *De Spect.*, 7; 5; *Epig.*, 8.30. Tertullian, *Adv. Val.*, 14; *Apol.*, 15. The presentation of the ravishment of Pasiphae is also recorded by Suetonius, *Nero.*, 12.

73 Ovid, *Trist.*, 2.507 ff.; Suetonius, *Aug.*, 99.

74 Suetonius, *Dom.*, 10; 15. Juvenal, *Sat.*, 1.36; 6.44.

75 Dio Chrysostomos, *Orat.*, 32.

76 Julius Capitol., *M.Ant.philos.*, 8.1; *Verus*, 8.7–11; Aelian, *Comm. Ant.*, 3.4.

77 Aelian, *Heliog.*, 25.4; Julius Capitol., *Max.duo*, 9.3–5.

78 Trebell. Pollio, *Gall.*, 8.3; *Tyr. trig.*, 9.1; Vopiscus, *Aurel.*, 50.4; *Carin.*, 16.7; 19.3.

79 Tiberius Donatus, *Ad Verg. Aen.*, 5.64; Euanthius in G. Kaibel, *Comicorum Graecorum Fragmenta* (1899), p. 65 ff.

80 *Cod. Theo.*, 15.7.2,4,5,8,9,13. Zosimus, 5.7.2.. But Julian urged the worshippers of the sun god to avoid the distractions of the stage and amphitheatre. *Epist.*, 52 and frags. in Hertlein's Teuber edition (1879), pp. 387, 389, 391.

81 Cassiodorus, *Var.*, 7.10. For Theodora, see Procopius, *Hist. Arc.,* 9.20 ff. Under Justinian the regulations which effectively forbade actresses to leave the profession were abolished, after provision had been made earlier (under the Emperor Justin) for them to enter a legally valid marriage. *Novellae*, 51; *Cod. Just.*, 5.4: *de nuptiis*, 23.1.

82 Cicero, *Pro Rab. Post.*, 35.

83 Pliny, *Epp.*, 6.21; 4.3.

84 Cf. G. Highet, *Juvenal the Satirist* (London, 1954), p. 274; M. Hubbard, *Propertius* (London, 1974), pp. 52–3, 151; and the important article by J. C. McKeown, 'Augustan Elegy and Mime', *Cambridge Philological Society Proceedings* 25 (1979), 71–84.

85 Jory, *op. cit.*, p. 147. The passage by Cicero is from *Paradoxa*, 25, and Jory substantiates his other assertions by citing further references from Cicero, ie. *Orator*, 14; *De Orat.*, 3.83, 3.86; *De Fin.*, 3.24; *De Off.*, 1.114; and *Acad.*, 2.20, 2.86.

86 Although they did not become identical. As A. W. Wallace-Hadrill has pointed out, 'Culture does not respond to the food-blender: you cannot throw in chunks of Greek and Roman, press a button, and come out at the end with a homogeneous suspension of bland pap.' 'Rome's Cultural Revolution', *Journal of Roman Studies* 79 (1989), 157–64; p. 164.

An excellent description of what occurred is given by Gordon Williams in *Change and Decline*, *op. cit.*, chapter 3, 'The Dominance of Greek Culture', pp. 102–52. Although many approved of the gradual assimilation of Greek culture, it was not uncommon for conservative voices both now and later to be raised against it. Juvenal was fond of condemning the perfidious Greeks, whom he characterized as 'a nation of play actors' (*Sat.*, 3.100). Tacitus grumbled that 'nowadays our children are handed over at their birth to some silly little Greek maid . . . they grow up in an atmosphere of sloth and pettiness, in which they gradually lose all sense of decency and all respect both for themselves and for others' (*Dial.*, 29).

87 Wallace-Hadrill, *op. cit.*, p. 159.

88 See Gordon Williams' contribution 'Phases in Political Patronage of Literature in Rome', in *Literary and Artistic Patronage in Ancient Rome*, ed. B. K. Gold (Austin, Texas, 1982), pp. 3–41, for an account of the role of patronage, and in particular, the influence of Augustus upon literary composition.

89 Williams, *Change and Decline*, *op. cit.*, p. 111.

90 Livy, 7.2.4. Tacitus too notes that the first such dancers were Etruscan at *Ann.*, 14.21. See the discussion of this event in chapter 1.

91 *Oratorum Romanorum Fragmenta*, 1.240, ed. Malcovati (Turin, 1955).

92 See note 49 above.

93 Sallust, *Cat.*, 25.2, and Macrobius, *Sat.*, 3.14.5.

94 For Afranius, Cassius Dio, 37.49.3. Cicero gives his opinion in e.g. *De Off.*, 1.150; 5.15; and *Pro Mur.*, 13. He speaks with contempt of Aulus Gabinius for

his love of dance, *De Dom.*, 60; *In Pis.*, 18.22.89; and *Pro Planc.*, 87, and attacks dancing in the nude, *In Cat.*, 2.23.26; *In Pis.*, 2; and *In Verr.*, 2.3.23.

95 Horace, *Sat.*, 2.6.71; cf. *Sat.*, 1.9.24–5. Ovid, *Ars Am.*, 1.595; 3.349..

96 Cf. Tacitus, *Ann.*, 14.21; Suetonius, *Div. Jul.*, 39.

97 It is interesting to note that the Romans used a Greek word, *Pantomimus* to designate it, while the Greeks referred to it as 'Italian Dance', reserving the Greek work, *Orchesis*, for their own varieties of dance. As Garton notes (*op. cit.*, p. 268) 'the two nuances of the word which seem best to justify it [are] "all-in-mime" and "mime-of-the-whole-story" '.

98 Cf. Xenophon, *Symposium*, 9.2, for an extensive account of a performance of the marriage of Ariadne and Dionysus by a troupe of children.

99 Athenaeus, 1.20 D. Cf. Suetonius, *Vir. Illust.*, frag. 3.

100 Tacitus, *Ann.*, 1.54 notes that Augustus had tolerated pantomimic performances in part 'to indulge Maecenas who was passionately in love with Bathyllus'.

101 Horace, *Epist.*, 2.2.125. Elsewhere Horace gives an account of an impromptu pantomic performance given by one Sarmentus, a rural jester who danced the cyclops (in a farcical contest) before Maecenas, Vergil, Varius, and Plotius Tucca (*Sat.*, 1.5.63). J. C. McKeown says of this 'the incident may or may not be historically true. The important point is that neither Horace nor his friends, including Maecenas, can have objected to having their enjoyment of this type of entertainment advertised and immortalised' (*op. cit.*, note 4).

102 Lucian (37–61; cf. note 105 below) gives a long list of pantomime subjects, including a vast range of Greek mythology together with a few subjects drawn from Roman, Egyptian, and Syrian myth. He concludes; 'To sum it up, he [the pantomime] will not be ignorant of anything that is told by Homer and Hesiod and the best poets, and above all by tragedy.'

103 Cassiodorus, *Var.*, 4.51.9.

104 Athenaeus, 20 CD; Plutarch, *Quaest. Conviv.*, 711 C.

105 The excerpts are from Lucian, *De Saltatione*, trans. A. M. Harmon in the Loeb edition *Lucian*, vol. 5 (London, 1936), pp. 209–89.

106 Lucian's accounts show that pantomime could sometimes employ several performers, and often had an elaborate musical accompaniment of lyricists, flautists, pipers, cymbalists, and players of the *scabellum*, a shoe with a metal sole used to mark the time; an indication of how important pantomime became may be seen in the fact that such *scabellarii* were organized into professional guilds.

107 *Anthologia Palatina*, ed. W. R. Paton (1916–18) 9.248.

108 Not the original, but a later dancer of the same name who was famous in the reign of the Emperor Domitian.

109 Juvenal, *Sat.*, 6.66.

110 Ovid, *Rem. Amor.*, 751–6.

111 Macrobius, *Sat.*, 2.7.12–16.

112 Suetonius, *Aug.*, 45. Augustus exiled Pylades from Italy for his offence in 18 BC, but later called him back. On another occasion, he was admonished by Pylades, 'You are ungrateful, Master. Let the people kill their time with us!' (Macrobius, *Sat.*, 2.7.19). By the end of his career, Pylades had accumulated such wealth that he sponsored performances himself, which were attended by the Roman elite (Cassius Dio, 55.10.11).

113 Tacitus, *Ann.*, 1.54.

114 Suetonius, *Tib.*, 47.

115 Juvenal observed (*Sat.*, 6.365 ff.) that a resident dancer tended to corrupt the whole household. 'From time to time women learn lascivious movements and whatever else the teacher knows. But take care for the teacher is not always to be

trusted. He may darken his eyes and dress like a woman, but his purpose is adultery.'

Pliny the younger has left an intriguing picture in one of his letters (*Epist.*, 7.24.4 ff.) of a wealthy old widow Ummidia Quadratilla, recently dead in her eightieth year, who had kept a troupe of pantomimes 'which she favoured more than behooves a woman of quality'. Pliny, who evidently viewed her behaviour with some incredulity and distaste, notes approvingly that her grandson was protected from such corrupting influences. 'When she viewed them she always sent him away to his studies.' He then continues, in a passage which conveys something of the disdain with which a portion of Roman society viewed the pantomimes;

> I was greatly surprised, as you will be, that at the last presentation of the Sacred Games, after a contest of pantomimes, as we came out of the theatre, he said to me 'You know, today is the first time I ever saw my grandmother's freedmen dance.' Such a man he is. But by Hercules, a very different sort used to crowd into the theatre in their acts of homage, there to applaud and admire, and all the while imitating every gesture of the lady with shrieks. But now all these theatrical *claqueurs* have got in exchange is a few small legacies, which they receive from an heir who was never a spectator!

He then adds that the house will now be returned to its former dignity.

116 Tacitus, *Ann.*, 1.77.
117 Tacitus, *Ann.*, 4.13.
118 Suetonius, *Calig.*, 11, 36, 54–5. Cassius Dio, 59.2.5; 59.5.5.
119 Tacitus, *Ann.*, 11.4; 11.36. Cassius Dio, 60.28.3–5; 60.31.5.
120 Tacitus, *Ann.*, 14.15.
121 Tacitus, *Ann.*, 13.24. Suetonius notes on the same subject that 'he would secretly attend the theatre in a sedan chair to view the arguments amongst the pantomimes, and encourage them from the top of the proscenium; when violence broke out, and fighting with stones and benches, he joined in by throwing things down on the audience' (*Nero*, 26).
122 *Ann.*, 14.18–19.
123 *Ann.*, 13.21.
124 Lucian, *De Salt.*, 63.
125 Tacitus, *Ann.*, 16.4; Suetonius, *Nero*, 21. Suetonius claims (23) that no one was allowed out of the theatre during his recitals. 'Women in the audience gave birth, and men were so bored with the music and applause, they slipped out from the rear of the theatre, or pretended to be dead to be carried away for burial.'
126 Suetonius, *Nero*, 25..
127 Suetonius, *Nero*, 24. The announcement was made personally by Nero at the Isthmian games at Corinth, an act for which Plutarch characterized him as 'one to whom the gods owed some reward, because he had freed the dearest and best to them of all his subjects' (*De Sera Numinis Vindicta*, 567 E).
128 Suetonius, *Nero*, 24.
129 Suetonius, *Nero*, 39.
130 Suetonius, *Nero*, 46; 49.
131 G. Williams, 'Phases in Political Patronage of Literature in Rome', *op. cit.*, p. 23.
132 Tacitus' phrase (which is characteristic) occurs in *Hist.*, 1.4. Pliny's account is in *Epist.*, 9.23.
133 Polybius in Athenaeus, 615 D; Horace, *Epist.*, 2.1.184–207; Horace, *Sat.*, 2.3.60; Tacitus, *Dial.*, 12.

134 Juvenal, *Sat.*, 7.87 ff. After serving six months the commander of a legion became a knight; under Claudius the practice had been changed, allowing an appointment to be made on an honourary basis, without service, to reward favourites. Statius died in AD 96 and it seems likely that Juvenal did not publish the satire until much later, probably around AD 117 in the time of Hadrian. He was banished, according to ancient tradition, because of this satire, although its direct object, Paris, was long dead. Perhaps Juvenal meant it as a disguised attack on the role of actors in the court of Hadrian; if so, the disguise failed, and the Emperor took offence. See G. G. Ramsay's discussion of the incident in the introduction to the Loeb edition of Juvenal, rev. edn (London, 1979), pp. xviii–xxi.

135 Suetonius, *Dom.*, 3; 7; 8; 10. Pliny the younger, *Paneg.*, 46. Domitian's wrath was such that he executed another unfortunate young actor simply for *resembling* Paris. Cassius Dio, 67.3.3; Martial, 11.13 records Paris' epitaph: 'The delight of the city and the wit of the Nile, art and grace, pleasure and joy, the fame and affliction of the Roman theatre, and all the Venuses and Cupids are buried here with Paris in this tomb.'

136 Cassius Dio, 68.10.2. *Hist. Aug. Hadrian*, 19.6.; *Anton. Pius*, 11.2; *Marcus*, 11.4; 23.6; 19.7; 23.7.

137 *Hist. Aug., Comm.*, 1.8; Herodian, 5.3.8. Commodus in AD 216 made a former slave and pantomime, Theokritos, the commander of the Roman army sent to Armenia, where he was decisively defeated. Cassius Dio, 77.21.2. *Hist. Aug. Alex. Sev.*, 34.2; *Carinus*, 19.2; 16.7. Libanius, *Or.*, 41.8 ff.; Ammianus Marcellinus, 14.6.19; Libanius, *Or.*, 64.80.

138 Julian, Frag. *Epist.*, 304 C.; John Chrysostom, 49.175 in J. P. Migne, *Patrologiae Cursus, series Graeca* (Paris, 1844–90), vols 47–64.

6 LATER STAGES AND STAGINGS

1 Cicero, *Tusc. Disp.*, 1.44.106; *Pro. Sest.*, 59.126. Horace, *Sat.*, 2.3.60

2 Cicero, *De Amic.*, 2.25.; *De Orat.*, 2.46.193.; *Ad Fam.*, 7.6.; *Parod.*, 3.26; *De Orat.*, 3.50.196.; *Acad.* 2.20 and 2.86.

3 Cicero, *Brut.*, 290; *De Orat.*, 3.221; *Pro Rosc. Com.*, 8.23. Cicero points out in his speech of about 77 BC that Roscius had performed for the past ten years for free, dedicating his art to the Roman people, by whom in turn he was greatly honoured. To have received money for his appearances on stage would have compromised his status as a knight. His colleague and rival Aesopus left an estate valued at twenty million sesterces. (Macrobius, *Sat.*, 3.14.) By way of comparison; the price of a slave varied from 800 to 2,500 sesterces, and the holder of a higher public office such as a procurator drew an annual salary, depending upon rank, of 60,000, 100,000, or 200,000 sesterces. Roscius gave Cicero his first important brief (*Quinct.*, 77), who later defended him in a private lawsuit, for which the oration survives; *Pro Rosc. Com.*.

4 Valerius Max., 8.7.7; Macrobius, *Sat.*, 3.14.12.

5 Cicero, *Ad Fam.*, 9.22. C. Garton offers an interesting commentary on Roscius and his art in the chapter 'How Roscius Acted Ballio', pp. 169–188, in *Personal Aspects of the Roman Theatre* (Toronto, 1972).

6 Valerius Maximus, 8.10.2. See also note 59 of chapter 5 for the unflattering comparison made between Hortensius and the mime artiste, Dionysia. For Aesopos' relationship with Cicero see *Auct. ad Her.*, 3.21.34, and *Pro. Sest.*, 56–58 (120–3).

7 Horace, *Epist.*, 2.1.82; Cicero, *Pro Sest.*, 56–8 (121–3); *De Divin.*, 1.37.80. Quintilian, 11.3.111.

8 Cicero, *Ad Fam.*, 7.1. Cicero suggests that instead of honouring the occasion by performing, Aesopus should have stayed away to honour his own reputation. In swearing an oath (either within a play, or as part of the preliminary ritual), his voice failed him.

9 Cicero, *Ad Fam.*, 7.1.2.

10 Horace, *Epist.*, 2.1.189–207. From 68 BC the first fourteen rows of the auditorium were formally reserved for knights. The senatorial order sat in the orchestra. See note 16. Elsewhere (*Epist.*, 1.6.40–1) Horace relates that the wealthy politician and patron L. Licinius Lucullus was asked to lend a hundred cloaks for use in a stage production. At first doubting he had so many, he later reported he found 5,000. 'Take some or all', he said. The same episode is mentioned by Plutarch, *Lucullus*, 39.

11 Livy, 7.2.13.

12 Peter Greenhalgh, *Pompey, The Roman Alexander*, (London, 1980) pp. 175–6. Long after his fall from power the theatre continued to bear Pompey's name. Tacitus notes (*Ann.*, 3.72.) that Tiberius partially rebuilt it 'on the grounds that no Pompey now had the means to do so; but its name was to remain the same.' It was restored again by Caligula, and rededicated by Claudius, burnt in the great fire of AD 80, and restored again by Titus. After further fires and restorations it was still in use as late as the sixth century, and a major landmark and 'tourist sight' throughout the Middle Ages. Much of it survives today, but concealed beneath the later buildings which encrust it. Two excellent restaurants make use of part of its vaulting, and, fittingly, a small modern theatre occupies another portion.

13 Plutarch (*Pompey*, 45.1–46.1.) lists some fourteen conquered nations represented at Pompey's triumph, and these may be the ones that were later depicted as allegorical statues when the theatre opened. Cf. Pliny, *Nat. Hist.*, 36.38.; 36.41. The dedication and choice of entertainments was carefully 'stage-managed' by the critic Spurius Maecius Tarpa, who was known to Cicero (*Ad Fam.*, 7.1) and mentioned later by Horace, (*Ars. Poet.*, 387; *Sat.* 1.10.38). Later emperors used the building in a similar way to glorify themselves. Nero had a huge representation of himself as the sun god depicted on the awning which covered the auditorium of Pompey's theatre, and actually gilded the entire interior surface of the building to honour Tiridates, King of Armenia. Cassius Dio, 63.6.1–2; Suetonius, *Nero*, 13.2.

14 Cf. Tacitus, *Ann.*, 14.20–1.

15 Paul Veyne, *Bread and Circuses*, abridged edn, trans. Brian Pearce (London, 1990), p. 212. Politicians dreaded sharing the aedileship with a wealthier colleague whose largesse would eclipse their own. Cf. Cicero, *Ad Fam.*, 8.3. Livy notes (38.35) that in one year due to *instauration*, the *Ludi Romani* were repeated in their entirety three times, and the *Ludi Plebeii*, five.

16 In this connection, see E. Frézouls, 'La construction du theatrum lapideum et son contexte politique', in *Théâtre et spectacles dans l'antiquité* (Leiden, 1981), pp. 193–214. Cicero notes troubles in Greek theatres in *Pro Flacco*, 7.16. He had himself experienced it at Rome. As noted earlier, in 68 BC under the Tribune L. Roscius Otho a decree had been issued reserving the first fourteen rows in the theatre for members of the equestrian order. Otho's law, the *Lex Roscia Theatralis*, may have confirmed or clarified existing practice; the orchestra was in any case already reserved for senators. Five years later, when Otho entered the theatre (possibly at the *Ludi Apollinares* for which, as Praetor in 63 BC he would

have been responsible) he was applauded by the knights, but roundly hissed by those sitting behind them. The confrontation would have ended in violence had Cicero, who was Consul, not summoned the audience to the Temple of Bellona, and there calmed them with a judicious speech. Plutarch, *Cicero*, 13; Macrobius, *Sat.*, 3.14.12; Pliny *Nat. Hist.*, 7.30.117; Cicero, *Ad Att.*, 2.1.3. See also, U. Scamuzzi, 'Studio sulla *Lex Roscia Theatralis*', *Rivista di Studi Classici* 27 (1969), 144 ff. Both the general population and the knights expressed their political opinion at the theatre by giving or withholding applause. In July, 59 BC, Cicero, noting that 'you can get the best idea of popular sentiment from the theatres and shows', observed that 'at Caesar's entry the applause dwindled away, but young Curio [C. Scribonius Curio who opposed Pompey and Caesar] was applauded like Pompey used to be. Caesar was much annoyed . . . [Pompey and Caesar] are irritated with the knights who stood up and clapped for Curio' (*Ad Att.*, 2.19).

Cassius Dio notes that the theatre was erected outside the city walls; 40.50.2.

17 The account of these events is taken from Cicero's speech, given five months after his return from exile; *Pro Sestio*, 50–9.

18 It was this connection which in part encouraged the scorn and opposition of the early Christians. Tertullian records Pompey's ruse of ensuring his theatre's survival by asserting that it was merely part of a temple. *De Spectaculis*, 10.5. Pliny the elder asserts that Pompey's games were given to celebrate the dedication of the temple (*Nat. Hist.*, 8.20). According to Suetonius (*Claud.*, 12), when Claudius rededicated the theatre after it had been damaged by fire and repaired,

> he first sacrificed in the Temple of *Venus Victrix* and in the shrines of Honour, Virtue and Felicity – all of which were built above the auditorium – and then walked down the aisle between packed and silent tiers, to inaugurate the games from a raised seat in the orchestra.

For the connection between theatres and temples, see J. A. Hanson, *Roman Theater-temples* (Princeton, 1959), pp. 13 ff. and 59 ff.

19 These had been first introduced in the temporary theatres by Q. Catulus about twenty years earlier (Pliny, *Nat. Hist.*, 19.23; Valerius Maximus, 2.4.6) and their presence in the permanent theatre is mentioned by Pliny, 33.54; Lucretius, *De Re. Nat.*, 4.75.-83; and Martial, *Epig.*, 9.38; 11.21.

20 Cicero, *De Divin.*, 2.5.23; Plutarch, *Caes.*, 66. The Senate decreed that it would never again meet in the *Curia Pompeii*, which was walled up. Augustus moved the statue to the main entrance of the theatre; Suetonius, *Caes.*, 81; *Aug.*, 31.

21 Ovid, *Ars Amat.*, 3.387; Propertius, 2.32.11–16; 4.8.75.

22 Cicero, *In Piso*, 27.65.

23 Cassius Dio, 39.38; Pliny, *Nat. Hist.*, 8.53; 8.64; 8.70; 8.72; 8.84; Plutarch, *Pomp.*, 52.

24 Cicero, *Ad Fam.*, 7.1. Cicero was particularly distressed by the pathos of the slaughtered elephants, of which Pliny too gives a moving account, asserting (perhaps with some exaggeration) that the spectators were so distressed by their plight that they rose up and cursed Pompey (*Nat. Hist.*, 8.20–1). Cassius Dio also claims they begged Pompey to spare the elephants (39.39.1). Elephants had, however, appeared in the circus before; in 99 BC at the games of Claudius Pulcher, and again in 79 at those given by the Lucullus brothers.

25 The contemporaneous historian and geographer Strabo (5.3.8) considered the building one of the chief glories of the city; some two and a half centuries later it was still praised by Cassius Dio (39.38.1) as a source of pride. As noted later in this chapter, at the end of antiquity, around AD 500, Cassiodorus the Roman

chancellor of Theodoric, King of the Ostrogoths, deemed it one of Rome's ancient monuments most worthy of preservation and restoration, although by then, like much of the city, it was in a sad state from plundering and neglect (Cassiodorus, *Var.*, 4.51).

26 Veyne, *op. cit.*, p. 260.

27 At the beginning of his career Caesar had enhanced the success of his aedileship by supplementing the statutory games with additional ones in memory of his father, who had died twenty years before. Caesar was Consul together with Pompey in 54 BC, but unlike the latter (glorying in Rome in the splendour of his new theatre), was busy in Gaul and later with the invasion of Britain. To compensate he sought to have constructed his own monuments without waiting for his triumph; a forum and basilica bearing his name. The spoils from Gaul financed these, which cost hundreds of millions of sesterces and rivalled Pompey's building in grandeur. Cf. Cicero, *Ad Atti.*, 4.16; Pliny, *Nat. Hist.*, 36.103; Suetonius, *Caes.*, 26.

In the course of defeating Pompey's forces, Caesar celebrated five triumphs; four of them in a single month. He gave a great variety of games: gladiatorial contests; plays performed in different languages (presumably Latin, Greek, and Oscan) at various places in the city; chariot races; athletic competitions; and a mock naval battle. Suetonius, *Caes.*, 37; 39.

28 Cicero, *Philip.*, 2.45.116 Suetonius, *Caes.*, 44; 'Caesar continually undertook great new works for the embellishment of the City. . . . His first projects were a temple of Mars, the biggest in the world . . . and an enormous theatre sloping down from the Tarpeian Rock on the Capitoline Hill.' It was completed under Augustus in 13 BC, who dedicated it to his nephew, Marcellus.

29 Ronald Syme, *The Roman Revolution* (Oxford, 1939), pp. 116; 468. Shortly after Caesar's murder Octavian sought at the *Ludi Ceriales* of 44 BC to display the golden chair which the Senate had voted to Caesar, together with the diadem offered by Mark Antony at the *Lupercalia*, but was prevented from doing so by the Tribune. A little later he gave lavish games in honour of Caesar, a repetition of the *Ludi Victoriae Caesaris*, and again tried to display the emblems. Although Antony attempted to prevent it, the plebs and veterans gave their support to Octavian, and when later in the day a comet appeared, the crowd declared Caesar's soul a god. Syme, *op. cit.*, pp. 116–17.

Augustus was at other times wary of unseemly demagogic display in the theatre. Suetonius records his horror when, after a comic actor had uttered the line 'O just and generous master!', the entire audience rose and applauded. 'An angry look and stern gesture soon subdued this gross flattery, and the following day he issued a strong reprimand.' On another occasion he was annoyed when upon taking his young adopted sons into the theatre, the crowd stood to cheer them. An even more awkward event took place when the audience approvingly encored what it thought was a reference to Augustus' sexual ambivalence.

An actor on stage was portraying a eunuch priest of Cybele, and as he played his timbrel, another actor exclaimed, 'Look, how this invert's finger beats the drum!'. Since the Latin could also mean, 'Look how this invert's finger *sways the world*!', the crowd took the line as a reference to Augustus, and broke into enthusiastic applause. (Suetonius, *Aug.* 53; 56; 68).

30 Pliny, *Nat. Hist.*, 7.34.

31 Tacitus, *Ann.*, 3.72; 6.45. The suggestion of wooden embellishment receives support from a fascinating account by the artist Francesco Piranesi concerning

his investigation of the remains of the Roman theatre at Herculaneum, which had been built in the time of Augustus, and subsequently refurbished in AD 41. Piranesi records that after it was discovered, and shafts were sunk to remove its rich decorations, substantial remains of wooden sets were found in front of the *scaenae frons*. He prepared a number of elaborate drawings attempting to suggest what these sets may have been like and how they functioned. *Teatro di Ercolano*, dedicated to King Gustavus III of Sweden, 1783.

32 Vitruvius, *De Arch.*, 5.5.7.

33 Pliny's account may suggest that Pompey's example of lavish display at his triumph had been followed by Scaurus. The remnants alone of his theatre were valued at 30 million sesterces (*Nat. Hist.*, 36.114–15). At his famous games Scaurus had caused a sensation with the exhibition of 150 leopards, the first ever seen at Rome. Pompey, in a further example of one-upmanship, used 410. (*Nat. Hist.*, 8.64).

34 The formal details of the Roman theatre were described at the end of the first century BC by Vitruvius, *De Arch.*, 5.3–9. He gives a precise account of its architectural features and their arrangement, which he contrasts with those of the Greek theatre. Important modern treatments of the subject and the evolution of the Roman theatre include Ernst Fiechter, *Die baugeschichtliche Entwicklung des antiken Theaters* (Munich, 1914), and Andreas Rumpf, 'Die Entstehung des Römischen Theaters', *Mitteilungen des deutschen archäologischen Instituts*, 3 (1950), 40–50. M. Bieber also provides comprehensive coverage in *History of the Greek and Roman Theater*, 2nd edn (Princeton, 1961), chapters 13 and 14.

35 G. Alföldy, *The Social History of Rome*, rev. edn, trans. D. Braund and F. Pollock (London, 1988), p. 101. By accepting money from the emperor the plebs became his clients. This formal dole, the *congiarium*, probably amounted to a few hundred sesterces; enough to survive on for several months.

36 Alföldy, *op. cit.*, p. 102 ff.; Suetonius, *Aug.*, 35–41; 44. See the discussion in D. Van Berchem, *Distributions de blé et d'argent à la plèbe romaine sous l'Empire*', Geneva University thesis, 1939, who concludes, p. 62; 'The audience at the games ought to represent a systematically arranged picture of Roman society.' The poet Ovid is unlikely to have pleased Augustus (concerned as he was with raising the moral tone of Roman life) by pointing out that the new theatres were fabulous places for amorous assignation, advising his gallants to 'above all do your hunting in the round theatres, in such places your hopes are amply met; there you will find someone for love or for play, to taste but once, or to keep, just as you wish' (*Ars. Amat.,* 1.89–92). In AD 8 Ovid (then Rome's leading poet) was suddenly banished by Augustus, and the suspicion has always been that one of the grounds for the Emperor's deep displeasure was the unseemly attitude expressed in Ovid's manual for lovers.

37 The origins of the ethos for such patronage lay in the last days of the Republic, when men such as Caesar and Pompey (and their followers) saw generous public benefaction as an important civic duty, as well as an expression of their authority and prestige. There had long been a tradition at Rome that booty should be used for public benefit, and the concept was extended now beyond ephemeral games and entertainments and the dedication of trophies, to permanent amenities as well as patronage of literary works. See E. Rawson, *Intellectual Life in the Late Roman Republic* (Baltimore, 1985), chapter 7, 'Towards Public Patronage'.

38 See the very informative discussion of civic patronage in Bryan Ward-Perkins, *From Classical Antiquity to the Middle Ages. Urban Public Building in Northern and Central Italy AD 300–850* (Oxford, 1984), pp. 3–13.

39 Plutarch, *Mor.*, 822.

40 Maecenas' advice is recorded by Cassius Dio, 52.30. See too the excellent discussion by Veyne, *op. cit.*, especially pp. 255–9. He quotes in note 254 J. Béranger, 'Fortune privée impériale et État' in *Mélanges offerts à Georges Bonnard* (Geneva, 1966):

> It was by means of the private law of inheritance that Augustus ensured his political succession, the principate being a conquest won in advance thanks to the resources which the *princeps* left to his heirs. Owing to the absence of a constitutional regulation (unthinkable because incompatible with the fiction of the *res publica*, an untouchable dogma) it was the *opes* that conferred, transmitted and perpetuated the principate.

41 A. Wallace-Hadrill, 'Rome's Cultural Revolution', *Journal of Roman Studies* 79 (1989), p. 159. For the ideological background to Augustus' innovations, see P. Zanker, *The Power of Images in the Age of Augustus*, trans. A. Shapiro (Ann Arbor, Mich., 1988).

42 The evidence is disputed, but this is, if anything, a conservative estimate. Pliny the elder, for example (*Nat. Hist.*, 36.15.115 ff.), asserts that Pompey's theatre alone could seat 40,000. If the number has been accurately transcribed from Pliny's original manuscript, it seems impossibly large; yet he would have known the theatre well. Augustus limited the splendour of other official shows, ordering that one praetor could not spend more than the other, or (using their own resources) more than three times the amount formally provided by the treasury. Cassius Dio, 53.2; 54.17. Tacitus records the end of private munificence at the beginning of Tiberius' reign (*Ann.*, 3.72).

43 Vitruvius, *De Arch.*, 5.5.7. His remarks occur in a discussion of theatre acoustics, where he notes that 'all public wooden theatres have a great deal of boarding which resonates naturally'.

44 The mid-first century AD politician and man of letters, Herodes Atticus, for example, in addition to works in Italy, bestowed his gifts on Greece: a redecorated stadium and a new Odeum for Athens; a theatre for Corinth; and a stadium for Delphi. Philostratus, *Vitae Soph.*, 2.1.

45 Garton, *op. cit.*, p. 269. In AD 47 Claudius in writing to the world guild reaffirms rights which had been 'granted by the deified Augustus'. See Pickard-Cambridge, *The Dramatic Festivals of Athens* (Oxford, 1953), p. 297.

46 Cassius Dio notes the formal wish for the emperor's good health, 72.2; cf. Phaedrus, *Fab.* 5.5, 'rejoice in security O Rome, for your prince is well'. See Veyne, *op. cit.*, pp.399–401.

47 Varro left extensive commentaries on many aspects of theatrical and dramatic history and practice; all of them, alas, reduced to fragments. In connection with scenery, see *Grammaticae Romanae Fragmenta*, ed. H. Funaioli (Leipzig, 1907); Varro, frags. 309–16.

48 Cicero, *De Prov. Cons.*, 14. For the connection of the *siparium* with the mime, see note 51 to chapter 5.

49 The theatre is discussed by Bieber, *op. cit.*, pp. 203–5.

50 Valerius Maximus 2.4.6.

51 Vitruvius, *De Arch.*, 5.6.8.

52 Julius Pollux, *Onomasticon*, ed. E. Bethe, *Lexicographi Graeci* 9 (Stuttgart, 1890), 4.124–32. The translation is by Michael Walton, and is taken from *Living Greek Theatre* (Westport Conn., 1987).

53 A useful analysis of the evidence for the *periaktoi* is D. Mullin, 'The Problem with *Periaktoi*', *Theatre Notebook* 38, no. 2 (1984), 54–60.

54 Vitruvius, *De Arch.*, 5.6.8.
55 This well-known painting has been widely discussed. See, e.g. P. L. Lehmann, *Roman Wall Paintings from Boscoreal* (Cambridge Mass., 1952), p. 82 ff.; E. Fiechter, *Die baugeschichtliche Entwicklung* (Munich, 1914), p. 42 ff.; L. Curtius, *Die Wandmalerie Pompejis* (Leipzig, 1929), p. 114 ff.; H. G. Beyen, *Die pompejanische Wanddekoration* (The Hague, 1938), p. 141 ff.; A. W. Pickard-Cambridge, *The Theatre of Dionysus in Athens* (Oxford, 1946), p. 225 ff; and Bieber *op. cit.*, pp. 124–6.
56 Lucius Annaeus Seneca, *Epist. Mor.*, 1.88.22.
57 Cicero, *Ad. Fam.*, 7.1.2; Cassius Dio, 39.38. For displays of animals in the theatre see Pliny the elder, *Nat. Hist.*, 8.65. Augustus presented a tiger on the stage of the theatre. Suetonius, *Aug.*, 43. Pliny records (*Nat. Hist.*, 36.116–20) that in 52 BC C. Scribonius Curio constructed two wooden theatres placed back to back. In the morning spectators saw dramatic performances; in the afternoon, the theatres were revolved to form an elliptical amphitheatre (Rome's first) where gladiatorial contests took place. The structure was still standing in June 51 BC according to Cicero, *Ad Fam.* 8.2.1.
58 Phaedrus, *Fabula*, 5.7. The song comprised the ritual affirmation by chorus and audience of the good health of Augustus, the 'Princeps'; hence the humour of the anecdote about the musician named Princeps, who following his accident, suddenly found the theatre rejoicing on 'his' behalf. He is otherwise known through the discovery of his epitaph, which is recorded by H. Dessau, *Inscriptiones Latinae Selectae* (Berlin, 1892–1916), no. 5239.
59 Suetonius, *Nero*, 12; *Claud.*, 34. Juvenal, *Sat.*, 4.122.
60 Strabo, *Geography*, trans. H. L. Jones (London, 1934), 6.2.6.
61 Josephus, *The Jewish War*, 7.139–47 trans. H. St. J. Thackeray (London, 1938).
62 Pliny the elder, *Nat. Hist.*, 9.32.16; cf. Martial, *Epig.*, 8.33.
63 An excellent discussion of these difficulties, together with a useful comparison of translations, is found in D. Mullin and J. M. Bell, 'The Problem with Pollux', *Theatre Notebook* 40, no. 1 (1986), 9–22.
64 Cf. Cicero's reference, mentioned earlier, to the appearance of the ghost of the murdered Deiphilus in the *Iliona* of Pacuvius; Cicero compares the behaviour of Appius Claudius (brother of the hated Clodius) as he skulked into the amphitheatre, to the ghost. 'He appeared suddenly as he crept up from beneath the boards, as if he were going to say, "mother, I implore you" ' (*Pro. Sest.*, 59.126). Appius' entry however (despite the *scholiasta Bobiensis*) was presumably into the seating area, whereas the actor playing the ghost would have emerged from beneath the stage.
65 Pollux, *Onomasticon*, 4. 124–32, trans. M. Walton.
66 Apuleius, *Meta.*, 10.30; 10.34.
67 Martial, *Epig.*, 8.33; 5.25; 9.38. Lucretius, *De Re. Nat.*, 2.416. Ovid, *Ars Amat.*, 1.103. Valerius Maximus, 2.6.4.
68 Aelius Donatus, *De Comoedia*, ed. P. Wessner (Leipzig, 1902–8), 1.29–30.

> Old men in comedy are dressed in white, as that is said to be the oldest style. Young men wear garments of contrasting colour. Slaves in comedy wear a short costume either because of poverty in early times, or to facilitate easy movement. Parasites wear their cloaks wound about them. White is the colour for a happy character; a man in difficulty wears ragged clothes. Purple is the colour for the wealthy, red for the poor. A captain wears a purple cloak [*chlamys*]. Girls are dressed in foreign fashion. A pimp wears clothes of different colours; a prostitute is given a yellow cloak to suggest her greed. Trailing robes are worn by characters in mourning to show their disregard for their appearance.

69 See T. B. L. Webster's concise account in *Studies in Later Greek Comedy*, 2nd edn (Manchester, 1970), pp. 119–24, or his comprehensive analysis in *Greek Theatre Production*, 2nd edn (London, 1970), with an extensive list of surviving visual evidence. Beare's discussion of the evidence for the introduction of the mask onto the Roman stage is very helpful (*The Roman Stage*, 3rd edn, London, 1968, pp. 303–309).

70 For his sources see A. W. Pickard-Cambridge, *op. cit.*, pp. 175–176.

71 Beare has an informative analysis of the various terms for theatrical dress and the dramatic genres which used them in *The Roman Stage*, *op. cit.*, Appendix D, pp. 264–6.

72 Cf. Horace, *Odes*, 2.1.12, and Ovid, *Ars Amat.*, 3.1.63. See too Pickard-Cambridge, *op. cit.*, pp. 228–34.

73 Lucian, *De Salt.*, 27., trans. M. Walton, *Living Greek Theatre*; Flavius Philostratus, *Apollonios Tyana*, 5.91.

74 Lucian, *De Salt.*, 30.

75 Apuleius, *Meta.*, 10.30–1. The account is markedly similar to the descriptions, a thousand years later, of Renaissance masques and *intermezzi*, with their emphasis on visual emblem and allegory.

76 Cf. St. Augustine, *Psalm 8*. When criticized by Augustus because of the unseemly rivalry between Hylas and himself, Pylades answered that the Emperor should be grateful that pantomime allowed the people to spend their time in such relatively harmless diversions. Macrobius, *Sat.*, 2.7.19.

77 As Bernard Andreae observes, 'The times called for ever more colossal constructions', and he cites by way of example the *Septizodium* erected by Septimus Severus around AD 210. Erected so that a visitor approaching the city from the south was confronted by its awesome grandeur, it was conceived very much in the style of a gigantic *scaenae frons*, over 100 feet high, almost 300 feet wide, with a vast decorated facade, and three great niches, the central one of which displayed a monumental statue of Severus himself (*The Art of Rome*, trans. R. E. Wolf, London, 1978, p. 516).

78 M. Cornelius Fronto, in the edition of M. P. J. van den Hout (Leiden, 1954), p. 200. Fronto records Trajan's observation that his power rested on the provision of entertainments no less than on more serious responsiblities. Failure to attend to the latter would be disastrous, whereas neglecting the former would only make him unpopular.

79 See Ammianus Marcellinus 16.10.13 on this right to free speech. Emperors such as Caligula or Vitellius who attempted to curb this right were viewed as particularly tyrannical by contemporary commentators. Cf. Suetonius, *Vit.*, 14., *Calig.* 27.

80 Tacitus, *Hist.*, 2.91. Elsewhere he notes (*Hist.*, 1.4) that when Nero died, 'the respectable portion of the common people and those attached to the great houses . . . were all roused to hope. The most degraded classes, addicted to the circus and theatre, together with the basest slaves . . . were saddened.' Cf. *Ann.*, 1.54, where Tacitus observes that Augustus felt it 'democratic' to be seen enjoying the common entertainments.

81 Cf. Tacitus, *Hist.*, 1.72. Caesar had offended the people by attending to official business at the games; Suetonius, *Aug.*, 45. Claudius pleased them by calling them his 'masters', and pandered and played to the crowd in a most undignified fashion. *Claud.*, 21

82 See the discussion in Veyne, *op. cit.*, pp. 411–15, on the rivalry between emperor and senators and its expression in provision of the games and how they were viewed. He offers too some very useful distinctions between types of

performance undertaken by emperors and how they were viewed at Rome, in notes 306–9, pp. 466–7. Nero's ultimate outrage in the eyes of conservative Romans was taking the public stage himself. At Rome the acting profession had always been viewed with contempt. Nero appealed to a different tradition, that of Greece, where participating in public festivals and contests, including music, recitation, and dramatic performances, had long been open to citizens, and indeed, provided an opportunity to win acclaim. Thus Nero's Greek tour, noted in the previous chapter, brought him honour in the old Hellenistic world, but appalled respectable Romans.

83 Josephus, *Antiq. Juda.*, 19.1.13; Suetonius, *Calig.*, 26.

84 See P. Brown, *The Making of Late Antiquity* (Cambridge, Mass., 1978), pp. 28–53, and Ward-Perkins, *op. cit.*, pp.14–20.

85 Ambrose, *De Off. Minis.*, 2.109.

86 Salvianus, *De Gub.Dei*, 6.39–45. For the ban, *Cod. Theo.*, 15.5.5.

87 The calendar of Philocalus AD 354, lists a total of 175 days each year for games of all types, 101 of which were scenic. Earlier, although the total number of *ludi* was less, the proportion of scenic entertainments had been higher; the growth of these in the Empire (although very substantial) was not as great as the rate of increase for contests in the amphitheatre and circus. See L. R. Taylor, 'The Opportunities for Dramatic Performances in the Time of Plautus and Terence', *Transactions American Philological Association* 68 (1937), 284–304, and *Corpus Inscriptionum Latinarum*, 1, 299–300.

88 *Cod. Theo.*, 6.4.4; Ammianus Marci., 15.7.2.

89 Ammianus Marcellinus, 14.6.19.

90 For example the politician and pagan opponent of Christianity, Symmachus gave splendid games in 393 and again in 401 on the occasion of his son becoming quaestor and subsequently praetor.

91 See Veyne, *op. cit.*, pp. 386–8.

92 Salvianus, writing in the mid-fifth century AD, lamented that when the vandals were attacking the walls of Carthage, the sounds of fighting outside rose together with the applause of spectators attending the games within; 'the voices of those dying and those reveling were mingled' (*De Gub. Dei*, 6.69.71). A sermon (no. 84) of Pope Leo the Great around AD 440 records that the Roman public preferred rather to crowd the circus than the churches on the anniversary of their deliverance from Alaric in 410. Ward-Perkins, *op. cit.*, p. 94.

93 See F. W. Deichmann, 'Frühchristliche Kirchen in Antiken Heiligtümern', *Jahrbuch des deutschen archäologischen Instituts* 54 (1939), p. 105 ff. and Ward-Perkins, *op. cit.*, pp. 85–91 for references to the imperial decrees and the conversion of pagan sanctuaries. The reference to restoration of Pompey's theatre is from H. Dessau, *Inscriptiones Latinae Selectae*, 793. For the games, see Claudian, *De Sex. Con. hon. Aug.*, 611–39.

94 *Cod. Theo.*, 10.3.

95 *Cod. Theo.*, 15.9.1; See too Ward-Perkins, *op. cit.*, pp. 98–9.

96 Apuleius, *Florida*, 17. Cf. the *Historia Augusta*, for *Carinus*, which lists a similar variety show in the late third century.

97 Claudian Claudianus, *Panegyricus Dictus Manlio Theodoro Consuli*, 323–30. Claudian appears to describe some elaborate pyrotechnic effect artificially contrived to suggest a conflagration.

98 Richard Krautheimer, *Rome, Profile of a City, 312–1308* (Princeton, 1980), p. 46. St Jerome lamented, 'It's the end of the world, words fail me, my sobs break in; I cannot dictate. The city to which the whole world once fell, has fallen.' Letter 127.12 from the Loeb edition of *Selected Letters*, trans. F. A. Wright (1954).

Rome, although never formally an imperial or royal residence after Maxentius (306–12) had remained the foremost city of the Empire, and the symbolic centre of the world.

99 Their ability to do so seems however to have been diminished, and after around 425, direct evidence of broad senatorial enthusiasm for the provision of games (apart from those holding the consulship) is lacking. Those bearing the now largely honourific titles of praetors and quaestors (or their families, when, as was usual, they were not yet adults) were obliged by law to provide games on election to the Senate. After the early fifth century, there is no further mention of the office of quaestor, but that of praetor continues at least to the Ostrogoths. The requirement to provide games came to be viewed as a burden by the sixth century, and there is evidence of growing reluctance as early as the end of the fourth. A section of the Theodosian Code (6.4.1–34) is concerned with the provison of games, and particularly with the reluctance of some new senators, especially those from the provinces, to pay for them.

100 For a very informative discussion of the situation in Ostrogothic Rome, see A. Cameron and D. Schauer, 'The Last Consul: Basilius and his Diptych', *Journal of Roman Studies* 73 (1982), 126–45. They note that in his formal letter to the new consul each year, Theodoric exhorted him to spend, since, after all,

> to the consulship we promote only those who are candidates for the dignity, those who know that their fortunes are equal to its demands. . . . This mode of spending money is a legitimate form of bribery. Be illustrious in the world, be prosperous in your life, leave an example for the happy imitation of your posterity.

The quotation is recorded by Cassiodorus, *Var.*, 6.1.

101 A letter from Cassiodorus commends Symmachus (the descendant of the politician of the same name, active a century earlier) for his munificence, for which he was reimbursed by Theodoric, the Ostrogothic king (*Var.*, 4.51); *Chron.* for AD 519. The games of 522 were given to celebrate the consulships of Boethius' two sons (Boethius, *Consol. Phil.*, 2.3). A number of carved ivory diptychs survive from this period which commemorated and represented entertainments given to mark consulships. These show horse racing, animal acts, and scenes from mimes and tragedies. Several are illustrated in Bieber, *op. cit.*, figs. 834–7, and discussed by R. Delbrück, *Die Consulardiptychen und verwandte Denkmäler* (Berlin, 1929). See too, Cameron and Schauer, *op. cit.*

102 Cassiodorus, *Chron.* for AD 519; *Var.*; 3.39; 4.51; 5.25; 7.10; 1.20; 1.31; 1.33. Cassiodorus was struck by the lamentable state of the theatre; 'Old Age, can nothing resist you, since you can shatter even this solid structure? One would have thought it more likely for mountains to subside, than this strong building to be shaken.' The mimes too seem to have been well past their glory; Casssiodorus speaks of them as now an object only of derision (4.51.10).

103 Procopius, *Vandal War*, 3.33.5.

104 See Ward-Perkins, *op. cit.*, pp. 111–16. The Christians found the gladiatorial contests 'uniquely horrible'. Cf. Prudentius, *Contra Symmachum*, 1128–9. In the East the hunts were banned by Anastasius in 498, but for a while the law appears to have been ineffective, with references to the practice as late as 537.

105 Cameron and Schauer, *op. cit.*, p. 140. While still a private citizen in 521, Justinian had given the most extravagant consular games in memory, but as Emperor, in a decree of 537, he limited the duration of such games to seven days with severe penalties for exceeding the time or scale stipulated. *Novellae*, 105.

106 Procopius, *Hist. Arc.*, 26.7–8.

107 Although provided for in Justinian's Pragmatic Sanction of 554 which organized the government of Italy, the Senate no longer appears to have functioned as a significant body, and is not mentioned after AD 600. See E. Stein, 'La Disparition du Sénate à la fin du sixième siècle', *Bulletin de la classe des lettres et des sciences morales et politiques de l'Académie Royale de Belgique* 5, no. 25 (1939).

108 Ward-Perkins, *op. cit.*, p. 108.

109 For the popularity of restoring the consulship, see Corippus, *Paneg.* 2.351 ff. 'I shall enrich the people and restore as consul the name denied to consuls for so long, that all the world may rejoice in Justin's gift.'

7 *POSTLUDE:* A THEATRE IN SEARCH OF AN AUDIENCE

1 A late eighth-century guide, the *Codex Einsidlensis*, mentions the theatres at Rome, as does a Benedictine itinerary of the late twelfth century. Both the theatres of Pompey and of Marcellus were eventually turned into fortified residences by great Roman families; by the thirteenth century, the Orsini occupied Pompey's theatre while the Savelli held that of Marcellus. The former also contained a church, and the latter, a meat market. The circus of Domitian became the Piazza Navona, the amphitheatre at Lucca was used first for storage and afterwards (to the present day) for housing, the theatre at Verona had a church constructed within it in the tenth century. For Rome see Rodolfo Lanciani, *The Destruction of Ancient Rome* (New York, 1899), pp. 142 ff. and 174 ff. A more general discussion is found in B. Ward-Perkins, *From Classical Antiquity to the Middle Ages. Urban Public Buildings in Northern and Central Italy,* A.D. *300–850* (Oxford, 1984), chapter 10, 'Spoliation and Reuse of Unwanted Buildings', pp. 203–29.

2 See, for example, H. Reich, *Der Mimus* (Berlin, 1903), pp. 785–6 and H. Jürgens, *Pompa diaboli. Die lateinischen Kirchenväter und das antike Theater* (Stuttgart, 1972), p. 250. The English scholar Alcuin, teaching in the court of Charlemagne, warned a pupil before embarking on a trip to Italy that 'It is better to please God than actors, and better to care for the poor than for mimers.' Quoted in Ward-Perkins, *op. cit.*, p. 118; the letter is found in *Monumenta Germaniae Historica, Epistolae* (Berlin, 1877–1919, repr. 1961), 4.439 *Epist.*, 281.

3 There are more than a thousand such plot outlines extant, preserved in manuscript collections dating between 1611 and 1735. These collections (which contain many *scenari* that had already been acted for a long time) are discussed *inter alia* in Kathleen Lea, *Italian Popular Comedy: A Study in the Commedia dell'Arte, 1560–1620*, vol. 1 (rpr. New York, 1962).

4 For an account of the theatrical work of the Roman Academy, see M. Dietrich, 'Pomponius Laetus und antiken Theater', *Maske und Kothurn* 3 (1957), pp. 245–67. A more general description is found in Charles Stinger, *The Renaissance in Rome* (Bloomington, Indiana, 1985). Laetus and twenty of his circle had been imprisoned by Pope Paul II in 1468 on the suspicion of 'Republican conspiracy, sexual immorality, and pagan irreligion' (Stinger, p. 8). They were released a year later and conducted their activities somewhat more cautiously thereafter. Printed editions of Terence usually included the fourth-century commentaries of Donatus, which had been rediscovered in 1433, and these provided a good deal of information about staging; as well as guidance in the construction of comic drama.

5 For accounts of theatrical activity at Ferrara, see *inter alia*, A. M. Coppo, 'Spettacoli all Corte di Ercole I', and F. Rositi, 'La Commedia Rinascimentale e le Prime Traduzioni di Plauto Rappresentate a Ferrara', both in *Contributi*

dell'Instituto di Filologia Moderna, ed. M. Apollonia, vol. 1 (Milan, 1968); A. Gennari, *Il Teatro di Ferrara* (Ferrara, 1883); E. G. Gardner, *Dukes and Poets in Ferrara* (London, 1902); W. Gundersheimer, *Ferrara: The Style of a Renaissance Despotism* (Princeton, 1973).

6 For a good account in English of the influence of Roman comedy upon Italian Renaissance playwrights, see M. Herrick, *Italian Comedy in the Renaissance*, (Urbana, Illinois, 1966), especially chapter 3, 'The Learned Comedy'.

7 It was written by Giovanni Sulpizio, and exhorts the Cardinal to

> Go ahead, then, and build a theatre! Yours compare with the achievements of the ancients, you have set up a theatre tent, and a painted scene. We need no gold or silver or ivory scene [references to ancient temporary stages] – just a modest place after the prescriptions of Vitruvius. . . . We need a theatre.

The preface is quoted by Richard Krautheimer in *Studies in Early Christian, Medieval, and Renaissance Art* (New York, 1969), p. 355.

8 For a thorough discussion of the relationship between the Terence woodcuts and these productions see T. E. Lawrenson and Helen Purkis 'Les Editions illustrées de Terence dans l'histoire du théâtre. Spectacles dans un fauteuil', in Jean Jacquot ed., *Le Lieu théâtral à la Renaissance* (Paris, 1964).

9 Cesare Molinari, *Theatre Through the Ages*, trans. Colin Hamer (London, 1975), p. 120. Molinari's chapters 10 and 11 provide an excellent and succinct summary of the relationship between Italian Renaissance theatre and the legacy of antiquity.

10 The building is described and illustrated in Fabrizio Cruciani, *Il Teatro del Campidoglio e le Feste Romane del 1513* (Milan, 1968).

11 In this we can see the confusion which sometimes resulted from attempts to reconcile ancient and modern practices which were incompatible. The logic of perspective dictated that the audience itself had to be arranged in relation to sightlines, with the best view being reserved for the most important members of the audience, and everyone else ranked accordingly. With a central vanishing point, the best positions for viewing the setting are those directly opposite that central point: this suggests a horseshoe or bell-shaped auditorium elogated along the middle axis of the perspective setting. The Roman auditorium, however, was not horseshoe shaped, but semi-circular, distributing its members in a broad arc opposite the wide, narrow stage upon which were displayed actors, but no perspective scene. Serlio, despite his use of perspective angle wings on a deep stage, preserved the shape of the Roman auditorium, and placed his most important spectators in the first row of the auditorium (the same place reserved by the Romans for their elite, since it provided a good view of the stage) whereas, in fact, the best point for viewing Serlio's perspective settings would have been from a row considerably higher up in the auditorium. The desire to emulate Roman practice was allowed by Serlio to override pragmatic considerations.

12 Ronald Vince, *Renaissance Theatre. A Histographical Handbook* (Westport, Conn., 1984), p. 12.

13 Inside the theatre a wide, open stage extends in front of a decorated facade. An elliptical orchestral area lies between the stage and the tiered seats of the auditorium or *cavea*. The theatre is actually contained within a rectangular building, but this is cleverly disguised by a curved loggia which crowns the auditorium. To further the illusion of being outdoors, at a later date clouds were painted on the ceiling.

14 The scenery is original, and was designed by Scamozzi apparently to represent the streets of ancient Thebes for the sumptuous production of *Oedipus*. At the same time, it closely resembles the classical architecture of the day which was everywhere the fashion, most notably at Vicenza itself in the magnificent buildings of Palladio. Perhaps Scamozzi (who claimed credit for the wings) intended his audience to glimpse an idealized vision of their own city, as in their theatre, both art and life as well as ancient Greece, Rome, and modern Vincenza all merged briefly together. An intriguing eye-witness account of the production is contained in A. Nagler, *A Sourcebook in Theatrical History* (New York, 1959), pp. 81–6; a full treatment is provided in A. Gallo, *La prima rappresentazione al Teatro Olimpico con i progetti e le relatione dei contemporanei* (Milan, 1973), and by L. Schrade, *La Représentation d'Edipo Tiranno au Teatro Olimpico* (Paris, 1961).

15 For the *Teatro Farnese*, see G. Lombardi, 'Il Teatro Farnesiano di Parma', in *Archivo Storico per le Province Parmesi publicato dalla R. Deputazione di Storia Patria* (1909), pp. 1–52; G. Ricci, *Theatri D'Italia* (Milan, 1971), pp. 105–12. The question of who was responsible for the system of movable flats installed at Parma and when, is disputed: credit is sometimes given to Giacomo Torelli. Earlier other inventors had attempted to provide scenery based upon a recreation of the ancient *periaktoi*. See Vince, *Renaissance Theatre*, pp. 26–8. The sliding wings at Parma were incorporated into what may have been the earliest example of the 'chariot counter-weight system' in which all the flats were attached to mobile cars beneath the stage, which in turn were linked to a central drum. When this was rotated, the scene changes on the stage above took place automatically, and, it seemed, almost by magic without any scene shifters visible to the audience. The system became standard throughout Europe.

16 Vince, *Renaissance Theatre*, p. 8. As Vince notes, in Sir Philip Sidney's *The Defense of Poesie*, written in 1583 and published in 1595, the two are fused.

> Poesy therefore is an art of imitation, for so Aristotle termeth it in the word *memesis*, that is to say a representing, counterfeiting, or figuring forth – to speak metaphorically, a speaking picture [cf. Horace]; with this end, to teach and delight. [cf. Horace]

17 Plautus was relatively unappreciated in France, but Terence much admired. During the reign of Francis I (1515–47) the same course discerned in earlier Italian practice was followed: Latin plays were studied, performed in Latin, and then in the venacular. Etienne Jodelle presented in 1552 both the first French language tragedy, *Cléopatre captive*, and the first comedy, *Eugène*; both based on Roman models. Terence also had figured in England, with a recitation of *Phormio* before Cardinal Wolsey in 1528 by the boys of St Paul's School, and performances (for Queen Elizabeth) in 1569 by the boys of Westminster in Latin; a tradition that continues to this day.

18 They comprise *Hercules Furens, Troades, Phoenissae, Medea, Phaedra, Oedipus, Agamemnon*, and *Thyestes*. A tenth tragedy, *Octavia*, based on events in the reign of Nero, is sometimes attributed to Seneca. Two useful recent studies are N. Pratt, *Seneca's Drama* (Chapel Hill, North Carolina, 1983) and D. Sutton, *Seneca on the Stage* (Netherlands, 1986).

19 The standard case against staging is put by O. Zwierlein in *Die Rezitationsdramen Senecas* (Mainz, 1966); that for it most recently by D. F. Sutton, *Seneca on the Stage op. cit.* The issue is also considered in the first collection of critical essays on Senecan tragedy published in English, *Seneca Tragicus* ed. A. J. Boyle (Clayton, Victoria, 1983).

20 H. H. Hine in a review article in the *Journal of Roman Studies* 77 (1987), 258.
21 T. S. Eliot, 'Seneca in Elizabethan Translation' in *Selected Essays*, 2nd edn, rpr. 1958, pp. 65–105; p. 68. Eliot's study remains extremely provocative and informative.
22 For the relationship between the works and contemporaneous events, see J. D. Bishop, *Seneca's Daggered Stylus: Political Code in the Tragedies,* Königstein, 1985, and D. and E. Henry, *The Mask of Power: Seneca's Tragedies and Imperial Rome*, Chicago, 1985.
23 Eliot, *op. cit.*, p. 71.
24 To these could be added a host of others, including Kyd's *Spanish Tragedy,* Webster's *The Duchess of Malfi*, and Tourneur's *Revenger's Tragedy*.

BIBLIOGRAPHY

Except when particular details are given in the notes, references to and quotations from ancient authors are from standard editions.

Alföldy, Géza. *The Social History of Rome*, rev. edn, trans. D. Braund and F. Pollock. London, 1988.

Andreae, B. *The Art of Rome*, trans. R. E. Wolf. London, 1978.

Andreae, B. and Kyrieleis, H. *Neue Forschungen in Pompeji*. Recklinghausen, 1975.

Arnott, W. G. *Menander, Plautus, and Terence*. Oxford, 1975.

Astin, A. E. *Scipio Aemilianus*. Oxford, 1967.

Barrow, R. H. *The Romans*. London, 1949.

Beacham, R. C. 'The Development of the Roman Stage: A Missing Link Restored', *Theatre Research International* 5, no. 1 (1980), 37–45.

Beare, W. *The Roman Stage*, 3rd edn. London, 1968.

Bell, J. M. and Mullin, D. 'The Problem with Pollux', *Theatre Notebook* 40, no. 1 (1986), 9–22.

Bentley, Eric. *The Life of the Drama*. New York, 1967.

Berchem, D. Van. 'Distributions de blé et d'argent à la plèbe romaine sous l'Empire', thesis, Geneva University, 1939.

Beyen, H. G. *Die pompejanische Wanddekoration vom II bis zum IV Stil I*. The Hague, 1938.

Bieber, Margarete. *History of the Greek and Roman Theatre*. Princeton, 1961.

Bishop, J. D. *Seneca's Daggered Stylus: Political Code in the Tragedies*. Königstein, 1985.

Bowersock, G. *Augustus and the Greek World*. Oxford, 1965.

Boyle, A. J., ed., *Seneca Tragicus: Ramus Essays on Senecan Drama*. Clayton, Victoria, 1983.

Brown, P. *The Making of Late Antiquity*. Cambridge, Mass., 1978.

Büchner, K. *Das Theater des Terenz*. Heidelberg, 1974.

Bulle, H. 'Von griechischen Schauspielern und Vasenmalern', *Festschrift für James Loeb*. Munich, 1930, pp. 33–7.

Cameron, A. and Schauer, D. 'The Last Consul: Basilius and his Diptych', *Journal of Roman Studies* 73 (1982), 126–45.

Carettoni, G. 'Due Nuovi Ambienti Dipinti Sul Palatino', *Bolletino d'Arte* 46 (1961), 189–99.

Carlson, Marvin. *Places of Performance, the Semiotics of Theatre Architecture*. Ithaca, New York, 1989.

Castellani, V. 'Plautus versus *Komoidia*: popular farce at Rome', in J. Redmond, ed., *Themes in Drama: Farce*. 10, Cambridge, 1988, pp. 53–82.

259

Chalmers, Walter R. 'Plautus and his Audience' in T. A. Dorley and D. R. Dudley, eds, *Roman Drama*. London, 1965, pp. 21–50.

Chiarini, G. 'Casina o dell metamorfosi', *Latomus* 37 (1978), 105–20.

Coppo, A. M. 'Spettacoli all Corte di Ercole I', in M. Apollonia, ed., *Contributi dell'Instituto di Filologia Moderna* vol. I. Milan, 1968.

Cruciani, F. *Il Teatro del Campidoglio e le Feste Romane del 1513*. Milan, 1968.

Curtius, L. *Die Wandmalerei Pompeiis*. Leipzig, 1929.

Deichmann, F. W. 'Frühchristliche Kirchen in antiken Heiligtümern', *Jahrbuch des deutschen archäologischen Instituts* 54, 1939.

Delbrück, R. *Die Consulardiptychen und verwandte Denkmäler*. Berlin, 1929.

Dietrich, M. 'Pomponius Laetus und antiken Theater', *Maske und Kothurn* 3 (1957), 245–67.

Dinmoor, W. B. *The Architecture of Ancient Greece*, 3rd edn. London, 1950.

Duckworth, George E., ed., *The Complete Roman Drama*. New York, 1942.

Duckworth, George E. *The Nature of Roman Comedy*. Princeton, 1952.

Dukore, B. *Dramatic Theory and Criticism*. New York, 1974.

Engemann, J. 'Architekturdarstellungen des frühen zweiten Stils', *Mitteilungen des deutschen archäologischen Instituts, römische Abteilung, zwölftes Erganzungsheft*. Heidelberg, 1967.

Fiechter, Ernst. *Die baugeschichtliche Entwicklung des antiken Theaters*. Munich, 1914.

Finley, Moses. 'The Silent Women of Rome', *Horizon* 7 (1965), 56–64.

Forehand, W. E. 'Plautus' *Casina*: An Explication', *Arethusa* 6 (1973), 233–56.

Fraenkel, Eduard, 'Zum Prolog des terenzischen Eunuchus', *Sokrates* (1918).

Fraenkel, Eduard, *Plautinisches im Plauto*. Berlin, 1922; trans. and rev. by F. Munari as *Elementi Plautini in Plauto*. Florence, 1960.

Franciscis, A. de. *Pompeian Wallpaintings in the Roman Villa of Oplontis*. Recklinghausen, 1975.

Frassinetti, P. *Fabula atellana: Saggio sul teatro populare latino*. Genova, 1953.

Frazer, J. C. *The Golden Bough*. 12 vols. London, 1914.

Frézouls, E. 'La construction du *theatrum lapideum* et son contexte politique', in *Théâtre et spectacles dans l'antiquité*. Leiden, 1981.

Fustel de Coulanges, N. D. *The Ancient City*, trans. W. Small. New York, 1964.

Gaiser, Konrad. 'Zur Eigenart der römischen Komödie' in H. Temporini, ed., *Aufstieg und Niedergang der antiken Welt I*. Berlin, 1972, pp. 1027–113.

Garton, Charles. *Personal Aspects of the Roman Theatre*. Toronto, 1972.

Gennari, A. *Il Teatro di Ferrara*. Ferrara, 1883.

Gentili, Bruno, *Theatrical Performances in the Ancient World*. Amsterdam, 1979.

Gigante, M. *Rintone e il Teatro in Magna Graecia*. Naples, 1971.

Gilman, R. *Common and Uncommon Masks*. New York, 1971.

Gomme, A. W. and Sandback, F. H. *Menander: A Commentary*. Oxford, 1973.

Gratwick A. D. 'Titus Maccius Plautus', *Classical Quarterly* 23 (1973), 78–84.

Greenhalgh, Peter, *Pompey, The Roman Alexander*. London, 1980.

Greenhalgh, Peter, *Pompey, The Republican Prince*. London, 1981.

Gundersheimer, W. *Ferrara: The Style of a Renaissance Despotism*. Princeton, 1973.

Handley, E. W. *Menander and Plautus: A Study in Comparison*. London, 1968.

Handley, E. W. 'Plautus and his Public: Some Thoughts on New Comedy in Latin', *Dionisio* 46 (1975), 117–22.

Hanson, J. A. *Roman Theater-temples*. Princeton, 1959.

Harsh, P. W. 'Angiportum, Platea and Vicus', *Classical Philology* 32 (1937), 44–58.

Henry, D. and E. *The Mask of Power: Seneca's Tragedies and Imperial Rome*. Chicago, 1985.

Herrick, M. *Italian Comedy in the Renaissance*. Urbana, Illinois, 1966.

BIBLIOGRAPHY

Highet, G. *The Classical Tradition. Greek and Roman Influences on Western Literature.* New York, 1949.

Highet, G. *Juvenal the Satirist.* London, 1954.

Horsfall, N. H. 'The Collegium Poetarum', *Bulletin of the Institute of Classical Studies of the University of London* 23 (1976), 79–95.

Hough, John N. 'The Development of Plautus' Art', *Classical Philology* 30 (1935), 43–57.

Hubbard, M. *Propertius.* London, 1974.

Hunter, R. L. *The New Comedy of Greece and Rome.* Cambridge, 1985.

Jocelyn, H. D. *Ennius.* Cambridge, 1967.

Johnston, M. *Exits and Entrances in Roman Comedy.* New York, 1933.

Jory, E. J. 'Associations of Actors in Rome', *Hermes* 98 (1970), pp. 224–53.

Jory, E. J. 'Continuity and Change in the Roman Theatre', in Betts, Hooker, and Oren, eds, *Studies in Honour of T. G. L. Webster.* Bristol, 1986, 143–52.

Jürgens, H. *Pompa diaboli. Die lateinischen Kirchenväter und das antiken Theater.* Stuttgart, 1972.

Kaibel, G. *Comicorum Graecorum Fragmenta.* Berlin, 1899.

Knoche, U. *Roman Satire*, trans. E. S. Ramage. Bloomington, Indiana, 1975.

Konstan, D. *Roman Comedy.* Ithaca, New York, 1983.

Krautheimer, Richard. *Studies in Early Christian, Medieval, and Renaissance Art.* New York, 1969.

Krautheimer, Richard. *Rome, Profile of a City, 312–1308.* Princeton, 1980.

Lanciani, Rodolfo. *The Destruction of Ancient Rome.* New York, 1899.

Lawrenson, T. E., and Purkis, Helen. 'Les Editions illustrées de Terence dans l'histoire du théâtre. Spectacles dans un fauteuil', in Jean Jacquot, ed., *Le Lieu théâtral à la Renaissance.* Paris, 1964.

Lea, K. *Italian Popular Comedy: A Study in the Commedia Dell'Arte, 1560–1620.* rpr. New York, 1962.

Lehmann, P. L. *Roman Wall Paintings from Boscoreale.* Cambridge, Mass., 1952.

Leo, Friedrich. *Plautinische Forschungen.* 2nd edn, Berlin, 1912.

Little, Alan McN. 'Perspective and Scene Painting', *Art Bulletin* 19 (1937), 487 ff.

Little, Alan McN. 'Plautus and Popular Drama', *Harvard Studies in Classical Philology* 49 (1938), 205–28.

Little, Alan McN. *Roman Perspective Painting and the Ancient Stage.* Maine, 1971.

Little, Alan McN. *Decor, Drama and Design in Roman Painting.* Maine, 1977.

Lombardi, G. 'Il Teatro Farnesiano di Parma', in *Archivo Storico per le Province Parmesi publicato dalla R. Deputazione di Storia Patria.* Parma, 1909, pp. 1–52.

Lowry, E. 'Iphigenee in Taurien', in *Jahrbuch des deutschen archäologischen Instituts* 44 (1929), pp. 87–103.

Ludwig, W. 'The Originality of Terence and His Greek Models', *Greek, Roman and Byzantine Studies* 9 (1968), 169–82.

Lugli, Giuseppe. 'L'Origine dei Teatri Stabili in Roma Antica', *Dioniso* 9, no. 2–3 (1942), 55–64.

Lyttelton, Margaret. *Baroque Architecture in Classical Antiquity.* London, 1974.

MacCary, W. T. 'Patterns of Myth, Ritual, and Comedy in Plautus' *Casina*', *Texas Studies in Literature and Language* 15 (1974), 881–9.

MacCary, W. T. 'The Bacchae in Plautus' *Casina*', *Hermes* 103, (1975), 459–63.

MacCary, W. T. and Willcock, M. M. *Plautus: Casina.* Cambridge, 1976.

Malandrino, C. *Oplontis.* Naples, 1977.

McKeown, J. C. 'Augustan Elegy and Mime', *Cambridge Philological Society Proceedings* 25 (1979), 711–84.

McLeish, K. *Roman Comedy.* London, 1976.

Millar, Fergus. 'The Political Character of the Classical Roman Republic, 200–151 BC', *Journal of Roman Studies* 74 (1984), 1–19.

Millar, Fergus. 'Politics, Persuasion and the People before the Social War (150–90 BC)', *Journal of Roman Studies* 76 (1986), 1–11.

Millar, Fergus. 'Political Power in Mid-Republican Rome; Curia or Comitium?', *Journal of Roman Studies* 79 (1989), 138–50.

Mitens, K. *Teatri Greci e Teatri Inspirati all' Architettura Greca in Sicilia e nell'Italia Meridionale c. 350–50 a.C.* Rome, 1988.

Molinari, Cesare. *Theatre Through the Ages*, trans. C. Hamer. London, 1975.

Momigliano, A. *Alien Wisdom: the Limits of Hellenization.* Cambridge, 1975.

Mommsen, Theodor. *The History of Rome*, trans. W. Dickson. London, 1880.

Mullin, D. 'The Problem with *Periaktoi*', *Theatre Notebook* 38, no. 2 (1984), 54–60.

Nicholl, Allardyce. *Masks, Mimes and Miracles. Studies in the Popular Theatre.* London, 1931.

Nicolet, Claude. *The World of the Citizen in Republican Rome.* London, 1980.

Norwood, G. *Plautus and Terence.* New York, 1932.

Pallottino, M. *The Etruscans*, trans. J. Cremona, ed. D. Ridgeway. London, 1975.

Pauly-Wissowa. *Real-Encyclopädie der classischen Altertumswissenschaft*, Stuttgart, 1894—.

Petrochilis, N. *Roman Attitudes to the Greeks.* Athens, 1974.

Pfuhl, E. *Malerei und Zeichnung der Griechen,* II. Munich, 1923.

Pickard-Cambridge, A. W. *The Theatre of Dionysus in Athens.* Oxford, 1946.

Pickard-Cambridge, A. W. *The Dramatic Festivals of Athens.* Oxford, 1953.

Pratt, N. T. *Seneca's Drama.* Chapel Hill, North Carolina, 1983.

Rawson, E. 'Theatrical Life in Republican Rome and Italy', *Proceedings of the British School at Rome* 53 (1985), 97–113.

Rawson, E. *Intellectual Life in the Late Roman Republic.* Baltimore, 1985.

Ribbeck, Otto. *Scaenicae Romanorum Poesis Fragmenta II, Comicorum Romanorum Fragmenta.* Leipzig, 1873.

Ribbeck, Otto. *Die Römische Tragoedia im Zeitalter der Republik.* Leipzig, 1875.

Ricci, G. *Theatri D'Italia.* Milan, 1971.

Richter, G. M. A. *Perspective in Greek and Roman Art.* London, 1970.

Rizzo, G. E. *La Pittura Ellenistico-Romano.* Milan, 1929.

Robertson, D. S. *Handbook of Greek and Roman Architecture.* Cambridge, 1943.

Romano, D. *Atellana fabula.* Palermo, 1953.

Rositi, F. 'La Commedia Rinascimentale e le Prime Traduzioni di Plauto rappresentate a Ferrara' in M. Apollonia, ed., *Contributi dell'Instituto di Filologia Moderna* vol. I. Milan, 1968.

Rumpf, Andreas. 'Die Entstehung des Römischen Theaters', *Mitteilungen des deutschen archäologischen Instituts* 3 (1950), 40–50.

Sandbach, F. H. *The Comic Theatre of Greece and Rome.* London, 1985.

Scamuzzi, U. 'Studio sulla *Lex Roscia Theatralis*', *Rivista di Studi Classici* 27 (1969), 144–56.

Schefold, K. *Pompejanische Malerei, Sinn und Ideengeschichte.* Basle, 1952.

Scullard, H. H. *Scipio Africanus: Soldier and Politician.* Bristol, 1970.

Segal, Erich. *Roman Laughter. The Comedy of Plautus.* New York, 1968.

Segal, Erich. 'Scholarship on Plautus 1965–1976', *Classical World* 74 (1981), 353–433.

Sifakis, G. *Studies in the History of Hellenistic Drama.* London, 1967.

Sihler, E. G. 'The Collegium Poetarum at Rome', *American Journal of Philology* 26 (1905), 1–21.

Slater, Niall. *Plautus in Performance.* Princeton, 1985.

Slater, Niall. 'Transformations of Space in New Comedy' in J. Redmond, ed., *Themes in Drama: The Theatrical Space* 9, Cambridge, 1987, pp. 1–10.

Spranger, P. P. *Historische Untersuchungen zu den Sklavenfiguren des Plautus und Terenz.* Wiesbaden, 1961.

Stein, E. 'La Disparition du Sénate à la fin du sixième siècle', *Bulletin de la classe des lettres et des sciences morales et politiques de l'Académie Royale de Belgique* 5, 25 (1939).

Stinger, C. *The Renaissance in Rome.* Bloomington, Indiana, 1985.

Sutton, D. F. *Seneca on the Stage.* London, 1986.

Syme, Ronald, *The Roman Revolution.* Oxford, 1939.

Szilágyi, Janos. 'Impletae modis saturae', *Prospettiva* 24 (1981), 2–23.

Taplin, Oliver. *Greek Tragedy in Action.* Berkeley, California, 1978.

Taplin, Oliver. 'Phallology, *Phlyakes,* Iconography and Aristophanes', *Cambridge Philological Society Proceedings* 33 (1987), 96–104.

Tatum, J. *Plautus: The Darker Comedies.* London, 1983.

Taylor, L. R. 'The Opportunities for Dramatic Performance in the Time of Plautus and Terence', *Transactions of the American Philological Society* 68 (1937), 284–304.

Toliver, Hazel. 'The Fabulae Palliatae and the Spread of Hellenism', *Classical Journal* 49 (1954), 303–6.

Trendall A. D. and Webster, T. B. L. *Phlyax Vases.* London, 1967.

Trendall A. D. and Webster, T. B. L. *Illustrations of Greek Drama.* London, 1971.

Veyne, Paul, *Bread and Circuses,* abridged edn, trans. Brian Pearce. London, 1990.

Vince, Ronald. *Ancient and Medieval Theatre. A Historiographical Handbook.* Westport, Conn., 1984.

Vince, Ronald. *Renaissance Theatre. A Historiographical Handbook.* Westport, Conn., 1984.

Wallace-Hadrill, A. 'Rome's Cultural Revolution', *Journal of Roman Studies* 79 (1989), 157–64.

Walton, M., ed., *Living Greek Theatre.* Westport, Conn., 1987.

Wardman, A. *Rome's Debt to Greece.* London, 1976.

Ward-Perkins, Bryan. *From Classical Antiquity to the Middle Ages. Urban Public Building in Northern and Central Italy A.D. 300–850.* Oxford, 1984.

Watson, A. *The Law of the Ancient Romans.* Princeton, 1970.

Webster, T. B. L. *Greek Theatre Production.* 2nd edn, London, 1970.

Webster, T. B. L. *Studies in Later Greek Comedy.* 2nd edn, Manchester, 1970.

Westaway, K. M. *The Original Element in Plautus.* Cambridge, 1917.

White, J. *Perspective in Ancient Drawing and Painting.* London, 1956.

Wickham, G. *Shakespeare's Dramatic Heritage.* London, 1969.

Williams, Gordon. 'Some Aspects of Roman Marriage Ceremonies and Ideals', *Journal of Roman Studies* 48 (1958), 16–29.

Williams, Gordon. *Change and Decline.* Berkeley, 1978.

Williams, Gordon. 'Phases in Political Patronage of Literature in Rome' in B. K. Gold, ed., *Literary and Artistic Patronage in Ancient Rome.* Austin, Texas, 1982, pp. 3–41.

Wiseman, T. P. *Clio's Cosmetics: Three Studies in Greco-Roman Literature.* Leicester, 1979.

Wiseman, T. P. 'Satyrs in Rome?', *Journal of Roman Studies* 78 (1988), 1–13.

Wright, J. *Dancing in Chains: the Stylistic Unity of the Comoedia Palliata.* Rome, 1974.

Zagagi, Netta. *Tradition and Originality in Plautus.* Göttingen, 1980.

Zanker, P. *The Power of Images in the Age of Augustus,* trans. A. Shapiro. Ann Arbor, Mich., 1988.

Zwierlein, O. *Die Rezitationsdramen Senecas.* Mainz, 1966.

INDEX

Note: Ancient names are listed for convenience under the form most commonly used; this precludes consistent treatment of Roman nomenclature. Where appropriate full names are provided in parenthesis.